HERMANN COHEN
AND THE CRISIS OF LIBERALISM

George Grosz "Strasse, Berlin" (1917) Drawing. © 2018 Estate of George Grosz /
Licensed by VAGA at Artists Rights Society (ARS), NY. Private Collection,
Courtesy Richard Nagy Ltd., London

NEW JEWISH PHILOSOPHY AND THOUGHT

Zachary J. Braiterman

HERMANN COHEN
AND THE CRISIS OF LIBERALISM

The Enchantment of the Public Sphere

—◊—

PAUL E. NAHME

INDIANA UNIVERSITY PRESS

This book is a publication of

Indiana University Press
Office of Scholarly Publishing
Herman B Wells Library 350
1320 East 10th Street
Bloomington, Indiana 47405 USA

iupress.indiana.edu

Manufactured in the United States of America

Library of Congress Cataloging-in-Publication Data

Names: Nahme, Paul E., author.
Title: Hermann Cohen and the crisis of liberalism : the enchantment of the
  public sphere / Paul E. Nahme.
Description: Bloomington : Indiana University Press, 2019. | Series: New
  Jewish philosophy and thought | Includes bibliographical references and
  index.
Identifiers: LCCN 2018049705 (print) | LCCN 2019005054 (ebook) | ISBN
  9780253039767 (e-book) | ISBN 9780253039750 (cl : alk. paper)
Subjects: LCSH: Cohen, Hermann, 1842-1918.
Classification: LCC B3216.C74 (ebook) | LCC B3216.C74 N28 2019 (print) | DDC
  193—dc23
LC record available at https://lccn.loc.gov/2018049705

1 2 3 4 5   24 23 22 21 20 19

CONTENTS

ACKNOWLEDGMENTS

THIS WAS NOT AN EASY book to write, and its author was not a particularly easy person to be around while doing so. Yet writing this book has been an emphatically social endeavor. It has been isolating and lonely at times but also provided the basis for cultivating meaningful friendships through intense conversation and thoughtful critique. Much like reading Cohen, therefore, it has been a frustratingly difficult and infinitely rewarding experience.

I owe thanks to so many more people than I could name here, but I want to express heartfelt gratitude to my friends and family—it is difficult to express in writing how much I owe to you and to those not listed here, so I hope this serves as a shortened list of folks to whom hugs are due.

First and foremost, I owe everything to the only legitimate Sovereign, the Holy One, who is blessed and merciful.

My love and appreciation to the friends I've made along the way who have inspired and challenged me to think ever more deeply: Rebecca Bartal, Shira Billet, Fannie Bialik, Sam Brody, Yoni Brafman, Sarah Imhoff, Matt King, Tim Langille, Ari Linden, Hannah Polin-Galay, and Justin Stein.

The Department of Religious Studies at the University of Kansas provided me with an incredibly warm and welcoming home when I first began this project. I am grateful to the colleagues and friends I made while there. Thanks to Jacquelene Brinton, Bill Lindsey, Tim Miller, Paul Mirecki, Hamsa Stainton, Dan Stevenson, Molly Zahn, and Michael Zogry for being wonderful colleagues.

Since coming to Brown, my colleagues in Religion and Critical Thought have been incredible conversation partners. I have learned an immense amount from Steve Bush, Mark Cladis, Tal Lewis, and Andre Willis, and their intellectual community has been indispensable. Thanks to Nancy Khalek for her mentorship and friendship; to Saul Olyan for his wisdom, support, and encouragement. To Dan Vaca for conversation and friendship. Thanks to my wonderful colleagues, who have helped make Brown an intellectual home: Rutie Adler Ben-Yehuda, Shahzad Bashir, Nathaniel Berman, Mary Gluck, Susan Harvey, Bonnie Honig, David Jacobson, Maud Mandel, Jason Protass, Rachel Rojanski, Michael Satlow, Adam Teller, Janine Sawada, Hal Roth, and Larry Wills.

Various chapters were presented in different venues. My thanks to the wonderful conversation partners I have had over the years I was writing this book, including James Diamond, John Efron, and Daniel Weiss. I am grateful for the number of opportunities to present chapters and pieces of this project in workshops, conferences, and public lectures. In particular, I want to thank Adam Shear, who hosted me at the University of Pittsburgh; Leora Batnitzky and Shira Billet for inviting me to a conference on Spinoza and Cohen at Princeton; Mark Roseman for inviting me to Indiana; and Elli Stern for inviting me to present some work at Yale, as well as to all those who participated and provided helpful feedback.

This book began as a dissertation project and probably would never have been completed were it not for the guidance, support, and direction of my teacher, David Novak. For taking a chance on a kid who shouldn't have made it to university and for encouraging me to flourish in the pursuit of difficult thinking, my unending thanks are due to him. He has been a true model of *Menschlichkeit*. My deepest thanks go to Bob Gibbs for introducing me to Cohen's system and for doing so with both philosophical rigor and humanity and for inspiring me to find in Cohen's thought a guide to understanding ethical and political problems of today; to Paul Franks for his precise reading and encouragement; to Ken Green for helping me sharpen my arguments about Cohen and liberalism. To Benjamin Pollock for pushing me to provide a broader contextual account of what was at stake in Cohen's thought.

I owe a great deal to my teachers at the University of Toronto in the Department for the Study of Religion, who taught me how to balance a commitment to concepts and to the people on whose lives those concepts have an impact, to balance the theoretical, the historical, and the anthropological. My sincere thanks to Joseph Bryant, Anver Emon, Pamela Klassen, Ruth Marshall, and Amira Mittermaier.

Many thanks to Eli Sacks for patiently reading multiple drafts of the book in various manifestations and for being a constant source of inspiration, critique, and encouragement. My deepest thanks to Fannie Bialek for being a true friend, always present philosophically and who helped me reimagine the opening chapters. Thanks to Molly Farneth for helpful comments and suggestions on an early version of chapter 1. Thanks to Elli Stern who read and commented on a draft of chapter 3. Ari Linden helped me rethink some translations and did so at the drop of a hat. My deepest thanks; all mistakes that remain are my own. Thanks to Elizabeth Berman for indispensable research assistance. My sincere thanks to Josh Kurtz for his keen sense of the written word, careful eye, and soulful insight; his assistance in the later stages of this book was invaluable.

My thanks to Aubrey Pomerance and to the Akademie of the Jewish Museum of Berlin for allowing me access to their library and rare books collection. Portions from early drafts of the introduction and chapter 4 appeared in a different form in the journal *Modern Theology*.

Martin Kavka and Randi Rashkover have been incomparable mentors, whose insight has helped me see this project through to its present form. Martin's mentorship and willingness to read, think, and give of his time, intellectual, and emotional support in such selfless ways has made me a better thinker and a more responsible pedagogue. Randi's penetrating and masterful command of the life of the concept has pushed me to be more explicit and to make thinking more ethical.

Shaul Magid has been a source of support and encouragement. With great wit and soul, he has helped me think deeper about what Jewish identity can and cannot mean.

Zak Braiterman has been an incredible supporter of this project, and my thanks are due to him for conversations that helped finesse the final manuscript. Dee Mortensen has been an incredible guide through the publication process and her patience, insight, and encouragement have been incomparable. Thank you.

Brauna, absolutely everything that I am today, without you I could never have become. My infinite thanks for your patience, wisdom, insight, guidance, and love. I just don't have the words to say all that needs to be said.

To my dearest Elias, Benjamin, and Clara: I can't tell you how happy I am to be able to play Legos, read books, and hang out now that this book is finished. My endless love to you. Nothing else in this world matters more than you.

ABBREVIATIONS FOR FREQUENTLY CITED SOURCES

Werke   Hermann Cohen, *Hermann Cohens Werke*, ed. H. Holzhey, 17 vols. (New York: G. Olms, 1978–).

KS 1–6   Hermann Cohen, *Hermann Cohens Werke, Kleinere Schriften*, vols. 12–17 of *Werke*, 6 vols.

KBE   Hermann Cohen, *Kants Begrundung der Ethik* (Berlin: F. Dümmler, 1877; repr. in *Werke* 2).

LrE   Hermann Cohen, *System der Philosophie, Erster Teil: Logik der reinen Erkenntnis* (Berlin: Bruno Cassirer, 1902; repr. in *Werke* 6).

ErW   Hermann Cohen, *System der Philosophie, Zweiter Teil: Ethik des reinen Willens* (Berlin: Bruno Cassirer, 1904; repr. in *Werke* 7).

JS 1–3   Hermann Cohen, *Hermann Cohens Jüdischen Schriften*, vols. 1–3, ed. Bruno Strauss with an introduction by Franz Rosenzweig (Berlin: C. A. Schwetschke & Sohn/Verlagsbuchhandlung, 1924).

RoR   Hermann Cohen, *Religion of Reason: Out of the Sources of Judaism*, trans. Simon Kaplan (Atlanta, GA: Scholars' Press, 1995).

HERMANN COHEN
AND THE CRISIS OF LIBERALISM

INTRODUCTION

Religion, Reason, and
the Enchanted Public Sphere

REFLECTING ON THE BIRTH PANGS of what would become a tumultuous revolt against the political establishment, an aging professor was invited to address an alienated student body. It had been a difficult year, politically. Academic lectures were becoming increasingly politicized and would-be leaders spent more time appealing directly to the most vulgar instincts and fears of their war-weary electorate than pursuing rational discussion of economic or military policy. Disillusioned by a culture of privilege and authoritarianism, the students were in search of guidance. But elements of their struggle were turning toward the decidedly nonrational, summoning the forces of experience, life, and feeling to counterbalance the increasingly xenophobic right-wing political parties' quests to build their own versions of populism out of similarly nonrational appeals to national identity. Acutely aware of the growing sense of crisis surrounding him, the professor undertook to diagnose the conditions of this social tumult, claiming, "Our age is characterized by rationalization and intellectualization and, above all, by the disenchantment of the world. Its resulting fate is that precisely the ultimate and most sublime values have retreated from the public sphere (*Öffentlichkeit*) either into the hidden realm of mystic life or into the fraternal feelings of direct and personal relations between individuals."[1] Rationalization and scientific intellectualization were supposed to present a position of moderation in public life, and yet the longing for enchantment was far from extinguished, it was just relocated.

Such was the tone in a year of crisis, 1917, when upheaval rocked a war-torn Germany. This professor was none other than the great German father of sociology, Max Weber, who was diagnosing what he perceived to be a structural problem in both the surging of militaristic nationalism and the countervailing force of revolutionary rhetoric. His fundamental point, cited repeatedly for its concision, is at once an observation of the crisis of legitimacy that occurs when the myths and beliefs about authority—whether scientific or political—are shaken and a plea to use caution in considering the alternatives. Thus it has come to represent a statement about the dynamics of secularization that accompanied the rise of liberalism and its ideal of reasoned consensus about the most important social and political values.

However, Weber also worried about the relationship between disenchantment and rationalization. Indeed, he was not simply celebrating disenchantment but also providing a critique of the ensuing assertion of new values to fill the vacuum left by tradition's apparent erosion. His analysis therefore portended a direct result of this disenchantment: that would-be prophets and seers would exploit the moment of disenchantment as the weakness inherent in liberal democracy, since "active mass democratization" also disenchants authority as such. And when the *belief* in institutions is called into question, then

> the political leader no longer becomes a candidate because he is esteemed within a circle of political notables and then, as a result of his work in parliament, becomes the leader. Rather, he wins his political power through mass-demagogic means and holds it on the basis of the trust and confidence of the masses. . . .
>
> Every kind of direct election of the highest authorities, and in fact every kind of political power that depends on the trust of the masses [and] not parliament . . . is on the way toward this 'pure' form of ceasa-ristic acclamation.[2]

His words would prove doubly sibylic, it seems, given the rise of totalitarianism immediately to follow Weber's own era as well as the resurgent nationalist populisms of our contemporary moment. But Weber's concerns over the connection between disenchantment and the crisis of parliamentary democracy—between the neutralization of spiritual forces and values commanding allegiance and the ensuing radicalization of mass democracy—turn on his plea to clarify the relationship between liberalism and democracy. This is because, as Carl Schmitt claimed, "Belief in parliamentarism, in government by discussion, belongs to the intellectual world of liberalism. It does not belong to democracy."[3] In other words, liberalism summons many voices to be heard, but democracies do not necessitate that all voices express rational opinions. Is there something fundamentally at odds between the enchantment of democratized participation and the sober, disenchanted labor of discussion and reasoning?

Weber's observations thus present us with a portrait of the crisis of secularization and rationalization stirred up in the discourse surrounding the rule of law in the German legal state (*Rechtstaat*) and the increasing role of the natural sciences in mapping societal self-understanding. They also describe disenchantment as a symptom of transformation in the intellectual history of liberalism. As an attempt to circumscribe the sheer force of will of authority and traditional entitlements, the liberal ethos represented by Weber should establish a space of sociality, where clarity and discussion might help rationalize which values are deemed most important for a polity. Thus, although the most sublime values, ideas, and spirits might be displaced by the insistence on rational legal equality and civic rights, these enchanted forces nevertheless find new homes in the realm of mystical, religious experience or in the worldly encounters of "direct and personal relations between individuals." Liberalism should not eradicate these forces but rather serve as a check on their hegemonic sanctioning by state institutions.

Liberalism's attempt to distinguish "the most sublime values" that state institutions (such as the German university of Weber's day) should hold from those that society should hold is therefore the root of this disenchantment. There is a clear division between public and private. It is perhaps understandable then why the German Jews of Weber's era were emphatic supporters of such a liberalism. Or, as Michael Brenner has suggested, at the very least German Jews were supporters of "their legal equality and acceptance in German society [which] depended to a large extent on the success of liberal politics."[4] This variety of liberalism, as Leo Strauss writes, "stands or falls by the distinction between state and society, or by the recognition of a private sphere . . . with the understanding that, above all, religion as particular religion [i.e., as either Christian or Jewish religion] belongs to the private sphere."[5] As Weber knew well, the rationalization of liberalism allowed German Jews to participate in the discussion about what values ought to count as sublime. Disenchantment therefore had its benefits. Yet according to Strauss, that same liberalism also left the Jews in a bind between desired membership in a state that would not discriminate against them and participation in a society that readily would.

What Weber and Strauss both observe at the heart of the discourse of Wilhelmine German liberalism, therefore, is that the *publicity* of politics is left disenchanted by reasoned consensus. However, that does not necessarily entail that the new space of social relations between persons should be disenchanted as well. For better and for worse, this means that unlike the disenchantment of politics, the social sphere remains enchanted. This is a considerable liberal inheritance, and it will occupy the story that follows. But it is also a glaring lacuna in the conception of liberalism we have inherited today. What should we make of the enchantment of social relations, and sociality more generally, and its role in transforming how religion is configured in the liberal public sphere?

The neglect of this enchanted dimension of liberalism stems from understanding religion as a private preoccupation of the individual rather than a social affair, a concern with legitimation, values, or collective identity.[6] Religion, so the story goes, is first pushed into a rationalized corner, whereby only a reformed theology in which religious beliefs, practices, and values are thoroughly historicized and stripped of any superstition can remain. By removing religion as an emphatically practical and public preoccupation—the sphere of politics and law—therefore, this privatization lessens the stringencies—and consequences—of observances and beliefs. In Strauss's description, liberalism therefore makes reason the litmus of religion (or, revelation as he calls it), if revelation is admitted as anything more than "universal morality" at all. Such a version of religion would seem to be weakened or watered down in the face of external pressures. Thus, as Strauss observed about the religion of the German Jews, "The need for external credentials of revelation (tradition and miracles) disappears as its internal credentials come to abound. The truth of traditional Judaism [becomes] the religion of reason or the religion of reason [becomes] secularized Judaism."[7] On this account, liberal "reason" presents itself as the neutral standard-bearer capable of adjudicating truth and therefore insinuates itself into religion. Liberalism, again, comes to represent the neutralization and disenchantment of the world. A "religion of reason," Strauss suggests, therefore compromises religion, thus secularizing, rationalizing, and disenchanting Judaism.

But it was also just such an emphasis on Judaism as a "religion of reason" that represented all that was noble and naive in the liberalism of the German Jews, Strauss claims. In their pursuit of belonging in German liberalism, however, the Jews sadly failed to answer the "Jewish Question" that resulted from the disenchantment of politics and the lingering enchantment of the social sphere. And perhaps most naive and noble of them all—and the most symbolic German-Jewish liberal—was Hermann Cohen, whose posthumous *Religion of Reason: Out of the Sources of Judaism* (1919) has been hailed as the foremost work of Jewish theology perhaps since Maimonides.[8] Cohen, Strauss claimed, demonstrated "most effectively how Jews can live with dignity as Jews in a non-Jewish, even hostile, world while participating in that world." But the virtue of this effort was shadowed by the fact that "in showing this he assumed indeed that the state is liberal or moving toward liberalism."[9] Cohen's philosophical elaboration of Judaism therefore demonstrated to Strauss the degree to which, as Michael Brenner writes, "The German Jews probably had stronger ties to nineteenth-century German liberalism than most other segments of the German population."[10] Indeed, Gershom Scholem described Cohen as "surely as distinguished a representative of the liberal and rationalistic reinterpretation" of Judaism as one could find.[11] And although many today still recognize Cohen as one of the most important modern Jewish philosophers, Strauss and Scholem are not alone in holding some negative opinions of his work.[12]

Cohen's philosophy has been ridiculed repeatedly for its optimism and trust in the advance of liberal democratic constitutionalism and the socialization of the state. With a deep commitment to philosophical reasoning as the vehicle for exploring science, history, and religion, Cohen's legacy would appear to square with depictions of liberalism as elevating reason over all else. But was it Cohen's thought that troubled so many, or was it his untimely association with this image of a rationalizing and disenchanted liberalism?

Understandably, Scholem's skepticism stems from his experience of a Weimar-era liberalism that failed to stymie the rise of National Socialism and the increasingly popular appeal of anti-Semitism. For his own part, Strauss's Weimar years led him to the belief that Jews of Cohen's persuasion were blind to the fact that "the liberal state cannot provide a solution to the Jewish problem, since such a solution would require the prohibition of every kind of 'discrimination' [such as anti-Semitism], i.e. the abolition of the private sphere, the denial of the difference between state and society, the destruction of the liberal state."[13] Those who sought to rescue Cohen's legacy, such as Franz Rosenzweig, decidedly distanced Cohen's later Jewish philosophy from this liberal legacy to the detriment of Cohen's philosophical voice.[14] Thus, in the lachrymose history of German Judaism, mention of Cohen is frequently limited to bellicose "I told you so" citations in accounts of what went wrong for the Jews of Germany in their wide-eyed infatuation with liberalism and belief in the possibility of reasoned discussion between German Christians and Jews.[15]

But the continued difficulty of taking Cohen's thought seriously and the sustained attempt to mark his ideas as woefully out of step with historical realities illustrates a larger problem for contemporary political discourse: a refusal to take seriously the lingering enchantment and spirit of trust and belief demanded by liberalism's social norms and institutions. Few liberals believe in spirits and even fewer trust those who do. Like Strauss, many liberals also cling to a notion of liberalism that fails to make clear the nature of the society that is distinguished from the state: religion remains confined to a "private" sphere, and, in liberalism's attachment to the rational individual, the lingering enchantment of sociality described by Weber is all but lost. Thus, the kind of reasoning implicit in the German liberal tradition from Kant to Hegel and certainly extending to German Jews from Mendelssohn to Cohen is deemed no more than another rung in the ladder to nowhere of liberalism's neutralizing history. But liberalism in Cohen's time was largely a language for imagining what a state could or ought to be. The existing German state of the period was hardly liberal.[16] And Cohen's vision of such a sociality was far from realized. What then should we mean by liberalism in nineteenth-century Germany?

Despite his associations with Weimar—including the Weimar constitution, whose fruits he would not himself enjoy—Weber was a liberal in the German Empire (1871–1919), and the crisis he diagnosed was pre-Weimar. Thus, any conceptual and historical treatment of the crisis of liberalism and the vicissitudes of a democratizing public sphere centered on

Weber's notion of enchantment ought to begin with imperial Germany, a period that attracts far less critical interest than Weimar from those concerned with the abiding conflict that followed liberalism's triumph in the North Atlantic world—namely, that between religion and politics. Yet Weimar remains unintelligible without a proper grasp of its (Weimar's) conditions. And to the extent that the conflict between religion and politics occupies the center of debate in imperial Germany, proper understanding of what Leo Strauss referred to as the era's "theologico-political predicament"[17] can only be attained with a reconsideration of liberalism's alleged disenchantment.

This is all the more significant then, when we consider that Cohen's life and career (1842–1918) spanned just about the entire length of imperial Germany (1871–1919). And Cohen's entanglements with German liberalism suggest a different trajectory than that described above. If Cohen was a liberal, he was certainly an enchanted one. If he sought to understand reason as the litmus for religion, both religion and reason would be defined in emphatically social and public terms. Indeed, he refused to abandon the transcendence of ideas, and his philosophy and social thought addressed the crisis of liberalism, secularization, and the rise of anti-Semitism with an unapologetic consideration of the role of Protestantism and Judaism in the *idea* of liberal culture. Cohen's idealism and his writings on Judaism in the modern world therefore provide a unique window onto a reimagined liberalism by making explicit both the Protestant roots and the minority Jewish expressions of a particularly German liberalism. Moreover, his willingness to tarry with forces of enchantment—with *ideas*—as the basis of the modern public sphere and its semiotic cultural forms tells a different tale about what liberalism could have been.[18] The goal of reimagining such a liberalism through this reading of Cohen is therefore to try and uncover an unrealized potential for liberalism, should it have a future.

This is a book that focuses on the enchantment and spiritual past of liberalism. In the chapters that follow, I put forward the argument that liberalism need be reduced to neither a covert ideology of disenchanted rationality nor the market capitalism regnant in North Atlantic democracies and the neoliberal transformation of individual rights in an "economization" of everyday life.[19] Rather, liberalism should be understood as an epistemology. Epistemology, as I understand it throughout the following chapters, is an attempt to ground knowledge in critically reflexive, hypothetical, and self-consciously revisable concepts subject to justification; it extends an act of protest into critique and the demand for reasons. Liberalism, as I will suggest, broadly describes the historical legacy of attempts to portray human sociality through reasoned claims about what the world could be and how its failures might be corrected. Such a worldview has a distinct history and set of values. And, in the chapters that follow, I argue for a redefinition of liberalism that makes explicit this history. I argue for an understanding of liberalism as a kind of idealism, and all idealisms require belief in and commitment to something intangible or spectral, namely, ideas. As an attempt to recover the implicit thrust of *belief, ritual, and tradition within a liberal epistemology*—where reasoning transpires at the level of the interpersonal, the social, and the ethical—I thus seek to retrieve a forgotten inflection of liberalism as a commitment to *reasoning, compromise, and corrigibility as eminently social practices.*

This book therefore proposes a reconsideration of the adage told of nineteenth-century German Protestant thought and culture by considering the case of Hermann Cohen. As a story about an alleged failure, it is therefore an opportunity to probe the extent to which liberalism could be a theory of corrigibility. That is to say, I do not propose to hold up Cohen as an exemplar of a determinate kind of Judaism or Jewish politics, nor of a successfully articulated theory of liberal politics, but rather to reimagine the relevance of Cohen's project (and its failures) to social and political life today.[20] A reconsideration of Cohen's thought is thus not only long past due but also urgently needed because contemporary liberalism is yet again at a breaking point and in need of reckoning with its past. With the crack in the foundations of the European supranational project decisively widened by the British exit from the EU and the rise of populisms nurtured by myth mongering and demagogy in the United States, and with the resurgence of nationalism on the right and the ever-increasing appeals to identitarian essentialisms on the left, there is good reason to reflect carefully on the future prospects of liberalism. If Weber's words no longer seem like antiquated assessments of a time long past, this is because the ghosts of crisis are restless. The legitimacy of liberal democratic institutions is once again a topic of debate and polemics. Increasing numbers of people throughout Europe and the United States are losing faith in the liberal constitutional model of state and society—of nations built on ideas rather than nostalgic narcissisms. Liberalism, it would seem, is on the cusp of failing—again. It therefore seems pertinent to reimagine what other, minor inflections of liberalism might teach us.

Cohen's idealism, along with its philosophical telling of the story of the German Jews, shows us a liberalism that requires faith: in ideas, spirits, and possibilities. We must *believe* in spirits in order to reap the benefits of the liberal vision; otherwise, we risk rendering Weber's words an unwitting prophecy yet again.

Cohen's thought also enables a theoretical intervention in conversations about religion, politics, secularism, and identity because his vision is the most sophisticated and systematic one offered by a Jewish philosopher in the modern age (at least since Moses Mendelssohn) and his influence exceeds the narrow scope of Jewish thought alone. His engagement with and revision of Kant's critical philosophy led Cohen to imagine a nonessentialized civic identity—a national identity built on an idea rather than a tribe—that provided a trenchant and rigorous critique of racism, anti-Semitism, hypernationalism, and reductionist materialism. Indeed, his influence and legacy in this regard remains palpable in the broad spectrum of twentieth-century social and critical theory. He is acknowledged explicitly in the work of the founding members of the Frankfurt School of Social Research.[21] His emphasis on the dialogical and on the priority of the Other finds its echo in the work of Mikhail Bakhtin[22] and Emmanuel Levinas.[23] His philosophical insights into the nature of conceptual justification and discursive rationality are increasingly recognized as embedded in the unconscious of American pragmatism,[24] and his historical orientation is indelibly stamped on Foucault's early notions of archaeology and genealogy.[25] But Cohen's thought is best understood when it is situated in its sociopolitical, historical, and intellectual context and when we engage the Jewish dimensions of Cohen's philosophy as an investment in public reasoning.[26] Thus, Cohen's attempt to advocate for a "Jewish" place in modern liberalism represents more than special pleading on the part of a Jewish minority. His command of Kantian philosophy drew unparalleled public recognition in his time, and his academic success and influence in Germany uniquely positioned him as an aperture through which to capture and narrate the philosophical, historical, and cultural constellations of German Jewry in the empire and the larger tumult of the period. Cohen, after all, was a public figure, and as such his voice deserves another hearing.

Furthermore, Cohen's engagement with liberalism was not ideological. Rather, he was a self-described "ethical socialist" and therefore committed to imagining what the state *ought to be*. Cohen envisioned the socialization of public laws but distanced society from the state. He appealed to religion as a source of culture but treated religion neither conservatively nor as a private and individualist affair; he venerated tradition but appealed to modern scientific reasoning and insisted that both were public bodies of knowledge. He was critical of the increasing partisanship of Wilhelmine[27] polemics but focused on democratizing the ideal foundations of an ethical society and culture. Cohen therefore sought not the caricature of a neutralizing liberal secularism—a doctrine of public neutrality—but what I instead describe as secularity, an epistemological condition in which religious minority and diversity could be expressed and recognized in the public sphere through the use of self-reflexive and transparent reasoning. This was also perhaps Cohen's most important, if overlooked, contribution to modern religious as well as political and social thought, for he envisioned such reasoning as anything but an attempt to neutralize the normative claims of religion. Unlike John Rawls's laudable attempt to disencumber the public sphere of any "comprehensive doctrines" or Carl Schmitt's more insidious desire to reenchant the public Leviathan as a secular vicar of Christ, Cohen's emphasis on ideals and concepts justified the use of public reasoning to *idealize* the claims of religious traditions. But this justification is not an imposition from the majority. Rather, I will argue that Cohen's account of religious reasoning is a practice of cultivating the relationship between historical sources of tradition and the normative needs of the future. Furthermore, Cohen's emphasis on the sociality of reason—on the public exchange of ideas— brings the enchantment of such a secularity into view. This enchanted public sphere is a space where reasoners *ought to* believe that they can persuade others with justified claims rather than merely trade conversation stoppers such as emotive conjecture or metaphysical assertion.[28] If they cannot persuade and are persuaded in turn, they should revise their commitments. Admitting this vulnerability and recognizing the reality of error, failure, and correction in our public reasoning must be the basis of progressive and reasoned social life, according to this story. Perhaps that is why I believe Cohen has something to teach us about liberalism, because his own errors and failures do not lesson his significance as an exemplar of idealism as a form of public reasoning. For Cohen's idealism, as I understand it, is *enchanted by a faith in and a commitment to ideas and reasons as the spirits that move society forward.*

My discussion of a reimagined liberalism therefore focuses on this moment in imperial Germany when liberalism was hardly recognizable by today's standards. My focus on secularity as an epistemology also describes a way of reasoning about what Weber described as the "most sublime values" while simultaneously tolerating opposition, critique, debate, and dissent about just what counts as the most sublime in value. Hence, the narrative I tell reframes a number of political and social movements, histories, and voices at times forgotten in our contemporary understanding of liberalism, such as philosophical idealism, the democratic socialist tradition, German Protestant theology, and the overall intellectual shift toward understanding human life within the purview of scientific study. Indeed, rather than a defined or singular political ideology, liberalism in the context of imperial Germany remained a desideratum that best expressed the need to address radical social transformations. More specifically, I focus on the epistemological meanings of liberalism and secularity because the minority German Jews took up the charge of the liberal *idea* and may have been the most capable of making these connections explicit.

As I contend in the chapters that follow, as a minority group committed to the ideals of reasoned discussion and debate, equal rights despite dissent, and the freedom to think independently of institutional dogmas, the German Jews were perhaps more deeply conscious of the relationship between liberalism and its spiritual roots in German Protestantism than anyone. This was because their experience of the secularization of Germany did not bring immediate religious freedom and legal emancipation. From the vantage point of their minority status, as David Sorkin has pointed out, German Jews explicitly recognized the fruits of a majority German culture of Protestantism, *Bildung* (cultural formation), and Enlightenment as the conditions for a liberal culture—if not a state—in which Judaism was finally permitted to partake of the reasoning of the public sphere.[29] As the carriers of a minority history through this process of German secularization, therefore, the Jews recognized both that Protestantism provided the epistemological basis for the spirit of liberalism—freedom of thought independent of institutional dogma—and that consciousness of the Protestant origins of religious freedom was necessary for liberalism to take root not just among Christians but anywhere. Rather than call for the dissolution of religion altogether, German Jews took up the cause of a Protestant liberalism, where religion occupied a public and social place.[30]

My story, therefore, examines the ways in which such seemingly disparate trajectories of socialism, liberal Protestant Christianity, and German Judaism might all share something fundamental, rooted in the historical import of the German Reformation and Enlightenment. Furthermore, I explore the contours of the Wilhelmine public sphere, including a very real process of secularization and a dialectic of (dis)enchantment that gave rise to confessional conflict, anti-Semitism, and illiberalism. In placing Cohen's thought in this context, I seek to retrieve the lingering enchantment in a rationalized society that his German-Jewish minority voice represents, even when such a society struggles and fails to recognize the diversity of participants in its rituals of public reasoning. In summary, one of the lessons learned from both Cohen and German-Jewish liberalism is that not all rationalizations are disenchanted.

It is therefore necessary to return to the conditions of liberalism's collapse in Weimar and to interrogate one of the structural deficiencies that would eventually beset a disenchanted liberalism, which I name as *secularism*. In doing so, I will critically evaluate the dimensions of both epistemic and social legitimacy and what might be needed to correct a disenchantment of the public sphere. As I argue in the chapters that follow, by addressing the underlying epistemological problem of enchantment and value in the modern world, Cohen's idealism provides an alternative path to a liberal conception of the public sphere. With his emphasis on the conceptual rigor of scientific modernity as well as the ethical imperative of utilizing such rigor transparently and with commitment to knowledge as a project of public reasoning, Cohen's idealism provides for a more systematic treatment of how knowledge is shaped in the public sphere. Indeed, Cohen's faith in ideas and the justification of reasoning demands a reconsideration of the rationalization of secular modernity, since, as idealists, even moderns must *believe* in ideas.[31]

While the crisis of mass democratization and the achievements of German liberalism contributed to the rise of demagogic power in Weimar Germany, what Weber's comments reflect—despite a general ignorance of the context for their assessment—is the degree to which the Wilhelmine era was the origin of the crisis of liberalism.[32] When associated with the post-war crises of Weimar Germany, liberalism has all too often been caricatured as culminating in parliamentary inaction and paralysis. But in imperial Germany, liberalism was not understood as the mandate of any one political party and certainly not of the legal system as such.[33] Indeed, aside from the brief ascendancy of the National Liberals during the early years of German unification under Bismarck, liberalism lacked a clear identity as a movement. Its failure to democratize Germany's public institutions left it out of sync with Germany's peculiar march toward industrialization and economic modernization. As far as political movements were concerned, in the years leading up to the war social democracy appeared increasingly to have picked up the torch of liberal democratization. Articulations of this so-called *Sonderweg* thesis of Germany's distinctive historical path thus often focus on the anti-modern and antiliberal animus of the various entrenched "social-moral milieus" of imperial German culture, as described by M. Rainer Lepsius.[34] These various and conflicting sites of cultural autonomy were like ideological islands lacking any common moral or political bridge beyond the entrenched interests of these varied communities. The liberal ideal of rational consensus, to put it somewhat reductively, never had a chance to unify these loosely connected worldviews and interests.

Liberalism, many scholars have claimed, therefore remained an ideal in modern Germany—or, rather, an anti-ideal. With the political realignment of Bismarck's government after 1878 away from a free market and toward the protection of the nobility and industrial classes, many historians have considered imperial Germany from those years forward as, following Fritz Stern's well-known description, patently "illiberal."[35] As a state of both institutions and of mind, this illiberalism, writes Stern, represented a "commitment in mind and policy against any further concession to democracy."[36] This disdain for the "liberal habits of tolerance, dissent, debate, openness," Stern continues, meant that Germans "lacked, in Bagehot's phrase, the nerve for open discussion."[37] Even German socialism, Stern claimed, was prone to such illiberal tendencies. Instead, many conservative Germans believed the traditional organization of the Junker class and the confessional milieus could only guarantee their interests through an authoritarian emphasis on honor, duty, and veneration of the received order. Dissent was made out to be "un-German." This aversion to discussion and critique—desiderata in the history of political thought—makes German liberalism something of an empty signifier. Indeed, liberalism in Wilhelmine Germany might be better described, following Ewald Grothe and Ulrich Sieg, as an "imagined enemy" (*Feinbild*).[38]

This imagined liberalism was often portrayed as a rationalist pursuit of political education for democracy directly opposed to the traditions and cultural sentiments of Germans. Liberalism therefore conjured an anxiety about the practice of parliamentary debate as a sign of disloyalty. Those committed to a liberal vision of reason—of deliberation, education, and *Bildungsbürgertum*, or civic education—were therefore destined to close ranks and turn their attention to the intellectual sphere, where the gap between the intelligentsia and the various moral-social milieus widened. Therefore, German liberalism ought to be framed according to its development in largely intellectual contexts, finding expression in the philosophical, scientific, and social concepts of the rational individual, social laws of change and commercial development, and a turn toward a more abstract conception of culture.[39]

How, then, ought we reconcile the image of Enlightenment citizen-subjectivity claimed as the basis for the modern nation-state with the economic individualism and emphasis on undeterred access to unregulated markets so often attributed to Locke's liberal ideals of "life, liberty, and property"? Is the epistemological or rational emphasis of Enlightenment liberalism identical with the political liberalism of Locke's *Second Treatise*? And if so, is liberalism plagued by the color-blind, secularist pretensions of its neutral (white) rights-holder?[40] In our time, liberalism has increasingly been framed almost exclusively according to the post–World War II European and American consensus that free-market economic principles have smoothed out the rough patches of what began as a commitment to the rational individual. But German liberalism, as James Sheehan notes, took root in Germany primarily in the era of the

Enlightenment, when figures such as Immanuel Kant first championed a public sphere in which ideas were both put forward and openly debated.[41]

With this emphasis on publicity and the cultivation of "public opinion," as David Sorkin notes, "German liberalism had an essential cultural component which distinguished it from an English or French liberalism whose origins lay more in the spheres of economics and politics."[42] Thus, while liberalism's underlying hermeneutic has also been characterized as one of self-legitimation and self-assertion,[43] this emphasis on publicity and the use of reason is the more firmly rooted principle for nineteenth-century German liberals. As Woodruff Smith has claimed, "one of the reasons most liberals thought that, despite differences, they belonged to the same movement and agreed on fundamentals was that the thinking embodied in their programs really did rest on a broad consensus about the validity of a set of assumptions, concepts, and inferences."[44] Liberalism in imperial Germany was therefore primarily an intellectual and theoretical pursuit. This was, as Habermas has shown, the era in which the public sphere, a space of social exchange of knowledge, opinion, and conjecture, truly took shape.[45] Although liberalism's understanding of reason and the abstraction of the citizen-subject has come under attack for its purported neutrality—a subject invariably white, male, and European—might there be something more to reason, when shaped in public and outside political parties, than what contemporary accounts lead us to believe? The full spectrum of the relationship between liberalism and public reasoning might include hues that are as yet imperceptible.

To better understand this account of liberalism, we need to turn away from contemporary connotations of political doctrine and acknowledge the social and intellectual spheres of nineteenth-century German liberalism. The social and intellectual foci for liberal and antiliberal paths alike were in large part epistemological. That is to say that liberalism, whether an imagined enemy or a new rational worldview, was debated because proponents declared it the basis for public reasoning itself. The depiction of liberalism as an attempt to "neutralize" the normative content of morality or religion in order to arrive at abstractly agreed on values and norms[46] first emerges in discussions of what should count as the normative roots of modern culture. Thus, many liberal Protestants sought to reconcile the dramatic transformations of modern life both with the rise of urbanization and industrialization and with the moral and social order provided by Christianity. However, the goal of these "cultural Protestants" was to present a compelling version of Christianity. They were seeking a justified and self-reflexive account of the Christian past in order to secure a place for tradition in shaping the modern world. One way to reassess the social and cultural meaning of German liberalism is therefore to consider the public debates over modernization and secularization, particularly during the rise of what is known as "cultural Protestantism."[47]

The concern with culture as an epistemological problem stemmed from a perceived loss of legitimate knowledge and values in imperial Germany. With the dismissal of Bismarck as imperial Chancellor and the repeal of the anti-Socialist laws, the late 1890s and early 1900s were set to become years of growth for new social movements and voluntary associations. As Todd Weir has recently demonstrated, a distinctly organized secularist movement emerged within the German public sphere at this time, vying for its own claim to a philosophical *Weltanschauung*.[48] Thus, movements in the name of monism, pantheism, and materialism popularized the metaphysical and epistemological transformations of the nineteenth century and articulated new scientific and moral values, which opened alternatives to traditional Christian religion.[49] Together with the rise of the German *Free Religious Movement*, these secularist organizations, if not anticlerical in nature, nevertheless challenged the institutional recognition of Protestantism and Catholicism as the established churches of Prussia and the dominant confessions of the German Empire as a whole.[50] This cultural constellation of forces therefore shaped the context in which liberal Protestantism sought to navigate a thicket of worldviews and articulate a place for religious continuity.

Whether liberal Protestants pursued an ideological liberalism or cultural hegemony in a struggle against Catholic institutional authority,[51] by the early 1900s debates in the sociology of religion and in philosophy were largely focused on how moral norms and historically developing values might best be understood and articulated amid the ideological force of political secularism. Liberal Protestantism, the sociology and history of religion, and German philosophy thus represent responses to perceived crises of objectivity, historicism, modernism, and secularization. And each response shared an appeal to some kind of methodological or epistemological standard that might help renegotiate the meaning of ultimate values without simply receding into theology. Addressing the crisis of *value* and the transformations of a bourgeois German society now embracing modern, scientific, and economic models of lifestyle, belief, and practice, the process of secularization required new methods of reasoning to address the diversity of worldviews that now competed for public recognition. Epistemological questions, in this context, were more than arcane philosophical debates; they concerned the legitimate basis for modern culture and society.

To the extent that epistemology was considered a basis for cultural values, however, philosophy most certainly had something to say in this story. Thus, as the dominant academic philosophical movement of the late nineteenth century, neo-Kantianism sought to negotiate between the spheres of cultural normativity and historical tradition, natural scientific thought and moral philosophy by reinterpreting the idealism of Immanuel Kant. With its scientific worldview, Hermann Cohen's Marburg school of neo-Kantianism provided a theory of normativity that sought to recuperate the reputation and role of philosophical method as arbiter of public discourse. Since Germany's failed liberal revolution of 1848, philosophical idealism had been associated with a weak and ineffectual liberal political project.[52] Neo-Kantianism sought to redeem idealism as a scientific and nonmetaphysical philosophy. Thus, the natural scientific model of "experience" sketched by Cohen's groundbreaking *Kant's Theory of Experience* (1873) provided neo-Kantian philosophy with a rigorous idealist basis for its account of human knowledge as a system of a priori categories and lawful cognitive models for mapping the world. Through Cohen's continued reinterpretation of Kant throughout the 1880s and the development of his own system of philosophy in the early 1900s, he helped popularize a neo-Kantanism that emphasized the construction and critique of knowledge (*Erkenntniskritik*), the rigors of science, and the role of philosophy as a coherent map of both concepts and values.

Cohen's idealism was unique in its emphasis on lawful objectivity and the unseating of subjectivity as the privileged point of philosophical analysis. Emphasizing the mathematically lawful conditions for cognition, Cohen's emphatically idealist Kant interpretation also insisted that the "things in themselves"—which Husserl and the young Heidegger would later seize as the sphere of authenticity for the Weimar generation—were regulative ideas.[53] For Cohen, the ideal and a priori categories of the understanding were the laws through which knowledge could be objectified and in turn publicly recognized as canonical. His transcendental method was therefore aimed at justifying the possibility of such a public canon of knowledge, and it is this public dimension of knowledge that I believe is so crucial to Cohen's contribution. Even the young Karl Barth, who would later bemoan his own neo-Kantian and liberal Protestant training, was rather compelled by the Marburger emphasis on methodology and "experience."[54]

However, as civil servants (*Beamten*), the professoriat was identified with the institutions of Wilhelmine Germany, and neo-Kantianism earned the reputation in Weimar as yet another malign offshoot of liberalism, albeit now tied to the authoritarianism and militarism of the German Empire. Together with the rise of sociological positivism and its shared emphasis on purely rational constructions of value, that neo-Kantian philosophers expressed their emphatic support for the German war effort in 1914 left an ashen taste in the mouths of those Weimar thinkers nurtured by prewar academic philosophy.

Thus, the neglect of Cohen's philosophy—both as an expression of German-Jewish intellectual liberalism and as a response to secularization—might be explained, as Frederick Beiser has suggested, by the devastation of the Great War and a younger generation whose hopes and imaginations had been singularly hijacked by the sobering realities of mechanized warfare's mass carnage and who could no longer put their faith in reason or a narrative of historical progress.[55] Forces of authenticity, emotion, and irrationality proportionate to the chaos of the war would be summoned instead and the advance of an age typically characterized by a correlative scientization and secularization culminated in the rise of mythic, racial, and spiritualist thinking. But the fault lines beneath the structure of reason had already begun to shift in the years leading to the war—the years of liberalism's incipient crisis.[56] And there is good reason to suspect, as I will show in the chapters that follow, that Cohen's thought lost its sphere of influence to the very forces it sought to prove unjustified, such as racial thinking, social Darwinism, and anti-Semitic nationalism, which all gained greater degrees of influence in this time of chaos.

In sum, Cohen's description of scientific knowledge was aimed at deploying critical philosophy and its transcendental method to the question, How is culture possible?[57] That is, Cohen considered culture to be the publicly constituted and historically delimited body of knowledge—both scientific and spiritual—of the modern world. At its zenith, Cohen's neo-Kantianism attempted to negotiate the spheres of cultural reasoning and claims to absolute value and authority by appealing to justified knowledge and treating "reason" as a public canon of historically developing knowledge rather than allowing any "authenticity" to be traced to the material world. Cohen's idealism uniquely aimed at critiquing the antiliberal offensive against justified, scientific, and historical reasoning mounted in the name of materialist and mythic accounts of identity and national values. By inveighing against attempts to imbue "things in themselves" with the notion of "given" value, Cohen's idealism insisted instead on a self-reflexivity of conceptual reasoning or the attempt to lay bare the historical provenance of ideas, their status in public reasoning, and their ability to help negotiate a more ethical culture. And, as I hope to show, this inquiry into the transcendental conditions of possibility for public, objective knowledge at the basis of culture represents an encounter between science and spirit that profoundly alters what it might mean to refer to Hermann Cohen as a liberal.

As the chapters to follow will show, Cohen's neo-Kantianism provides an emphatic response to the crisis of secularization, its illiberal backlash, and the ensuing forces of reenchantment with an appeal to science or public knowledge as the ground of culture.[58] Thus, this book argues that the seemingly arcane philosophical epistemology of Cohen's thought endows his overall project with the resources for what is perhaps the most rigorous defense of a modern, liberal worldview in the early twentieth century.

LIBERALISM AS
A THEOLOGICO-POLITICAL PREDICAMENT

The Weimar era's association of Wilhelmine liberalism with neo-Kantianism, liberal Protestantism, and German Jewry as expressions of formalism or positivism stems from another significant critique of the liberal ideal of reasoned consensus: what Leo Strauss described as the "theologico-political predicament." As one of the better known repercussions of the social and historical process of secularization, this predicament describes the transformation of institutions and canons of knowledge that previously commanded legitimate authority for social and individual self-understanding through their theological sanction. In Strauss's telling, the theologico-political predicament indicts a liberalism that presents itself as disenchanted and unencumbered by a spiritual past or by beliefs and rituals. It is this disenchanted liberalism that failed to quell the stirring of antiliberal forces that later successfully toppled the liberal project of Weimar Germany. Strauss therefore believed this predicament required a move beyond what he believed was simply "too strong"[59] of an idealism on Cohen's part; an idealism that Jacob Taubes similarly ridiculed for its complicity in the "liberalism" of Wilhelminian naivete.[60] Thus, given the critical study of values and historically situated accounts of knowledge debated in neo-Kantianism, the sociology of religion, and liberal Protestantism, the theologico-political predicament also describes the alleged failure of liberalism to fill the vacuums of value and objectivity created by the recession of traditional authority from institutions and knowledge.

As I argue in the following chapters, however, Cohen anticipated such developments, and his critique of materialism and metaphysics must be understood as part of a critical response to the secularist dimension of the theologico-political predicament described by Strauss. In large part, we find Cohen's implicit critique of secularism in his description of Protestantism, which he understood as a broad cultural heritage that was not simply a confession of Christianity. Rather, Cohen described Protestant culture as the intellectual motive for distinguishing between science and faith as sources of knowledge. Protestantism, in other words, is the catalyst for liberalism. Thus, Strauss and others trace the separation of rationality and enchantment to Luther's distinction between faith and knowledge as the basis for the theologico-political predicament. However, Cohen's project demonstrates the degree to which the distinction between faith and justification was an epistemological revolution that enabled reason to become something public; that is, because Protestantism freed individual thought from the dogma of the church, Protestantism indirectly made room for Judaism within the space created between the institutions of modern society and the dogmas of Christianity. Cohen therefore traces the development of public religious reasoning to its Protestant *roots* and insists that this broader history is implicit in idealist philosophy, especially that of Kant. Religion, for Cohen, remains part of the story of liberalism.

Cohen's engagement with Protestantism has not served his legacy well, however. Though characterized as a hopeful, if not naive, attempt to articulate a modern Jewish philosophy of religion that decisively presented itself as a modern, liberal worldview, Cohen is also accused of effectively forwarding a secular and liberal as opposed to authentic Judaism. By *secular*, however, it seems that such critiques mean that Cohen's thought is *too Protestant*. Consider, for example, Gershom Scholem's claim that

> to the extent that the rationalism of the Jewish and European Enlightenment subjected the Messianic idea to an ever advancing secularization, it freed itself of the restorative element. It stressed instead the utopian element, though in a totally new way that is foreign to the Middle Ages. Messianism became tied up with the idea of eternal progress and [the] infinite task of humanity perfecting itself. In this process, the concept of progress, itself a non-restorative element, became central for rational utopianism. The restorative factors lost their effect to the degree that the national and historical elements of the Messianic idea were superseded by a purely universalistic interpretation. Hermann Cohen, surely as distinguished a representative of the liberal and rationalistic reinterpretation of the Messianic idea in Judaism as one could find, was driven by his religion of reason into becoming a genuine and unhampered utopian who would have liked to liquidate the restorative factor entirely.[61]

Cohen's idealized messianism, which Scholem refers to as an expression of Enlightenment rationalism, is characterized as a kind of liberal universalism, a utopianism that not only supersedes the "national and historical elements" but secularizes the messianic idea. As we will see, the messianic inflection of Cohen's "God-idea" is crucial to Cohen's idealism because it helps negotiate between the historical norms not only of Judaism but also of Christianity. It provides the ideal of consensus between reasoners capable of idealizing their pasts as concepts usable in the future. This irked Scholem for reasons that he may not have been able to fully name. For Cohen's idealism—as Scholem surely knew—was neither ahistorical nor neutral in its content. Cohen's messianic God-idea was in no way an attempt to dissolve its (messianic God-idea) roots in Jewish sources. But if an appeal to God as an emphatically decisive idea for human history was considered too liberal for Scholem, this was due to its normative designs. For Cohen's God never materializes at some historical moment but instead exists always as an ideal beyond human volition, an infinite ethical demand placed forever upon moral and political actors. Cohen's God suffers no secularization by being an idea; rather Cohen's

God shows us the degree to which ideas are by definition enchanted. Enchantment, however, simply requires more from us; it requires justified thinking. Hence, God represents the critique of mythic thinking that Cohen disavowed as metaphysics or the antiliberal refusal to engage in justified thinking.[62] If anything, Cohen's liberalism is expressed in the twin goals of justified conceptual thinking and the reconciliation of morality with science. Such rationality is, therefore, perhaps *too* enchanted for Scholem's liking.

Whatever Scholem's grievances, his comments reveal how the explicitly Protestant dimension of modern German Judaism, for which Cohen in particular has been criticized, has been misunderstood. Following the broader contemporary trends of the study of religion, Protestantism has continued to garner a reputation in Jewish studies as an insincere dimension of Jewish modernity. Thus, Cohen's idealizing interpretation of Judaism in Protestant terms has been characterized as a hollow expression of Jewish "religion." However, by reframing Cohen's liberalism around the question of religious reasoning, we begin to develop a better sense of what is at stake in his philosophy: namely, a pursuit of idealism as enchanted reasoning.

REASONING AND ENCHANTMENT

The epistemological focus of my story is minor inflections, protests, contestations, and the recognition of different reasons. But the claim that reasoning is not only a social practice but also an ethical *labor* arises in Cohen's account of idealism and its connection to German Protestantism. Idealism, with its focus on the transcendence of ideas to empirical, historical specificity (as well as political institutions), imprints reasoning with a lingering enchantment. Liberal Protestantism therefore adopts a number of new attributes. As Pamela Klassen has shown, liberal Protestants may have distinguished their "rationalities" from the "superstitions" of other Christians, but they were nevertheless enchanted by anthropologies of the spiritual body. And when we consider the scientific pursuit of medicalized healing, as Klassen has, we find the texture of the spirit everywhere.[63] Within the rationality of the biomedical pursuit—the apex of scientific rationality—the spirit of intangible disease, healing, and communicability vested its power. Science remained a sphere of enchantment.

So, too, in the pursuit of an ethical labor of cultural creativity and compromise, the prospect of building something that does not yet exist but that *ought to* gives such reasoning the characteristic of being enchanted with possibility. It is something to believe in.

This enchanted liberalism should help pluralize the project of liberalism associated with Protestantism. While in Klassen's account we find in the globalizing and rationalizing Christian project of modernization a reason beholden to spirits of another kind, the inflection of Protestantism *as* liberalism reveals something similar: by placing religion and reason in a space of reflexivity where opposites meet—whether rationality and enchantment, spirit and matter, or idea and history—Protestantism enables the shift toward a self-reflexivity in knowledge. This, at least, is the view of Protestantism on the part of its minor inflections. For Cohen, Protestantism becomes a style of *reasoning*, whereby the publicity of knowledge becomes available to a minority as well as a majority.

When treated as a style of reasoning, the Protestant contours of liberalism describe, to borrow a phrase form Wilfred Sellars, a "logical space of reasons, of justifying and being able to justify what one says."[64] Sellars's description of the space of reasons expounds on a view of knowledge that looks both to the past and to completed states of knowing for justification. Akin to Sebastian Luft's suggestion,[65] we might adapt Sellars's account to Cohen's understanding of reason as a work in progress—and a work within a pluralized public sphere—and describe Protestant epistemology, a liberalism conscious of its roots having opened a space of epistemological action, and the legacy of the liberal public sphere as such a space of *reasoning*.

—⚹—

Chapter 1 therefore explores the interweaving of Protestantism and the self-reflexivity of liberalism by showing that usual depictions of Cohen's liberalism as Protestant—which often caricature it as a one-sided conversation in which Jews become Germans either by assimilating and giving up religion or by reducing Judaism to an abstract reason—are false. Rather, by focusing on the role of Protestantism in Cohen's depiction of both German and Jewish *ethé*, I show instead how Cohen's Jewish writings—including his early essay on Heine (1867), his later essay on Spinoza (1915), his infamous "Germanism and Judaism" (1916), and his late essay "The Jew in Christian Culture" (1917)—provide a description of Protestantism as a syncretistic philosophical worldview that is something more than Christianity. In other words, to ground Cohen's liberalism in Protestantism is not quite the same as grounding it in Christianity. This is because Protestantism represents the separation of scientific and philosophical *reasoning* from the historically established values, norms, and truths deemed theologically dogmatic. By focusing on Cohen's engagement with Heine and Spinoza, I trace a genealogy of Protestant Judaism that explains Cohen's sense of modern Protestantism as an idealistic worldview in which Judaism can be introduced *as itself*, now that German modernity has emancipated knowledge from the confines of Christian theological dogma. For Cohen, liberalism is best expressed in philosophical idealism because reasoning remains enchanted *with ideas*.

That being said, Cohen was also worried about an alternative—and perhaps more familiar—result of Protestantism: the secularization or disenchantment of the modern world. In his later writings, Spinoza's pantheism is the screen onto which Cohen projects this worry. Cohen was concerned that pantheism (or what he would also call metaphysics) had transformed the newfound freedom accorded reason into a new dogmatism that risked naturalizing and nationalizing reason, which, in relegating religion to the irrational, left Judaism with a new quandary of having to metaphysically assimilate to the "true religion" of universal reason. As a result, Cohen's own attention to the role of Protestantism in the history of philosophical idealism enables him to embrace a different account of reasoning represented by a minor Protestantism, *a Protestantism without Christianity and consequently also a liberalism without secularism.*

Cohen therefore depicts German Judaism as animated by an epistemology of protest where, in the space of reasoning, opposites meet, and the Hellenic spirit of *Deutschtum* collides with the Prophetic spirit of *Judentum*; or, as James Joyce would have it, "Jewgreek is Greekjew. Extremes meet!" The very labor of placing two extremes into contact with each other, of reflecting each seemingly independent tradition's ability to make claims on the other, illustrates the work of reasoning to transcend each tradition's particularities. This is the enchantment afforded by Cohen's version of idealism. And it is this facet of idealism that I seek to forward as a version of liberalism rooted in a Protest(ant) epistemology.

But the act of reasoning that protests the past, seeking ever more de-mocratized knowledge, is also implicit in an alternative description of the problem of secularization. This alternative stems from the disenchant-ment of knowledge and truth. Chapter 2 therefore considers the dialectic of enchantment and disenchantment that is enabled by Protestantism's epistemological opening. While one consequence is the liberal distinc-tion between institutional dogmas and the space of reasoning into which freedom of religion might be articulated, another consequence is the unmooring of scientific truth and knowledge from the constraints of the past. Hence, the recognition of the Reformation as a historically contin-gent moment of epistemological protest makes possible two paths of Prot-estant liberalism: one that enables religious reasoning and the other that enables the culmination of philosophy as a metaphysics of secularism. Chapter 2 therefore surveys the scientific and philosophical discourse surrounding Cohen's development of his system of critical idealism and *Religion of Reason* (1919) in order to show how he navigated the crisis of value he anticipated resulting from the secularization of Protestantism.

In the late nineteenth century, philosophy became the site of critical debate about the legitimate concepts and values for grounding scientific as well as social/moral knowledge. Cohen's complex philosophical method was an intervention into these debates. His idealism—specifically his account of judgment—is integral to an account of *reasoning* about values *that occurs over time.*[66] Thus, Cohen saw in the canon of scientific knowl-edge a *public* body of knowledge, and he saw access to it as potentially ever more democratized. Cohen's version of idealism lays bare how a community (a) transmits the sources of its values and norms, (b) debates those sources, values, and norms, and (c) justifies those sources, values, and norms so that the reasoning community can be democratized or liberalized.

Thus, in response to the path of secularized reason that presents itself as value-neutral and universal, Cohen's idealism develops what I refer to as an epistemological secularity. As a secular mode of reasoning about collective knowledge, Cohen's idealism refuses to demand that religious communities check the authority of their values and norms at the door of entry to the public sphere but it also insists that those values and norms cannot be rooted in the unjustified assertion of mythic origins in the blood, soil, or identity of a people's past. Rather, this reasoning transpires in reflecting on the historical sources of both religious and liberal values. This effectively *minoritizes* would-be absolute or majoritarian values. That is to say, by reflecting on where values come from and how they came to be established in knowledge, the universality of those values is given a past and a particularity. And this is the work carried out by what I describe as Cohen's method of idealization: by turning to the sources of a tradition and showing the constructed nature of values over time, the method frees ideas themselves from any pretense to embody the eternal. *This minoritization of values is the democratization of those values.* A majority value or norm can then be redeployed by the minority. While an emphasis on justification is certainly implicit in the rise of modern philosophy,[67] Cohen's insight stems from his insistence on the Protestant roots of this critique and the fact that his minor inflection of it presents a secularity uninterested in neutralizing the past.

German Christians and German Jews, in their own self-understanding, depicted the secularization of philosophy, science, society, and morality in very different ways. For many German Christians, the secularizing path of Protestantism meant that even though public life and faith would be distinct, the legitimate authority of law and state remained rooted in a common Christianity. If secularization meant that this legitimacy was in question, then a crisis of public knowledge—both scientific and moral— was at hand. For Jews, secularization meant something else entirely. The secularizing path of Protestantism meant that Jews could now participate in the public life of German civilization as writers, teachers, lawyers, and artists, but not exclusively as Jews. Jews did not experience their rights as entitlements but rather as publicly acquired and socially constructed. Jews thus *became* good Protestants in order to become modern and liberal citizens. Heinrich Heine's well-known quip that "baptism was an entry ticket into European culture" was much more than jest.

However, the anxiety over this assumed "Christianness"[68] of German secularity fueled a widespread conception that Jews qua Jews could not accept the legitimate authority of the state and the moral foundations of civil society; perhaps they were actively opposed to it, even. Indeed, this was the root of the late nineteenth-century "Jewish Question."[69] Theoretically described, therefore, the Jewish Question helps name the theologico-political predicament of a minority religion within a liberal regime, since it forces a series of questions about the legitimacy of a truly secular public sphere. Can a regime be truly neutral toward religions? Or is there always a background history or set of commitments? Can there be a definition of *neutrality* that does not derive its normative basis from some claim of hegemony or absoluteness? Can reason be value neutral and still serve as a bulwark against a more insidious transvaluation of values?

The Jewish Question therefore exposes the social imaginary of liberal culture. By forcing these spectral presences into the light, however—with sometimes violent repercussions—the Jewish Question is therefore a correlate of the theologico-political predicament. That is, following Randi Rashkover and Martin Kavka's description, the theologico-political predicament concerns the determination of "whatever constitutes a community's point of ultimate concern, without which the community has no identity or meaning." Such concern is confirmed as ultimate through the "willingness for participation in collective sacrifice for the sake of causes that are taken to address the core of a community's identity."[70] In the public sphere of Wilhelmine Germany, nationalism provided one form of "ultimate concern" in the wake of Christianity's institutional and social transformations. But the identity of the nation was debated because it traced the boundaries between state and society, nation and religion. The Jews, as true liberals, were therefore accused of neutralizing the nation.

The rise of anti-Semitism is therefore yet another dimension of the dialectic of enchantment and disenchantment in liberalism. Anti-Semitism also drew on an imagined past and, in pursuit of justifications befitting the modern era, sought scientific confirmation through the ascendant intellectual worldviews of pantheistic metaphysics, humanism, monism, and materialism. As different manners of recasting knowledge's past, however, such invocations of the past could be neither *justified* nor *argued against*. In answer to the perceived crisis of modernization in Germany, the imagined values that consolidated a common national history also isolated the Jews as enemies of the nation. Based on the classic paradigm of romantic nationalism imagined by Johann Gottlieb Fichte, German anti-Semitism exploited the idea of a nation as the "eternal element to which [a member] entrusts the eternity of his self and his continued activity, the eternal order of things in which he lays his own eternity."[71] The nation became a new "eternal life" since "the divine has appeared in the people." But in this inverted world, in which nationalism traced an enchanted alternative to a disenchanted modernity, the theologico-political predicament encountered one of its most insidious responses in the form of anti-Semitism.

German liberalism and secularism therefore provide the theorist an opportunity to make explicit the dialectic of enchantment and disenchantment. This dialectic is a condition of the protest and contestation of the public sphere, where reasons, myths, and ideas of collective imagination proliferate. And this relationship between imagined belonging within Germany and collective imagination also exposes the vicissitudes of depicting enchantment as opposed to rationality, since the unity that all communities project for themselves—the "ultimate concern"—is, as Benedict Anderson writes, a product of imagination. The nation is "imagined because the members of even the smallest nation will never know most of their fellow-members, meet them, or even hear of them, yet in the minds of each lives the image of their communion."[72] Imagination reveals the degree to which the theologico-political predicament of liberalism has never been disenchanted; rather, the predicament concerns whether negotiated *reasons* can be compelling enough for a community to build and share its identity, to admit that their collective enchantment with such reasoning is something worth *believing in*. The alternative, as the history of anti-Semitism shows, is to assert an identity as absolute, exclusive, and grounded in something prior to any reasoning. Opting for the latter, anti-Semitism depicted liberalism as aiming blindly at serving everyone and, in fact, benefiting no one except the Jews, who were decidedly otherwise than members of a shared identity or reasoning.

Chapter 3 explores Cohen's idealization of Protestantism and Judaism as a response to and critique of anti-Semitic identitarianism. Now turning to the civic and political stakes of Cohen's account of "Germanness," this chapter outlines a basis for a critical idealist account of citizenship, belonging, and ethical cultural formation (*Bildung*). Tracing Cohen's response to attacks on Jewish liberalism, the chapter outlines Cohen's own critique and revision of the Kantian separation of legality from morality. Worrying that this incipient positivism in modern law and ethics effectively neutralized the ethical content of law, Cohen adopted a different strategy than other liberals. As a distinction seemingly necessary for liberal individualism, Cohen's worries over the threat of this positivism directly relates to his concern with the rise of nineteenth-century anti-

Semitic antiliberalism and the latter's use of irrational elements, such as blood and myth, to unite law and (*völkisch*) morality. As reactions to the debates over secularization and the "crisis of values" in Wilhelmine Germany, Cohen's focus on the *purpose* of law and judgment leads to a revision of Kant's categorical imperative in which its content generates from its form: the idea of humanity in one's own person. By relating Cohen's revised Kantianism to his depiction of the Jewish minority struggle for civil rights and the problem of freedom of conscience, this "difference within law" both becomes the basis for a new public reasoning about moral value and refutes materialistic arguments about crudely construed racial identity. In contrast to the historical arguments over the relationship between law and nation—or the racial appeal to blood and morality—the chapter concludes with Cohen's claim that *law consists of ideal actions that build citizenship and identity into the purpose of law: to socialize the state toward humanity.*

In the looming anti-Semitic critique of liberalism as having neutralized the point of ultimate concern, Cohen rightly detected a metaphysical and mythic threat to reasoning. I refer to this threat as the lure of reenchantment. That is, Cohen knew that without purpose and an ultimate concern, one must decide in favor of an alternative. If liberalism presents itself as having neutralized the possibility of conflict in the name of something universal, then to posit an alternative is to engage in an immanent critique that offers another enchanted placeholder at best. But if liberalism presents itself as a worldview conscious of its past and explicit commitments, then liberalism points us to its method of decision as an act of *reasoning*.

As a sphere of action, this space of reasoning is not only a logical space but also an ethical one. If negotiated consensus and parliamentary debate *commit* us to the belief that public reasoning is the space in which reasons can be given, taken, justified, and shared, then abiding by such a methodological maxim no longer remains a logical *necessity* but becomes a norm of ethical *possibility*: namely, to abide by honest, critical, and justifiable reasoning in the pursuit of a truth that ought to be. For Cohen, ethics provides the method for justified thinking, and its active pursuit of this truth is what he refers to as "ethical socialism." This socialism manifests, however, not at the level of state politics but within the conceptual structure of sociality itself. Hence, Cohen demonstrates that within the conceptual structure of consciousness, citizenship, and identity there is a sociality through which the *I* is first constituted. By renegotiating the relationship between law and morality as well as Kant's categorical imperative, Cohen demonstrates that the idea of humanity provides the ideal for self-formation and upends the notion of liberal individuality. Thus, as a distinctly minor inflection of German liberalism, this ethics of culture defines the *labor* of public reasoning that I unpack from Cohen's epistemological idealism.

Idealism therefore provides a crucial clue to identifying the dynamics of a minority's experience of secularization, and Cohen's account provides a hermeneutic to describe how majoritarian norms as well as the minoritarian response can be negotiated through a model of historical and normative consciousness and justification (or correction) of the social order.[73] Committed to the quintessentially modern questions of German national identity and civic belonging as Cohen was, it is important to note how these very questions also animate his interpretation of the task of modern Jewry—namely, questions about the work of reasoning as a public labor in science, law, social morality, and the development of culture. Cohen believed such questions could only be negotiated through idealism, whose vantage point is emphatically transcendental and helps reasoning comb through the thicket of reasons, values, histories, and contestations that inform modern culture by rigorously justifying and unpacking our concepts.

Chapter 4 concludes the book by arguing that Cohen's conception of religion provides an idealist and constructive account of social reason-giving in the public sphere. Revitalizing the enchantment of liberalism, Cohen's ethical idealism enables us to speak unapologetically about religious pluralism in public reasoning. I show how Cohen provides a systematic critique of the majoritarian discourse of neutrality toward religion. In contrast to the latter, Cohen turns to the rabbinic concept of the Noahide, or the resident alien recognized by both ethical culture and public law. The Noahide represents a concept of public reasoning that need not participate in political myth since the Noahide is not a theory of identity but of a *publicly* recognizable legal person. The Noahide is, however, a figure of minority. And as a minority projection on the part of a factual minority, this idealization of the Noahide helps Cohen negotiate the self-reflexivity of religious reasoning that does not seek to impose itself as a new majority. Contrasting Cohen's thought with Carl Schmitt's political theology and John Rawls's political liberalism, the chapter concludes by building on Cohen's idealized monotheism as a public norm of culture in order to develop an account of consensus in public reasoning.

In sum, I am attempting to navigate specific shifts in epistemic structures in the nineteenth century in order to uncover the roots of a reimagined liberal secularity; not a politically organized movement, which I refer to as secularism, but an epistemic order, a space of reasoning. In Cohen's thought, because ideas legitimate the cultural institutions, practices, and beliefs of modernity, these ideas must come from somewhere and are only justifiable if they are grounded in some holistic framework. Thus, while liberalism has been criticized for lacking transparency about its Christian—and emphatically Protestant—past, what I believe has been overlooked in common genealogies of the secular are the minority voices caught up in this spiritual past of liberalism, which do not remain silenced when we make that past explicit. Rather, as Cohen's thought and the German-Jewish experience of liberal Protestant modernity shows, the minority voices invite new epistemological contestations of the rationality and enchantment of modernity. These are questions that were in fact never fully settled in Cohen's time, but it is all the more important that we continue to ask them today.

This new interpretation of Cohen's philosophical idealism as a constructive vision of self-reflexive and critical thinking navigates between neutralizing liberal secularism and political theology. Its emphasis on idealism grounds modern cultural and political legitimacy in norms and ideas of human spirit and ethical possibility. Such a form of public reasoning for religion and liberalism provides a necessary corrective to the neutralization of spirits by secularism but also serves as a critical control on the unjustified appeal to myth and blood in racial essentialisms. By virtue of surpassing the flesh and blood of human artifice, ideas are the spirits of the religious past that help us navigate a postsecular future. Cohen's idealism therefore represents an attempt to understand the secularization of concepts and to reintroduce the role of religion in public life by making Jewish thought a genealogical link in the extended chain of modern idealism, the lever of liberal constitutional thought and values in the contemporary world.

In the chapters that follow, I suggest that Cohen's ethical idealism and monotheism, criticized by Weimar-era Jewish thinkers as empty formalism and liberal abstraction, reveal a deeper set of normative concerns and constraints animating Cohen's philosophy of Judaism and that Cohen's efforts to expose the feeble basis of metaphysics, materialism, and anti-Semitic antiliberalism have failed to gain due consideration in understanding the crisis of liberalism. By considering the struggles of imperial Germany, including the rise of anti-Semitism and nationalism, the rapid secularization of Wilhelmine society and politics, and the legacy of liberal and antiliberal arguments over citizenship, racial identity, and civic recognition, I argue that Cohen's thought provides an epistemological basis for a new kind of liberal secularity that does not neutralize the idiom of public reasoning. But most important for the overall reassessment of liberalism is, I believe, that Cohen's epistemological self-reflexivity accomplishes a critique of theological and political essentialisms urgently needed in contemporary discourse. It is a critique that demands not only justified and self-reflexive thinking as the basis of public reasoning but also belief and trust as the spiritual origin of modern, liberal culture—virtues badly needed in yet another time of looming crisis.

NOTES

1. English translation slightly modified from Max Weber, "Science as Vocation," in *The Vocation Lectures*, ed. David Owen and Tracy B. Strong, trans. Rodney Livingstone (Indianapolis: Hackett, 2004), 30.

2. Max Weber, *Parlement und Regierung im neugeordneten Deutschland. Zur politische Kritik des Beamtentums und Parteiwesens* (1918), in *Max Weber*, ed. Johannes Winckleman (Berlin: Duncker & Humblot, 1918), 393. Cited in Ellen Kennedy, introduction to Carl Schmitt, *The Crisis of Parliamentary Democracy*, trans. Ellen Kennedy (Cambridge, MA: MIT Press, 1988), xxii–xxiii.

3. Schmitt, *Crisis of Parliamentary Democracy*, 8.

4. Michael Brenner, *The Renaissance of Jewish Culture in Weimar Germany* (New Haven, CT: Yale University Press, 1996), 37–38.

5. Brenner, 6.

6. I will use the term *religion* in much the way that late nineteenth-century thinkers used the term, to designate the sphere of recognizable ritual and belief, which was designated by the scholarly discourse surrounding "religion." However, through my reading of Cohen, I begin to gesture at the degree to

which even when historicized, the term religion animates spheres of life, identity formation, and communal advocacy that defy attempts to place religion within a scholarly category. On the discursive production of "religion" more generally, see Talal Asad, *Genealogies of Religion: Discipline and Reasons of Power in Christianity and Islam* (Baltimore: Johns Hopkins University Press, 1993). See also Donald S. Lopez Jr., "Belief," in *Critical Terms in Religious Studies*, ed. Mark C. Taylor (Chicago: University of Chicago Press, 1998).

7. Leo Strauss, "Preface to the English Translation," in *Spinoza's Critique of Religion* (Chicago: University of Chicago Press, 1997), 8.

8. See letter to Alexander Altmann dated 22 Feb. 1952. Quoted in Marc B. Shapiro, *Between the Yeshiva World and Modern Orthodoxy: The Life and Works of Rabbi Jehiel Jacob Weinberg, 1884–1966* (Oxford: Littman, 1999), 173.

9. Leo Strauss, "Introductory Essay," in *Religion of Reason: Out of the Sources of Judaism*, by Hermann Cohen, trans. Simon Kaplan (Atlanta: Scholars' Press, 1995), xxxviii.

10. Brenner, *Renaissance of Jewish Culture*, 37, 41.

11. Gershom Scholem, "Toward an Understanding of the Messianic Idea in Judaism," in *The Messianic Idea in Judaism, and Other Essays on Jewish Spirituality* (New York: Schocken, 1971), 1–36, 26.

12. See Gershom Scholem, "On the Myth of German-Jewish Dialogue" in *On Jews and Judaism in Crisis: Selected Essays*, ed. Werner J. Dannhauser (New York: Schocken, 1976), 63: "The Jews have always been listeners of great intensity, a noble legacy they brought with them from Mount Sinai. They listened to many kinds of voices, and one cannot say that has always served them well. . . . I will forego the treatment of that deeply moving chapter that is designated by the great name of Hermann Cohen and the way in which this unhappy lover, who did not shun the step from the sublime to the ridiculous, was answered."

13. Strauss, "Preface to the English Translation," 6.

14. On the debates over Rosenzweig's interpretation of Cohen and its lasting contentiousness and the concept of "correlation" as the particular point of focus for this interpretation, see Alexander Altmann's now canonical essay "Hermann Cohen's Begriff der Korrelation," in *In Zwei Welten: Siegfried Moses zum fünfundsiebzigsten Geburtstag*, ed. Hans Tramer (Tel Aviv: Bitaon, 1962), as well as Andrea Poma, "Correlation: A Method and More Than a Method," in *Yearning for Form: Essays on Hermann Cohen* (Dodrecht, Netherlands: Springer, 2006), 61–86. For contemporary examples of how this revised interpretation of Cohen has only furthered understanding of Rosenzweig, see for example Robert Gibbs, *Correlations in Rosenzweig and Levinas* (Princeton, NJ: Princeton University Press, 1992); Leora Batnitzky, *Idolatry and Representation: The Philosophy of Franz Rosenzweig Reconsidered* (Princeton, NJ: Princeton University Press, 2000). For a helpful overview of the different

interpretations of Cohen's thought, see Daniel H. Weiss, *Paradox and the Prophets: Hermann Cohen and the Indirect Communication of Religion* (New York: Oxford University Press, 2012), 3–35. On Rosenzweig's attempts to imbue Cohen's posthumous work with a Weimar modernism, see Peter E. Gordon, *Rosenzweig and Heidegger, Between Judaism and Philosophy* (Berkeley: University of California Press, 2003).

15. On Cohen's historical context and the rise and fall of his influence, see Hans Liebschütz, "Hermann Cohen and His Historical Background," in *Publications of the Leo Baeck Institute Year Book XIII* (London: East and West Library, 1968); Amos Funkenstein, *Perceptions of Jewish History* (Berkeley: University of California Press, 1993), chap. 7; David N. Myers *Resisting History: Historicism and Its Discontents in German-Jewish Thought* (Princeton, NJ: Princeton University Press, 2009); Michael A. Meyer and Michael Brenner, eds., *German-Jewish History in the Modern Times: Integration in Dispute, 1871–1918* (New York: Columbia University Press, 1997), chap. 10.

16. As Susannah Heschel has emphasized (personal communication), Wilhelmine Germany was an empire and thus the logic of imperialism importantly determines the limits and possibilities for political and social agency in the Reich. This means that characterizations of the "liberal state" correspond to the imagined state in the discourse of liberalism, which, as will become clear throughout, I describe as a diffuse intellectual movement rather than a defined political ideology. On the implications of a colonial encounter between the Jewish minority and German majority in the nineteenth century, see Susannah Heschel, "Revolt of the Colonized: Abraham Geiger's Wissenschaft des Judentums as a Challenge to Christian Hegemony in the Academy," *New German Critique* 77 (1999): 61–85.

17. Strauss, "Preface to the English Translation," 1.

18. On the semiotic ideology of Protestant modernity—the link between habits, practices, and materiality—see Webb Keane, *Christian Moderns: Freedom and Fetish in the Mission Encounter* (Berkeley: University of California Press, 2007).

19. See Wendy Brown, *Undoing the Demos: Neoliberalism's Stealth Revolution* (New York: Zone Books, 2015).

20. In this respect, I take Sarah Hammerschlag's reading of Derrida and the dangers of exemplarity to heart and see a similar model in Cohen's thought. See Sarah Hammerschlag, *The Figural Jew: Politics and Identity in Postwar French Thought* (Chicago: University of Chicago Press, 2010), especially chapter 5. That is, *because* of its emphasis on minority, it interrogates what the exemplarity of a successful Jewish politics or account of any specific Jewish identity could mean by showing that majorities can also be minoritized. On the role of cultural particularity in mapping the universal in Derrida and Rosenzweig (and Cohen's legacy therein), cf. Dana

Hollander, *Exemplarity and Chosenness: Rosenzweig and Derrida on the Nation of Philosophy* (Stanford, CA: Stanford University Press, 2008).

21. John Abromeit, *Max Horkheimer and the Foundations of the Frankfurt School* (New York: Cambridge University Press, 2011); cf. Paul Mendes-Flohr, "'To Brush History against the Grain': The Eschatology of the Frankfurt School and Ernst Bloch," *Journal of the American Academy of Religion* 51, no. 4 (1983): 636–40.

22. Katerina Clark and Michael Holquist, *Mikhail Bakhtin* (Cambridge, MA: Harvard University Press, 1984).

23. See Leora Batnitzky, *Leo Strauss and Emmanuel Levinas: Philosophy of the Politics of Revelation* (New York: Cambridge University Press, 2006); Gibbs, *Correlations in Rosenzweig and Levinas*.

24. See Robert B. Brandom's acknowledgment in Brandom, *Reason in Philosophy: Animating Ideas* (Cambridge, MA: Harvard University Press, 2009), 108n12. Natan Rotenstreich also observed the similarity between Cohen and Habermas, in Rotenstreich, "Recht, Gesetz, und Individuum: Zu Hermann Cohens praktischer Philosophie," *Zeitschrift für Religions- und Geistesgeschichte* 46 (1994): 97–106.

25. See Michel Foucault, "Une histoire restée muette," *La Quinzaine littéraire* 8 (1966): 3–4, reprinted in *Dits et Écrits I, 1954–1975*, ed. Daniel Defert and François Ewald (Paris: Gallimard, 2001).

26. Largely responsible for the continued interest in Hermann Cohen in the English-speaking world, Steven S. Schwarzschild gestured toward this reading of Cohen. See Steven S. Schwarzschild, "Franz Rosenzweig's Anecdotes about Hermann Cohen," in *Gegenwart im Rückblick: Festgabe für die Jüdische Gemeinde Berlin 25 Jahre nach dem Neubeginn* (Heidelberg: Lothar Stiehm Verlag, 1970), 209–18; Steven S. Schwarzschild, "The Title of Hermann Cohen's 'Religion of Reason: Out of the Sources of Judaism," introduction to Cohen, *Religion of Reason: Out of the Source of Judaism*, 1–20. Helmut Holzhey has also dedicated much of his more recent research to bringing both Cohen's Judaism and neo-Kantianism into better focus in European scholarship, where Cohen's neo-Kantianism still enjoys greater attention. See Helmut Holzhey, "Der Systematisch Ort der 'Religion der Vernunft' in Gesamtwerk Hermann Cohens," in *"Religion der Vernunft aus den Quellen des Judentums." Tradition und Ursprungdenken in Hermann Cohens Spätwerk*, ed. H. Holzhey et al. (New York: Georg Olms, 1998). Similarly, Andrea Poma and Pierfrancesco Fiorato treat Cohen's Judaism as part of the systematic influence on his philosophy; see Pierfrancesco Fiorato, *Geschichtliche Ewigkeit: Ursprung und Zeitlichkeit in der Philosophie Hermann Cohens* (Würzburg: Königshausen & Neumann, 1993) as well as Andrea Poma, *The Critical Philosophy of Hermann Cohen*, trans. John Denton (Albany: State University of New York, 1997). Likewise, Dieter Adelmann's *"Reinige dein Denken": Über den Jüdische*

hintergrund der Philosophie von Hermann Cohen (Würzburg: Könighausen & Neumann: 2010). Michael Zank has sought to give a more concentrated place to Judaism in Cohen's overall thought. Zank also attempts to date Cohen's "return" at the early- to mid-1890s, when Cohen begins to address the concept of atonement in his work. See Michael Zank, *The Idea of Atonement in the Philosophy of Hermann Cohen* (Providence, RI: Brown University Press, 2000), 107–151; cf. George Kohler, *Reading Maimonides in 19th Century Germany: The Guide to Religious Reform* (New York: Springer, 2012), 140n37. Similarly, Dieter Adelmann's *"Reinige den Denken": Über den jüdischen Hintergrund der Philosophie von Hermann Cohen*, ed. Görg K. Hasselhoff (Würzburg: Königshausen & Neuemann, 2010). See also George Kohler's review of Adelmann's "Reinige deine Denken" in *Modern Judaism* 31, no. 1 (2011): 109–13.

27. Throughout, I will refer to Wilhelmine or Wilhelminism to describe the period of 1890–1918, the period of time following Otto von Bismarck's resignation and during the reign of Wilhelm II.

28. On the contemporary relevance of such an account of sociality in political theory, see Jeffrey Stout, *Democracy and Tradition* (Princeton, NJ: Princeton University Press, 2004).

29. See David Sorkin, *The Transformations of German Jewry, 1780–1840* (Detroit: Wayne State University Press, 1999), 19. On Wilhelm von Humboldt's influential designation of *Bildung* or formation in the nineteenth century, see David Sorkin "Wilhelm von Humboldt: The Theory and Practice of Self-Formation (*Bildung*), 1791–1810," *Journal of the History of Ideas* 44 (1983): 55–73. For the significance of *Bildung* for German Jews, see George L. Mosse, *German Jews beyond Judaism* (Bloomington: Indiana University Press, 1985).

30. Leora Batnitzky, *How Judaism Became a Religion: An Introduction to Modern Jewish Thought* (Princeton, NJ: Princeton University Press, 2011).

31. On the question of modernity as a philosophical problem imbricated in the history of idealism, see Robert Pippin, *Idealism as Modernism: Hegelian Variations* (New York: Cambridge University Press, 1997), 11–16.

32. See Uffa Jensen, "A Communicative Gap: Bourgeois Jews and Protestants in the Public Sphere of Early Imperial Germany," *History of European Ideas* 32 (2006): 295–312.

33. The National Liberals and Progressive People's Party, as well as the German Social Democrat Party and Center Party, variously represented the center and left, and, with the exception of the latter, which garnered the support of the Catholic population in large part due to its attempt to negotiate a Catholic minority politics during and after the *Kulturkampf*, the remaining parties were in large part representative of the Jewish vote. See Jehuda Reinharz, *Fatherland or Promised Land? The Dilemma of the German Jew, 1893–1914* (Ann Arbor: University of Michigan Press, 1975).

34. M. Rainer Lepsius, "Parteinsystem und Sozialstruktur," 64, cited in Geoff Eley, "Notable Politics, the Crisis of German Liberalism, and the

Electoral Transition of the 1890s," in *In Search of a Liberal Germany* (New York: Berg, 1990), 187–216, 189.

35. Fritz Stern, *The Failure of Illiberalism: Essays on the Political Culture of Modern Germany* (New York: Columbia University Press, 1992), xvii. Cf. Heinrich August Winkler, *Liberalismus und Antiliberalismus: Studien zur politischen Sozialgeschichte des 19. und 20. Jahrhunderts* (Göttingen: Vandenhoeck & Ruprecht, 1979).

36. Stern, *Failure of Illiberalism*, xvii.

37. Stern, xx.

38. Grothe and Sieg, "Liberalismus als Feinbild—eine Einleitung," in *Liberalismus als Feinbild* (Göttingen: Wallstein Verlag, 2014), 1–18.

39. Woodruff D. Smith, *Politics and the Sciences of Culture in Germany, 1840–1920* (New York: Oxford University Press, 1991), 11.

40. On the problem of liberalism's claimed color-blindness and the limits of its purported universality, see Charles W. Mills, *Black Rights, White Wrongs: The Critique of Racial Liberalism* (New York: Oxford University Press, 2017).

41. James Sheehan, *German Liberalism in the Nineteenth Century* (New York: Cambridge University Press, 1978), 7.

42. Sorkin, *Transformations*, 19.

43. Hans Blumenberg, *The Legitimacy of the Modern Age*, trans. Robert M. Wallace (Cambridge, MA: MIT Press, 1985); Grothe and Sieg, "Liberalismus als Feinbild," 7–8.

44. Smith, *Politics and the Sciences*, 19.

45. Jürgen Habermas, *The Structural Transformations of the Public Sphere: An Inquiry into a Category of Bourgeois Society* (Cambridge, MA: MIT Press, 1989).

46. On the neutralization of politics see John P. McCormick, *Carl Schmitt's Critique of Liberalism: Against Politics as Technology* (New York: Cambridge University Press, 1997).

47. On the relationship between liberalism and cultural Protestantism, see Gangolf Hübinger, *Kulturprotestantismus und Politik: Zum Verhältnis von Liberalismus und Protestantismus im wilhelminischen Deutschland* (Tübingen: Mohr Siebeck, 1994); Marc D. Chapman, *Ernst Troeltsch and Liberal Theology: Religion and Cultural Synthesis in Wilhelmine Germany* (New York: Oxford University Press, 2001); David N. Myers, "Hermann Cohen and the Quest for Protestant Judaism" *Leo Baeck Institute Yearbook* 46, no. 1 (2001): 195–214. See also Todd H. Weir, *Secularism and Religion in Nineteenth-Century Germany: The Rise of the Fourth Confession* (New York: Cambridge University Press, 2014). On the relationship between liberalism and cultural Protestantism in shaping Cohen's own responses to antiliberalism and anti-Semitism, see Nahme, "God Is the Reason: Hermann Cohen's Monotheism and the Liberal Theologico-Political Predicament," *Modern Theology* 33, no. 1 (2016): 116–39.

48. Weir, *Secularism and Religion*, 66.

49. On the various transformations of these terms in the eighteenth and nineteenth centuries, especially pantheism and monism, see Weir, *Secularism and Religion*; Todd H. Weir, ed. *Monism: Science, Philosophy, Religion, and the History of a Worldview* (New York: Palgrave Macmillan, 2012); Frederick C. Beiser, *The Fate of Reason: German Philosophy from Kant to Fichte* (Cambridge, MA: Harvard University Press, 1987).

50. On the relationship to the Free Religious movement, see Hübinger, *Kulturprotestantismus und Politik*, 275.

51. Helmut Walser Smith, *German Nationalism and Religious Conflict: Culture, Ideology, Politics, 1870–1914* (Princeton, NJ: Princeton University Press, 1995); Michael B. Gross, *The War against Catholicism: Liberalism and the Anti-Catholic Imagination in Nineteenth-Century Germany* (Ann Arbor: University of Michigan Press, 2004). See also Todd H. Weir, "Germany and the New Global History of Secularism: Questioning the Postcolonial Genealogy," *Germanic Review* 90 (2015): 6–20, 16, where he discusses the sociologist Ferdinand Tönnies, for example, who was interested in building a *spiritual* and ethical culture distinct from the metaphysics and materialism. Ferdinand Tönnies, *Mitteilungen der Deutschen Gesellschaft für ethische Kultur* 1, no. 1 (Nov. 20, 1892) cited in Weir, "Germany and the New Global History of Secularism," 16; Weir describes this critique as a "neutralization" of secularism by attempting to synthesize different moral norms. Perhaps too vague to describe the methodological thrust of neo-Kantianism's epistemological project in this regard, Weir's thesis is important for recognizing Hermann Lübbe as having first put forward this observation. See Hermann Lübbe, *Säkularisierung: Geschichte eines ideenpolitischen Begriffs*, 2nd ed. (Munich: Karl Alber, 1975).

52. On the critique of German Idealism as an instantiation of incipient liberalism, see Klaus Kristian Köhnke, *Entstehung und Aufstieg des Neukantismus: Die deutsche Universitätsphilosophie zwischen Idealismus und Positivismus* (Frankfurt am Maim: Suhrkamp, 1986).

53. On the transformation of Cohen's Kant interpretation on his way to sketching his own critical idealism, see Geert Edel, *Von der Vernunftkritik zur Erkenntnislogik: Die Entwicklung der theoretischen Philosophie Hermann Cohens* (Berlin: Editions Gorz, 2010). On the definitive rejection of the thing-in-itself in *Kants Begrundung der Ethik*, see Helmut Holzhey, *Cohen und Natorp*, 2 vols. (Basel: Schwabe, 1986), as well as Poma, *Critical Philosophy of Hermann Cohen*.

54. Simon Fischer, *Revelatory Positivism? Barth's Earliest Theology and the Marburg School* (Oxford: Oxford University Press, 1988).

55. Frederick Beiser, "Weimar Philosophy and the Fate of Neo-Kantianism," in *Weimar Thought: A Contested Legacy*, ed. Peter E. Gordon and John P. McCormick (Princeton, NJ: Princeton University Press, 2013), 115–32, 116.

56. On the growing rhetoric of crisis in both philosophy and society, compare Albert Lewkowitz, "Die Krisis der modernen Erkenntnistheorie," *Archiv für systematische Philosophie* 21, no. 2 (1915) cited in Peter E. Gordon, "Science, Finitude, and Infinity: Neo-Kantianism and the Birth of Existentialism," *Jewish Social Studies* 6, no. 1 (1999): 30–53; Karl Joël, *Die philosophische Krisis der Gegenwart, Rektoratsrede* (Leipzig: Felix Meiner, 1914); See also Fritz Stern, *The Politics of Cultural Despair: A Study in the Rise of the Germanic Ideology* (Berkeley: University of California Press, 1974); Peter Eli Gordon, *Continental Divide: Heidegger, Cassirer, Davos* (Cambridge, MA: Harvard University Press, 2010), 43–44.

57. Sebastian Luft, *The Space of Culture: Towards a Neo-Kantian Philosophy of Culture (Cohen, Natorp, & Cassirer)* (New York: Oxford University Press, 2015), 61.

58. See chapter 3. On Cohen's conception of science and reason as a public canon of knowledge, see his forward to Friedrich Albert Lange, *Geschichte des Materialismus und Kritik seiner Bedeutung in der Gegenwart*, 2nd ed. (Iserlohn: Baedeker, 1875), x. While Peter Gordon depicts Cassirer as having softened Cohen's scientism, this public dimension of Cohen's understanding of science remains largely unexplored. Gordon also contends that Cassirer represents a politics of Enlightenment liberalism that is in many ways indebted to Cohen. See Gordon, *Continental Divide*.

59. Strauss, "Introductory Essay," xxxvi.

60. Jacob Taubes, *The Political Theology of Paul*, trans. Dana Hollander (Stanford, CA: Stanford University Press, 2004), 62.

61. Scholem, "Toward an Understanding," 26.

62. Both myth and metaphysics are terms that I will explain at length in the following chapter, however, it is important to emphasize that Cohen's thought deems metaphysics to be a betrayal of idealism, grounding knowledge in the principle of self-consciousness, the "I," and thus reflecting a closed circle of cognition, taking the self as both alpha and omega of knowledge.

63. Pamela E. Klassen, *Spirits of Protestantism: Medicine, Healing, and Liberal Christianity* (Berkeley: University of California Press, 2011).

64. Wilfred Sellars, *Empiricism and the Philosophy of Mind*, ed. Robert B. Brandom (Cambridge, MA: Harvard University Press, 1997), 76. Cited in Luft, *The Space of Culture*, 241.

65. Luft, *The Space of Culture*, 2.

66. Although Cohen's *Logik* outlines a theory of Truth that might indeed be construed as eternal and unchanging, this logical concept of truth remains an ideal that does not preclude the possibility of articulating an ethical conception of truth in the social sphere. On the difference between logical and ethical truth, see Hermann Cohen, *System der Philosophie, Zweiter Teil: Ethik des reinen Willens* (Berlin: Bruno Cassirer, 1904; repr. in *Hermann Cohens*

Werke, ed. H. Holzhey, 17 vols. [New York: G. Olms, 1978–], vol. 7), 23. Page numbers are to the reprint edition.

67. For a description of the relationship between tradition and justification in the context of European philosophical thought, see Thomas Pfau, *Minding the Modern: Human Agency, Intellectual Traditions, and Responsible Knowledge* (Notre Dame, IN: University of Notre Dame Press, 2015).

68. "Christianness [*Christenheit*] in our day," wrote Theodor Mommsen in 1880, "no longer has the same meaning it once had, nevertheless, it is the only designation we have to denote the international civilization of our day that unites millions and millions of the highly populated globe." Cited in Uriel Tal, *Christians and Jews in Germany: Religion, Politics, and Ideology in the Second Reich, 1870–1914*, trans. Noah Jonathan Jacobs (Ithaca, NY: Cornell University Press, 1975), 50–51.

69. Peter Pulzer, *Jews and the German State: The Political History of a Minority, 1848-1933* (Detroit: Wayne State University Press, 2003), 29–31.

70. Randi Rashkover and Martin Kavka, introduction to *Judaism, Liberalism, and Political Theology* (Bloomington: Indiana University Press, 2015), 5.

71. Johann Gottlieb Fichte, *Addresses to the German Nation*, ed. Gregory Moore (New York: Cambridge University Press, 2008), 104.

72. Benedict Anderson, *Imagined Communities: Reflections on the Origin and Spread of Nationalism* (New York: Verso, 2006), 6.

73. Robert Erlewine has highlighted the formal rationalism in Cohen's "ethical monotheism" as one such strategy for engaging religious pluralism in modernity. What Erlewine finds in Cohen's monotheism is therefore a willingness to recognize and to grapple with difference. But while Erlewine is right to find in Cohen's monotheism an explicit confrontation with difference, his use of the rubric of tolerance might fall short of the larger picture of liberalism that deems consensus as its ideal. Robert Erlewine, *Monotheism and Tolerance: Recovering a Religion of Reason* (Bloomington: Indiana University Press, 2010).

MINOR PROTEST(ANT)S

Cohen and German-Jewish Liberalism

HERMANN COHEN HAS NOT BEEN remembered fondly, and his philosophy has not received the recognition in its afterlife that it knew and
deserved in its own time. That may be due to the fact that many of those
with whom Cohen expressed political differences about German-Jewish
social struggles for civic recognition and integration have, for the most
part, controlled the telling of his life and work. It also hasn't helped that
the same telling tends to focus on the apparent historical tone-deafness
of Cohen's wartime tract, "Germanism and Judaism." Projecting an image of Jewish and German cultural and intellectual entanglement, Cohen's vision for a Jewish future in Germany was quickly tarnished by the
rise and success of the National Socialists, giving it the appearance of a
dilapidated liberal fantasy. Furthermore, to the extent that the Zionist
movement insisted the Jewish Question was insoluble and had forever
marked Jews as outsiders in European countries, many Zionist thinkers
represented—and continue to represent—Cohen's vision as evidence
of a failed integration of Jews into Germany and Europe.[1] Others have
intimated that Cohen might even bear some figural guilt for the supposed
naivete of German Jewry.

By contrast, in his day Cohen's role as one of the foremost exponents
of neo-Kantianism, then the reigning German academic philosophy,
earned him respect across Europe. His interpretation of Kant's philosophy presented idealism as a new vision of public access to knowledge, a democratization of science, and an appeal for justified reasoning.

However, as Paul Mendes-Flohr has observed, while the legacy of Cohen's neo-Kantianism has fared somewhat better than his alleged liberalism, Cohen's optimistic vision of Germanism and Judaism has been the subject of some ambivalence. Some of his closest associates, such as his student and friend Franz Rosenzweig, found Cohen's vision to be a sign of "infinite *chutzpah*," or hubris, in its devising of a purely philosophical representation of German identity and culture.[2] As Rosenzweig wrote to his parents, who were rather Cohenian Germans themselves, "All but [Cohen's] philosophy" is emptied out of *Deutschtum* such that "it is easy for him to regard himself a better German than the Germans themselves. For a Cohenian is naturally a better German."[3] In other words, Cohen's claims to Germanness—as well as Jewishness— were inseparable from his understanding of philosophy.

The same philosophical rigor attracted the ire of the postwar Weimar generation, who caricatured it as the trappings of an empty liberal rationalism. For some, this liberalism was inseparable from Cohen's Jewishness. For example, as Peter Gordon notes, "Heidegger indicated that Neo-Kantianism was a 'leveling' philosophy 'tailor made for liberalism,' which could only be combated through an influx of what he called 'native-born' teachers."[4] In other words, neo-Kantianism—of which Cohen was most prominently a representative—was marked as "liberal" and "Jewish," and responsible for both neutralizing philosophy and leveling German identity. Most interpreters of Cohen in fact have accepted the claim, although in less insidious form, that his ambitious philosophy was the root of his liberalism, the source of his naive account of German identity, and the vehicle for his Judaism. Some have even dismissed his thought, as one particularly negative assessment would have it, as "blinded" to political realities in its strictly philosophical gaze.[5] However, amid Rosenzweig's and Heidegger's contrasting disparagements of Cohen is an emphatically philosophical remainder: both German and Jew were philosophical identities for Cohen, and the very claim that philosophy might have something to say about identity led to the charge that Cohen was a liberal. What then should we make of this dual legacy—of Cohen's alleged guilt both of using philosophy to unsettle the essence of German or Jewish identities and of having philosophically reconstructed those same identities through his liberalism?

The association of Judaism with liberalism, and liberalism with some-thing foreign to Germany, reflects a broader anxiety in the nineteenth century. The alleged disenchantment, rationalization, and positivism of a philosophy such as neo-Kantianism left many of Cohen's readers dissatis-fied with his portrait of German-Jewish identity, because they saw it as a hyphenated identity constructed in the abstraction of reason alone. While some perceived a threat to Germanism, others feared its effects on Juda-ism. Either way, liberalism and disenchantment were the alleged culprits. However, if we ask what German and Jewish identities—identities that were emphatically tied to both the secularizing space of the imperial state and the liberal ideal of civic rights—might really have meant to people living in the late nineteenth and early twentieth centuries, we are forced to interrogate the transformations of modern Germany, the liberalism and antiliberalism of its intellectual as well as religious culture. And, in doing so, we discover something overlooked in Cohen's precocious un-derstanding of the relationship between religious (Jewish) minority and civic (German) identity in a liberal state. That is, German liberalism, as I begin to show in this chapter, was a distinctly Protestant tradition.[6]

The relationships between religion, nation, and civic rights inter-twined in the history of the Reformation, and Cohen recognized the development of German Protestant culture as a watershed moment in political history, especially as concerned the Jews. Thus, we must consider how Cohen, in building his case for a German-Jewish identity, aligned Judaism and Protestantism as the dual sources of a culture of religious freedom, civic equality, and democratization. Rosenzweig recognized as much when he suggestively wrote in his introduction to Cohen's *Jew-ish Writings*, "all modern Jews and German Jews more than anyone are Protestants."[7] Cohen's story suggests, therefore, that the German Jews were deft negotiators of such transformations, and Cohen's philosophy provides one model for such negotiation.

Although the implicit connection between liberalism and Protestant-ism has contributed to caricatures of Cohen's thought, that relation-ship must be unpacked.[8] What might Protestantism signify for Cohen's account of German-Jewish identity, especially when we take seriously Rosenzweig's insistence that Cohen's philosophical thought is what makes him a "better German"?[9] What might it mean for Jewish identity if Cohen understood modern Jews to be Protestants? And what should liberalism mean, in turn?

In an attempt to answer such preliminary questions, this chapter probes what a Cohenian Protestantism looks like and suggests that Cohen's so-called Judeo-Protestant[10] vision is in fact an important conceptual anchor for what would become an all-encompassing, if too often overlooked, dimension of his thought: namely, his grounding of German-Jewish identity in a liberal epistemology. Both *liberal* and *epistemology* are terms that I work to define and expound in the discussion that follows. Provisionally, I would like to understand liberalism in terms of its democratizing impulse. That is, I want to frame Cohen's thought as a project of democratizing knowledge and broadening access to sociality or participation in the shaping of public culture.[11] Epistemology, by contrast, describes the space and principles of reasoning underlying our understanding of sociality. Thus, when applied to knowledge, Cohen's liberalism democratizes reasoning, crucially allowing others to join the space of reasoning. Interpreted both conceptually and in the historical context of Wilhelmine Germany, I therefore suggest that Cohen sees in Protestantism an epistemological shift in the history of German philosophy and religion toward a democratized public reasoning in which freedom of thought becomes possible. As a result, a minority religion such as Judaism could gain public recognition and, further, the means to participate in the reworking of Protestant Germany.

It is therefore important to stress that a Cohenian Protestantism, such as we glean here, is not the same as Christianity. But neither is it simply a protosecularism, which we might understand as both a political doctrine of neutrality with regard to religious goods and an attempt to mitigate their advocacy in the public sphere. Rather, in tracing Cohen's earliest essays to his later "Germanism and Judaism," I argue that, to the extent that Protestantism provided the epistemological worldview that separated faith from knowledge and made idealist philosophy possible, religion and epistemology—religion and *reasoning*—become deeply intertwined in Cohen's account of Jewish and German identities. Grounding Cohen's liberalism in Protestantism is therefore not quite the same as grounding it in Christianity. This is because Protestantism represents the separation of scientific and philosophical *reasoning* from the historically established values, norms, and truths deemed theologically dogmatic.

To make this case for the implicit connection between liberalism and Protestantism, I begin by outlining a genealogy of Protestant Judaism through Cohen's early engagement with Heinrich Heine and Baruch Spinoza. Pointing to a different story about Judaism, religion, and liberalism's epistemology, I describe Protestantism as an epistemological condition for liberalism to take root, and trace this narrative to Cohen's reading of Heine. In his reading of Heine, Cohen began to describe Protestantism as an opening for the articulation of freedom of thought, freedom of religion, and a space of reasoning for modern Jews. With these epistemological contours of Cohen's account of Protestantism more squarely in view, we will then be able to reassess Cohen's liberalism and configuration of public reasoning in the following chapters.

While this liberal epistemology of democratized reasoning helps negotiate religious differences in public and articulates a kind of public reasoning or secularity, Cohen also worried about the secularization or disenchantment of the modern Protestant world. Whereas Spinoza's pantheism at first seemed like a promising avenue for Jewish integration into German philosophy, Cohen's later writings seize on Spinoza as the symbolic head of what alternative worldviews might emerge from secularization. Cohen grew concerned that pantheism (or what he would also negatively refer to as metaphysics) had cast subjective reason as a new dogma that risked naturalizing and nationalizing reason. Furthermore, in relegating religion to the irrational, pantheism would place Judaism in a new quandary, that of metaphysical assimilation to a hyperrational liberalism. As a result, I conclude the chapter by suggesting that Cohen's nuanced attention to the role of Protestantism in the history of German Idealism enabled him to embrace a different account of religion's place within political and public reasoning: a Protestantism without Christianity and so also a liberalism *without secularism*.

JUDAISM AND THE SOURCES OF PANTHEISM

Understanding the nuance with which Cohen expressed both German and Jewish identities is crucial to a reassessment of his thought first and foremost because, to many, Cohen "symbolized more than anyone else the union of Jewish faith and German culture."[12] German Jews, however, have been cast as liberals caught up in the wave of assimilation and secularization that would ultimately betray them.[13] Cohen's story thus shows us the nuance required in any treatment of German Jewry.

Hermann Cohen was born in Coswig (Anhalt) in 1842 to a traditional Jewish family in a historically significant Protestant region. Coming of age amid the generation of Germany's failed liberal revolution of 1848, Cohen's philosophic quest to acculturate to a modern, German spirit was no doubt refracted through the popular ideals articulated by German-Jewish liberals such as the politician and champion of freedom of conscience, Gabriel Riesser (1806–63).[14] As a result of that lingering revolutionary sentiment, Jewish liberalism would remain something of a work in progress, requiring Cohen to stake out a path of his own.[15] Coswig's geographical location between Dessau and Wittenberg—the homes of Mendelssohn and Luther, respectively[16]—lends a symbolic quality to Cohen's life and thought, since his family played an active role in the cultural life of their town and strove to balance their commitments between a traditional Judaism and a German national pride.[17] As for many German Jews, the Protestant culture that would lend itself to Bismarck's later reshaping of German national identity presented Cohen and his family with something of a less foreign or at least less theologically threatening culture than did Catholicism and its medieval history of difficult relations with Jews.[18] To the extent that it was the land of Martin Luther that made possible the emancipation of the Jews of Anhalt in 1810 (albeit with a little help from Napoleon) and Prussia in 1812,[19] many Jews had reason to see German Protestantism as a promising development of Christian culture.

Indeed, it was this openness of Protestant Germany that enabled Cohen to enter the Protestant Friedrich-Gymnasium in Dessau before attending from 1857 to 1861 the recently established Jewish Theological Seminary in Breslau, home to leading voices of the science of Judaism (*Wissenschaft des Judentums*) such as Zecharias Frankel, Heinrich Graetz, Jacob Bernays, and Manuel Joel. The Breslau seminary was founded with the intention of serving as a bulwark against the reforms advocated by the Frankfurt Rabbinical Assembly and, in particular, against Abraham Geiger's particular flavor of liberal Judaism, which would later blossom into a distinct movement of Reform Judaism. Thus, Cohen's Jewish education at the institution suggests that his own understanding of liberalism did not derive from a denominational notion of Jewish religion.

Nevertheless, his longing for a path to modern Germany and his attraction to its intellectual vehicle—philosophy—led Cohen away from rabbinical ordination at the seminary first to the University of Breslau, then to Friedrich-Wilhelms-Universität in Berlin, and finally to defend his doctoral dissertation at the University of Halle-Wittenberg in 1865.[20] Despite his disinterest in becoming a theologian, Cohen gleaned from Frankel the significance of Judaism as a "world-historical process" of spirit, a notion that would leave a lasting impression on the philosopher in search of a properly "scientific" standpoint.[21]

Cohen's commitment to philosophy as the path to participation in modern German culture led him to Berlin, where he was drawn to the anthropologically inclined school of cultural psychology (*Völkerpsychologie*) of Moritz Lazarus and Heymann Steinthal, themselves active supporters of German-Jewish liberal politics.[22] Working under the sway of the school's scientific focus on culture, Cohen anonymously published one of his first essays, entitled "Heinrich Heine and Judaism."[23] In the essay, Cohen considered Heine—once a member of the Organization for the Culture and Science of Judaism, conflicted convert to Lutheranism, national poet, and social and literary critic—as a Jewish thinker.[24] It was a somewhat controversial thesis, to the extent that Heine himself had given up his Judaism and been baptized in order to accept what he famously referred to as his "entry ticket" to European culture. Published in 1867, four years before German unification, Cohen's anonymously published essay on Heine was an important site for the young thinker to begin tracing the cultural significance both of religion in the modern world and, in particular, of Judaism's place within modern German cultural consciousness. In fact, a careful reading of the essay demonstrates that what would become Cohen's infamous defense of both a German and a Jewish ethos in 1915–16's "Germanism and Judaism" was long in the making. Moreover, Cohen's early essay both represents a nuanced political vision and outlines an often overlooked dimension of what would become Cohen's version of liberal social and political thinking, which is democratic, legal in orientation, and frames reasoning as a historical tradition. Thus, even before Cohen had completed his first work on Kant, his liberal vision already centered on the role of philosophy as a vehicle for public religious reasoning.

Cohen's attention to the relationship between political freedom and religion in his early writings can also be interpreted better in light of the fact that Germany in the 1860s underwent unprecedented changes, with the North German Confederation somewhat suddenly morphing into an empire of Germans. Anxiety over the nation and its spirit was certainly not limited to Jews alone. As Alon Confino has argued, in the years preceding German unification, configuring what a national culture and identity might look like relied largely on the cultural imaginings of various German regions: each region projected its own specificity on the idea of national "unity."[25] In such varied projections, the idea of Germany envisioned by Catholic Bavarian hopes and anxieties obviously differed dramatically from that of northern Prussian Protestants. Yet, in the years of unification, the consequence of Prussian ascendancy was a rapidly modernizing, industrializing, and militarizing culture. Additionally, Bismarck's campaign of Prussianization and "Practical Christianity" created an institutional Protestantism that indelibly stamped the public life of imperial Germany. This left Catholics and Jews in a minority position, forced to justify their place within the state over and again.

Cohen therefore turned to philosophy as the means for negotiating between Jewish and Christian specificities and demonstrated this in his essay on Heine. Cohen begins his essay by acknowledging that his description of Heine's "Judaism" would need to be qualified. Heine, after all, was a Lutheran by baptism, and his most well-known writings, such as *Germany: A Winter's Tale*, were seen as patriotic German national literature. Nothing therein was overtly Jewish. But Heine's participation in the Cultur-Verein was a point of pride for German Jews, and the anti-Jewish sentiment of some members of the non-Jewish intelligentsia meant that few were shy to allege Heine's literary deficiencies might stem from his Jewish heritage. But Heine's status as something of a national poet laureate and his account of Protestantism as central to modern German history was revered by many. Cohen's thesis therefore made explicit what many German Jews may have felt they could not say in their still markedly Jewish voices.[26] That is, Judaism and Protestantism shared not only a great thinker but also a conceptual vocabulary with which to pursue a common truth and justice in the world: the freedom of (from) religion.

By drawing on Heine as an advocate for a philosophical position from which to defend such a vision of Judaism in a Protestant world, Cohen was effectively employing the kind of religious reasoning that he would later

refine. And so, while Heine's participation in the Cultur-Verein, for example, might be marshaled as evidence of a continued intellectual investment in Judaism,[27] Cohen's main treatment of Heine's relation to Judaism
is interesting because it focuses on a philosophical point of entry for this
Jewish genealogy. He writes,

> In our time—and strictly speaking, this is so in any age where a still
> amenable science humbly goes along with the religious development
> of a people—a religious form of thought (*religiöse Gedankenform*), even
> the most potent and farsighted, cannot limit the spiritual horizon: from
> all sides of cultural life the illuminating rays penetrate modern man
> and gather into effective reflexes within his spirit. However, amidst the
> many other cultural means that condition our whole cultural formation
> (*Gesammtbildung*), the religious element remains of greater capacity,
> which we must examine and assess in the varied expressions of the en-
> quiring and effective spirit, if we seek to become clear about the inner
> motives and the disposition (*Gesinnungswerth*) of human actions.[28]

Cohen's description of religion as a resource that can help clarify the
conceptual, historical, and social values of cultural formation (*Bildung*)
is significant. Jews of this period valued the intellectual ideal of *Bildung* as
a sign of their investment in German national culture and its ideals, after
all.[29] But Cohen's description, importantly, is not specific to Judaism.
Rather, Cohen's emphasis is on the broadly construed intellectual forces
shaping the modern world, from science to religion. Cohen therefore
begins by contextualizing Heine's writing in a world where this struggle
between science and tradition is beginning to become palpable. Heine is
a modern writer (*In unsere Zeit*) and, like Cohen and his ostensible readers, he is concerned with the "spiritual horizon of our age," where science
emerges from a constellation of disparate cultural resources, not yet fully
emancipated from the theological dogmas that surround it. Cohen therefore sees in Heine's Jewish upbringing an example and occasion to mark
a connection to such religious resources and to acknowledge that they
did not limit Heine's achievements. Yet, while not suggesting that Heine
continued to practice Judaism, Cohen also describes the lasting potency
of this religious element. Cohen's interest is with the way modern human
beings (*den modernen Menschen*) are suffused by historically refracted
cultural life and spirit, and so his discussion of Judaism as an account of
religion should be treated in philosophical terms.[30]

With this broader philosophical meaning of Judaism in mind, we can therefore better understand why Cohen emphasizes a seemingly minor citation in Heine as the crux of his Judaism. That is, Cohen focuses on the conceptual space opened by a peculiar reference to the work of Spinoza in Heine's *Concerning the History of Religion and Philosophy in Germany*. In this survey of distinctly German thinkers such as Immanuel Kant, Johann Gottlieb Fichte, Friedrich Wilhelm Joseph Schelling, and G. W. F. Hegel, Heine names the "concealed religion" of the German idealists as "pantheism." He writes, "No one says it, but everyone knows that pantheism is an open secret in Germany. . . . Pantheism is the concealed religion of Germany."[31] That is, the worldview in which nature and divinity, human and God, are interwoven, and the worldview associated most readily with the Dutch and Sephardic Jew Spinoza, is a keystone in the foundation of German Protestantism and German Idealism. Neither the same as Christianity nor the absence of religion altogether, Heine's pantheist dimension of this history, Cohen suggests, is an important intersection of the intellectual histories of Judaism and German philosophy. For although Spinoza's reception history was mixed, and Cohen himself would later criticize Spinoza's pantheism, the young Cohen found in Heine's citation of Spinoza a positive point of entry for Judaism into philosophy.

Although pantheism helps name the changing relationship between philosophy and religion(s) in Germany, the young Cohen was hardly a full-throated supporter of either Spinoza or pantheism. Heine's pantheism, according to Cohen, is not the same as Spinoza's metaphysics, with which Cohen finds fault. Rather Heine's engagement with Spinoza was "less concerned with the system than . . . with Spinoza's way of seeing things [*Anschauungsweise*], which I designate by the name of pantheism."[32] This pantheistic "way of seeing things" therefore establishes a philosophical connection, a cultural bridge for concepts culled from a shared historical past to be redeployed in both Spinoza's and Heine's time. Pantheism is therefore a link via Spinoza to Judaism such that, even if establishing Heine's personal links to Judaism remains problematic, hermeneutically "does not one wonder how we can venture to say that an ancient religion should be able to act as significant to the worldview of modern man. Indeed we might, were it not for the fact that religious

ideas are so often intertwined with all of our representations!"[33] As Cohen reads Heine, the philosophical and cultural resources of religion that
continue to shape modern thought are located in the term *pantheism*. As
a "way of seeing things," Heine was treating pantheism as a conceptual
contribution providing Judaism space to negotiate between religion and
philosophy.

Cohen therefore tells us that Heine's pantheism and invocation of Spinoza should not be taken at face value. While Heine's other works sometimes invoke the figure of the "Hellene" as a reference to the naturalism
and aesthetic sensibilities that many attributed to Goethe as a form of
paganism or pantheism, Heine's seems to be a very un-Hellene interpretation of pantheism.[34] Such a rhetorical strategy, Cohen writes, should not
mislead us about what pantheism really encodes; it is not a pagan pantheism that would divinize the material world but, rather, something quite
different. This, Cohen explains, should not surprise us. In Heine's work,
"every beautiful expression [reminiscent of] mythological eras is however, still only a *mythological* one." That is, throughout Heine's writing,
"the spirit of modern life has breathed its air [*eingehaucht*] into the ancient
world."[35] And while Heine is no doubt resuscitating some concepts and
images from the past, according to Cohen, pantheism is encoding something else, some other inflection of religious and cultural resources that
in fact refocuses the spiritual intensity of ideas away from any material
limitation. Heine's pantheism, in this reading, is a "monotheistic-Jewish
pantheism" that seeks not to vindicate the naturalism or materialism of
the natural scientist but to express a progressive conception of human
emancipation.[36]

Why might this reference to pantheism be so significant for Cohen?
After all, we might assume that if one were to pursue a syncretistic worldview then a logical option for blending together elements of Judaism and
Christianity might be a turn to pantheism—a God in everything and
in all. But pantheism was a controversial term with a significant history.
Thus, before turning to Cohen's seemingly paradoxical description of a
"monotheistic-pantheism" and his engagement with Heine's history of
German philosophy, we must first consider the controversial meaning
of pantheism in the history of nineteenth-century German philosophy
more generally.

PANTHEISM AND THE SECULARIZATION OF PHILOSOPHY

It should not be taken for granted that philosophy, in the second half of the nineteenth century, might help articulate a positive Jewish contribution to German history and culture. It had been a little over eighty years since Friedrich Heinrich Jacobi and Moses Mendelssohn had exchanged their series of letters and essays on the question of Spinoza's pantheism and triggered a crisis in European intellectual history. Known as the *Pantheismusstreit* (Pantheism Controversy), the 1785 argument ostensibly concerned whether or not their mutual friend, the celebrated German writer Gotthold Ephraim Lessing, had admitted prior to his death that he was in fact a committed adherent of the philosophy of Spinoza.[37] If the well-respected Lessing had indeed declared in favor of Spinoza's philosophy, which Jacobi called "nihilism" and "pantheism," Lessing could not be considered a believing Christian. Moreover, a philosophy such as Spinoza's could not serve as the handmaiden of theology, as had been philosophy's traditional role. Spinoza and his inflection of philosophy came to represent, especially on account of Mendelssohn's defense of Lessing, a step beyond Christianity or Judaism.

While stepping beyond Judaism or Christianity may have been deemed to be in fact a leap into atheism, the German idealists Fichte, Schelling, and Hegel saw something else in Jacobi's musings on Spinoza. By the early nineteenth century, Hegel remarked that "you have either Spinozism or no philosophy at all,"[38] since a philosophy of the infinite presented a strategy for freeing thought from the confines of dogmatic, scholastic theology. In other words, the pantheism of Spinoza's infinite intelligibility—the notion that everything in nature could be rendered intelligible—was celebrated by some and denigrated by others because it presented a subjective freedom for human thought to achieve communion with the infinite. Pantheist philosophy therefore stepped outside of Christianity, just as Spinoza has stepped outside of Judaism.

While pantheism became a controversial strategy for negotiating a way out of dogma, Jacobi's arguments in the Pantheism Controversy were largely responsible for this fate. Indeed, German Idealism's legacy as a kind of secularizing metaphysics was due in large part to Jacobi's persuasive depiction of the challenge to Christian theology posed by idealism. Describing Spinoza's philosophy as a chain of infinite determinations of logical judgment, Jacobi argued that these ideal determinations effaced or annihilated the immediate reality of the things we perceive and experience. Jacobi labeled this form of metaphysics "idealist," by which he meant that logical categories and concepts, independent of the particular objects of experience, allegedly determine and produce the objects of experience. Rather than immediate reality, objects are rendered by thought as "sensibilia."[39] Without the immediate reality of the world, Jacobi wrote, such idealism is "nihilistic."[40] Idealism and pantheism were therefore connected by virtue of the fact that Jacobi had grounded a coherent portrait of reality in ideas, even if his goal was to prove that idealism was a form of atheism.

Spinoza was thus considered by many the eighteenth-century paradigm of heresy. However, German philosophers in pursuit of freedom of thought, or subjective freedom, found in Spinoza a defender of scientific truth grounded in human reason. Jacobi had simply shown how Spinoza enabled an idealist monism[41] in which knowledge and consciousness cohere with nature and action in a single principle—the infinite—as it articulates itself in human freedom, or thought.[42] The process of secularization, or the freeing up of philosophy to articulate arguments that contradict or transform theology, thus began with a descent into negativity and purported disenchantment: pantheism was charged with being atheism.

The charge that pantheism was a nihilistic or atheistic philosophy continued to haunt Spinoza's legacy well into Heine's time.[43] What to make of this atheism therefore became an important question with which philosophers had to grapple. Emphasizing the systematic connection between ideas as the ground of the world of experience, including its social and historical forms of life and knowledge, Hegel's philosophy had taken up Jacobi's reading of Spinoza and enriched it. Using this idealist reading of Spinoza, Hegel elaborated his own account of the "reconciliation" of ideal and real—tradition and science—as different representations in and of the self-consciousness of modern European society. This bold assertion of philosophy as a vehicle both for overcoming the conflict between religion and science and for providing European society with a narrative about its own canons of knowledge, however, did not allay the tensions felt by traditional pietist Christians who saw such an assertion of reason as crass heresy. For Hegel, revealed Christian religion and the canons of positive scientific knowledge presented differing conceptions of the world, the self, and society.[44] His thought was therefore aimed at mediating these two modes. However, the claim that Hegel harmonized and reconciled the ideal and the real in philosophy both ignited a political attack on the part of pietist theologians such as Ludwig von Gerlach against Hegel's influence on Protestant theologians at the University of Halle[45] and began the Halle Affair of 1830, in which "rationalist" philosophy was attacked for its seeming rejection of revealed religion altogether.[46] Spinoza's claim that all possible causes and effects that strive for unification in the infinite are intelligible when viewed from a perspective of the eternal (sub specie aeternitatis) was taken by many orthodox Lutherans as a claim to have replaced the eternal with human thinking and thus equivalent to atheism.[47]

We can see in the charge of atheism a compelling example of how philosophy was implicated in the secularization of German thought and society. By shifting the frame of reason and reality away from a transcendent legitimacy toward an inherent explanatory order, Spinoza's "immanent frame" triggered debate about the extent to which knowledge and truth might be determined first and perhaps only in human thinking.[48] The license with which the German idealists therefore undertook to argue for a robust human freedom grounded in thought alone was met by a theological establishment entrenched against what it perceived as the liberalism of Hegelian and post-Hegelian thought.[49] Liberalism was therefore both tied to philosophy and marked with the charge of atheism and anticlericalism.[50]

These debates only further intensified when, in 1838, Heinrich Leo attacked Hegel's young disciples, accusing them of atheism and pantheism.[51] Some of Hegel's students would try to quell the seeming radicalism of this shift to subjective freedom by claiming the reconciliation of idea and actuality was a renewal of Christian religion,[52] whereas others identified this same reconciliation as a humanizing or materializing shift that rendered divinity a human projection on nature and existence[53] and, in consequence, demonstrated positive (revealed) religion to be a myth.[54] In Ludwig Feuerbach's telling, young Hegelian and conservative reactionaries were now in full-fledged confrontation, and the equation of pantheism with atheism became ever more prominent as a symbol of liberal and conservative charges.[55]

Pantheism now posed an explicitly metaphysical challenge to theology. That is to say, metaphysics emerged as a specific sphere of philosophical inquiry into the inner coherence of thought, the development of knowledge, and the foundations of truth about God, human beings, and the world. Claiming that the infinite could be reconciled or even intuited by the finite act of human thinking created a new landscape for human reason, in which even divinity was rendered intelligible. Whereas the young Hegelians had employed historical criticism to demonstrate that traditional religion was a determinate moment in the history of spirit culminating in its own negation, liberal Protestant theologians continued to work under the influence of Hegel's rival, Friedrich Schleiermacher, who ensured that the association of pantheism and Spinoza would keep religion as a constellation of the public sphere.[56] Pantheism had become an almost ubiquitous term and its association with religious heterodoxy firmly established. For example, by 1843 Feuerbach would simply assert, "Pantheism is theological atheism, it is theological materialism, it is the negation of theology but from the standpoint of theology. Since it makes matter, which is the negation of God, into a predicate or attribute of the divine being . . . [this] divinization of the actual (*Wirklichen*), of the materially existent—materialism, empiricism, realism, humanism—and the negation of theology are, however, the essence of the modern era. Pantheism is, therefore, nothing other than a divine being and a religiophilosophical principle that is sublated into becoming the essence of the modern era."[57] For Feuerbach, the modern era represented a condition in which religion and philosophy comingled, and theology was confronted by the challenge of a growing scientific attitude that viewed empirical and material reality as the standard by which to judge all products of knowledge. Pantheism therefore represented the dialectical expression both of divinity as a principle of reason and the internal coherence of the empirically real world. This was not simply a form of theological negation but the methodological blueprint for a veneration of free thinking. As the essence of modernity, pantheism therefore connoted the actualization of human reason, turning a negation of divinity into an affirmation of human freedom. The anthropological turn ushered in by Feuerbach, related as it is to overcoming both philosophical pantheism and philosophy itself, culminated in the modern project of the sciences to leave no stone unturned, to allow criticism and science to shine a light on all concepts and all experiences. This was the birth of an explicitly human-centered account of a universal knowledge, or metaphysics. It was the beginning of an era of a secular, seemingly anticlerical, metaphysics.

When Heine set out to tell a version of this history of German philosophy to his French readers while living in exile in Paris, he was well aware of the controversy surrounding the term *pantheism*. To describe it as Germany's "open secret" and "concealed religion" in 1834, therefore, was rhetorically pointed and polemically noteworthy. Furthermore, Heine's insistence that this pantheism emerged from the philosophical insight of Spinoza was no doubt an impish embrace of the alleged heresy of philosophy. But while Heine cited this heretical moment in the history of German philosophy as a watershed, Cohen seized on this reference as reflecting something perhaps still unconscious for Heine. Attentive to how pantheism gave philosophy a new parity with religious thought, Cohen's interpretation is important because it turns Heine's pantheism into a carrier of Judaism rather than a vehicle for atheism or a philosophical supplement to Christian religion, as it was interpreted in Heine's own time. Cohen sees evidence of this in the rhetorical clues Heine includes to mark this relationship to Spinoza, whose writing Heine describes as having a "certain mysterious aura" in which "the air of the future seems to flow over us." Heine therefore wonders whether "the spirit of the Hebrew prophets still hovered over their late-born descendant [Spinoza]."[58] For Cohen, these lines are telling. In them he interprets Heine as his genealogical forebearer, since Heine's citation of Spinoza is not for the purposes of

> entering the particulars of the great system that bears the immortal name of Spinoza; but he [Heine] rather describes the general significance of the Spinozist idea for the development of humanity, revealing his most deep sympathy and intuitive vision when he opens up such a cultural historical vista [in linking Spinoza to the Hebrew Prophets].
>
> Thus he sensed, *without this feeling ever obtaining in clear representations,* in the nature and the striving of Spinozist thought the spiritual parity with the old writers and thinkers of the monotheistic faith.[59]

Heine's Judaism is therefore located in this reading of Spinoza as a symbol of both the prophetic past as well as the emancipatory future. Pantheism is thus not to be understood as an attempted negation of religion. Rather, Cohen's sees Heine as offering an implicitly political understanding of pantheism wherein the goal of uniting all humankind, first articulated by the Hebrew prophets, finds its philosophical voice in modern history. And by placing Spinoza and Heine on a continuum with prophetic monotheism, Cohen tells his readers something crucial about the two most well-known Jewish figures to have made a mark on European history—two figures who shared a peculiar relationship to Judaism. Neither in Cohen's telling was truly a Christian: Spinoza because he never converted, and Heine because of his self-declared allegiance to a Spinozist framing of his Hellenism.[60] The latter, Cohen tells us, signals that Heine was not really a pantheist who saw everything in nature as God. Rather, Heine had taken up pantheism as a gauge for "the course of human development." This "Jewish-pantheistic" bridge into "monotheistic-pantheistic" thought leads beyond the confines of Judaism or Christianity into a broader philosophical articulation of the freedom of thought, which Cohen designates as monotheism.[61] Jewish monotheism, rather than atheism or metaphysics, therefore helps articulate a space between religion and philosophy without negating religion.

By tracing a space between religion and philosophy, I am suggesting that Cohen's reading of Heine should be understood as a kind of social politics. That is, his reading of Heine attempts to identify a set of conceptual resources with which to address the place of a Jewish minority amid the religious majoritarianism of Christianity. And because Christianity continued to frame debates over emancipation, equality, and freedom of religion, what Heine's introduction of Spinoza into the history of German Protestantism and philosophy announced was a moment of philosophical protest of the dominance of Christian theology even in philosophy. Thus, in the face of Jews' continued struggle to find a way to be themselves in a still culturally Christian world, Cohen's turn to Heine and pantheism as a resource for his own time is significant because it shows the degree to which philosophy became a language for such debates and concerns. It was in philosophy that Cohen saw Heine's description of pantheism draw a connection between freedom of thought and social liberation that would lead the Jews, along with all of humanity, to a true political freedom. As Cohen writes, "Under the influence of Spinozist thought, in the 'forest of highest heavenly thoughts,' he deepened the socialist conception of the equal enfranchisement of all classes into a cosmopolitan one of the equality of all peoples, and all the more

deepened this into a *metaphysical* conception of the divinity of all people!"[62] In Cohen's reading, Heine's invocation of Spinozist pantheism
circumvents the charge of atheism by emphasizing the "divinity" of all
peoples or, as Heine described, a "democracy of gods" as the goal of this
emancipatory pantheism.[63] Thus, while philosophy was in the process of
articulating a protosecular mode of expression, it was a language of political and social reasoning not without religious or metaphysical trappings.
This mode of expression was rooted in the vindication of subjective, human thinking but enchanted by an image of future emancipation. Cohen
therefore sets out to uncover the genealogy that links Spinoza's pantheism
and Heine's Hellenism to a particularly Jewish condition of negotiating
religion and the public work of philosophizing.

Pantheism becomes a path for Judaism to enter Cohen's reading of
Heine. However, Cohen leads us in a circuitous, winding direction
through narratives of spiritualism and materialism, social progress and
philosophical idealism, pantheism and monotheism. Nevertheless, the
single most important feature that both drives his argument forward and
draws out the affinities between the "prophet of pantheism and that of
monotheism, between Spinoza and Moses," is the claim that "according
to the monotheistic account of the representation 'God', this 'God' is a
spirit."[64] Pantheism and monotheism are connected by Heine's treatment
of God as spirit because, as Cohen outlines, this spirit transcends time
and place and opens up a *belief* (*Glaube*) in the future—a belief that can,
because it by definition *must*, transcend the world of material.[65]

In this respect Heine's turn to pantheism is not, Cohen tells us, a turn
to materialism. Quite the contrary, Heine's disdain for the medieval
church—for the contemptible denigration of the corporeal and its vices
despite the stifling materialism of church authority and its enforcement
of heresy on the body—paints a picture of Heine as the defender of a new
kind of belief: a belief in *ideas*. Indeed, Heine notes that it was "knowledge, the perception of things by means of reason, science, [that] gives
us in the end the pleasures which faith, Catholic Christianity, has for so
long cheated us of."[66] Heine therefore champions "a belief," Cohen tells
us, "in the progress of humanity, in the equal right [*gleiche Berechtigung*]
of all to earthly flourishing, preserved in his heart, *this is his truth*."[67] This
kind of pantheism is expressly political and humanistic and envisions a
time when the God of All becomes a God *for* all. "That," Heine writes,

"will be the revolution, the great daughter of the Reformation."[68] The political accent to Heine's pantheism is therefore crucial to Cohen's interpretation because this belief in future emancipation and emphasis on the democratic progress of human beings is located in Heine's "*idealistic Spinozism*."[69] Idealism thus retains the enchantment of divinity (and not divinity itself) in reasoning.

Cohen's attempt to elaborate this same pantheism as a philosophical entry point for Judaism was therefore a particularly charged claim even in its own time. As we saw, this is because Heine was not alone in claiming Spinoza and pantheism exemplified a peculiar model for German philosophy to articulate a freedom of thought. However, given Spinoza's multidimensional legacy, while Heine may have cited his pantheism as an example of the lingering enchantment of a "concealed religion," many equated Spinoza with a particular metaphysical system interrelating (or conflating) history and actuality, substance and ideality, law and nature.[70] But for Jews like Cohen, Spinoza's name symbolized first and foremost a philosophical path toward emancipation. No matter how he might be interpreted, Spinoza also represented the possibility of seeking divinity, freedom, the infinite or absolute—in short, the supplemental transcendental signifier of *God*—independently of theology. And Heine acknowledged the particularly cryptic possibilities of pantheism when he simultaneously presented Spinoza's pantheism as the open secret of German philosophy as well as a concealed religion. Heine recognized that there was indeed "a way of seeing things" between theology and science. What might this middle way be called, if not secular?

PANTHEISM AND PUBLIC REASON

As we saw above in the controversy swirling around the term *pantheism*, German Idealism was thus imbricated in the birth of liberalism in Germany, freeing thought from the determinations of theology. This was implicit in Heine's narrative. With its newfound wiggle room between theology and politics, philosophy expressed the liberal continuation both of the Enlightenment ideals of self-assertion and maturation of autonomous thought and of the foundational ethos of publicity of opinion. Kant, for example, declared public reason the definition of enlightenment, because it signifies a public use of freedom. Publicizing one's thought expresses respect for humanity, as if simply opening one's mouth and letting reason run its course embodies enlightenment. "Reason and freedom"—particularly the freedom to openly express reason in public—led the charge. Thus, defining enlightenment, Kant wrote "that a public should enlighten itself is more possible; indeed this is almost inevitable, if only it is left its freedom. . . . For this enlightenment, however, nothing is required by *freedom*, and indeed the least harmful of anything that could even be called freedom: namely, freedom to make *public use* of one's reason in all matters."[71] The public use of freedom— allowing the individual the autonomy to use reason in *public*—therefore begins a new style of discourse, a language that frees itself of theological or metaphysical presuppositions. One must prove their points and be judged by standards of reason rather than assert them on good authority. As a result, public reason props itself up as the objective criterion by which to judge all reality, whether social or metaphysical. Reason gains the legitimacy to identify other cultural expressions of rationality. As a consequence, religion is differentiated as one among many public expressions of reason.

However, although the German public sphere was no longer homogeneously Christian, with philosophy and metaphysics now contending for space therein, this fact should not suggest that it was secularist, if by that term we mean "neutral toward religion."[72] Nor should we assume that Jews were recognized as equal participants in the public sphere. But the role of public opinion and the possibility of forming an opinion independent of established religion did take on a distinct meaning for Jews. However, this characteristic of the public sphere demonstrates the ambivalent core of German liberalism. That is, although one's public opinion and engagement in debate is supposed to secure a path to consensus, the presumption nevertheless remains that a "public opinion" is an established addressee of such debate.[73] In other words, access to public opinion remained unequal because of whom was considered part of the public sphere. And, although Germany may have been a nation in flux, the symbolic power of Christianity remained palpable; religion was still very much public.

The tensions surrounding philosophy as a force for secularization should help us understand why Cohen was concerned about the lure of metaphysics. The metaphysical thrust of German Idealism, culminating in an explicitly humanized atheism, was therefore just one telling of the history of German philosophy as the elaboration of reason. It thus is that much more significant that Cohen chose Heine's narrative of German Idealism as his guide. Instead of placing Heine within the narrative of the secularization of German Protestantism, Heine becomes, in Cohen's work, a champion of a distinct philosophical voice that negotiates between theology and philosophy. In other words, Cohen deftly avoids engaging pantheism as a theological problem within Christian or post-Christian thought without falling into what he would later describe as the "trap of metaphysics." Rather, by attributing a distinctly monotheistic coloring to Heine's description of pantheism, Cohen effectively names German Idealism as the means with which to inflect religion anew, through rather than in opposition to reason. However, even at this early stage of his thinking, Cohen grasped that such issues of knowledge production were publicly disseminated and popularly consumed. Philosophy would have to maintain its position as a vehicle for negotiating such precarious knowledge. Thus, knowing philosophy would need to become the explicit form of public reasoning, Cohen's description of "pantheistic-monotheistic" thought emphasizes monotheism and pantheism as different ends of a conceptual spectrum that make a different account of public reason possible. That is, for Cohen monotheism provides the standard by which public reason becomes accessible to the many rather than the few.

In Heine's account of pantheism, public reason can be found in the distinction between theological dogma and freedom of thought. While pantheism signifies a democratizing subjective freedom and thinking, Cohen insists that monotheism extends this process into the future—which is to say, into the sphere of the not-yet. Monotheism tells the story of what pantheism *ought to be*: the possibility of public reason and freedom of thought being accessible to all. To the extent that Heine's God is "spirit," according to Cohen, pantheism and monotheism are implicitly connected, both historically and conceptually,[74] by this link between unity and totality or the "all" (*pan*). This is, Cohen writes, because

> it was the development of monotheism, even as it diverged from the normal course of its logical direction amidst several historically conditioned conflagrations, that first made the viewpoint [*Anschauungsweise*] possible in which a catechism of modern religion could take shape, and for it to

become among *all* confessions that which is most exalted for each one to believe. If we were to outline pantheism, in that this theory should find consistent expression, we must do so according to its historical presuppositions developed out of monotheism. But since we believe Heine's Judaism to be explained by his pantheistic approach, the reverse path must be taken.[75]

For Cohen, Heine had articulated a dialectical relationship between monotheism, pantheism, and humanism in which political emancipation and revolution would lead to the "unity" of human fraternity.[76] Whether as the unity of God or the unity of nature—whether as spirit or matter—monotheism had achieved for itself the spiritual unity to bring about a historical continuity between seemingly diverse moments of religious history.[77] This, Cohen claims, is what Heine's references to Hellenism are all about; they are clues to this deeper monotheistic sentiment. As Cohen asks, could Heine really invoke Hellenic antiquity as a model for the political progress he envisioned for humanity? Is such a concept even "possible in a time and a literature, in which there is no *humanistic* representation of mankind, in which the human race is a natural-historical concept?"[78] For Cohen, Heine's pantheism fuses the unity implicit in Jewish monotheism together with a social idealism. This is what makes monotheism a bridge between confessions, since it is in essence an idealism.[79] That is to say, pantheism articulates a principle shared with Jewish monotheism: the ideal of the unity of all peoples, all of the human spirit, which is akin to the unity projected by idealist thought. By naming pantheism *as if* it were a program of social idealism and emancipation, Heine retrieved the trace of a Jewish monotheism in his understanding of German philosophy and therefore inflected an "*idealistic* Spinozism."[80]

In summary, by transforming monotheistic pantheism into a form of idealism, Cohen therefore emphasized the political thrust of Heine's introduction of Spinoza into this narrative of German philosophy. In this regard, Cohen was unique among interpreters of Heine.[81] For Cohen, pantheism and the political vision of emancipation for all are linked to Heine's Judaism. And here we begin to see the political stakes of monotheism and idealist philosophy for Heine as well as for Cohen: idealism becomes a public discourse regarding how humanity *ought to be*. The vision of emancipation proposed here is a future one and ever expanding. This is the political stake of reading Heine as a Jewish thinker, and we can see how such a narrative about pantheism diverges from the secularizing and anticlerical account of the German idealists. Cohen sees in pantheism a form of religious reasoning.

Philosophical idealism provided Cohen a language with which to not only advocate for Jewish inclusion but also defend a moral and religious consciousness implicit in the German national identity. Cohen's reading of Heine and Spinoza therefore emphasizes the distinctly spiritual or idealist dimension of pantheism as a way of stepping beyond the limitations of dogma and institutional churches while still retaining a vision of public engagement that was very much enchanted by religion. That is, through pantheism Cohen came to recognize that reasoning could remain enchanted with ideas—with possibility, with images of a better future—and that such a reasoning was not just a rationalization of the present. Cohen saw in Heine's future-oriented liberal socialism a program for the democratization and emancipation of all peoples. For Jewish minority politics, this kernel of pantheistic idealism presented a distinctly philosophical vehicle for negotiating Jewish minority difference without collapsing German identity into atheism. This was because the social space of reasoning between religion and philosophy remained enchanted with idealism.

PROTESTANTISM AND EPISTEMOLOGY

From the discussion so far, we might have expected Cohen to embrace Heine's pantheism as articulating a neutral philosophical space between Judaism and Christianity. This would certainly square with some characterizations of a liberal Jewish position.[82] However, Cohen suggested something quite different. Rather, he insisted that Heine's pantheism was in fact monotheistic because of its norm of unity, which brought diverse peoples access to reason. While Heine's pantheism makes a "belief" in progress fundamental, Cohen saw Jewish monotheism as the model for this movement toward the emancipation of thought. Philosophy's enchantment with ideas, spirit, and the freedom of thought dovetailed on this point as well. Thus, monotheism and idealism share an aura of enchantment that this otherwise liberal pursuit of equal rights and freedom of thought might have lost with a turn to metaphysics and the displacement of theology. However, to understand the role of what I am calling the enchantment of Cohen's idealism, we must first scrutinize Heine's use of Protestantism as the conceptual vehicle for this "belief" in ideas as an emancipatory political vision.

As we will see, Protestantism plays a crucial role in Heine's narrative, and the relationship between pantheism and German Protestantism, I want to suggest, is key to Cohen's understanding of idealism. That is, while Heine stresses the uniquely German dimensions of the protest and reform of thinking that led from the Reformation to German Idealism, Cohen emphasized the connection between this protest and its emancipatory politics in the form of Jewish, "monotheistic-pantheism." However, as Cohen would explicitly describe in his later works, it is Protestantism that first opens the space for Judaism to be articulated in philosophical and historical terms. I therefore suggest in this section that the common denominator linking the young Cohen's account of pantheism and later account of Protestantism is the epistemological revolution commenced by the Reformation, in particular its introduction of *freedom of thought*. Characterized in this way, Protestantism opens up a space of reasoning, an epistemological discourse that navigates between religions within the language of philosophy.

In Heine's expository work on religion and philosophy in Germany, he gives explicit voice to an emancipatory pantheism as it permeates Protestantism and philosophical idealism. In Germany, Heine claims, civilization reached a milestone when idealist philosophy emerged from the intellectual revolution of Protestantism. And in the combination of German Protestantism and idealism, Heine asserts, we find a revolutionary harbinger that humanity might achieve universal subjectivity and a freedom only abstractly imagined in premodern European monarchies. It was therefore not Christianity per se that impressed Heine. The young Heine once promised his fellow convert Eduard Gans that he "would never crawl to the cross,"[83] and, although he would later convert, he nevertheless reserved a cynicism about having done so. Heine thus shared with his contemporaries and fellow Jews of the Cultur-Verein an implicit Hegelianism that would guide their interpretation of their historical moment as an opening for the articulation of Jewish emancipation.[84] In other words, as Jeffrey Sammons notes in his biography of Heine, "joining Protestantism meant joining the emancipatory tradition in German and European thought, from Luther, the Enlightenment, and Lessing to modern philosophy and liberalism."[85] Philosophy was thus a natural outgrowth of the world-historical significance of Protestantism—a protest tradition articulating the "formal" appearance of what Gans claimed "only philosophy can provide us with adequate knowledge [of], and in accordance with this knowledge everyone may construct his own subjective religion."[86] Humanity, in Heine's words, had grown "weary of all Eucharistic wafers and longs for more nourishing food, for real bread and good meat."[87] Idealist philosophy therefore represented the logical extension of the process begun with the Reformation en route to its culmination in political revolution, which would emancipate all subjectivity as such.[88] In Heine's attempt to reconcile Reformation and revolution, we can therefore see that Hegel's influence on Heine's understanding of German philosophy was significant, especially given the link between Protestantism and the subjective freedom that Heine would name as freedom of thought.

Despite his perceived atheism, which we saw above, Hegel claimed Protestantism had provided a crucial philosophical reconciliation between a subjective, inward freedom personalized in the model of Christian redemption and the public world of the modern state and its laws.[89] Describing this "Protestant Principle,"[90] Hegel claims that Protestantism provided a self-sufficient ethical life—which was only an abstract, inward, subjective freedom—with objective and public institutions in which to be reconciled with custom and public ethical mores. In other words, the foundations of Hegel's concept of the state.[91] Modern ethical life (*Sittlichkeit*) actualizes the principle of freedom in community with others, which Protestant religion formalizes in the role of a social sphere such as the church. But this objective recognition of moral autonomy amid historical social norms is also facilitated by the public laws of the state. Protestantism therefore provides the modern state with a model for the reconciliation of subjective freedom and objective laws.

While Hegel's emphasis on the reconciliation of subjective freedom and objective right was certainly influential on Heine, according to Heine the Protestant Reformation carried out a primarily spiritual revolution that made possible a new epistemological or philosophical configuration of freedom. As Heine writes, "A methodical people like us had to begin with Reformation, only after that could it occupy itself with philosophy, and only after completion of the latter could it go to political revolution."[92] The Reformation had emancipated the soul "by permitting freedom of inquiry in the Christian faith and by liberating the minds of men from the yoke of authority, [and thus] it enabled freedom of inquiry in general to take root in Germany and made it possible for science to develop independently."[93] In other words, Protestantism began an intellectual revolution by placing knowledge at the center of human freedom. Protestantism opened the door for spirit and matter to live under the same roof. Luther's insistence that faith constituted the inner life of the human being and was therefore distinct from the public knowledge of works created a space between institutionalized knowledge and the individual's experience of grace. For Heine, this distinction was revolutionary because it recognized a new sphere of freedom: "when Luther declared that his doctrine could be refuted only by the Bible itself or on grounds of reason, human reason was granted the right to explain the Scriptures, and reason was acknowledged as the supreme judge in all religious controversies. Thus, there arose in Germany so-called spiritual freedom or, as it is also called, freedom of thought. Thought became a right, and the authority of reason became legitimate."[94] For Heine, Luther's proclamation of *Sola Scriptura*, or that "only scripture" was needed for revelation, was a defense of reason and the establishment of a new regime of freedom of thought. And this recognition of reason as capable of standing on its own in dealing with the most holy truths of scripture signaled a shift toward this world—a world of history, embodiment, and living people. Freedom of thought, for Heine, is therefore the freedom *for* thought. Knowledge had been secured as the right to think, and the refutation of external, heteronomous authority afforded subjective freedom to reason. For Heine, Luther's revolution was therefore an epistemological one: faith and knowledge were now the right of the individual.

While Heine attributes the revolutionary freedom of thought to Luther, this is not to say that Luther's contributions were solely subjective. As Heine writes,

> Martin Luther gave us not merely freedom of movement, but also the means to move, that is, he gave the spirit a body. He put the thought into words. He created the German language.
> He did this by translating the Bible.[95]

By translating the Bible, Luther gave the individual not only a platform for individual reasoning but also a national language and literature. This act of embodying the freedom of thought in the German language also created a national revolution, according to Heine.[96] Spirit and body, mind and matter, faith and reason, find their way into the world of nation and language with Luther's Bible. And if Germany's March Revolution, which Heine actively supported in 1848, had failed to achieve its goals, the spiritual revolution was well underway, and the vision of equality and emancipation for all predicated on Heine's pantheism became a way to articulate the inchoate connection between Protestantism and philosophy.

As a path for emancipation, the freedom of thought founded in Protestantism was of universal benefit, but it was particularly significant for the Jews. Heine's emphasis on the particularly German history of this revolutionary shift in thinking was an important symbol of the legacy of philosophical idealism for German Jews more generally and for Cohen in particular. For Cohen, the connection between idealism and monotheism was given even greater integrity by Heine's insistence that German Idealism, and its concealed religion of pantheism, developed out of the Protestant tradition. In tracing this genealogy of idealism to pantheism and Protestantism, Heine had effectively opened the door for Judaism to find its rightful place within the history of Protestantism as well.

Praising Luther's translation, Heine claims that Luther reformed the idea of religion as such; through this transformation, "the Indo-Gnostic element disappeared, and we see the Judaic-Deistic element again becoming prominent."[97] Again, Cohen notices the indelible influence of Judaism within this account of the Reformation. According to Heine, at the very moment the Reformation gave people the freedom to think and made the German of the Bible the language in which to do so, the Jewish people were also given a right to think and to contribute to thinking. In Heine's praise for Luther, he claims that the "great national act of the Reformation, the 'creation of the German language,' returned to the Jews, their great world-service, the possession of the Bible."[98] This, Cohen interprets, was the moment at which the Jews joined the movement of protest as well. This was the moment when, as Heine writes, "Like a ghost that watches over a treasure … this ghost nation [*Volk-Gespenst*] [who] sat in their ghettos and guarded the Hebrew Bible" were called on to rejuvenate the German language itself. As a result of this conjuring, the "German scholars could be seen stealthily creeping down to unearth the treasure in order to acquire knowledge of Hebrew."[99] Citing these lines, Cohen sees in Heine's Luther an acknowledgment of Jewish provenance in the transformation of the German language. Taking on an ancient shade of biblical Hebrew, *modern* German became a hybrid language. Thus, as Cohen concludes, for Heine "Medicean Catholicism was Hellenic and Germanic Protestantism was Jewish, in its simple chastity, as he refers in many instances to the Jews and the Germans [*Germanen*] as people of ethical life [*Sittlichkeit*]."[100] In sharing a common ethical language, Jews and Germans both became Protestants.

When we take this reading of Heine as methodologically formative, we gain not only a better grasp of what is at stake in Cohen's negotiation of monotheism and pantheism but also insight into how Judaism and Germanism are inflected by an idealism that remains enchanted. That is, Protestantism represents an epistemological revolution by giving thought its independence from dogma and institution. Turning to the Bible alone, Protestantism enshrines the monotheistic unity of reason, which ought to be accessible to all, as the freedom of thought. And in retrieving the ancient Hebrew Bible as a common source of this freedom of thought, Protestantism implicitly recruits the Jews into its protest. This epistemology, however, remains enchanted by the spirit of pantheistic monotheism, a vision of emancipation that remains beyond the sphere of what is actual and present. Thus, only idealism, in Cohen's telling, presents a common language of ethical life shared by Germans and Jews. And this epistemological idealism is rooted in monotheism.

PROTEST(ANT) REASONING

The relationship between pantheism and Judaism—and between monotheism and idealism—was the driving narrative of Cohen's essay on Heine. Having opened up an avenue for Judaism to be introduced into philosophy by way of an "idealistic Spinozism," Cohen gestured toward a philosophical path beyond Christian religion and anticlerical secular metaphysics. For Cohen, idealism came to represent a mode of reasoning focused on the transhistorical value of ideas, especially the future value an idea may have for changing the present. But Heine's narrative revealed a specifically German intellectual history of idealism. This account of German Idealism also emphasized its implicit Protestant roots as the epistemological revolution that freed human thought to pursue knowledge independently of the strictures of theology. Moreover, although Cohen's early essay focused on the role of Spinoza within that history of German Idealism and Protestantism, Cohen would dedicate his career to unearthing the various dimensions of idealism as a public reasoning through the philosophy of Kant, whose critical project of Enlightenment emphatically declared the freedom to make public use of reason as the mandate of philosophy. After exploring Heine's influence as a context for Cohen's developing ideas, we can better understand this turn to Protestantism and Germanism in Cohen's later thought, as well as his use of monotheism to navigate between the ideal constructs of Germanism and Judaism, by beginning to interrogate his refinement of Kantian idealism.

In his infamous 1915–16 essay "Germanism and Judaism," for example, Cohen united these two spiritual exemplars in what has been seen by some as a quasichauvinistic nationalism.[101] Addressed to American Jews during World War I and intended as a defense of German culture and civilization as a bulwark in the cause of Jewish emancipation, Cohen focused on the question of national ethos and wedded the fates of the Germans and the Jews—both lacking complete political self-determination in the early modern period[102]—to the legacy of the German Enlightenment, cosmopolitanism, and idealism. Cohen's understanding of idealism as a lens through which to view these pasts was built on his system of philosophy, however, and its nuance has led to much misunderstanding of Cohen's argument.

By the time of Cohen's "Germanism and Judaism," he had developed a system of philosophy which he described as a "critical idealism," which theorizes ideas as "hypotheses" or constructive grounds of all research and discovery. Ideas ground the scientific discovery of "what is."[103] Arguing that Plato intended just such an account of ideas when he referred to them as the *hypokemenon* or groundwork for what is,[104] idealism, according to Cohen's explanation, distinguishes the being of ideas from all other beings. Cohen remarks that the being of ideas, in this Platonic sense, is not unlike Judaism's distinction between the unique being of God and all other beings in that "outside of [God's] being, there is no other being; that all other being, as Plato would say, is only *appearance*."[105] Given Kant's explicit acknowledgment of Plato as the guide for his own transcendental idealism,[106] Cohen asserts that there is an implicit affinity between Judaism and German Idealism, which monotheism helps articulate. But

Cohen's is a complicated understanding of the meaning of the "being of ideas," and it is more fully elaborated in his systematic philosophy, in which he had painstakingly developed his own theory of critical idealism.

According to Cohen, the history of idealism need not culminate in a turn to metaphysics, which can be roughly characterized as a form of subjective idealism, which the German idealists writing after Kant had seemingly proposed. Rather, Cohen developed an interpretation of Kant's critical philosophy that insisted upon this distinctive being of ideas. Kant's publication of the *Critique of Pure Reason* (1781) had transformed German intellectual history with its argument for a rigorous critique of knowledge. By *critique* Kant understood the work of tracing limits to human knowledge. His aim was to differentiate between knowledge-claims that could be tested as possible experiences and claims to "speculative knowledge," which critique would reveal to be based on certain "dogmatic" assumptions. Kant's critical project thus sought to avoid the kinds of speculative assertions that might lay claim to a divine-like knowledge of all things, at least as far as knowledge of the natural world might be concerned. For Kant, human reason is emphatically finite and as far as natural scientific knowledge was concerned, Kant sought to determine the limits of reason's claims. By emphasizing an account of human experience that privileged natural science as its map, Cohen therefore struggled to show how Kant's limiting of human reason was not a complete reduction of the spiritual scope of reason, history, and ideas to a physiological human reflex. Yet in emphasizing the distinctive being of ideas, Cohen recognized in Kant's idealism both a model of transcendence as something more than a concern for theological abstraction or historical mythology and a more rigorous account of knowledge than the appeal to brute or vulgar materialism against which his mentor, Friedrich Albert Lange, had cautioned. Kant's idealism bolstered Cohen's grappling with the shifting authority of science and religion, and he channeled his energy into reconstructing Kant's idealism to that end.

While Heine had also narrated the rise of idealism as fundamentally grounded in Kant's critical philosophy, Heine was persuaded that Hegel's system of idealism had achieved its purported reconciliation of substance and subject. However, by the second half of the nineteenth century, Hegel's system and penchant for seemingly metaphysical language had fallen into disrepute with the privileging of the natural sciences in philosophy. Thus, Cohen's publication of *Kant's Theory of Experience* (1871) provided a robust defense of an antimetaphysical and scientifically oriented idealism. It was admittedly a lopsided reading of Kantian philosophy, prioritizing Kant's *Prolegomena to Any Future Metaphysics* and its explicit defense of physics as a science related to the critical project. However, with the publication of the book Cohen helped consolidate the steady return to Kant that had been brewing in the decades between the revolution and the founding of the German Empire in 1871.[107] It also provided an account of philosophical idealism that was emphatically nonmetaphysical.

Having established himself as a foremost interpreter of Kant's philosophy, Cohen secured a post at the University of Marburg in 1873 (a rarity for a Jew) with the help of his friend and mentor, Lange, upon whose death, Cohen was promoted to his chair in 1876 (a watershed moment for Jews in the German academy).[108] With the institutional security previously only dreamed of by Jewish intellectuals in Germany, Cohen turned the bulk of his time and attention to what would become his professional concern: the interpretation of Kant and a looming crisis of philosophy.

Cohen's efforts to forward a philosophical return to Kant were largely successful, and the German academic philosophy of the Wilhelmine period was dominated by the movement known as neo-Kantianism. This movement, especially Cohen and his Marburg school's variety, was more than a simple return to Kant, however. It was a reinterpretation and transformation of Kant's idealism. Indeed, Cohen's own systematic philosophy, which he developed between 1902–12, took many critical steps past Kant and even framed some of its innovations as critiques of Kant. Most notably, Cohen transformed Kant's transcendental idealism, which probes the conditions of possibility for judgment, into a philosophical method for the critique of a body of knowledge, such as natural science.

The "transcendental method," Cohen claims, takes an extant body of knowledge, such as natural science, as the subject of critique and then inquires into its conditions of possibility. While Kant was focused on the minutiae of judgment—the syllogistic structure of logical judgments—, Cohen expands the meaning of *critique* into a method of analysis of claim making and the justification of concepts within an objective body of knowledge. Therefore, when Cohen describes ideas as having a quality of "being," he means that ideas are the fundamental stuff of what we count as knowledge: the idea of a mathematical curve, for example, is the basis for understanding in the world of physics how objects fall or travel distances but not necessarily the ground for how a basketball player understands the arc of a free throw. Ideas are, however, only hypothetical grounds. They have the "value of being," which is to say ideas are conceptual norms that must be tested against the developing canons of knowledge—in science, ethics, and aesthetics—of historical human experience. The latter are the "facts" with which the transcendental method commences. The value of being is established for the relevant canon of knowledge that treats those objects as meaningful, and thus critique transpires as an analysis of the judgments relevant to those forms of knowledge.[109]

According to Cohen, judgments are the foundation of thought since they pursue the concept of something by asking what it is not.[110] As Cohen explains, the work of justification in thinking—the work of logic—is to analyze the conditions of any one concept to the point at which a relative negation is found to differentiate it from being nothing at all or that concept's total negation.[111] By recognizing what the concept is not, we can better account for its conditions and explain why it has value at all. What Cohen calls "the judgment of origin" is therefore already a question of *what* thinking has assigned with value, namely its value as *something rather than nothing*.[112] Cohen's logic must be understood, therefore, as a pure idealism that anticipates, rather than represents, the objects of perception because they are anticipated by validated concepts, which make up a body of knowledge.[113] Hence, Cohen's logic of anticipation assigns value to ideas.

With its emphasis on the value of ideas for a specific canon of knowledge, Cohen's critical idealism also interrogates knowledge as something shared between people. As historical agents of reasoning—as actors in the logical activity of thinking—we participate in a body of scientific knowledge, which means that forms of consciousness and reason are public and objective canons of knowledge. As norms or hypotheses to be tested and justified against the canon of historical norms, knowledge is thus socially constituted, and logic is socially practiced, because it is transcendent to any particular subject, the latter being produced by the system of idealism itself.

This account of idealism, and the being of ideas, animates Cohen's "Germanism and Judaism." Germanism and Judaism are ideas in need of testing and justification. Thus, Cohen's essay sets out to justify these ideas since they are the dynamic "origins" of a rational (re)construction of the experience of such historical identities. They are not static or eternal "essences." Because these ideas are constructible and, as hypotheses, fluid,[114] Cohen places the idea of Judaism in conceptual kinship (*Verwandtschaft*) with Germanism in order to test those ideas against what they are not. Neither Judaism nor Germanism is a theologically determined entity but rather a tradition that consists of conceptual elements and resources.

Akin to his early essays on Heine and God and soul, Cohen's later "Germanism and Judaism" also focuses on the conceptual value of these ideas. Considering both as national *idealities*, Germanism and Judaism are norms or hypotheses that Jews and Germans *ought to be* striving toward.[115] As philosophically constituted constellations of norms, institutions, and historical meanings that are being generated and regenerated in pursuit of future ideals for society as a whole, the German state as it is cannot be taken as the sum total of what Cohen envisions Germanism to be.[116] Rather, Cohen is envisioning what Germany *could be*. And to the extent that Germany is the historical progenitor of critique and idealism—the historical source of the Protestant revolution that secured the freedom of thought—neither Germanism nor idealism is identical with some given thing called German being or existence. Rather, Germanism is an idea in need of justification because it remains a goal or ideal rather than a fully constituted entity. Judaism thus similarly remains a work in progress. As the origin of monotheism, Judaism provides the configuration of a God for all, who transcends particularities such as nation and tribe. Yet as ideals, both Germanism and Judaism are refined and refashioned through the protest or demand for these ideals to be expanded beyond what they currently are. Also, taken together, how these ideals ought to be, Cohen claims, must be revised in light of reasoning. However, Cohen focuses primarily on Germanism because it provides the readiest example of a cultural and philosophical context in which such self-refinement is implicit and thus is the means with which Judaism could reframe its meanings.

Much like Heine, Cohen emphasizes that Germanism combines a particular linguistic and religiocultural trajectory into a philosophical movement that culminates in Kant's Copernican revolution. But the ideal of

Germanism remains, for Cohen, a work in progress almost by definition, since it seeks to secure justification and faith as the modes of freedom of thought. Germanism is therefore another way of describing Protestantism. And in Kant's philosophy Cohen locates the refinement of this Protestant epistemology first alluded to by Heine. As Cohen writes, "With the Reformation, the modern human being became animated by the *distinction* between modes of *certainty* in human cognition, namely, between certainty in the exact *sciences* and certainty in all *questions of faith*."[117] The Reformation, therefore, is larger than Germany alone; it is the condition of modern human existence, in which certainty and knowledge are recognized as finite and disciplinarily articulated. This freedom of thought to pursue certainty in the sciences therefore demands justification as the condition for this freedom. And Kant's philosophy seeks to express this delimiting of knowledge by way of "critique." Cohen's philosophy therefore advocated a truly critical standpoint by extending Kant's principle into a critique of culture as well. Culture—especially German culture, in this case—should be treated as a constellation of diverse bodies of knowledge, each subject to critique and in need of justification.

Despite—or, perhaps because of—Cohen's emphasis on an "ideal" Germanism, he saw his philosophy as working "against the grain" of his time while simultaneously steering a course through the storm of controversy that would continue to build in social, political, and cultural debates of his day.[118] To pursue such idealist purposes and ends that were far from actual, Cohen's vision of an ethical culture capable of anchoring both scientific and religious transformations enabled by the Protestant Reformation hinged on a cultural return to a more rigorous idealism, such as he found in the philosophy of Kant. This is because, as Cohen writes,

> The problems of our time are, on the one hand, on the theoretical side: the problem of basing science upon its own most simple principles, whose precise and clear determination is thereby aspired to; and on the other hand, on the practical side: the validity of making the core truth of faith in God into the living and literal truth of love of the neighbor (*die Nächstenliebe*), that is to say: the regeneration of the nations (*die Völker*) on the basis of the ethical ideal of socialism.
>
> In both directions—although the combatants don't always know it— the Kantian worldview stands as the shibboleth of the present and the solution to the future.[119]

The problems of Cohen's day were concerned with reconciling science and tradition, whether in the form of religion, ethics, or social progress. Thus, for Cohen, theory and practice—science and ethical culture—represent the spheres of philosophical tensions that result from a secularizing public sphere. But they are also the result of Protestantism's distinction between faith and knowledge. Within the transcendental method, which identifies the conditions that make the present state of knowledge possible, Cohen therefore sees the key to resolving conflicts between bodies of knowledge and a path toward the transformation of religious love into an ethical socialism. In other words, Cohen assigns both science and religion with roles in German culture.

Because Kant's idealism builds on the Protestant distinction between faith and knowledge, according to Cohen, this idealism sustains rather than abrogates the possibility that religion might articulate reasons that could count as knowledge. The practical side of Kantian reason therefore pursues the ideal of a love of God, or faith, that *should* ground a love of the neighbor, or ethics. The theoretical side pursues the certainty of knowledge, or justification, that Cohen deploys as the basis for a public reasoning accessible to all in culture. Because of this distinction and its safeguarding of both a method for justifying knowledge claims as well as a social morality, Kantian idealism therefore becomes a basis on which to demonstrate both that religious difference is part of the great legacy of Protestantism and, thus, that other religions such as Judaism might become a public contributor to the social body of knowledge. Indeed, according to Cohen, the Reformation and the Enlightenment did not seek to discard religion but rather to introduce a more rigorous form of cultural life through what Kant deemed the principled autonomy of ethics as a form of cognition. This, Cohen claims, is "the Protestant character of Kant's thought. Thus, it puts an end to the medieval subterfuge of 'double-truth in every sense. Ethics becomes coordinated within the system, although its character of certainty is different from that of logic. But that it could be coordinated within the system at all is due to the methodological analogy of their mutual principles."[120] Whereas this distinction between theoretical and practical reason—logic and ethics—suggested to many post-Kantians that an insurmountable dualism plagued transcendental idealism, Cohen understands the analogy of principles undergirding logic and ethics as a *methodological* autonomy of the natural sciences from the humanities. As distinct disciplines taking shape in Cohen's time, both natural science and the humanities, in his account, nevertheless share an ideal of method and thus a common purpose: namely, critically justified truth. While truth in logic remains a systematic demand,[121] a question of methodological validity, the ethical inflection of ideas seeks justification through a labor of reasoning. For Cohen, this commitment to method and purpose despite distinct epistemic canons is the innovation of a Protestant modernity and the German "nation of Kant."[122] Describing religion as a cultural resource rather than a theologico-political power to enforce dogmatic truths in either science or morality, Cohen therefore draws inspiration from Kant's idealism for what he calls a theory of ethical socialism—a socialism firmly rooted in a normative idea of a monotheistic God shared between Christian and Jew.

In Cohen's hands, Kant's idealism therefore animates a critique of knowledge that invites a new understanding of public debate and justification as expressly idealist endeavors. And it is this relationship between Protestantism, as an epistemological condition for justification, and idealism, as the method of justification, that Cohen locates in Kant's work. Culture and sociality can be articulated through the lens of idealism, both theoretical and practical, because Kantian reason is a scientific and objective body of knowledge. Whether Kant's "priority of practical reason" or his insistence on the a priori and categorical determination of laws of reason as well as of nature (and their independence from each other), idealism becomes the method for constructing an epistemology of modern culture. As Cohen writes, "Through the distinction between both these types of certainty [natural-scientific and religious], the idea of Protestantism gave the first sure ground to the scientific knowledge of culture to all modern peoples. All development of religion, if no less even all development of ethics, is conditioned by the construction of this idealism of culture. Without the distinction between moral, and therefore also religious [certainty] and otherwise scientific certainty, there is no sincerity and no personal conscientiousness for people of modern culture."[123] Free from institutional and dogmatic censorship, Cohen's account of Protestantism invokes the freedom of reason to pursue truth in all its forms. But, hardly an account of the neutralization of reason, this means that Protestantism establishes the legitimacy of modern culture as the pursuit and exchange of ideas or *reasons*. Modern culture is idealism, for Cohen. And, to the extent that Protestantism expresses the properly idealistic principles that distinguish the being of nature from the being of ethics, the autonomy of ethical and religious knowledge means that cultural knowledge must be understood as *justifiable knowledge*. Ethics best represents this task of cultural knowledge insofar as ethics represents the space of purposive thinking about how knowledge can be better— how it *ought* to be. But knowledge can only be transformed by *enacting* that knowledge in justification and reasoning. The spirit of Protestantism therefore lives on in what amounts to a different expression of religion in the sphere of human reasoning: as an epistemological idealism. This idealism develops the freedom of conscience introduced by the Reformation into a critical labor of thinking justifiably, of reasoning and idealizing culture, history, and politics. But it also lives on as a spirit of belief that progress in knowledge—more accessible and more critically justified knowledge—is possible.

Cohen's idealism is therefore Protestant in connotation because it is an epistemology of justification. By recognizing distinct types of certainty— one predicated of faith and the other of knowledge—Protestantism also demonstrates an implicit hermeneutic principle at the base of modern culture. That is, by separating according to rules and standards of adjudication the public, historical, and social development of knowledge from a theological certainty that no human institution could justify, Protestantism implicitly recognized legitimate and illegitimate ways of making claims—scientific, social, and ethical—in modern culture. This distinction between kinds of reasoning, however, is mediated by the shared investment in justification, which Cohen, like Hegel, seeks to affirm as the inheritance of modern ethical life.[124] Emphasizing justification in reasoning, Cohen's idealism therefore stresses the need for a distinct process by which a concept is accounted for and its various predicates and inferences justified. This process of publicly asking for and critiquing reasons is what Cohen describes as the idealism of German culture, and it is in such a culture that he envisions Judaism to be at home, such that "the Jew, as well as the Catholic, must imbue themselves with the historical insight and impartiality with which the *turn* (*Tendenz*) of the Reformation suffuses, as it were, all religious thought and deed."[125]

To illustrate the Protestant form of justification that animates such a cultural affinity between Judaism and Germanism, Cohen describes the work of "idealization," a conceptual process in which the normative content of a historical idea—a religious myth, practice, or belief—is reworked in view of the idea's historical development and then placed within the scope of a contemporary justificatory claim. If we recall the controversial development of liberal Protestant theology described above, such as that of David Friedrich Strauss or Schleiermacher, Cohen describes the example of Christ's suffering in moral terms. That is, the moral personality and model of responsibility represented by this ideal of Christ's suffering is an idealization that brackets the question of the historical Jesus. As Cohen writes, "For this orientation historicity is not the effervescent source of a literary text; rather, reason, in all its subjectivity, in all of its depths and shadows, is. For Luther himself, Christ had become an ideal figure of faith."[126] Rather than appeal to a standard of empirical science for determining the truth or falsity of religious faith, reason sets a standard of judgment in matters of faith and science according to each one's respective norms. Hence, Cohen sees in Protestantism a definitive shift in both intellectual and social history. He writes,

> Within Christian culture, the Reformation has brought about a specific Protestant culture. This consists not only of a general cultural spirit in science, literature, and art but also in nothing less than the most intimate conditioning of religion. The alternative of works or faith is a battle slogan, a catchword, whose real sense and value remain misunderstood so long as the bulwarks, against which and for which the battle was led, remain veiled. . . .
>
> Against the sovereign church and its works of faith, Protestantism oriented itself by faith alone. As the authority and the sovereignty of the Church and its salvific works are disdained as the basis of faith, Protestantism opposes to these its own spiritual-intellectual principle: the personhood of the individual in opposition to the abstract power of the Church. The personhood of the individual, however, unavoidably entails the dimension of subjectivity, with all its ambiguities. This subjectivity, with its dangers but also with its classical tendencies, is the destiny of Protestantism. Personhood is lifted out of the universal generality of the Church. Individuality is awakened and called to its own, unique responsibility.[127]

It is the unique responsibility of the individual—the particular amid the "universal" and "abstract" power of the Church—that signals the cultural hermeneutic of Protestantism. Protestantism vindicates difference, according to this reading, by emphasizing the responsibility of the individual to think. Whether as a subject or self,[128] this individuation and the development of conscience is fundamental to the "Protestant culture" that Cohen discusses.[129] The responsibility of the individual is to *reason* their way to faith, rather than be determined by institutional authority. Thus, the process of developing an individual responsibility out of the abstract universality of the Church is a demonstration of the work of idealization. This responsibility means that the ideal behind the historical norm must be reasoned out and into the subjectivity of the individual.

While this responsibility of the individual allows an epistemological opening, Protestantism also signals a danger in this vindication of subjectivity. Hence, Cohen's Protestantism emphasizes yet another common feature of both German and Jewish idealities: monotheism. This fundamental thread of monotheism conceptually links Cohen's early essay on Heine and his later essays and helps allay the ambiguities in the individuation of responsibility beyond institutional authority. Intertwined in philosophy's past, Cohen claims, Judaism and Protestantism share monotheism as a conceptual norm that helps negotiate historical as well as political difference but without completely reducing this responsibility to isolated individualism. Rather, this freedom of thought and faith makes possible the freedom necessary for a new form of *public* reasoning. By making access to public reason the goal of human sociality, monotheism also insists on idealization, or the work of taking responsibility for ideas and believing in their contribution to the progress of knowledge. Idealization lifts both Germanism and Judaism out of their particularities and puts forward a space in which they confront each other's reasons. As Cohen writes,

> Thus we can make the Protestant faith in its historical world power understandable to us through our monotheism and without prejudice make a home within it. We can undertake the finest idealization of this Protestant faith, give it our sympathy, and contribute for our own part to its further development, without, by contrast, giving up the historical duty of idealization altogether in Catholicism. We remain as absolute monotheists, in that we reject every form of identity as [of any] mediation between God and man, in an impartial objectivity toward these Christian conflicts, so that we can openly speak of the free historical view of the progress of this religious development.[130]

Protestantism is aligned with pure idealist monotheism because both warn against the mediation of the individual and God. While Protestantism rejects the institutional mediation of the church, in rejecting the identity between man and God, monotheism implores the individual to take responsibility for their thinking as beholden to a norm that transcends them. The goal of an absolute monotheism is thus to mitigate any attempt to incarnate either God in man or the self-assertion of human reason as equivalent to a divine justification. Instead, the historical view of religious development is an attempt to justify religion through human judgment alone, which is to say in the human sociality of judgments. Cohen therefore develops monotheism into a conceptual resource for developing a theory of knowledge: transcendence, separation, and the difference signified by a monotheistic God nevertheless projects a future unity for human reasoning to strive toward.[131] The combination of transcendence and justification (or method) finds an ideal unity in this historical duty of idealization, and by emphasizing the work of reasoning as a responsibility that awakens and calls the individual to take responsibility, this same monotheism dissolves the stability of "Jew or Christian, Jew or German" without reducing the one to the other. This emphasis on idealism and transcendence over and against metaphysics and immanence dispels the "bogeyman for the Jew, namely that he is a foreigner in Christian culture, and that much more in German Protestantism, [this image] must disappear."[132] Monotheism transcends these particularities.

Although the young Cohen might have tolerated Heine's depiction of Spinozist pantheism as a promise to equalize all objects of knowledge, Cohen's continued interest in a Protestant Judaism is strictly monotheistic. This monotheism both idealizes difference and enables the shared, "unconditional duty of mankind" to be the *goal* of ethics—of "the historical hope for a unified mankind."[133] By projecting this unified mankind as a goal of justification of difference in the past, we see the *norm* of the future emerge: Judaism and (German) Protestantism idealize unity as a project and goal. Cohen's account of Protestantism therefore becomes a condition for public reasoning, where idealism leverages the past for the sake of the future.

In sum, Cohen's conception of a German, a Jew, and a German Jew is animated by his idealism. Idealism, however, represents the space of reasoning that transcends the differences of historical particularity,

religious or national. Carved out of a history that begins with Protestantism, refined by Kant and upheld by an ideal of German culture, this new
space of reasoning signals that a German is defined as one who reasons
their way toward an ideal of the nation. Thus, the monotheistic emphasis on idealization, announced by Cohen, helps transcend the divide
between Christian and Jew. Idealism, therefore, becomes a democratizing form of thinking for Cohen. This is why he considers idealism a
"national inheritance," since the nation—including its protestation of the
church's hegemony—is an idea; a *public* idea. As he writes in his 1916 essay
"German Idealism and Classical Thought," by referring to *German* Idealism
Cohen is assuming "the national moment [represented] in a scientifically basic concept, in idealism, and objectifying it."[134] While idealism
represents a German contribution to culture, the spiritual understanding of knowledge, creativity, and sociality in Cohen's understanding of
culture is a confluence of reasons, ideas, and meanings that have been
refracted through time and into our present.[135] As both a philosophical
and a Jewish question, therefore, Cohen maintains that the idea of the
nation means "it is undoubtedly my right and even my duty as a religious
individual, let alone as a professing Jew, to charge my Fatherland with
the ideal task of protecting and preserving the Jewish group so that the
religion of the One and Only God may be preserved."[136] In other words, a
nation is legally constructed from the idealization of historical sources of
many "nationalities," and religion retains a spiritual task in this endeavor
of construction.[137] The preservation of religion by the state is thus more
than a question of policy for Cohen. A plea for neutrality will not secure
the recognition of Judaism, nor will the moral content of general culture
be continuously refined and bettered without the historical sources of
religion. Rather, for Cohen, the mandate of the state itself is to represent
an ethically constituted form of consciousness that idealized by its many
constituents, reaching into the past to secure a more diverse background
conversation for the generation of public norms of morality and social
organization.[138]

   This account of reasoning as an activity or a form of labor in its own
right is not a neutralization of the past; rather, this demand is for social actors to engage in a *spiritual labor* of practical and public reasoning
about religion and culture.[139] Cohen recognized that articulating the
democratized version of idealism he found in Heine and later Kant would

require a reckoning with the public stakes of the new reasoning enabled by Protestantism. Therefore, his account of reasoning would require him to step beyond Spinoza definitively. In other words, Cohen's Protestantism became eminently social and political or, at least, the basis for negotiating religion in the public sphere.

THE POLITICS OF PUBLIC PROTESTANTISM

In Cohen's telling, Protestantism is a protest against majoritarian reasoning. That is to say, in its explicit focus on the transformation of knowledge and reason, Cohen's description of Protestantism significantly provides a moment of separation between the practices of reasoning and the identities of reasoners. Protestants are no longer simply Christians but, rather, members of a movement of independent, free thinkers. Jews become Protestant to the extent that they continue this tradition of protesting the majority by laying claim to knowledge and reason independent of belonging to a religious faith called Christianity.

Cohen's characterization of Protestantism is also that of a worldview that grounds, as we can now see, an epistemology of liberalism. That is, Protestantism articulates a space not only between the practice of reasoning and identity but also between the individual and the state in which the human and divine relationship is negotiated anew. Protestantism therefore describes a public transformation of the political and social order. However, the religious freedom opened up in this new social and political space between state and individual, at least according to Cohen's account, provides new opportunities for religion to be articulated in public, not private. Indeed, Cohen's Protestantism functions more as an epistemological freedom than a strictly individualist freedom. That is, the individual must now be defined in the context of the public reasoning that will shape her rather than in terms of the free-floating abstraction of an individual who comes before the law and is then shaped anew.

While Protestantism therefore provides the catalyzing thrust for Cohen's account of philosophical idealism to carve out the space of the public sphere, Cohen also notes a "danger" and "ambiguity" in the legacy of Protestantism. As we saw earlier, liberalism was indelibly associated with the trajectory of German philosophy, and the latter also drew from Protestantism's epistemological opening. German Idealism took a different path into metaphysics, and its disenchantment with theology led to accusations of atheism and anticlericalism. Pantheism, along with the reception of Hegel's idealism, had given Spinoza the reputation of a founding father to this metaphysics. And this metaphysical account of freedom and human reason became deeply entwined with liberal political thought.

Cohen grew skeptical of the metaphysical trajectory of pantheism, especially its political manifestations. Warning of the ambiguities of subjectivity in his later account of Protestantism, Cohen's early assessment of pantheism, as I present it, should surprise readers familiar with Cohen's more mature works. Nevertheless, pantheism first helped Cohen name the epistemological opening for the freedom of thought and emancipation of reasoning that he would later explicitly associate with his account of idealism and German Protestantism. This shift in Cohen's thinking is important for the fact that Spinoza represented one possibility for Jews to become individuals: to embody subjective freedom by unencumbering themselves of religion. This, Cohen began to worry, was too high a price for Jews to pay for emancipation. Another understanding of the relationship between religion and the state was needed.

In his later rereading of Spinoza, Cohen attributes Spinoza's greatest error—and the threat posed by his pantheism—to his reduction of all knowledge, whether natural-scientific, Biblical, religious, or ethical, to the monistic unity of infinite intelligibility. Neither transcendence nor a distinction between logical and ethical methods—between faith and knowledge—was possible in such a system. Without a distinct sphere of ethical or religious knowledge in reason—of ideas distinct from materiality—pantheism simply collapsed the Kantian organization of theoretical and practical reasoning. Without a distinction between nature and human will, only the natural sciences and the technological model of causal necessity could legitimate modern epistemology. Without an objective body of knowledge, only the individual could validate their own judgments in the light of the infinite within them. In short, human life would be left explained only in terms of necessity in which "statistics become the morality and theology of the modern age [*die neuer Zeit*]."[140] In Cohen's view, such a philosophical elaboration of Spinozism confused the relationship between faith and knowledge in a manner similar to its confusion about ideas and reality and ideality and facts. Ideas, insofar as they transcend the material conditions of history and nature, cannot be reduced to given natural facts, according to Cohen. As Cohen writes, a metaphysics such as Spinoza's collapses the realm of ideas, of spirit, into the material realm of substance and "turns the human being and the human Spirit into a mode of substance. In the unity of substance alone lay being and truth, and only in the relation to substance, which signifies not only its self and the self of the human being in general, but that it is therefore only through heteronomy that the law of its will can be found and sought. It is always in the world, which shall comfort the restriction of the self."[141] The challenge of pantheism therefore lies in Spinoza's metaphysical system, in the inherent relation of substance to its modes. In his *Ethics*, Spinoza masterfully weaves the infinite substance of all reality into the fabric of the finite. Interpreting nature as the "modes" of the infinite substance in their determinate manifestations, yet identical with the world in toto, Spinoza's account of lawfulness for the human will, in Cohen's understanding, posits an identity with nature and is thus "heteronomous." Because Spinoza did not distinguish human spirit from natural substance, according to Cohen, his metaphysics had confused what a human being *is* and what it *ought to be*, since "with a circle, I may not ask what it ought to be; rather, only what it is. In its being lies its law. There against, the law of human beings lies not in their being, rather in their ought."[142] By collapsing the ideal into the real, Spinoza's real philosophical error, Cohen claimed, was to make volition (will) and thought one identical substance (*intellectus et voluntas unum et idem sunt*).[143] All determinate particulars are interwoven, at least from the perspective of the infinite, as subsumable within the chain of causation, back into the infinite self-emerging of substance.

With Spinoza at the helm of such a metaphysics of immanence and materialism, Cohen worried about the associated charge of neutralization that would soon follow such a political theory when it attempts to address and recognize the role of religion. Therefore, Cohen's growing ambivalence about Spinoza was also rooted in the political consequences of Spinoza's philosophy.[144] Naming "Spinoza the leader of the contemporary era," Cohen claimed that the pantheistic reduction of all knowledge to substance and its modes meant that "all problems of religion, as of philosophy thus are splinted together (*schienen*) to arrive at a unifying solution."[145] For Cohen, it was this unifying solution that posed the greatest threat and motivated the "betrayal" of Judaism he attributes to Spinoza's *Theological-Political Treatise*.[146]

The mature Cohen therefore judged Spinoza to have committed two errors, the first scientific and the second political. First, Spinoza had fundamentally inverted Jewish monotheism by placing natural knowledge, indeed nature altogether, on par with the knowledge given to human beings by an ideality: God or prophetic revelation. In Cohen's account, Spinoza internalized and privatized what was always meant to be a public canon of knowledge, the Bible. Yet the consequence of this inversion went beyond a metaphysical substitution: Cohen also charged Spinoza with having subordinated the role of philosophy to both his reconstruction of theology and of politics.[147] Here again, Cohen saw Spinoza to have internalized and privatized something that was meant to remain public: namely, the sociality of religion. As David Biale has suggested in his reading of Spinoza, pantheism and materialism imbricate Judaism within a process of "secularization" in which "materialism thus defines the metaphysical philosophy of the secular, [while] humanism defines the political theory of the secular."[148] Cohen similarly develops a critique of Spinoza taking aim at both a metaphysical (theological) and a political reduction such that it might be said that the naturalizing turn of Spinoza's pantheism paves the way for the neutralizing turn of liberalism. In other words, the political consequences of pantheist metaphysics must be confronted.

In his 1915 essay on Spinoza, Cohen therefore claims Spinoza willfully misinterpreted what Descartes referred to as the "natural light of reason," understanding nature as "the order and the disposition that God established within created things."[149] By reinterpreting this Cartesian criterion of certainty, Spinoza transforms natural knowledge into divine knowledge or prophecy, which "is recognized as divine only in the sense that it is *natural* for *all* human beings, insofar as all human beings have a share in God's nature."[150] There is nothing special about prophetic knowledge, for it is "no more exalted than the knowledge of all other humans."[151] The consequence of this naturalization of prophetic knowledge, which Cohen reads as the extension of Spinoza's pantheism, is that it reduces the particularities of Judaism to error or historical contingency such that "the religion of the Jews belongs only in their own state."[152] Additionally, the nature of divine law is transformed into an intellectual apprehension of a pantheistic principle—namely, that "divine law is grounded in our

Geist [Spirit]," which is to say that "the human *Geist* and God are *by defini-tion identical*, inasmuch as He exists in this *Geist*."[153] By placing God in the human spirit, Spinoza effectively collapses the distinction between God and the individual. Furthermore, by abrogating the continued rel-evance of Jewish law, Spinoza paints a picture of an irrational Judaism in broad and blunt brushstrokes. For Spinoza, the state must therefore police religion both because "the *Church* must be challenged as a state within the state" and because the historical origin of this problematic "lies in the theocracy of *ancient Judaism*."[154] This is the basis for Spinoza's purported liberalism, which configures religion as subordinate to the state and the purview of the individual alone.

While many nineteenth-century rationalist Protestants and liberal thinkers celebrated this dimension of Spinoza's thought both for ex-pounding a natural religion and for seeking to separate religion and state, Cohen perceived this move as a betrayal of both Judaism and liberalism altogether. For Spinoza, revealed religion consists only of obedience—which is to say, the ritualized practice of obedience to the strictures of law.[155] Such an obedience, which begins out of fear of God, does not express true freedom, however.[156] Rather, such religion is necessary for the masses that have no patience for intellectual demonstration of eternal truths.[157] In the concluding chapters of his *Tractatus*, Spinoza therefore seeks to identify the role of philosophy over and against that of religion within the state. Philosophy is supposed to be situated within the state as the vehicle of free spirit, of the freedom of each person to think as they see fit and to philosophize by articulating the form of reason that brings all citizens closest to the "natural state."[158] Yet, as Cohen reads such propositions, Spinoza's metaphysical pantheism upends any form of public reason.

By reimagining religion as a "natural religion"[159] and by outlining a natural condition of the state and its attendant conception of natural right, Spinoza's liberalism transforms religion and state into "reason-less" constructs according to Cohen. As Cohen argues,

> If philosophy should thereby be separated from theology by its own *de-cree*, then not only does this not accommodate religious *liberalism*, but so too it simultaneously establishes a barrier between the *cultural education of the people* [*Volksbildung*] and science [*Wissenschaft*], which is what now counts as philosophy and will hereafter be allocated the role of a learned

guild. This distinction between universal education and scientific insight is the *basic deficiency of this theory of state* as it is of this *theory of religion*. The state must remain an aristocracy, because the masses cannot live according to reason. And religion only teaches obedience; but may have absolutely nothing in common with speculative insights. The same ground makes both religion and the state reason-less. This relation of the state to religion is the consequence explicitly drawn.[160]

In Cohen's interpretation, Spinoza misidentifies the nature of the theologico-political problem. That is, because Spinoza sees philosophy as the proper sphere of truth, which must be sheltered by the state, religion is relegated to the sphere of faith and separated from praxis as much as it is from reason. For Spinoza, religion concerns obligation, duty, and fear,[161] whereas "true religion" is philosophy; it is the freedom to inquire into necessity and truth.[162] Therefore, on Spinoza's model religion and science are opposed to each other, and philosophy and science are placed out of grasp from the common people. Left with positive religion as their sole source of moral and political education, they must simply "obey." For Cohen, this philosophical elitism undermines Spinoza's entire liberal theory. By contrast, Cohen argues that philosophy must serve the purpose of *Volksbildung* if state-sanctioned philosophy is not to eliminate religion. Cohen therefore worries that Spinoza has metaphysically assimilated religion to politics and then christened reason with divine justification.

Because his metaphysics both precluded the fear of God from being a cognitive or rational stance at all and rejected the defects of sin and responsibility as the consequences of rote obedience to revealed law, Spinoza disregarded the possibility of Judaism being called a "rational religion."[163] Indeed, by discounting the possibility of religion maintaining reasons different from those dubbed theologically and politically true, Spinoza's definition of true religion is in fact aristocratic and blind to "the social spirit contained in the Mosaic political constitution" as well as to the "anti-aristocratic and anti-clerical socialism rooted in the politics of the prophets."[164] In one camp's celebration of radical enlightenment,[165] Cohen viewed with suspicion this version of Judaism (and Christianity) as well the Heinean liberalism neutralized by Spinoza's version of a pantheistic "true religion."[166] Nonetheless, what Cohen worried over most was the consequent portrait that this painted of Judaism in the German philosophical imagination.

The very fact that Spinoza, perhaps the most recognizable modern Jew, secularized and politicized religion concerned Cohen. And in Cohen's eyes, Spinoza's pantheistic "true religion" posed an additional threat to German Jewry. If Jews are to participate in such a philosophical and political myth of pantheism as the basis of a liberal state rather than to convert to Christianity, then this option would seem to require the Jews' *metaphysical assimilation* as well. However, in contrast to Spinoza, Cohen's thought demonstrates that Protestantism is a tradition with multiple dimensions, and its epistemological roots lie primarily in the space created between state and individual: the space of reasoning, or sociality.

CONCLUSION: THE DUAL PATHS OF PROTESTANT LIBERALISM

Cohen's liberalism is primarily epistemological and indebted to the minor history of Protestantism that I have sketched above. Whatever liberalism has been understood to mean for German Jews, Cohen's portrait of a liberal, self-reflexive German-Jewish identity is explicit about its Protestant sources. In other words, Protestantism, for Cohen, made possible a world in which freedom of thought would be guaranteed—a world, that is, in which the transcendence of ideas to political institutions would be guaranteed. This space of reasoning independent of state sanction therefore opened up a space between the state and the individual as well: namely, the social. This is a public sphere in which different thoughts can be expressed but are also—and perhaps more importantly—available to all.

However, the relationship between the independence of scientific reason and state policy beset Wilhelmine liberals with a dilemma.[167] They could either acknowledge outright the role that Protestantism played in shaping this new epistemological terrain or they could credit Protestantism with freeing reason, which had always already lay in wait for such an opportunity, only to sever reason from religion and guard it under lock and key in what Weber famously described as an "iron cage."[168] Perhaps liberalism was, therefore, destined to be an amnesiac condition.

As I have argued, Cohen saw in Heine and Spinoza two sides of the Protestant coin, and each one's minor inflection laid bare a different possibility. On one face of it, Spinoza represented the fruits of an emancipated reason free to pursue a new objectivity and true religion in the form of metaphysics. But this metaphysics, Cohen began to observe, would be indelibly stamped with a theological form of absoluteness and exclusivity against which Protestantism had originally rebelled. Furthermore, it placed subjective freedom of the individual over and against the state without a means of access to the very reason and philosophy that was deemed true religion. Neutralizing difference and history, Spinoza's metaphysical system and the pantheism that was later attributed to him threatened not only the normative force of critique but also Judaism's inclusion within idealism as the sentinel of transcendence. The consequences of this story—the humanization of theology in the form of metaphysics and the secularization of the public sphere—is a familiar one, and it would appear to confirm Weber's concern: namely, that this version of Protestantism would culminate in either a liberal secularism or the neutralization of religion altogether.

Yet Cohen showed us another story as well. In Heine's minor Protestantism, the sphere of ideality freed up a space of enchantment between state and church. Reasoning remained aware of its past and in search of an emancipatory future. Thus, Cohen pursued a reading of Heine in which Judaism finds expression in modern idealism not to support the neutrality of philosophical method but, rather, to articulate a basic norm of modern culture and make public use of it in reasoning. This norm was transcendent and ideal; not only a monotheistic God as a transcendent source of morality but also the transcendent relationship of ideas, especially moral ideas, to human history and political institutions. This transcendent space of reasoning represented a new freedom for Jews, and Cohen saw this opening as a legacy of the Protestant Reformation. Idealist philosophy, Cohen believed, thus articulated a shared cultural inheritance between Judaism and Protestantism. This version of the story of Protestantism therefore culminated in a separation between faith and knowledge, an epistemological opening that made possible the transcendence of ideas and the development of a space of reasoning.

Cohen's emphasis on the latter story—on the protest and demand for justification—ensures that reasoning, as idealism, remains enchanted. This is due to Cohen's insistence on the transcendence of ideas, whose clarity and justification are demanded by a sociality emphasizing critique as a virtue.[169] Protestantism ensured this path of enchantment by making "conscience the foremost matter for advancing the development of the nation-principle (*Volksprinzip*) into the ideal concept of the national state."[170] The ideal concepts of the state, society, and the nation therefore enabled a path of enchanted reasoning for Jews as well as Christians.

With this emphasis on education, the freedom of thought, and even conscience, the social space of reasoning can best be understood through its deployment as a critique of science—the canon of public knowledge that most emphatically demands justification—which I will explore in greater detail in the following chapter. But we can see from the account above that science in the nineteenth century ought to be understood as the capacity to reason independent of both state and church. In this Protestant determination of reasoning as something transpiring in between these institutions, Cohen's own descriptions of science are best reflected in what we have seen above as a defense of philosophical idealism. Idealism plays the crucial role of a labor of articulating the very norms, histories, and interpretive traditions that it critiques. To the extent that reasoning is idealist, it is self-reflexive and provides an account and justification of where our norms come from and how we *ought* to use them. Implicit in Cohen's account of Protestantism, therefore, is an understanding of modern religion as inseparably linked to the social spaces in which reasoning seeks to articulate social needs and goods.[171]

Nevertheless, the familiarity of the first story, in which Protestantism culminates in liberal secularism, stems from the prominence it has attained in contemporary genealogies of religion in modernity. Protestant religion, we are told, both privatizes religion and emphasizes an interiorized faith.[172] In this story, Protestantism's distinction between state and society yielded a private sphere in which "individuation and privatization of subnational filiations and beliefs entailed in belonging to the new universal state . . . required what might be called the Protestantization of the Jew."[173] The normative role that such a definition of religion has come to play in contemporary scholarship has led to the conflation of Protestantism and liberal secularism. Some scholars even describe this "secularized conception of religiosity" and "privatized and individualized concept of religion" as interchangeable with Protestantism.[174]

Yet Protestantism in Cohen's time was embedded within the public institutions of the German Empire, which informed conceptions of national identity and public law and helped determine Bismarck's foreign and domestic policies. This form of Protestantism was not just a set of abstract propositions to which the individual assented or not; it was the face of culture and power. It is therefore important to reconsider the role of Protestantism in Wilhelmine Germany in terms more akin to what José Casanova has referred to as a modern public religion.[175] In Casanova's identification of religion as a developing social form that seeks to configure secular political institutions, modern religion finds itself entering the public sphere as a source of political and normative claims on public goods. Hence, Protestantism still configures the "differentiation of the secular and religious spheres."[176] This illustrates how secularization is a historical process that helps explain the political ramifications of religious arguments in modern culture.[177] This description of the political function of religion more accurately accounts for the role of Protestantism in imperial Germany, where the Evangelical Church had become a limb of the state and where Bismarck's Prussianization campaign solidified the cultural symbol of a Christian Germany.[178]

In contrast to the story that links Protestantism and liberalism on account of a shared emphasis on the private sphere, Cohen's narrative develops the epistemological opening of Protestantism into an account of how knowledge and its production can be democratized. It is also self-consciously repurposing Protestantism as a majority narrative of Germanism and showing its implicit minor variations, such as the Protestant Judaism that Cohen imagines. The emancipation of science from theological dogma is therefore also related to the emancipation of the Jews, for both represent social access to forms of reasoning and laboring in the public sphere that were previously impossible.[179] In Protestantism, Cohen therefore sees a cultural ideal—or what Charles Taylor might call a "modern social imaginary" that cannot be severed from its connection to the social formations to which it gave rise.[180] Protestantism is therefore more than the specific history of Christianity; as an idealizing culture, Protestantism is representative of the freedom of religions, whereby Judaism can legitimately find a voice with which to express itself in public. Protestantism is something more than Christianity, that is, because Protestantism is also the language of public reasoning.

In a sense, Cohen helps us distinguish between secularity and secularism as two paths dialectically positioned and made possible by Protestant liberalism. We might characterize secularism as an extension of the pantheist metaphysics outlined above. Therefore, secularism ought to be considered as part of a developing state policy of neutrality toward religion. As we will see in the next chapter, one major problem with this representation of neutrality is that it obscures Protestantism's role in shaping this very face of liberalism. On the other hand, secularity—such as Cohen implies in his reading of Heine and idealist monotheism—should be seen as a philosophical epistemology that designates a shift away from Christian theology to the freedom of thought and science without seeking to eclipse religion as such. Secularity does so because its epistemology depends on the historical reflexivity of the tradition of reasoning itself. Thus, secularity must be traced back to Protestantism because the history of protest put forward by the Reformation made possible the introduction of new ways of thinking and reasoning—new ways of reasoning about religion independent of state sanction. This is the liberal path that Cohen pursued in imagining German-Jewish identity.

Protestantism therefore emerges as a root of a liberal secularity but need not, in the form of a Cohenian minor Protestantism, culminate in secularism. Secularity need not be anticlerical nor in favor of the neutralization of religion. But as we saw in his developing critique of Spinoza's pantheism, Cohen would come to worry about the problem facing Jews in a liberal state. The association of secular reason with pantheism therefore raises a social as well as a philosophical question about this Protestant epistemology. For Jews to become modern Germans, they would be required to assimilate both culturally and metaphysically. In order to better understand the dual-pronged Jewish experience of liberalism named by Cohen, the next chapter will trace this other dimension associated with Spinoza's pantheism in the growing liberalism of the nineteenth century: namely, the turn toward the immanence of secular, neutral reason. This metaphysics of secularism, I suggest, stems from the dialectic between science and religion—the two paths of Protestantism—which fully blossomed during Cohen's lifetime.

NOTES

1. On Cohen's arguments against Zionsim, see Hartwig Wiedebach, *The National Element in Hermann Cohen's Philosophy and Religion*, trans. William Templer (Boston: Brill, 2012). For one particularly negative citing of Cohen, see Yoram Hazony, *The Jewish State* (New York: Basic Books, 2000), 91–93; cf.

Jakob Klatzkin, *Hermann Cohen* (Berlin: Jüdischer Verlag, 1919), 89–94; see also Isaac Husik, "Klatzkin's Hermann Cohen," in *Jewish Quarterly Review* 12, no. 1 (1921): 119–21.

2. Paul Mendes-Flohr, *German Jews: A Dual Identity* (New Haven, CT: Yale University Press, 1999), 78.

3. Rosenzweig to his parents, September 20, 1917, in *Briefe und Tagebücher*, vol. 1 (The Hague, Netherlands: Martinus Nijhoff, 1979), 443–44, cited in Mendes-Flohr, *German Jews*, 78.

4. Peter E. Gordon, "Neo-Kantianism and the Politics of Enlightenment," *Philosophical Forum* 39, no. 2 (2008): 223–38, 236.

5. Micha Brumlik, "1915: In *Deutschtum und Judentum* Hermann Cohen Applies Neo-Kantianism to the German Jewish Question," in *Yale Companion to Jewish Writing and Thought in German Culture, 1096–96*, ed. Sander Gilman and Jack Zipes (New Haven, CT: Yale University Press, 1997), 336–42.

6. Throughout, I will refer to "Protestantism" and "Judaism" as idealized figures, to echo the philosophical elaboration in Cohen's work. While I certainly do not claim there could ever be a singular "Protestantism" or "Judaism"—nor a singular "liberalism"—to speak of, my goal is not to eliminate the plural histories of Protestantism and Judaism with these designations but rather to show how Cohen went about idealizing "Protestantism" so that he might provide a minor inflection of how some Jews in Germany could negotiate Protestantism's historical and philosophical significance for themselves.

7. Franz Rosenzweig, "Einleitung," in *Hermann Cohens Jüdischen Schriften*, vols. 1–3, ed. Bruno Strauss (Berlin: C. A. Schwetschke & Sohn/ Verlagsbuchhandlung, 1924) (hereafter cited as *JS*), xxviii.

8. Viewed as an attempt to retrofit Judaism as a confession of liberal Christianity, some, such as David Myers, suggested that this "Protestant" influence on Cohen is that of the more diffuse trends of cultural Protestantism. See David N. Myers, "Hermann Cohen and the Quest for Protestant Judaism," *The Leo Baeck Institute Yearbook* 46 (2001): 195–214. Others, such as Hans Liebschütz, attempted to explain Cohen's liberalism as derived from a direct imitation of "liberal" Protestant theological methods. Hans Liebschütz, "Hermann Cohen and His Historical Background," *Leo Baeck Institute Year Book* 13 (1968): 11. Jacob Taubes, for example, wrote off Cohen as providing little more than the political advocacy of a liberal Wilhelmine civil servant. See Jacob Taubes, *The Political Theology of Paul*, trans. Dana Hollander (Stanford, CA: Stanford University Press, 2004), 62. On Taubes's critique of Cohen, see Elias Sacks, "'*Finden Sie mich sehr amerikanisch?*': Jacob Taubes, Hermann Cohen, and the Return to German-Jewish Liberalism," *Leo Baeck Institute Year Book* 57 (2012): 187–221.

9. On the "Protestantism" of modern Judaism, see Leora Batnitzky, *How Judaism Became a Religion: An Introduction to Modern Jewish Thought* (Princeton, NJ: Princeton University Press, 2011). On the relationship between

Germany and the Reformation, see Hartwig Wiedebach, *The National Element in Hermann Cohen's*, 87–166; Robert R. Geis, "Hermann Cohen und die deutsche Reformation," in *Gottes Minorität: Beiträge z. jüdische Theologie u.z. Geschichte der Juden in Deutschland* (Munich: Kösel Verlag, 1971), 136–51. Whereas Robert Erlewine has recently presented one of the most nuanced readings of Cohen's "Germanism and Judaism" by pointing to how the Protestant Reformation becomes a basis for Cohen to narrate a German identity that is spiritual, ideal, and thus divergent from racializing accounts of German national identity, we are still left with the distinct impression that Cohen's vision of Protestantism is either a restoration to predetermined rational Jewish roots or a version of historicized Christianity. Robert Erlewine, *Judaism and the West: From Hermann Cohen to Joseph Soloveitchik* (Bloomington: Indiana University Press, 2016), 21–25.

10. Jacques Derrida, "Interpretations at War: Kant, the Jew, the German," in *Acts of Religion*, ed. Gil Anidjar (New York: Routledge, 2002), 135–88.

11. Thus, instead of a political ideology, Woodruff Smith refers to the "liberal theoretical pattern" of nineteenth-century German intellectuals. See Woodruff D. Smith, *Politics and the Sciences of Culture in Germany, 1840–1920* (New York: Oxford University Press, 1991). See also chapter 2.

12. Leo Strauss, "Preface to the English Translation," in *Spinoza's Critique of Religion* (Chicago: University of Chicago Press, 1997), 17. Cf. Mendes-Flohr, *German Jews*, 59.

13. Steven E. Ascheim, *At the Edges of Liberalism: Junctions of European, German, and Jewish History* (New York: Palgrave Macmillan, 2012), 7–8. Amos Elon, *The Pity of It All: A Portrait of the German-Jewish Epoch, 1743–1933* (New York: Picador, 2003), 255; Henry Morgenthau, "The Tragedy of German Jewish Liberalism," *Leo Baeck Memorial Lecture 4* (New York: Leo Baeck Institute, 1961).

14. H. I. Bloch, *The German Jew: A Synthesis of Judaism and Western Civilization, 1730–1930* (Oxford: Littman Library, Oxford University Press, 1984), 178.

15. Jehuda Reinharz, *Fatherland or Promised Land? The Dilemma of the German Jew, 1893–1914* (Ann Arbor: University of Michigan Press, 1975), 5.

16. Something noted by David N. Myers, *Resisting History: Historicism and Its Discontents in German-Jewish Thought* (Princeton, NJ: Princeton University Press, 2003).

17. For example, in 1870 Cohen's father, Gerson, the cantor of the synagogue in Coswig, decided despite scruples stemming from his halakhic observance to join the community in the local church to pray for the fatherland during the Franco-Prussian war. For this and other biographical details of Cohen's early life see Michael Zank, *The Idea of Atonement in the Philosophy of Hermann Cohen* (Providence: Brown Judaic Studies, 2000), 54, 48–76. For further biographical information on Cohen's life, see Franz Orlik, *Hermann*

Cohen (1842–1918): Kantinterpret, Begründer der "Marburger Schule", Jüdischer Religionsphilosoph (Marburg: Universitätsbibliothek Marburg, 1992). Cf. Myers, *Resisting History*, 41.

18. On the polemic against Catholicism as a boundary marker for modern Jews, see Ari Joskowicz, *The Modernity of Others: Jewish Anti-Catholicism in Germany and France* (Stanford, CA: Stanford University Press, 2014), 126.

19. A partial and short-lived emancipation that triggered resentment of the French incursion into German national consciousness and soil, catalyzing the Hep riots of 1819 and the subsequent curtailment of certain emancipatory gains. Cf. Peter Pulzer, *The Rise of Anti-Semitism in Germany and Austria* (Cambridge, MA: Harvard University Press, 1988), 32.

20. See Orlik, *Hermann Cohen*, 24–33; Zank, *The Idea of Atonement*, 65–66.

21. See Cohen's 1861 letter to Eduard Steinthal, Coswig, in *Briefe*, ed. Martha and Bruno Strauss (Berlin: Shocken, 1939), 14.

22. Till van Rahden, "Germans of the Jewish *Stamm*: Visions of Community between Nationalism and Particularism, 1850 to 1933," in *German History from the Margins*, ed. Neil Gregor, Nils Roemer, Mark Roseman (Bloomington: Indiana University Press, 2006).

23. Hermann Cohen, "Heinrich Heine und das Judentum" (hereafter cited as "Heine") originally published anonymously in *Die Gegenwart* 1 (1867), reprinted in *JS*, 2:2–44, and *Hermann Cohens Werke*, ed. H. Holzhey, 17 vols. (New York: G. Olms, 1978–) (hereafter cited as *Werke*) 12: *Hermann Cohens Werke, Kleinere Schriften*, vols. 12–17 of *Werke*, 6 vols. (hereafter cited as *KS*), 1:193–258. On the influence of Steinthal on Cohen's *Religion of Reason*, including a focus on the *Sprachform* of the Hebrew language, see Dieter Adelman, "H. Steinthal und Hermann Cohen," in *Hermann Cohen's Philosophy of Religion: International Conference in Jerusalem, 1996*, ed. Stephane Moses and Hartwig Wiedebach (New York: Georg Olms, 1997), 1–34. On the methodological focus of the *Völkerpsychologie* school, bringing together *Sprachwissenschaft* and anthropology, see Ivan Kalmar, "The Völkerpsychologie of Lazarus and Steinthal and the Modern Concept of Culture," *Journal of the History of Ideas* 48, no. 4 (1987): 671–90. For the relationship between the desire for Jewish emancipation in Steinthal and Heymann's programmatic studies of culture see Egbert Klautke, *The Mind of the Nation: Völkerpsychologie in Germany, 1851–1955* (New York: Berghahn, 2013), chap. 1 in particular.

24. Joskowicz, *The Modernity of Others*, 125–29.

25. Alon Confino, *The Nation as a Local Metaphor: Württemberg, Imperial Germany, and National Memory, 1871–1918* (Chapel Hill: University of North Carolina Press, 1997).

26. On the ambivalent (be)longing of Prussian Jews for the Vaterland and the often fraught question of German identity in the years of emancipation, as well as for an overview of the conflicts over German identity, citizenship, and Judaism for Jewish converts to Lutheranism, see Deborah Hertz, *How Jews*

Became Germans: The History of Assimilation and Conversion in Berlin (New Haven, CT: Yale University Press, 2007), 122, 198–201.

27. Cohen, "Heine," 238–47.

28. Cohen, 198.

29. George L. Mosse, *German Jews beyond Judaism* (Cincinnati: Hebrew Union College Press, 1985), 4.

30. Compare Cohen's account of the deductive critique of a concept within the framework of a people's history in Cohen, "Mythologische Vorstellungen von Gott und Seele psychologisch entwickelt" in *Werke* 12: *KS 1, 1868–1869*, 277.

31. Heinrich Heine, "Zur Geschichte der Religion und Philosophie in Deutschland," in *Heines Werke in fünfzehn Teilen*, ed. Helene Herrmann and Raimund Pissin, 15 vols. (Berlin: Deutsches Verlagshaus Bong & Co., 1927), 9:213. English translation as "Concerning the History of Religion and Philosophy in Germany," in *The Romantic School and Other Essays*, The German Library 33, trans. Helen Mustard (New York: Continuum, 2002), 181.

32. Heine, "Zur Geschichte," 213.

33. Cohen, "Heine," 237.

34. Cohen, 220.

35. Cohen, 215.

36. Cohen, 223.

37. For an excellent overview of the *Pantheismusstreit*, see Alexander Altmann, *Moses Mendelssohn: A Biographical Study* (1973; repr., Portland: Littman Library of Jewish Civilization, 1998), 638–711; Frederick C. Beiser, *The Fate of Reason: German Philosophy from Kant to Fichte* (Cambridge, MA: Harvard University Press, 1987); Frederick C. Beiser, *German Idealism: The Struggle Against Subjectivism, 1781–1801* (Cambridge, MA: Harvard University Press, 2002); Michah Gottlieb, *Faith and Freedom: Moses Mendelssohn's Theological-Political Thought* (New York: Oxford University Press, 2011); George Di Giovanni, introduction to Friedrich Heinrich Jacobi, *Main Philosophical Writings and the Novel Allwill* (Montreal: McGill-Queen's University Press, 2009). See also Allen Wood's concise summary of the Pantheism Controversy in his introduction to "What Is Called Orientation in Thinking?" in *Religion and Rational Theology, Cambridge Edition of the Works of Immanuel Kant*, ed. Allen Wood, George Di Giovanni (New York: Cambridge University Press, 2001).

38. G. W. F. Hegel, *Vorlesungen über die Geschichte der Philosophie, Dritter Theil*, ed. Carl Ludwig Michelet, 2nd ed. (Berlin: Duncker & Humblot, 1844), 362. Cf. Emile Edmond Saisset, *Essai de philosophie religieuse* (Paris: Charpentier, 1859), xii.

39. Jacobi writes "The moment man sought to establish scientifically the veracity of our representations of a material world that exists beyond them, and independently of them, at that very moment the object that the demonstrators wanted to ground disappeared before their eyes. They were left with mere subjectivity, with *sensation*. And thus they discovered *idealism*."

Friedrich Heinrich Jacobi, *David Hume on Faith, or Idealism and Realism, A Dialogue: Preface and also Introduction to the Author's Collected Philosophical Works* (1815), in *Main Philosophical Writings*, 105.

40. Jacobi, *David Hume on Faith*, 105.

41. See Paul W. Franks, *All or Nothing: Systematicity, Transcendental Arguments, and Skepticism in German Idealism* (Cambridge, MA: Harvard University Press, 2005), 86. Cf. Rolf-Peter Hortsmann, *Die Grenzen der Vernunft: Eine Untersuchung zu Zielen und Motiven des Deutschen Idealismus* (Frankfurt am Main: Anton Hain, 1991).

42. Friedrich Heinrich Jacobi, *The Doctrine of Spinoza in Letters to Herr M. Mendelssohn*, in *Main Philosophical Writings*, 1:105n1; Franks, *All or Nothing*, 85–91.

43. Compare Gottlob Benjamin Jäsche, *Der Pantheismus: nach seinen verschiedenen hauptformen, seinem Ursprung und Fortgange, seinem speculativen und praktischen Werth und Gehalt, Eine Beitrag zur Geschichte und Kritik dieser Lehre in alter und neuer Philosophie*, 3 vols. (Berlin: Reimer, 1826), in which he attempts to trace a "purified" form of pantheism to Spinoza; and Heinrich Ritter, *Die Halb-Kantianer und der Pantheismus: Eine Streitschrift, veranlaßt durch Meinnungen der Zeit und bei Gelegenheit von Jäsche's Schrift über den Pantheismus* (Berlin: Trautwein, 1827), 19–24, who sees Jäsche's attempt to differentiate between "dogmatic" and "critical" pantheism in readings of Spinoza as equally problematic conclusions.

44. Georg F. W. Hegel, *Elements of the Philosophy of Right*, ed. Allan Wood (New York: Cambridge University Press, 1991) para. 360; see also Thomas A. Lewis, *Religion, Modernity, and Politics in Hegel* (New York: Oxford University Press, 2011).

45. See *Evangelische Kirche-Zeitung* (hereafter cited as *EKZ*) 5/6 (1827): 38; *EKZ* 6:50; *EKZ* 14/15, no. 65 (1834): 515–16. See also Robert M. Bigler, *The Politics of German Protestantism: The Rise of the Protestant Church Elite in Prussia, 1815–48* (Berkeley: University of California Press, 1972), 102, 104–5; Annette G. Aubert, *The German Roots of Nineteenth-Century American Theology* (New York: Oxford University Press, 2013), 188.

46. See the outline of the debate as reported in *Allgemeine Literatur-Zeitung*, no. 82 (May 1839): 41–48.

47. Beiser notes that "attacks on Spinoza became a virtual ritual, [and] there was an abundance of defamatory and polemical tracts against him. Indeed, by 1710 so many professors and clerics had attacked Spinoza that there was a *Catalogus scriptorium Anti-Spinozanorum* in Leipzig. And in 1759, Johann Anton Trinius counted, probably too modestly, 129 enemies of Spinoza in his *Freydenkerlexicon* (Leipzig: Cörner, 1759). Such was Spinoza's reputation that he was often identified with Satan himself. Spinozism was seen as not only one form of atheism but the worst form." See Beiser, *The Fate of Reason*, 48.

48. Charles Taylor uses this term of art to refer to the modern social imaginary or moral order of concepts, symbols, and institutions that are perceived as self-authorized and, indeed, the result of an inward turn toward grounding modern morality in reason alone. This order is perceived as a natural order, and the term aptly applies to Spinoza. See Charles Taylor, *A Secular Age* (Cambridge, MA: Harvard University Press, 2008), 542–43.

49. As Warren Breckman has observed, the opposition between personalism and pantheism as claims to have reconciled ideal and actual set the tone of debate among the young Hegelians. Consider Ludwig von Gerlach's rejection of Savigny's attempt to root the legitimacy of law in the *Volkgeist*: "This teaching, which, in pantheistic fashion constructs a system essentially form the historical evolution of nations without regard for their eternal origins or for universally human, divinely created and therefore permanent institutions (personality, patriarchy), cannot provide adequate defense against the revolutionary essence of our century." While indicting Savigny's historicism as "pantheism" Gerlach's appeal to the "eternal origins" of "divinely created institutions" such as personality of the monarch and the justifications of the estates system shows the degree to which Cohen saw this human-divine continuum continually approximated by conservative thought. Gerlach quoted in John E. Toews, "The Immanent Genesis and Transcendent Goal of Law: Savigny, Stahl, and the Ideology of the Christian German State," *American Journal of Comparative Law* 37, no. 1 (1989): 139–69, 162. For a discussion of the conservative ideology of personalism as political theology, see Warren Breckman, *Marx, the Young Hegelians, and the Origins of Radical Social Theory* (New York: Cambridge University Press, 2001), 9–15, 63–71.

50. Further events such as David Friedrich Strauss's critique of divine personality in *Leben Jesu* simply emptied a canister of gasoline on an already healthy flame. See Breckman, *Marx, the Young Hegelians*, 134–35.

51. Heinrich Leo, *Die Hegelingen: Actenstucke und Belege Zu Der S. G. Denunciation Der Ewigen Wahrheit* (Halle: Eduard Anton, 1839); Helmut Reinalter, *Die Junghegelianer: Aufklärung, Literatur, Religionskritik und politisches Denken* (Frankfurt am Maim: Peter Lang, 2010), 91–93. See also the contemporary portrayal of the debate in "Systematische Theologie: Der Leo-Ruge'sche Streit" in G. F. H. Rheinwald, *Allgemeine Repertorium für die theologische Literatur und kirchliche Statistik* (Berlin: Verlag von Friedrich August Herbig, 1840), 28-43.

52. Karl Rosenkranz, *Psychologie: oder, Die Wissenschaft vom subjektiven Geist* (Königsberg: Verlag der Gebrüder Vornträger, 1863), 328. Hermann Hinrichs, *Die Religion im inneren Verhältnisse zur Wissenschaft* (Heidelberg: Karl Groos, 1822), 204. See Hegel's foreword to Hinrichs, where he explains that revelation cannot be the source of truth in religion if it is not at the same time the product of thinking, willing, and knowledge, which would seem to internalize Spinoza's argument in the *Tractatus Theologico-Politicus* (cited

hereafter as *TTP*); see Haym's attempt to read into Hegel's Berlin lectures a dialectic and critical account of Hegel's use of the pantheistic connotations of Karl Friedrich Goeschel's *Aphorismen über Absolutes Wissen und Nichtwissen im Verhältnisse zum christlichen Glaubenserkenntniß* (Berlin: Franklin, 1829) in Rudolf Haym, *Hegel und sein Zeit* (Berlin: Rudolph Gaertner, 1857), 431.

53. Consider the example of Ludwig Feuerbach, *Gedanken über Tod und Unsterblichkeit aus dem Papieren eines Denkers, nebst einen Anhang theologisch-satyrischen Xenien* (Nürnberg: J. A. Stein, 1830), 3, 16, 25, 35. See also John E. Toews, *Hegelianism: The Path Toward Dialectical Humanism, 1805–1841* (New York: Cambridge University Press, 1980), 195–97.

54. David Friedrich Strauss, *Das Leben Jesu, für das deutsche Volk bearbeitet*, 3rd ed. (Leipzig: Brockaus, 1874) 22, 150–51.

55. Ludwig Feuerbach, *Ueber Philosophie und Christenthum, in Beziehung auf den der Hegel'schen Philosophie gemachten Vorwurf der Unchristlichkeit* (Mannheim: Hoff & Heuser'schen Buchdruckerei, 1839) originally published in the *Halleschen Jahrbüchern für deutsche Kunst und Wissenschaft*, nos. 61–62 (March 1839); see also Marx W. Watofsky, *Feuerbach* (New York: Cambridge University Press, 1977), 160. On the controversy more generally, see Walter Jaeschke, *Reason in Religion: The Foundations of Hegel's Philosophy of Religion*, trans. J. Michael Stewart and Peter C. Hodgson (Berkeley: University of California Press, 1990), 377. See also the comments of the journalist K. E. Jarcke quoted in Bigler, *The Politics of German Protestantism*, 193.

56. Schleiermacher writes, "The high world spirit permeated him [Spinoza], the infinite was his beginning and end, the universe his only and eternal love, in holy innocence and deep humility he was reflected in the eternal world and saw how he too was its most lovable mirror." Friedrich Schleiermacher, *On Religion: Speeches to Its Cultured Despisers*, ed. Richard Crouter (New York: Cambridge University Press, 2003), 24.

57. Ludwig Feuerbach, *Grundsätze der Philosophie der Zukunft* (Zürich: Verlag des litteratischen Comptoirs, 1843), 23.

58. Cohen, "Heine," 173.

59. Cohen, 199.

60. Thus, Cohen derided Chamberlain's downplaying the role of Spinoza's pantheism in Goethe's Hellenism as an attempt to excise the Jewish dimension of German history. See Cohen, "Streiflichter über jüdische Religion und Wissenschaft: 13. Der Jüde in der christlichen Kultur, IV" in *Neue jüdische Monatshefte* 17 (1916–17): 509–14, reprinted in *Werke* 17: *KS 6, 1916–1918*, 419–24, 434. Translations herein slightly modified from the English version, "The Jew in Christian Culture," trans. Alan Mittleman, *Modern Judaism* 23, no. 1 (2003): 51–73, 67.

61. Cohen, "Heine," 227.

62. Cohen, 219.

63. Heine, "Zur Geschichte," 9:226.

64. Cohen, "Heine," 201.

65. This is not to downplay Cohen's youthful interest in scientific material-ism under the influence of Lazarus and Steinthal. Rather, it is all the more sig-nificant that Cohen emphasizes this idealist dimension in Heine's pantheism while still developing his own critical distance from materialism. Cf. Zank, *The Idea of Atonement*, 70–71.

66. Heinrich Heine, *Die Romantische Schule*, in *Heines Werke*, 9:50. English translation in Heinrich Heine, *The Romantic School*, 42.

67. Cohen, "Heine," 211.

68. Heine, *The Romantic School*, 42.

69. Cohen, "Heine," 228.

70. Cohen, *Begriff der Religion im System der Philosophie* (herafter cited as *BdR*), *Werke* 10:14.

71. Immanuel Kant, "An Answer to the Question, What Is Enlighten-ment?" in *Practical Philosophy, Cambridge Edition of the Works of Immanuel Kant*, vol. 8, ed. Allen Wood and George Di Giovanni (New York: Cambridge University Press, 1996), 36–37.

72. See Hermann Lübbe, *Säkulerisierung: Geschichte eines ideenpolitischen Begriffs*, 2nd ed. (Munich: Karl Alber, 1975). See Todd H. Weir, *Secularism and Religion in Nineteenth-Century Germany: The Rise of the Fourth Confession* (New York: Cambridge University Press, 2014), 13–14.

73. Jürgen Habermas, *The Structural Transformations of the Public Sphere: An Inquiry into a Category of Bourgeois Society* (Cambridge, MA: MIT Press, 1989), 237.

74. Hartwig Widebach and Helmut Holzhey note that Cohen had elabor-ated such a theory of continuity between Eleatic pantheistic-monotheism and Spinoza's monotheism already in his doctoral dissertation, See editorial note in Cohen, "Heine," 55–58.

75. Cohen, 216–17.

76. Cohen, 234–35.

77. Cohen, 234–35.

78. Cohen, 214.

79. As Willi Goetschel has remarked, "one can recognize in [Heine's] use of pantheism more than merely a compositional device, for it operates as a kind of code name for a complex that cannot be otherwise explicitly expressed." This code, according to Goetschel, is for Heine's "strategic Hegelianism." See Willi Goetschel, *Spinoza's Modernity: Mendelssohn, Lessing, and Heine* (Madi-son: University of Wisconsin Press, 2004), 256.

80. Cohen, "Heine," 228.

81. Goetschel, *Spinoza's Modernity*, 262.

82. Cf. Ned Curthoys, *The Legacy of Liberal Judaism: Ernst Cassirer and Hannah Arendt's Hidden Conversation* (New York: Berghahn, 2013), 1–3, 9–10.

83. Hertz, *How Jews Became Germans*, 198.

84. Eduard Gans, "A Society for the Furthering of Jewish Integration" in *The Jew in the Modern World: A Documentary History*, ed. Paul Mendes-Flohr and Jehuda Reinharz (New York: Oxford University Press, 2011), 240–43.

85. Jeffrey L. Sammons, *Heinrich Heine: A Modern Biography* (Princeton, NJ: Princeton University Press, 1979), 109.

86. Transcript from a meeting of the Cultur-Verein, Dec. 22, 1821, printed in Siegfried Ucko, "Geistesgeschichtliche Grundlagen der Persönlichkeit Gottes bei Philipp Marheineke," in *Neue Zeitschift für systematische Theologie und Religionsgeschichte*, 10 (1970): 313–47, 19. Cited in John Edward Toews's discussion of Gans and Leo in Toews, *Hegelianism*, 126–27.

87. Heine, "Zur Geschichte," 9:215; Heine "History of Religion and Philosophy," 178.

88. See Heine to Heinrich Laube, November 23, 1835, in *Heinrich Heine. Säkularausgabe, Werke*, ed. Fritz H. Eisner, vol. 21, no. 1 (Berlin: de Gruyter, 1970). Cited in Breckman, *Marx, the Young Hegelians*, 183.

89. This is the case in Hegel's lectures on the philosophy of religion from 1827. See Thomas A. Lewis, "Religion, Reconciliation, and Modern Society: The Shifting Conclusions of Hegel's Lectures on the Philosophy of Religion," *Harvard Theological Review* 106, no. 1 (2013): 37–60.

90. On Hegel's account of the Protestant principle as the reconciliation of subjective freedom and the public laws of the state, compare *Philosophy of Right*, para. 270 and *Encyclopedia*, para. 552. Cited in Walter Jaeschke, "Christianity and Secularity in Hegel's Concept of the State," *Journal of Religion* 61, no. 2 (1981): 127–45, 136–37.

91. The failure of the 1848 revolution resulted in much disillusionment with Hegel's emphasis on the state. Cf. Breckman, *Marx, the Young Hegelians*. Hegel, however, was not simply calling for the institutionalization of the extant Evangelical Protestant Church as a state church. Hegel himself was skeptical of such an arrangement and his critical remarks on religion in politics in his *Philosophy of Right* reflect a growing anxiety over the restrictive Karlsbad decrees and the increasing prominence of dogmatic religion in political life. On Hegel's reconsideration of the public role of Protestantism, see Lewis, *Religion, Modernity, and Politics*, 240–43. See Walter Jaeschke, "Christianity and Secularity in Hegel's Concept of the State," *Journal of Religion* 61, no. 2 (1981): 127–45, 136–37. Lewis, "Religion, Reconciliation, and Modern Society," 47, 59–60. Compare *Philosophy of Right*, para. 270 and *Encyclopedia*, para. 552.

92. Heine, *Zur Geschichte der Religion und Philosophie*, 275; Eng., 242. Heine continues: "The heads that philosophy used for speculation can be cut off afterward by the revolution for any purpose it likes. But philosophy could never have used the heads cut off by a preceding revolution."

93. Heine, *The Romantic School*, 24; *Heines Werke*, 9:50.

94. Heine, "History of Religion and Philosophy," 154–55.

95. Heine, 157.

96. Indeed, Georg Lukács would later describe the historical novel as providing a point of access for the commoner to participate in a larger historical narrative about their own conscious participation in society. See Georg Lukács, *The Historical Novel* (Boston: Beacon, 1963). Benedict Anderson similarly highlights the rise of vernacular languages and literatures as a means of participating in an imagined community, see Benedict Anderson, *Imagined Communities: Reflections on the Origin and Spread of Nationalism* (New York: Verso, 2006), 79–80.

97. Heine, *Zur Geschichte*, 9:191.

98. Cohen, "Heine," 247.

99. Heine, "History of Religion and Philosophy," 158.

100. Cohen, "Heine," 248–49.

101. This skepticism is most apparent in reactions to an essay published toward the end of Cohen's life, in 1916, in what is perhaps the most infamous piece of Cohen's legacy, which has often condemned his memory to infamy. See Husik, "Klatzkin's Hermann Cohen," as just one early example. Indeed, much of Scholem's lament over Cohen's memory stems from what he dubs this "shameful" tract. See, from 1918-1919, Gershom Scholem, "Farewell: An Open Letter to Dr. Sigfried Bernfeld and against the Readers of this Journal," reprinted in *On Jews and Judaism in Crisis: Selected Essays*, ed. Werner J. Dannhauser (New York: Schocken, 1976), 59; Gershom Scholem, "On the Myth of German-Jewish Dialogue," in *On Jews and Judaism in Crisis*, 63.

102. Compare Geoff Eley's discussion of how Germans negotiated nation and citizenship and Fritz Stern's account of the failure of civic virtue to take root in German conceptions of citizenship in Eley, "Making a Place in the Nation: Meanings of 'Citizenship' in Wilhelmine Germany," in *Wilhelminism and Its Legacies: German Modernities, Imperialism, and the Meanings of Reform, 1890–1930; Essays for Hartmut Pogge von Strandmann*, ed. Geoff Eley and James Retallack (New York: Berghahn Books, 2003), 16–33; and Stern, introduction to *The Failure of Illiberalism: Essays on the Political Culture of Modern Germany* (New York: Columbia University Press, 1975).

103. Hermann Cohen, "Deutschtum und Judentum," parts 1 (originally published 1915) and 2 (originally published 1916) in *JS* 2:237–318; reprinted in *Werke*, part 1 in *Werke* 16: *KS* 5:465–560; part 2 in *Werke* 17, *KS* 6:109–32 (hereafter cited as *DuJ* 1 or 2). *DUJ* 1:474; published in English as "Germanism and Judaism," in *Reason and Hope: Selections from the Jewish Writings of Hermann Cohen*, trans. Eva Jospe (Cincinnati: Hebrew Union College, 1992), 176–77. Compare Cohen's discussion of hypotheses in Plato in *System der Philosophie, Erster Teil: Logik der reinen Erkenntnis* (Berlin: Bruno Cassirer, 1902; repr. in *Werke* 6), 87–88 (hereafter cited as *LrE*).

104. Zank, *The Idea of Atonement*, 251.

105. Cohen, *DuJ* 1:478.

106. On the Platonism of Marburg neo-Kantianism, more generally, see Karl-Heinz Lembeck, *Platon im Marburg. Platon-Rezeption und*

Philosophiegeschichtsphilosophie bei Cohen und Natorp (Würzburh: Königshausen & Neumann, 1994).

107. Beiser, *The Genesis of Neo-Kantianism*, 3.

108. This was not without some resistance. See Peter Pulzer, *Jews and the German State: The Political History of a Minority, 1848–1933* (Detroit: Wayne State University Press, 2003).

109. *LrE*, 83–84.

110. *LrE*, 84–87. Judgments (*Urteilen*) both hold apart (*teilen*) pieces of a concept at the same time that the act of judging brings them their original unity (*Ur-teil*). Reinier Munk has characterized Cohen's understanding as a form of preservation of separate pieces (*die Erhaltung der Teilen*) of an original separation (Ur-*Teil*). See *LrE*, 60; Reinier Munk, "Alterity in Hermann Cohen's Critical Idealism," *Journal of Jewish Thought and Philosophy* (*JJTP*) 9 (2000): 251–65. The judgment of "origin" (*Ursprung*), which is the immanent principle of thinking, describes thinking as a generative *movement* from a whole down to its parts, determining the grounds on which to move back up again to a unifying act of judgment. See Helmut Holzhey, *Cohen und Natorp*, 2 vols. (Basel: Schwabe, 1986), 1:190; Andrea Poma, *The Critical Philosophy of Hermann Cohen*, trans. John Denton (Albany: State University of New York, 1997), 88–89.

111. As an *action* of tracing the conditions for something down to what it is not in order to determine that it is not "no thing," Cohen explains how the "infinite judgment," or the negation of a relative privation (what is, is not nothing; which the prefix *in-* seeks to approximate in describing the in-finite) is the infinite, or generative origin of a "some thing." The "not-nothing" becomes a relatively meaningful something for thinking.

112. *LrE*, 84.

113. *LrE*, 154–88. Cohen's interpretation of Kant pays closer attention to the system of principles, and the anticipations of perception in particular, than it does the transcendental aesthetic. Indeed, the aesthetic is more or less removed from Cohen triadic stages of the a priori. On the role of infinitesimals and anticipation in Cohen's thought, see Marco Giovanelli, *Reality and Negation—Kant's Anticipations of Perception: An Investigation of its Impact on the Post-Kantian Debate* (New York: Springer, 2011), 162–78.

114. Cf. Steven Schwarzschild, "Germanism and Judaism—Hermann Cohen's Normative Paradigm of the German-Jewish Symbiosis" in *Jews and Germans from 1860 to 1930*, ed. David Bronson (Heidelberg: Winter, 1979), 129–72.

115. Schwarzschild, "Germanism and Judaism," 152–56; Wiedebach, *The National Element*, 120.

116. Schwarzschild, 120.

117. Cohen, *DuJ*, 1:476.

118. Hermann Cohen, foreword to *System der Philosophie, Zweiter Teil: Ethik des reinen Willens* (Berlin: Bruno Cassirer, 1904; repr. in *Werke 7*) (hereafter cited as *ErW*), 2nd ed., x (page numbers refer to the reprint edition).

119. Hermann Cohen, "Biographisches Vorwort" to Friedrich Albert Lange, *Geschichte des Materialismus und Kritik seiner Bedeutung in der Gegenwart* (Leipzig: J. Baedeker, 1887), viii.

120. *LrE*, 605.

121. *LrE*, 395–98

122. A phrase Cohen would later defend against Heinrich von Treitschke's indictment that beneath Jewish pretense to Enlightenment was a cultural chauvinism resisting assimilation. See chapter 3.

123. Cohen, *DuJ*, 1:476–77.

124. This Hegelian dimension of Cohen's thought was first observed by Franz Rosenzweig in his introduction to Cohen's *Jewish Writings*; see Rosenzweig, "Einleitung in Die Akademieausgabe der Jüdischen Schriften Hermann Cohens," reprinted in *Kleinere Schriften* (Berlin: Schocken, 1937), 304.

125. Cohen, *DuJ*, 1:476.

126. Cohen, "The Jew in Christian Culture," 69 (Eng.).

127. Cohen, 67–68 (Eng.).

128. As we will see in the coming chapters, selfhood for Cohen is a complex conceptual articulation of a subject out of an objective structure of knowledge. See Steven S. Schwarzschild, "The Tenability of Hermann Cohen's Construction of the Self," *Journal for the History of Philosophy* 13, no. 3 (1975): 361–84.

129. Compare *DuJ*, 1:476.

130. Cohen, "The Jew in Christian Culture," 439 (Ger.)/69 (Eng.); translation slightly modified.

131. *ErW*, 214.

132. Cohen, "The Jew in Christian Culture," 445 (Ger.)/72 (Eng.).

133. Cohen, 446 (Ger.)/72 (Eng.).

134. Cohen, "Der deutsche Idealismus und die Antike," in *Werke* 17: KS 6, 1916–1918, 150.

135. On the significance of religion for refracting the scope of human cultural phenomena throughout history, see Cohen's remarks at the beginning of *BdR*, 4–6.

136. Cohen, *DuJ*, 2:186 (Eng.).

137. Cohen, *DuJ*, 1:523. See Hartwig Wiedebach's extensive discussion of the relationship between nation and nationality in Cohen's account of religion in *The National Element in Hermann Cohen's Philosophy and Religion*, trans. William Templer (Boston: Brill, 2012).

138. See chaps. 3 and 4.

139. *ErW*, 587–88.

140. *ErW*, 290.

141. *ErW*, 331.

142. *ErW*, 16; see Cohen's extended comments to the same effect in his 1877 work, *Kants Begrundung der Ethik* (Berlin: Dummler, 1877), 162.

143. Spinoza, *Ethics*, part 2: prop 49, corollary, cited in Cohen, "Spinoza über Staat und Religion—Christentum und Judentum," first published in *Jahrbuch für jüdische Geschichte und Literatur*, no. 18 (1915): 56–150, and reprinted in *JS* 3:290–372 and *Werke* 16: *KS* 5:319–426; see also *ErW*, 459, 117.

144. Cohen had few reservations about heaping scorn onto Spinoza, and the term *pantheism* became a lightning rod for Cohen's polemics against radical materialism and spiritualism in later works; for these shifts, see Ernst Simon, "Zu Hermann Cohens Spinoza-Auffassung," *Monatsschrift für Geschichte und Wissenschaft des Judentums* 79/43, no. 2 (1935): 181–94; Myriam Bienenstock, "Hermann Cohen sur le panthéisme. Sens et usages du terme dans sa reception de Spinoza," *Revue de métaphysique et de morale* 69, no.1 (2011): 29–45, 32, 37–38; as well as Hans Liebschütz, "Cohen und Spinoza," *Bulletin für die Mitglieder der "Gesellschaft der Freunde Des Leo Baeck Instituts"* 12 (1960): 225–38, in which Dilthey's characterization of pantheism becomes a prominent concern. Cf. Beate Ulrike La Sala, *Hermann Cohen Spinoza-Rezeption* (Berlin: Alber, 2012), 138–47.

145. *ErW*, 458. In Cohen's 1915 essay, he refers to Spinoza's attempt to conflate sovereign authority and "true religion" to discourage the state from overlegislating or interfering with religious difference. Cohen is suspicious of this apparent neutrality on the part of the state since it promotes the freedom to philosophize at the expense of religion as a source of popular education. See Spinoza, *Tractatus Theologico-Politicus*, chap. 20 in particular. I return to Cohen's reading below.

146. Cohen, "Spinoza über Staat und Religion," *Werke* 16: *KS* 5:410–11/*JS* 3:361.

147. Leo Strauss, "Cohen's Analysis of Spinoza's Bible Science," in *Leo Strauss: The Early Writings, 1921–1932*, trans. Michael Zank (Albany: State University of New York Press, 2002), 139–72, 142.

148. David Biale, *Not in the Heavens: The Tradition of Jewish Secular Thought* (Princeton, NJ: Princeton University Press, 2011), 26.

149. Cohen, "Spinoza über Staat und Religion," *Werke* 16: *KS* 5:350/*JS* 3:313.

150. Cohen, "Spinoza über Staat und Religion," *Werke* 16: *KS* 5:351/*JS* 3:314, 358; Cohen cites Spinoza's offhanded remark concerning Moses and Jesus both communing with God "face to face" and this reference to Maimonides therein. See Spinoza, *TTP*, 363.

151. Cohen, "Spinoza über Staat und Religion," *Werke* 16: *KS* 5:351/*JS* 3:314.

152. Cohen, *Werke* 16: *KS* 5:375/*JS* 3:333.

153. Cohen, *Werke* 16: *KS* 5:377/*JS* 3:334.

154. Cohen, *Werke* 16: *KS* 5:389/*JS* 3:344.

155. Spinoza, *TTP*, 64, 66–67.

156. See Strauss, *Spinoza's Critique of Religion*, 208–9; Spinoza, *TTP*, 66.

157. Spinoza, *TTP*, 67–68.

158. Spinoza, 227–28.

159. Cohen, "Spinoza," *Werke* 16: *KS* 5:337, 341/*JS* 3:302–6.

160. Cohen, *Werke* 16: *KS* 5:344–45/*JS* 3:309.

161. Cf. Strauss, *Spinoza's Critique of Religion*, 208. While I am more interested in Cohen's interpretation than in Spinoza's thought itself, a nuanced reading of Spinoza's philosophy can be found in Nancy K. Levene, *Spinoza's Revelation: Religion, Democracy, and Reason* (New York: Cambridge University Press, 2004).

162. Spinoza, *TTP*, 229.

163. Strauss, *Spinoza's Critique of Religion*, 207–9.

164. Cohen, "Spinoza," *Werke* 16: *KS* 5:388–89/*JS* 3:344.

165. Jonathan Israel, *Radical Enlightenment: Philosophy and the Making of Modernity, 1650–1750* (New York: Oxford University Press, 2001).

166. Cohen even attempts to rescue Christology from Spinoza by highlighting the difference between God's holiness and the holiness of God, to which Cohen returns in his *Charakteristic Ethik Maimunis*. See Cohen, "Spinoza," *Werke* 16: *KS* 5:358–60.

167. See Lübbe, *Säkularisierung*, as well as Weir, *Secularism and Religion*, 13.

168. Max Weber, *The Protestant Ethic and the Spirit of Capitalism*, trans. Talcott Parsons (New York: Routledge, 1992), 123.

169. See *ErW*, 535.

170. Cohen, "Einleitung mit kritischem Nachtrag zu Langes Geschichte des Materialismus," in *Schriften zur Philosophie und Zeitgeschichte*, ed. Albert Görland and Ernst Cassirer, vol. 2. (Berlin: Akademie Verlag, 1928), 296.

171. *ErW*, 506–8, 587; Hermann Cohen, "Der Jude in Christlichen Kultur," translated in Alan Mittleman, "'The Jew in Christian Culture' by Hermann Cohen: An Introduction and Translation," *Modern Judaism* 23, no. 1 (2003): 51–73, 67. See also chapter 3.

172. See Talal Asad, *Genealogies of Religion: Discipline and Reasons of Power in Christianity and Islam* (Baltimore: Johns Hopkins University Press, 1993).

173. Wendy Brown, *Regulating Aversion: Tolerance in the Age of Identity and Empire* (Princeton, NJ: Princeton University Press, 2006), 52.

174. Saba Mahmood, *Politics of Piety: The Islamic Revival and the Feminist Subject* (Princeton, NJ: Princeton University Press, 2005), xiii–xiv.

175. José Casanova, *Public Religions in the Modern World* (Chicago: University of Chicago Press, 1994).

176. Casanova himself sometimes associates bourgeois individualism and the privacy of religion with an undifferentiated Protestantism (see Casanova, *Public Religions*, 96). Yet he nevertheless describes public religion to involve the reintroduction of norms and values into the social fabric via political mobilization.

177. Casanova, *Public Religions*, 19, 21–22.

178. Referring to Adolf Stoecker, see Uriel Tal, "Religious and Anti-Religious Roots of Anti-Semitism," in *Religion, Politics, and Ideology in the Third Reich: Selected Essays* (New York: Routledge, 2004), 178.

179. Cf. Ernst Troeltsch, "Die Bedeutung der Protestantismus für die Ent-stehung der modernen Welt," in *Historische Zeitschrift* 97 (1906), 1–66; trans-lated as *Protestantism and Progress: The Significance of Protestantism for the Rise of the Modern World* (Fortress Press, 1986).

180. Charles Taylor, *Modern Social Imaginaries* (Durham, NC: Duke University Press, 2004).

TWO

—w—

THE DIALECTIC OF ENCHANTMENT

Science, Religion, and Secular Reasoning

THE EPISTEMOLOGICAL OPENING IDENTIFIED BY Cohen's minor Protestantism reveals a space of reasoning between institution and individual—a space for science and religion to both gain independence. Such a space of reasoning distinct from the state-sanctioned forms of thought that collapse religion into politics shows the necessity for justified knowledge and modes of reasoning in a project of democratization. But this need for justification, which I suggested should characterize Cohen's worldview as liberal, is hardly limited to politics alone. Indeed, as I have suggested, liberalism need not be conceived only in terms of party politics and ideology. Liberalism, rather, is an epistemological condition. But as I have endeavored to outline in the previous chapter, this epistemological condition had more than one consequential path: one into secularity represented by Heine and one into secularism represented by Spinoza. But, in large part, both those paths were trodden at the level of knowledge production, in the sciences and philosophy.

Protestantism's distinction between faith and knowledge made possible the kind of reasoning with which Cohen would mine religion as a conceptual resource for German national culture—including Judaism as one such expression. Yet there was also another repercussion of this epistemological opening: the rise of the sciences, both natural and humanistic, as a challenge to Christian moral and social conceptions of truth. This confrontation between science and traditional Christianity in the late nineteenth century contributed to what many scholars characterize as a time of legitimation crisis in liberal bourgeois Germany, more generally.[1] Challenging the dogmas that had validated conceptions of world, man, and society, the advance of scientific knowledge transformed the later nineteenth century in which Cohen was writing.

The confrontation between science and religion is crucial to my story because scientific knowledge and liberal social politics were deeply entangled in Wilhelmine Germany, as the account of secularization explored in the previous chapter began to reveal. This secularization of knowledge gave rise to newfound assertions of human subjectivity, sociality, and rationality as the grounds and arbiters of truth and falsity. This chapter therefore sets out to examine the dialectic of enchantment—the dissolution of theological legitimacy and reenchantment of science with metaphysical materialism—that underlays the ideological transformations of the later nineteenth and early twentieth centuries, especially regarding the role of religion in the public sphere.

If the previous chapter demonstrated that the space of reasoning opened up by Protestantism ought to be considered enchanted because of its emphasis on transcendence and ideality, this chapter turns to the underside of the dialectic of enchantment: the epistemological formation of a purported value neutrality in the sciences and philosophy and an insistence on what Charles Taylor describes as a shift away from the transcendent toward an "immanent frame."[2] I aim to show how the freedom of thought that both brought about a democratization of knowledge in the nineteenth century and made it possible for Jews to claim access to the public stuff of sociality and reasoning independent of religious identity also catalyzed an antiliberal pursuit of new forms of objectivity in blood, soil, and race with the help of scientifically rendered forms of objectivity tied to materialism or monism. This chapter begins a critique of one path of liberalism toward an immanent, secularist, neutral reason, which has left this version of liberalism incapable of reconciling itself with its own past. What I mean by this is that the fragility of a liberalism claiming epistemic neutrality, whereby all voices are declared welcome in its conversation—even those same voices that seek to negate the liberal worldview altogether—, stems from a loss of perspective on the particulars of its historical origin. By attempting to pass itself off as a new universal form of rationality, capable of replacing its previous allegiance to Christian theological dogma, this face of liberalism conceals its identity as a minor tradition of epistemological protest in Christian history. By hiding this Protestant past behind its claim to hegemonic neutrality, this form of liberalism therefore silences the very minority voices it first enabled to speak freely in the name of protecting a majoritarian claim. In negotiating this paradox at the heart of the dominant narrative of liberalism, therefore, my aim in the previous chapter was to show how minority voices such as Cohen's make the relationship between liberalism and Protestantism explicit. In this chapter, I move toward a critique of what happens when liberalism fails to acknowledge its roots and thus presumes a majoritarian view of its forms of reasoning.

To illustrate this limitation to nineteenth-century liberalism, I first examine the relationship between scientific discourse—including the natural and social sciences as well as philosophy—and the neutralizing epistemic moment within liberalism. In doing so, I aim to show how the space of reasoning opened up to Jewish participation also stamps the Jewish Question as the limit to that neutralizing liberalism. Showing how Cohen recognized both the lure of neutrality as well as the threat of its culmination in humanism and materialism, I explore Cohen's idealism as a counterpoint to this immanent turn in liberalism. Insisting on the persistence of transcendence and ideality—of ideas as the source of our belief in the possibility of change in the world—I argue that Cohen's idealism is a critical rejoinder to the modes of scientific and philosophical thought that in his time bestowed increasing legitimacy on nativist nationalism and anti-Semitism. Jewish participation in the democratization of reasoning enabled by Protestant liberalism thus also reveals this concealed core of liberal ideological commitments to materialism, empiricism, and rationalism as contingent moments in the dialectic of enchantment.

In contrast, I gesture toward the blueprint for an alternative—if yet to be actualized—liberalism based in Cohen's democratizing and socializing account of scientific knowledge and idealist reasoning. This reasoning finds enchantment in ideas rather than materiality. Before turning in the next chapter to the explicit social and political arguments on behalf of Jewish minority representation that extend from Cohen's philosophy, I want first to examine the problems implicit in the shifting scientific and philosophical discourse of his time, the purported source of legitimacy of the ideological transformations taking shape. This chapter therefore argues that the crisis of legitimacy attributed to liberal secularism can be better navigated when we minoritize secular forms of thought.

MATERIALISM AND
THE METAPHYSICS OF SECULARISM

The second half of the nineteenth century was an era of crisis in German intellectual history. While theological orthodoxy had been in retreat since the Enlightenment, philosophy now presumed the authority to take over as the sentinel of truth. Thus, science and religion encountered one another in an ever-intensifying cold war. And because of the efforts of the German idealists, and the legacy they inherited from Kant, philosophy at midcentury sought to fashion itself as the sole pillar of reason, a science (*Wissenschaft*) in its own right. The various Hegelianisms that came to prominence at midcentury saw in the secularization of philosophy and the emphatically human and worldly mapping of the divine-human nexus a sign that metaphysics was the clarion call of liberalizing idealism.

Along with the rise of idealism, therefore, came the increasingly diffuse influence of liberalism—a worldview premised on the freedom of thought and the individual prowess of subjectivity. Framed as a vindication of the individual perched above the political institutions of the age, the spiritual self-understanding of this theoretical pattern of liberalism (as the vehicle of *Bildungsbürgertum* or civic and cultural formation) permeated the German sciences and must thus be distinguished from the liberal political ideology of pre-1848 Germany. As Woodruff Smith writes, "The liberal theoretical pattern was not the same thing as liberal ideology." Smith describes this theoretical pattern as more loosely characterized by "its assumptions about the rational individual as the unit of social explanation, its central aim of discovering social laws, and its approach to social change and equilibrium."[3] In other words, liberalism must not be limited to the ideological forms more familiar in twentieth-century political thought. Rather, liberalism pervaded the scientific discourse of the time, a discourse that consisted of newfound appeals to human rationality, physiology, material immediacy, and natural harmony as the root of legitimate and objective knowledge. Implicit in this form of liberalism, therefore, is a self-understanding presumed to be neutral or objective knowledge—neutral because it presupposes only reason and the individual, and objective because both were presumed to be universal.[4] In other words, this intellectual liberalism saw itself as authorized by a method that was scientifically neutral, despite that method being rooted in the very principles it sought to prove valid.

How might we account for this liberal theoretical pattern of neutrality and its internal paradox? In order to ascertain the shift toward neutrality, we must understand this reaction in contrast to its conditions. While we could characterize the metaphysical idealism of the mid nineteenth century as an explicit attempt to ground the harmony of nature and human sociality in the rational individual, by the 1850s the scientific self-representation of philosophy as capable of both scientific and political freedom was beginning to buckle under such weighty metaphysical pretensions. Self-consciousness may have provided a principle for rational thought to legitimate itself and its designs on political freedom in the purity of abstraction; however, in light of the failures of Germany's 1848 revolution, German Idealism now appeared as an embattled bourgeois form of wishful thinking. The speculative power of subjectivity had dreamed boldly but found its waking life stymied by the forces of traditionalism and authoritarian monarchy. In such a disenchanted climate, any intimation of metaphysics or the promised deduction of political rationality as well as scientific objectivity from the principle of subjective freedom increasingly incited suspicion. However, it is important to note that this dual claim to political freedom and scientific objectivity was a systematic one for the German idealists, and this ethos was perhaps the sole remnant of their labors: to wield both the sword of freedom and truth at once.

The philosophical foundations of late nineteenth-century political and scientific thought must therefore be oriented around an understanding of how the era's purported rejection of metaphysics—or the appeal to any form of spiritual phenomena—is dialectically related to the simultaneous representation of self and society as neutral and depoliticized. That is to say, we must understand how the shift toward the study of the more immediate or concrete realities of self, society, and economic life drew their epistemological forms from a worldview that remained deeply metaphysical. Indeed, as I suggest below, the appeal to nature and materialism must be seen as the negative moment in a dialectic of enchantment.

The shift away from an explicit and toward an implicit metaphysics can be mapped within the history of philosophy in the later nineteenth century. While there already existed an antimetaphysical trajectory of

Kantianism in the work of Jakob Friedrich Fries (1773–1843) and Johann Friedrich Herbart (1776–1841), alongside the Romantic and Speculative idealists[5] of the early nineteenth century,[6] the predominant focus of philosophy in the 1850s and 1860s was the return to Kant in order to overcome the systems devised by the German idealists. *Wissenschaft*, which had been emphatically linked by Hegel to the "life of the idea" and by Wilhelm von Humboldt to the project of cultural development and *Bildung*, needed rejuvenation. First principles grounded in the abstraction of self-represented thinking would no longer suffice. If later nineteenth-century German philosophy wanted to maintain its claim on the title of science, philosophy would have to model the specialized sciences by focusing on foundational facts.[7]

Empiricism now replaced speculation, at least in name. Philosophers, jurists, and scientists were moving away from systematic thinking grounded in ideal principles as a model for knowledge and turning instead to the empirical natural sciences, beginning with and deducing knowledge from empirical facts alone.[8] Thus, epistemology or the theory of knowledge (*Erkenntnistheorie*), as it was called, was elevated to the rank of a pure science and sought certainty in the facts of nature.[9] In a wave of intellectual self-assertion, perhaps not unfamiliar to contemporary readers, this turn to facts and the real world was championed as a step on the way to overcoming the purported superstition and irrationality of religious forms of thought that had once dominated German minds. By contrast to systematic idealism, materialism and scientific naturalism therefore appeared to purify philosophy of metaphysical as well as ideological, theological, and political residues. While Hegel maintained that his idealism was indeed a scientific worldview of *Wissenschaft* intended to reconcile these various forms of thought, the fact that he built his system up from a principle rather than a fact left scientific purists to question whether "in addition, these systems follow a nonscientific, political or critical intent?"[10] Systematic assertions of freedom as a principle of philosophical knowledge were viewed as at worst nothing but whimsy or speculative apologetics for the monarchy and at best projections of subjective freedom.[11] Tellingly, Cohen's teacher in Berlin, the esteemed philosopher Friedrich Adolf Trendelenburg (1802–72), would declare that philosophy must recognize "the fact of the sciences is the basis of logical problems."[12] Despite his own metaphysical commitments, Trendelenburg saw philosophy's task as clarifying the methods of the sciences rather than presupposing itself capable of intuiting science's first principles.[13] The time had come for a purer science: an idealism free from such metaphysical values.

In contrast to free-floating or subjectively grounded values, the facts of science became central. And out of this historical context, neo-Kantianism emerged as the dominant voice in German academic philosophy. However committed to Kant it was, neo-Kantianism oscillated between idealism and positivism.[14] That is to say, while priority was given to the Kantian conception of the a priori validity of cognition and knowledge, just as important was the ability to lay claim to knowledge of actual facts, cultural products, and the human progress being made in the sciences and economics. No longer honored with scientific primacy, philosophy was pushed into a corner; in order to reestablish its role as the agent of critique, clarifying the limits and goals of all knowledge, philosophy would have to reorient its commitment to the study of values on the basis of empirically justifiable facts.[15] Philosophy became an emphatically methodological expression of critique.

The focus on method that became synonymous with neo-Kantianism arose from the movement's description of philosophy as an agent of clarification, justification, and metadescription of the conditions for science.[16] Natural science therefore stepped into the forefront as the epistemological ground of all disciplines, and so philosophy's privilege would be guaranteed by tending to the needs of this master. But natural science of the time was not a ready-made discipline. Rather, it was in the throes of a contentious transformation.

Published in 1859, Charles Darwin's *The Origin of Species* revolutionized how natural scientists and philosophers understood the natural world by, in Darwin's own words, challenging the opinion of "the great majority of naturalists who believed that species were immutable productions and had been separately created."[17] Darwin deemed change—the adaptation of organisms to their geographical and historical specificities—foundational to material nature. His account of nature therefore placed movement, struggle, and transformation squarely within the frame of materiality itself, which led philosophers and scientists to renegotiate erstwhile theories of transcendent cause for change in the world. The newfound scope of natural order no longer sought change in a time immemorial or in the ethereal; rather, both a law of continuity and a transformative progression toward harmonization of organic and inorganic nature were mapped within the immanence of the physical world itself. Science and philosophy were thus treating empirical facts as counterevidence for spiritual or transcendent laws explaining nature. However, as a conversation rooted in the opposition to metaphysics and theology, it was nevertheless implicitly linked—by virtue of recognizing them as obstacles—to these forms of thought as well. Natural science therefore retained the principle of a lawfully regulated natural world, albeit while transforming the lawfulness of transcendence into that of immanent materiality.

Materialism was therefore more than just matter; it was matter infused with a spiritual form of lawful order. There was still a guiding hand, just more proximate. Crystallizing this intellectual moment of conflation between spirit and matter, within which Cohen undertook his early study of Kantian idealism, was one of the more significant crises of the late nineteenth century to emerge from this growing constellation of biology and Darwinism: the *Materialismusstreit* (Materialism Controversy). The Materialism Controversy entranced the German academic community.[18] The controversy centered around a public address of 1854 in which the German physiologist Rudolf Wagner (1805–64) declared that, while natural science had progressed immensely in the nineteenth century, scientists should refrain from promoting materialistic theories that would call into question biblical doctrine or traditional Christian conceptions such as the immortality of the soul. Wagner saw materialism—the appeal to a physiological, empirical reduction of thought and human agency to natural and biological impulses—as a reductionist threat to the autonomy of religious thought. Science and religion represented two distinct paths. And to support his view, he appealed to the Protestant distinction between faith and knowledge. Faith and science, Wagner claimed, require separate criteria for certainty, a double bookkeeping for the scientist's leap of faith in religion amid empirical evidence pointing to the contrary.[19] As Wagner put it, "To the question of what tax is due science and what is due faith, the Savior's command holds valid: give to Caesar what is Caesar's and to God what is God's."[20] For Wagner, the crisis looming for scientific advance was more than an epistemological one. If the lawfulness of nature supplanted the lawful regulation of human affairs, his concern was that religious life as such would be undermined. Hence, the materialism of the nineteenth century was in need of critical control to stave off a free fall into secularization.

Upon hearing Wagner's address, the chemist Karl Vogt (1817–95) fired a blistering retort that declared Wagner's distinction an appeal for censorship that set limits on empirical evidence and research and was thus void of intellectual integrity.[21] Through Vogt's reduction of psychological processes to the materiality of the brain, for example, he claimed no immaterial soul could be maintained.[22] This was clear evidence that science was on an unalterable course. An avowed political radical and erstwhile associate of Pierre-Joseph Proudhon and Mikhail Bakunin, Vogt maintained that the latest physiological evidence clearly demonstrated both that the religious doctrines Wagner held so dear were nothing but myths and that science was the root of a new worldview. For Vogt, materialism was the enemy of myth and its conservative guarantors.[23] With the imprimatur of Marx and Engels, radical political movements were thus endorsing materialism as the basis on which to advocate for purportedly objective and lawful human activity. The shift toward democratization was linked to the turn to the human, worldly material of life itself.

The ramifications of this controversy were broad. The worldview rooted in materiality and the immanent explanatory order tied to it was all-encompassing. In light of such scientific transformation, even proponents of a renewed religious and spiritual mission were openly advocating a turn to materiality as the basis for any claim to objective truth. The position was compelling scientifically and gained popular support as well. This was due in large part to the efforts of the zoologist Ernst Häckel (1834–1919), one of the most dominant voices in the last decade of the nineteenth century, who crystallized the challenge that material science posed to religion. Häckel had stirred yet further controversy over materialism with his lecture "Über die Entwicklungslehre Darwins"[24] and rose to great fame in Germany for his monistic doctrine of materialism. Häckel sought to reconcile theology and science within a monistic and materialistic doctrine. His *Die Welträtsel*, first published in 1899, would become one of the best-selling books of the Wilhelmine period.[25] The strength of his doctrine rested on the popularization of science as a metaphysics of materialism. That is, Häckel sought to ground a spiritual life in material laws both by overcoming the apparent dualism between spirit and matter and by attempting to revive the "profound thought of Spinoza [to which] our purified monism returns after a lapse of two hundred years."[26] As a theory of scientific materialism as well as a theology, what was once an expressly metaphysical system became for Häckel a new ground of methodology and epistemology in the social sciences. And whereas Spinoza's name had been absorbed into and eclipsed by the legacy of pantheism, Häckel explicitly revived it. His monistic theology likewise united materialism and pantheism. And since the natural sciences had risen to the apex of the university, Häckel's declaration that "pantheism is the world-system of the modern scientist" was perceived as a direct challenge to the philosophical establishment.[27] Hence, his popularity did not impress academic philosophers and theologians— particularly the neo-Kantians—whose ire he sparked on account of his bold attacks on Kant's dualistic philosophy. But Häckel had nevertheless succeeded in promoting a popular vision of the harmony between science and spirituality.[28]

For example, as Todd H. Weir has recently shown, the relationship between popular science and philosophy, along with the development of the Free Thought and liberal Free Religion movements in Germany, was due in large part to the coherent worldview presented by monism and pantheism.[29] By the time of the *Kulturkampf*, the political struggle between Bismarck and the Catholic Church, the relationship between materialism, Free Religion, and monism was growing ever more identifiable as a strand of a popular secularist movement.[30] As an organization, the German Monists League, founded by Häckel, believed to have found a synthesis between religion and science.[31] The monists claimed religion and science were compatible when grounded in a materialist epistemology.[32] Uniting nature and science, however, meant that biological and causal calculations of the best means to the greatest ends based on empirical experience and a posteriori observation had replaced moral absolutes as the basis for adjudicating human actions.[33] Popular science converged with popular religion, and, with the growth of such popular associations, this new worldview of metaphysics and science adopted the same hue in challenging traditional definitions of religion. While the impulse of liberals and social democrats was to cast religion as a private affair and the state as separate from the church, the popularization of scientific monism was anything but private. And as a social formation of public life, monism followed the example of traditional religion by making its worldview public.[34]

In the midst of this turn toward materialism, monism, and Darwinism, philosophy therefore underwent its own identity crisis in which ethics, philosophy, and theology were all primed to suffer a devastating blow at the hands of the natural sciences. The methods of natural science were mounting an increasingly explicit challenge to the various historically received truths about the natural, social, and confessional world. A proliferation of various intellectual crises[35] followed in the latter half of the century, and Spinoza's name was once again attached to these developments. Indeed, Cohen would go on to note explicitly that Spinoza's ideas had even become a major source of modern anti-Semitism, for which his pantheism was centrally at fault.[36] These various transformations all shared in common a specific demand for an objective and legitimate grounding of knowledge, value, and truth. Whether moral and spiritual, scientific and historical, or social and political, the demand for truth and reason was paramount. Thus, these symptoms of a legitimation crisis within bourgeois society reflect not only an academic dispute but also the transformation of the German public sphere and the implicit role of—and opposition to—religion in these debates.[37] What was to ground this new liberal model of a rationally organized state and society if not something deep within nature—the nature of reason itself? Philosophy, as the vehicle for the public campaign of enlightenment throughout the nineteenth century, now had to reckon with the ghosts of a past it believed it had put to rest for good.

If natural science had become a new religion fit for the modern world and materialism had become a dominant paradigm, many philosophers believed that a return to Kant provided the model for how philosophy should function in such fraught terrain. Philosophers such as Otto Liebmann believed that Kantianism had always been a philosophy of science and that philosophy ought to interrogate the conditions that make science possible.[38] These conditions should be clarified and justified, especially in order to free science from the metaphysical trappings of post-Kantian German Idealism. But, while Liebmann disparaged the idealist direction of Kant-interpretation as intimating an explicitly metaphysical program that turned away from empirical contingency toward abstract necessity, thinkers such as Friedrich Albert Lange believed that idealism represented a strategy for refitting philosophy on the basis of natural science. By rebuking the skeptical challenge posed by materialism to the reconciliation of science and faith, Lange's *History of Materialism and Critique of its Meaning in the Present* (1866) detected a threat to philosophy and natural science not in the methodological orientation of idealism but rather in the crude reductionism of materialism that was sweeping popular conceptions of science.[39]

Lange insisted that Kant's philosophy enabled a coherent defense of ideas, moral faith, and the spiritual life of an ethical idealism that might combat either the crude "ethical materialism or 'secularization' as theologians call it"[40] or the "dead unity of the Free Congregations."[41] That is, Lange was concerned that, with the steady descent into complete reduction of ideas and human sociality, spirit, and imagination to the material of the senses, the enchanted life of ideas and spirit was being slowly desiccated. He worried expressly about the problem of looming disenchantment and the cruder forms of reenchantment that lay in wait. He writes,

> There is the additional difficulty, whether the abolition of all religion, however desirable it may appear to many well-meaning and thinking men, is at all possible. . . .
>
> If we suppose such a course of proceeding, it would be very doubtful whether it would not necessarily produce, in spite of scholastic enlightenment, a popular reaction in favor of a thoroughly fanatical and narrow-minded conception of religion, or whether ever fresh, perhaps wild, but at the same time vigorous, shoots would not spring up from the roots that had been left behind. Man seeks the truth of reality and hails the extension of his knowledge so long as he feels himself free. But let him be chained down to what can be attained by the senses and the understanding, and he will revolt, and will give expression to the freedom of his imagination and his spirit, perhaps, in still cruder forms than those which have been successfully destroyed.[42]

Lange sensed the vicissitudes of secularization that lay in wait for materialism.[43] Religion would not be eliminated but rather graft the human longing for value, transcendence, and meaning onto ersatz forms of crude and wild fantasy. Indeed, Lange's suspicions would be confirmed, as we will see, if not in the rise of monism then certainly in the turn of the *völkisch* national movements toward the reenchantment of natural science. Lange therefore insisted that the scientific criticism introduced by Kant—along with his assertion of materialism as a mode of critical reflection on the world as it has been rendered in knowledge—was not an advocacy for the dissolution of religion. Rather, Lange's critique was double-pronged: on the one hand, the state ought to "require from their clergy a certain standard of scientific culture," and, on the other hand, he insisted that "only with the dissolution of the political church is an unconditional freedom of creed possible."[44] Lange thus made clear the importance of the secular—as a mode of scientific freedom of inquiry that encouraged disestablishment of a state church as the arbiter of scientific, religious, and political dogmas. However, Lange also insisted that the standpoint of the ideal would help focus the "idea of human fellowship" in conjunction with a defense of natural science and its empirical focus. Together, Lange believed science and faith would nurture the effects of idealism within the material world of social change that the times demanded, bringing knowledge to all peoples and sharing with them the "necessary condition of human intercourse."[45] "The community of the species in knowledge," he wrote, "is at the same time the law of all interchange of ideas."[46] For Lange, religion thus provided a control on scientific knowledge by helping to emphasize the implicit sociality of knowledge. This was the importance of idealism for Lange's nuanced understanding of scientific materialism, and it was a direct response to and anticipation of the perceived threat of materialism and monism.[47] And his insistence on the standpoint of the ideal as a control on both crude materialism and state-sponsored religion bore the marks of the Protestant tradition traced earlier. At least this was the view of his protégé Hermann Cohen.

Lange's philosophy was of great importance to Cohen, who shared Lange's concern that materialism, much like Spinoza's pantheism, had collapsed nature into a metaphysics of secularism. That is, by trying to unite the natural and human sciences through the singularity of materialism, Lange and Cohen detected in metaphysics a looming ideological crisis for the sciences. The problem of metaphysics would continue to adopt very specific resonances, at once political and philosophical, for Cohen, since by the 1880s economists and legal theorists alike were debating the merits of scientific materialism, historicism, and psychologism in their disciplinary approaches. But according to Cohen, such discussions took place without any self-awareness of the philosophical roots of these *isms*. At the very moment his philosophical career was gaining greater recognition in the German university, Cohen would therefore lament that "the future of the universities is at stake in this question [of philosophy]. Make no mistake about this. The teaching of natural science in today's universities suffers from a lack of respect for philosophy among the subjects' representatives, owing to a deficiency in understanding and in cultural edification [*Bildung*]. It is well-known that philosophical studies are often begrudgingly recognized, impeded and dissuaded."[48] Should science want truly to serve as the backbone of culture then, as a corrective to this state of affairs, Cohen claims, a proper scientific education ought to begin with the history of philosophy. In Cohen's telling, the history of science should commence— as Lange had begun his own history of materialism—with an understanding of how Aristotle's *Physics* transformed Platonic idealism into an anthropological theory of cognition that treats natural history as the metaphysics of physics.[49] Materialism, in other words, was a philosophical formation that was projected on nature, rather than the yield of nature's crop itself. Cohen thus insisted, like Lange did, that philosophy must focus on the ideas that animate a theory of natural science, experience, and human activity. Ideas must occupy the center of philosophy's attention.

Fundamentally, popular science and epistemology suffered from what Cohen claimed was a disappearing cultural consciousness of philosophical history. And yet much more was at stake than ignorance of the provenance of an academic discipline. For Cohen, this shift toward an immanent explanatory order for natural phenomena, as well as human institutions and cultural life, intimated the degree to which scientific materialism had grown into a theology in its own right, leaving traditional religion to seem redundant and antiquated. Lange's fears were coming true. And a new constellation linking materialism to organic matter, historicism to historically individuated persons and events, and monism and pantheism to unified accounts of spiritualized matter and materialized spirit, all presented themselves as modern principles for knowledge. Human sociality and ethical culture suffered a devastating blow, Cohen observed, at the hand of "the zoological-anthropological sense of the natural being," and this was due to the model of "causality [that] had become the *Leitgedanke* [central theme] of the modern world."[50] If Cohen had expressed any ambivalence toward pantheism in his early work, the metaphysical eclipse of pantheism's idealist tendencies had become irreversible for him by the 1880s. Idealism and pantheism, which was largely identified directly with materialism, were now squarely opposed.[51] The lawfulness of materialism was a direct threat to scientific and moral culture as such.

Cohen's fears were hardly abstract. While Vogt, one of the leading figures in the Materialism Controversy, may have styled his materialism as a pathway toward a radical politics, one of his most famous students, Houston Stewart Chamberlain, would go on to not only endorse his teacher's biophysical thesis concerning consciousness but also develop this materialist conception of natural science into the basis of his treatment of the "racial question." Before long, Chamberlain was joined by a chorus of voices drawing the scientific conclusion of such materialism: he claimed biological, anti-Semitic racism merely deduced a fact of nature, and the competitive hope for the continuity of the human species demanded it.[52] Indeed, the confluence of myth and popular science, as we will see in the following chapters, would become a major presupposition of the anti-Semitic political movement. And, even if Chamberlain would not admit it due to his own prejudice,[53] Cohen would argue in a lecture of 1910 that Spinoza's ideas were at the root.[54] Indeed, Chamberlain's views did not seem implausible given Vogt's insistence on finding categories and principles in the things themselves, or the world around us. In other words, while Kant had insisted on distinguishing between the world as it is in itself and the world as it appears to us, the scientific materialists had drawn a dramatic conclusion about the relationship between concepts and objects and between words and things. They had collapsed them together.[55]

In collapsing ideas that map the world into the world itself, the very catalyzing shift of Protestant epistemology was inverted. That is, as Peter Harrison describes, when Protestant biblical interpretation ceased to employ allegory, the literal meaning of the biblical word left the natural world without the order and meaning the biblical word had once served. No longer sign or symbol, natural objects were now reconfigured by mathematical number and taxonomic category and, thus, given new meaning. This, claims Harrison, is how modern science was born.[56] But, with the descent into materialism and the attendant claim to have found certainty and objectivity in the union of organic and inorganic matter—in nature and society, science and morality—the implicit claim made by the materialists and monists was that the essence of things lay in their very physical existence. The implicit metaphysics of materialism had therefore achieved two fundamental shifts: matter was now the irreducibly immanent sphere of human existence as well as being the new arbiter of meaning and value. Material was now both the subject and object of the sciences, both natural and moral.

IDEALIZATION AND THE PROBLEM OF VALUE

Cohen's idealism should be understood as a response to theoretical and moral questions raised by the Materialism Controversy of the 1850s. As Frederick Beiser has noted, this controversy had an influence on the later nineteenth century analogous to that between Friedrich Jacobi and Moses Mendelssohn less than a century before.[57] Given the rise of the materialist and empiricist paradigm of the natural sciences, Cohen's concern with Spinoza and pantheism can in part be seen as an attempt to preserve the Protestant epistemology that made possible the independence of science from institutional strictures and dogmas. Yet, it can also be seen as part of a larger concern to avoid the complete collapse of moral into material lawfulness by carving out a distinct space in which to renegotiate ethics, religion, and the autonomy of the human spirit. In order to rescue the legacy of Protestant epistemology amid philosophy's identity crisis, therefore, Cohen would weigh in on the question of the sciences with an appeal to idealism, much as Lange insisted, as a standpoint guaranteeing the sociality and democratization of knowledge.[58]

Amid the rise of materialism and the prestige accorded the empirical within the natural sciences, therefore, Cohen's understanding of idealism is rather significant. Whereas materialism sought both to secure the objectivity of knowledge in the immanence of the world of organic material and to adduce laws and principles of human sociality therefrom, Cohen's critical idealism, which he began articulating in earnest with the publication of his 1888 book on the history and concept of infinitesimal calculus, turns instead to the fact that the natural sciences exist as a body of knowledge concerned with the meaning of nature and the physical world. Cohen sees the role of philosophical idealism as providing the conceptual resources for analyzing how this knowledge of nature is possible; in other words, philosophical idealism clarifies the value attached to nature in a system of judgments and principles organized by mathematics and physics. Thus, we must understand Cohen's idealism as a concern with the conditions that make knowledge possible. Focusing on ideas that are necessarily extracted from their individuated historical conditions, Cohen's interest in science is thus a far cry from materialism. Rather, Cohen is interested in how material first achieves scientific value through the laws and principles of mathematics and physics, which are ideas about matter. Materialism had imagined the world of things in themselves as enchanted by a lawfulness all its own. Cohen, by contrast, again highlights that enchantment is located in the relation of ideas to other ideas. What matters is the conceptual meaning of matter.

Concepts or functions, instead of a self-constituted substance,[59] set the tone for Cohen's generation of neo-Kantians to conceive of philosophy as a critical justification of knowledge as such. Cohen followed the lead of Hermann Lotze, whose logic was premised on the claim that the truth conditions of concepts do not depend on existents.[60] Particularly in the Marburg school of Cohen and his colleague Paul Natorp (1854–1924), epistemology became a kind of meta-epistemology, a mathematical modeling of the functions of judgment in knowledge. This view of philosophy was influential in both Marburg and the southwestern school, and Heinrich Rickert, whose thought was highly influential on Max Weber,[61] followed Cohen's example and eliminated any reference to Kant's thing-in-itself as an object or empirically given entity to which representation corresponds.[62] As Rickert articulated, any transcendental theoretical value of truth is beckoned forth in the epistemological subject in the form of "stance-taking" (*Stellungsnehmen*). Philosophy must provide the clarity for how such stances are taken with regard to value but not with regard to material. What elicits this stance is the *Sollen* or ought, an emphatically ideal concern with what *should be* but is not yet.[63] The ought is the formal impetus to take a stance with regard to values. It is the object of knowledge and the structural form of validity.[64] Neo-Kantianism, more generally, can therefore be understood as a philosophy concerned with the generation and justification of values.

While Cohen also championed an epistemological philosophy to marshal a turn away from both metaphysical idealism and materialism, he nevertheless worried that the purity of *Erkenntnistheorie* as a quest for values and stances actually neutralized the lawfulness of concept formation. Cohen worried that any description of value formation without a concept of lawfulness implicit in concepts themselves left the process neutral. That is to say, Cohen expressed concern for the ethical and historical phenomena that may fall under the rubric of such a philosophy:

if there are no implicit goods to scientific reasoning, then is progress in knowledge governed by accident alone? If there are no implicit goods in the act of reasoning about social institutions, should the fact of poverty and wealth determine just deserts and their institutionalization? By eliminating the teleology of material causality, Cohen did not wish to reduce the notion of purpose altogether. What, if not an implicit value in reasoning about justification itself, would be the source of normative control on which values should count as meaningful or valid? Is logical coherence sufficient, and what, in turn, makes coherence valuable?

For Cohen, the critical task of Kantian idealism was to delimit cognition and knowledge as a normative enterprise that answers such questions. In other words, philosophy has its own implicit norms, and *justifying* the conditions of certainty should be treated as a normative task. History and ethics, as much as natural science, are therefore normative forms of knowledge in Cohen's thought.[65] But the validity of logic and the methodological articulation of concepts must be secured. As such, justification presupposes but is more than a plea for logical coherence.

To address this normative concern, Cohen describes philosophy not just as a theory of what knowledge is but also as a theory of how knowledge *came to be*. By better understanding how scientific knowledge developed, we gain better insight into what ought to count as knowledge in the future. This historical dimension of Cohen's thought therefore leads him to describe his *Erkenntniskritik*, or critique of knowledge, as the task of idealizing science. That is to say, science must be treated as an ideal body of knowledge that has accrued historically through trial and error—change and argument—and treated as an objectified entity that exists independently of those particular historical moments. This *idealized* construction of reason can then be treated as a fact. Therefore, in contrast to materialist reductions of science to psychologized epistemology, Cohen's account of science is both ideal and historical, and critique serves to idealize and objectify reason therein. Cohen writes,

> while Kant himself still debated with psychological representations and conjectures, by following his sense in the spirit and the letter of the critical system, we *objectify reason* [*Vernunft*] within science. The *critique of reason* is *critique of cognition* [*Erkenntniskritik*] or of science. Critique puts to task that which is pure within reason to the extent that it discovers the *conditions of certainty* upon which cognition as science rests.

Thus the critique of cognition distinguishes Kantian idealism from all other forms of idealism; it explicates and defines the contents of that which is *transcendental*. Idealism, at bottom, dissolves things into phenomena and ideas. *Erkenntniskritik*, by contrast, deconstructs [*zerlegt*] science according to the presuppositions and the grounds that are admitted within the laws of science and to which the former are destined. Idealism directed by the critique of cognition thus does not have for its objects things and processes, not even to its advantage those of consciousness pure and simply, but rather, scientific facts.[66]

The proper function of critical idealism is to serve as a critique of science, of the presuppositions of science and its conditions of possibility. Rather than begin with material objects or things, Cohen's idealism therefore takes science as a fact. Yet science is something ideal to the extent that it both operates according to principles and concepts and, through these, construes objects as meaningful for its conceptual operations. Idealism therefore becomes a philosophical method by which the grounding of science can be secured. And in contrast to materialism and psychologism (which equates nature and thinking) Cohen's account of critique is one that works on a body of knowledge, something objectified and idealized. The laws of science must be carefully critiqued in order to ascertain the meaning of certainty, or what the southwestern school of neo-Kantianism described as validity (*Geltung*). Critical idealism, to put it succinctly, is concerned with justification.

A question emerges from this account of knowledge, however: in limiting knowledge of natural facts to the value of an object for knowledge, do we not also allow for a gap to persist between the conceptual world and a world beyond our grasp? Does such a gap not reify the mysticism of either a thing-in-itself or of a metaphysical world beyond cognition?[67] In response to such questions, Cohen suggested that a theory of critical idealism must shift the idiom of the conversation away from the emphasis on thought or consciousness as a speculative abstraction that is set over and against the world of experience and, instead, place greater emphasis on the fact that scientific knowledge of the world of experience—with its principles, concepts, and schemas—has succeeded in achieving a deeper understanding of the natural world. In other words, Cohen focused on the ideas that *lay a foundation* for thinking and judging about *possible experience* but not for speculating about immaterial or improvable substance. The latter is characteristic of metaphysics and, as Cohen claims, "Idealism stands in a methodical opposition to all that goes by the name of metaphysics."[68] If the category of substance is analyzed properly, then there is no longer a need to postulate such a division between thought and matter: matter *is* to the extent that it is *thought scientifically*.

For Cohen, idealism distinguishes itself from metaphysics with critique: that is, with the critical unearthing of the origin of ideas by looking at their past and present sources of validity. Rather than searching for the essence of things in a sphere of hidden reality, Cohen finds in ideas the conscious past of knowledge.[69] In the shift away from metaphysical substances or essences underlying things and ideas, Cohen thus turns to history, the spiritual archive of knowledge. This move to history precludes the lure of materialism by avoiding the "methodological falsehood"[70] of "naturalism and materialism [that] goes hand in hand."[71] That is to say, Cohen avoids the reduction of human spirit and lawfulness to causal necessity. Ideas are part of a historical development of reasoning, which is why the fact of science presents idealism with its own history, the history of reason.

Cohen's account of metaphysics is therefore not just a claim about the spiritual or abstract sphere of consciousness; it is also a description of the heterogeneity of material claimed by materialism. Introducing both spirit and matter into the same object of reality transforms the world of natural science into a world of substance—a world intelligible only to theology or dogmatism. For Cohen, science is therefore one canonical way of describing the world, and reason must be considered the source of normativity for that knowledge. Reason is what provides science with a character and an identity. Yet, crucially, Cohen insists that reason must not be abstracted or rendered additive to the world of experience. Rather, reason is a critically delimited and historically developing body of knowledge, for which the history of science provides evidence. Thus, in his introduction to the third edition (1918) of his major work, *Kants Theorie der Erfahrung*, Cohen describes the history of science as the history of reason itself. He writes, "And so history becomes a broader concept that encompasses philosophy and science at the same time. If we, however, reunite the latter two in a unity, in the concept of scientific reason, then the ideal of a cognition of the history of philosophy achieves substantive determinateness. The *history of scientific reason* thus emerges as the ideal of all cognition [*Erkenntnis*]."[72]

In Cohen's use of historicity *of* reason, the development of scientific knowledge becomes the history of its development, and philosophy becomes the interpreter of that body of knowledge as an ideal, the ideal of knowledge. Without reducing reason to a material faculty of human psychology or to the empirical positivism of singular historical agents, Cohen transforms this principle of scientific reason into the foundation for a theory of judgment. Reason is an ideal, and it is a lawful ideal in that it serves as an objective standard by which scientific reason is developed, tested, and justified. A history of this lawfulness becomes the domain of science—the study of *how* reason came to be this way, of how reason became normative—since lawfulness and normativity are the basis for reaching consistency in judgments. Historical reason therefore becomes a history of norms. And for Cohen, the history of reason can only be told as the tale of idealism, which is the study of such normative ideas.

We can begin to see the relationship between Cohen's idealism, his early writings on Heine, and the religious concepts that have been mobilized in modern thought. Similar to his account of the transhistorical role of concepts that helped him explore Heine's introduction of Judaism into philosophy, Cohen's account of the history of reason provides a more robust definition of knowledge as constituted by this interfacing of concepts between past and present. Knowledge, following the minor Protestantism described in chapter 1, achieves independence from the institutions and persons that seek to determine what is true and false. Knowledge becomes a public possession by becoming a historical body of ideas and norms developed and argued, justified and reconciled.

More broadly considered, Cohen's idealism shows us that neo-Kantianism integrated the lessons of nineteenth-century historicism into its theory of ideas.[73] Such an idealism seeks clarity about where and when our ideas emerged to help us make consistent judgments in the natural and human sciences. Both Rickert and Cohen, as the foremost representatives of their schools, shared an attention to the differences between natural science and ethics, history, and culture.[74] Yet the nuance of Cohen's work emerges both in his attention to the broader conception of reason as a cultural possession and in his claim that science is a historically objectified body of knowledge, a public reason that crystallized this ideal of culture.[75]

This public dimension of reason in Cohen's idealism is connected to the historical scope of science. Cohen understood the objectivity of Kant's categories of the understanding with which we judge the world to have emerged in time and to have been produced through the social ratification of knowledge. For Cohen, science therefore describes a historical and cultural institution of knowledge. He writes,

> The transcendental method does not carry out its research according to the principles of human reason [*menschliche Vernunft*], but rather according to those principles with scientific value [*wissenschaftliche Geltung*] that condition the groundwork of the sciences.... The sciences, however, lay present in printed books. Asking after what makes them into sciences, what their character of universality and necessity is based upon, from within which concepts their sphere of valid knowledge-worth can be derived, of which movements and peculiarities of cognition each of the historical Facta of knowledge can be explained by the sciences, in their validity: these reflect a methodological question, the question which the sciences, wherever they have set out to consider their own principles, to experience their shaping impetus, that becomes the transcendental question; this and nothing else.[76]

Reason and science are emphatically public, or at least socially constituted through the interface of history and ideality. The transcendental *method*, for Cohen, unearths the historical principles and concepts that have given way to the validity of scientific knowledge. This insight is crucial to a proper understanding of Cohen's neo-Kantianism and helps reconfigure the sociopolitical stakes of his project, as we will see further on. This emphasis on the printed books—the facts that have been put forward in a public, discursive form—changes the status of reason. Reason is neither the possession of a person or people nor reducible to laws of nature; rather, reason is a public body of knowledge that is accessible to all who can access books.

Cohen's rejection of human reason as a basis for considering the scope of the transcendental method stems from his rejection of crude materialism. Instead of privileging some pregiven object of material nature that science works on interpreting, Cohen casts scientific discourse as the very source of the concept of an object—something that must be shaped by the categories of mathematical number—just as language would serve to cast the world of representation. The changing discourse of science—and not some mystified nature in need of monistic doctrine to interpret the world—was the real basis on which the popular scientific associations, Free Religious congregations, and other liberals, sought scientific validity for their worldviews. Therefore, Cohen believed it was a corrigible discourse but one susceptible to ideological manipulation as well. It was similarly a discourse adopted by intellectual anti-Semites in their appeal to social Darwinism. Hence Cohen feared that if scientific reason were construed as something rooted in the human being—whose own substantial and material existence as a tribal or anthropological being is now deemed absolute—then science is rooted in nothing more than an enchanted myth of that people's genius, or human reason. For Cohen, the historical, categorical, and social emphasis on science as a canon of reason reorients the *critical thrust* of Kant's transcendental idealism. The focus of critique is to both perform the *justification* of knowledge and, in effect, critically remind us that knowledge is never purely given but rather comes from somewhere. This, for Cohen, is why the normativity of reason and, likewise, its sociality is something that transcends any particular individual or people.

In sum, Cohen's critical idealism is framed as the conceptual labor of justifying and critiquing—clarifying and analyzing—the conditions that make science possible. These conditions are the ideas, hypotheses, principles, and categories that have been exhibited in the history of science and accrued as a worldview through which nature and experience are conceived. Therefore, the value of the objects of knowledge is specific to the particular canon of knowledge at issue. Reason is thus a multifaceted historical accrual of such knowledge, and the values that are treated as meaningful are those that continue to help knowledge gain ratification and clarification in a public discourse. In other words, science is discursive, and the work of critique is a public labor of justifying knowledge through active participation in the exchange of reasons.

Cohen's idealism secured for itself the right to pursue the analysis and justification of the ideal—of the spiritual concerns of human thought—without falling prey to metaphysics. To further illustrate this distinction between idealism and metaphysics, therefore, we must turn to Cohen's account of idealism as a study of ideas distinct from any intimation of reductionism, which is evident in Cohen's account of normativity. This normative dimension of Cohen's idealism combines the public nature of knowledge, its historical elaboration, and its continued justification and reasoning.

NEUTRALIZATION OR IDEALIZATION?

While Cohen's account of science demonstrates the relationship between publicity, history, and value, it is important to reflect on how such an idealist account of public knowledge differs from the liberal theoretical pattern I referred to above. For many Wilhelmine intellectuals, the lure of monistic materialism was its insistence on a worldly synthesis of value and material. With the concrete and immediate facts of nature as an apparent basis, and a robust conception of a dynamic nature along with it, materialistic monism provided an answer to the crisis of legitimacy: the facts of nature are the source of our judgments and concepts. That is, as the empirically minded would have it, just how the world is. However, as we also saw above, the turn to scientific method also insisted that nature take over the shape of transcendence. That is to say, nature became a vast horizon on which human rationality was projected and from which it was also alienated. Nature was more than what was simply given, it was also a source for how things ought to be and to continue to be.

Cohen's account of reason as implicitly historical, however, shifted the tenor of the conversation surrounding the source of legitimate values. While Cohen's emphasis on the history of science as the model of reason gestures toward the public and social nature of his understanding of ideality, his thought is most compelling on this score when we consider how reason, history, and publicity also relate to the social, ethical, and religious resources for a public knowledge. That is, once we better grasp the social and public nature of knowledge production in Cohen's thought, we'll be in a better position to assess both the larger issues of neutrality, secular reasoning, and value associated with liberalism and also how Cohen's idealism differs from these immanent elements of liberalism. In this next section, therefore, I want to turn from Cohen's understanding of logic in relation to natural science and instead contrast the social-scientific negotiation of value and value neutrality to Cohen's account of idealization, especially in his ethical philosophy. Idealization, I ultimately suggest, represents the kind of self-reflexivity that allows historical sources to be consciously presented within the frame of a normative assertion. The norm must come from somewhere, guiding both the method of inquiry and the value produced for claiming social goods. Cohen's thought calls attention not only to the dialectic of enchantment and disenchantment in Wilhelmine German thought but also to the pitfalls of a neutralizing turn in the sciences of the time.

While I suggested that the context of the Materialism Controversy should be seen as setting the parameters for how natural scientific thought contributed to secularization, Cohen's thought and intellectual formation should also be seen as squarely within the ambit of the birth of German sociology. Insofar as Cohen, like the neo-Kantians, shared a theoretical critique of metaphysics and materialism in turning to the validity of judgments and the epistemological basis of values, these methodological contributions were crucial to the development of the social sciences. Cohen's method of idealization, for example, shares many conceptual parallels with the historical-conceptual method developed by Max Weber, a point that some of Cohen's critics have also noted.[77] However, Cohen's and Weber's differences are significant, as we will see.

Largely under the influence of his colleague at Freiburg, Rickert,[78] Weber also developed a method of abstracting ideal types from historical action in order to reach a causal explanation of social phenomena. In his theory, Weber claims that historical and social phenomena require "the isolation (that means, abstraction) of the individual components of the course of events, and for each component the orientation toward rules of experience and the formulation of clear concepts without which causal attribution is nowhere possible."[79] The study of historical institutions must yield lawful principles that can explain *how* society develops. The "concepts and 'laws' of pure economic theory are examples of this kind of ideal type,"[80] since the actual physical labor and exchange in which human beings engage is not itself lawful until a typical case is determined as a measure for future cases. The typical case is therefore an ideal one for Weber.[81]

Weber's understanding of these ideal-typical laws that govern scientific explanation was a manifestation of his own theoretical pattern of liberalism. That is, Weber's account of ideal-typical lawfulness was directly related to his negotiation of the disenchantment he described as resulting from the increasing rationality of the modern world. In his "Science as

Vocation" lecture, Weber thus notes that "science today is irreligious," a fact that "no one will doubt in his innermost being, even if he will not admit it to himself."[82] A theory of ideal types should therefore provide a value-neutral viewpoint with which to regulate science. For Weber, this is due to the fact that

> scientific progress is a fraction, the most important fraction, of the process of intellectualization which we have been undergoing for thousands of years....
>
> The increasing intellectualization and rationalization *do not*, therefore, indicate an increased and general knowledge of the conditions under which one lives.
>
> It means something else, namely, the knowledge or belief that if one but wished one *could* learn it at any time. Hence, it means that principally there are no mysterious incalculable forces that come into play, but rather that one can, in principle, master all things by calculation. This means that the world is disenchanted.[83]

For Weber, science is not in a position to answer the questions of ultimate value in life; science cannot tell us how we ought to live; that is, science cannot teach us ethics. Science suspends our awe and wonder before the world that surrounds us. And with a *belief* in the possibility of explaining all there is—of the infinite intelligibility of the world—science, Weber worries, loses a sense of limitation that mystery and myth, spirits and magic had represented for former generations. This, Weber opines, provides armature for a new kind of zealotry, combining the authority of the scientist with the bombast of a false prophet. He writes, "Today the routines of everyday life challenge religion. Many old gods ascend from their graves; they are disenchanted and hence take the form of impersonal forces. They strive to gain power over our lives and again resume their eternal struggle with one another."[84] Thus, value-neutral science must guard against the academic prophecy of values that Weber attributes to the work of his colleagues. Science should be guarded from assertions of value and, instead, directed toward achieving greater clarity in the examination of those domains of life where ultimate value can be sought. Science cannot supply these values, however. This clarity is the best one could hope for, since, as Weber notes, "only on the assumption of belief in the validity of values [is] the attempt to espouse value-judgments meaningful. However, to *judge* the *validity* of such values is a matter of faith ...

it certainly does not fall within the province of an empirical science [to do so]."[85] Disenchantment, in Weber's assessment, leads to an ideology of belief in science. Value neutrality is thus necessary for scientific thought to remain sober.

Weber's Protestant sensibilities might have enticed him to make such a distinction between science and value.[86] His theory sought to guard against the encroaching irrationality and looming "war of the gods" that might seek to reoccupy the sphere of value judgments. Thus, his theory insists on the distinction between the historical study of values and the assertion of those values as a matter of faith.[87] Ideal types, he claims, are therefore distinguished from "the idea of an ethical imperative, of a 'model' of what 'ought' to exist." As an analytical construct, the ideal type is only "'ideal' in the strictly logical sense of the term." Science ought to humble itself and seek only to map "relationships which our imagination accepts as plausibly motivated and hence as 'objectively possible.'"[88] This humility of science, claims Weber, is a necessary bulwark against the "old gods" ascendant in new, "impersonal forms." Neutrality, for Weber, thus guards against secular prophets.

According to Todd Weir, if German history can be reinterpreted according to what he calls a "quadriconfessional model" that includes organized secularism alongside Catholicism, Protestantism, and Judaism, then we can see Weber's account of secularization as his attempt to defang and neutralize secularism by insisting that value judgments of the kind purported by secularists and monists as the basis for their scientifically legitimated worldviews were in fact nothing but projected values.[89] Only science could stand above the fray of the disenchanted war of gods, thus ensuring an objective and neutral perspective. In this respect, he shared Cohen's worry over the rise of scientific worldviews. But Weber may not have understood his own commitment to value neutrality as a belief in its own right, which is an issue that Cohen too worried about.

In contrast to Weber's commitment to—we might even say *belief* in— the value neutrality of scientific thought, Cohen's understanding of idealism and the mechanics of idealization takes a different route and insists on the normative significance of the ideals extracted from historical and cultural institutions. And whereas Cohen's account of logical concepts and laws hold valid for the justification of natural science, his social and ethical thought makes explicit its normative and value commitments. That is, while Weber repeatedly insists on a value-free methodology[90] in which the ideal type becomes a descriptive type aimed at both approximating something essential in a past social action or economic trend and explaining it causally, Cohen maintains that the very insistence on causality belies the claim to neutrality. This is because Cohen considers causality to be a natural scientific concept, and ideality in the sphere of historical and social normativity has an autonomous existence in relation to the actuality of the event or historical process. Achieving the status of a norm, an idea gestures not to a causal past but to a future implementation—or, at the very least, to a temporal horizon where past and future collide.[91] In Cohen's three-part *System of Philosophy* (*Logik*, 1902; *Ethik*, 1904; *Aesthetik*, 1908), he thus contrasts natural causality to this model of ideality time and again. While the causal model of natural science emphasizes the direct connection between events—a necessary relationship between cause and effect—the ideal norms in the realm of the human sciences (the sphere of ethics) are not empirical causes. They occupy a different relationship to actuality. Norms inscribe a future tense into the overall historical provenance of an idea. That is, by treating ideas as the conceptually developing archives of the past, those same ideas come to serve as indices for how future actions grounded in such ideas *ought to be*.

Cohen's account of ideality begins his system with logic, since, as he describes, logic denotes "thinking about the laws of thinking."[92] Without sensibility as a source of cognition, Cohen does away with the primacy of representation for idealist thought.[93] There is no given or thing-in-itself. Eliminating Kant's dualistic structure of intuition and concepts—sensibility and understanding—Cohen instead describes thinking in terms such as *anticipatory* and *generative*.[94] Thinking does not begin by simply analyzing a given object but rather by analyzing a concept of an object. By analyzing a concept of something, thinking generates its content according to the discourse—the principles, categories, and concepts—of science. Following Kant, Cohen describes this form of thinking as judgment. Judgment (*Urteil*) begins with a question, *What is?*, and this question "lays the ground of judgment."[95]

Cohen describes this process in his *Logic of Pure Cognition* (1902) through "the judgment of origin."[96] This is the origin of the concept, which asks, *What is?*, and "the deeper answer to this question," Cohen claims, "is the Idea."[97] That is to say, for Cohen the principle of origin and the infinitesimal approximation of something to nothing enacted by a judgment, leads the question *What is?* toward something (*Etwas*) rather than nothing (*Nichts*), and, insofar as it is a meaningful something, it is a normative concept. The normative status of ideas therefore originates in judgment.[98] Once concepts are established as valuable—as something rather than nothing—they gain value as the grounds for thinking. They also serve as a measure for justifying other judgments. This lawfulness of thinking (*Denkgesetze*)[99] builds on a series of judgments, relating judgment and concept.[100] Hence, the growing canon of concepts that are justifiably upheld and judged as something rather than nothing must ensure the justifiability of the chain of judgments.[101] The reliability of judgments is therefore a normative enterprise in its own right, according to Cohen. This method of critique is what Cohen refers to as the body of scientific knowledge, which represents a canon of historical content that is itself publicly recognizable.[102]

Hence, while affirming the sociality of reasoning as an objective idealism, Cohen takes the additional step of emphasizing thinking as fundamentally defined by *lawfulness*; a lawfulness found *in* thinking rather than in the materiality of the world. Nevertheless, thinking is neither the self-revealing force of judgments belonging to some preconstituted *I*, nor is it embodied by a pure, determinate, and mediated universal *I*. Rather, our justifiably held ideas are part of a canon that we share with others in the history of knowledge. This ideal lawfulness provides a shared validity to reasoning on which we can rely because we can trace its past in the history of science. Thus, for Cohen, the logic of science develops as a historical series of hypothetical groundings (ideas) that have been judged in concepts and categories, laws and functions. Our hypotheses are tested against historical and natural experiments proving our categories are valid (or not) to the extent that they are recognizable. History is therefore crucial to all thinking, whether logical or social, both because this testing takes time and because the validity of these tests must be ratified with others.

While this normativity of ideas helps provide the parameters for scientific method, Cohen's understanding of ideality becomes even clearer in treating the lawfulness of judgments both in the natural and the human sciences. This is because Cohen claims logic can only provide the *validity* of the concept. However, the idea of validity remains incomplete without its normative justification through logic's relation to ethics.[103] This, Cohen claims, is the meaning of the idea as a hypothesis, which Plato understood as leading any account of logical justification all the way back to the idea of the good.[104] For Cohen, ethics pursues the truth that logic can help justify. Cohen therefore remarks that it is peculiar that Hegel's logic does not contain an ethics,[105] since logic produces the unity of the object of cognition but requires ethics in order to generate the subject of self-consciousness.[106] Cohen therefore emphasizes that thinking is a movement, a process that employs logic (defined as thinking about the laws of thinking) in pursuit of certainty. This is foundational for science, which requires justification or truthfulness in the sense of an ethical good faith and transparency necessary for a cultivating science as part of cultural consciousness. As Cohen claims, "Without scientific truth (*Wahrheit*) there can be no truthfulness (*Wahrhaftigkeit*) and without truthfulness there can be no truth."[107] Truth is therefore intimately tied to sociality, or ethics. The goal of attaining logical certainty is thus to ensure that idealism strives for correct judgments and justifiable concepts in shaping all branches of consciousness. Consciousness is a goal to be idealized through the system of philosophy—of idealism—in which the "ideal human being of culture can be brought to an idealization."[108]

In this respect, Cohen's emphasis on the normativity of ideas both gives ethics a particularly privileged position as a critique of the public canons of knowledge such as history, positive law, and theories of law and state (*Rechts- und Staatstheorie*) and distinguishes itself from Weber's account of ideal types by emphasizing that logical validity has not cornered the market on the production of value. In other words, ethics becomes the logic of *social science*, according to Cohen.[109] While Cohen and Weber agree that concept formation of the laws of nature idealizes the conditions under which natural acts *should* occur, they differ when it comes to the social. In the case of norms of human spirit and sociality, according to Cohen, the lawfulness of ideas that provide the conditions under which actions should occur can never be neutral. This is because human actions do not operate according to laws of logical necessity but rather according to what Cohen calls the "basic law of truth,"[110] whereby logic outlines the necessary conditions for ethics to pursue the good.

To explicate the unique character of human historical and ethical actions, Cohen explains how norms serve as foundational principles in both logical and ethical shapes of concept use. As Cohen writes, "Norms are in and of themselves laws; they are but the mathematical archetype of a law, in so far as angular dimensions would take shape as a prescript and guiding principle. In norms, right [*Recht*] legitimizes the concept of law. It channels away from this logical meaning of the norm, when the emphasis is placed on the linguistic grammatical, stylistic form."[111]

Norms are thus fundamental to the judgments of logic as well as ethics. But the norms themselves are not judgments; rather, Cohen insists that the doubled meaning of the norm as a principle and a rule (of measure) is precisely what makes the ideality of the norm so important to his system.[112] While in natural science Cohen sees the logical norm as a kind of mathematical condition for laws of necessary relations (such as angular dimensions or other axioms), in ethics and positive law the norm not only adopts a linguistic characteristic—say, as a command—but also signifies modality.[113] That is, logic operates with necessity as its norm. Ethics and law, by contrast, are normative in a different way—thus the modality of exceptionless universality (*ausnahmslose Allgemeinheit*) characteristic of an ethical norm is not the same as causal necessity.[114] In other words, the norm for human action *ought* to hold as valid even if human beings fail to observe that norm. That failure does not constitute an exception to the validity of the norm. Rather, the norm remains. But in natural scientific cognition the exceptions to the norm constitute moments of possible experimentation and might warrant the revision of principles. The difference between these expressions of normativity lies in the *purpose* of the norm. And the difference between logic and ethics surrounds the characteristics of what is and what ought to be.

To explore the ethical ramifications of this description of normativity, it may be helpful to concretize the debates in which Cohen found himself treading new territory. The distinction between purpose and cause was central, for example, to debates in the social sciences over how historical phenomena might lead to theoretical models of explanation. Weber criticized both the German Historical School of economics, represented by Wilhelm Roscher's almost biological empiricism to explain human economic phenomena,[115] as well as Gustav Schmoller's later attempt to introduce an ethical dimension to economic theory by employing a quantified study of *Moralstatistik* in history.[116] Schmoller's methodology insisted that the epistemological basis of the social sciences should begin with both legal and economic material history, which would account for the religious, moral, and cultural norms that undergird human economic life through an accumulation of data.[117] Schmoller saw this as an empirical scientific viewpoint.[118] By contrast, the more senior head of the Austrian school, Carl Menger, argued against Schmoller and insisted that only systematic and logical first principles could underlay a scientific study of human culture and economic activity.[119] Theory must come first. Thus, while historicism was aligned with the material and empirical sciences and logic and idealism were aligned with metaphysics or abstraction, it was clear from Max Weber's later argument against Schmoller that the fundamental presupposition of these social-scientific debates was that fundamental laws grounded human existence in an immanent causal order.[120]

Cohen criticizes those involved in the debate for being fixated on causality as a model for understanding human action. Instead, he asks whether, in this attempt to amend the statistical research in economic theory by introducing freedom as a causal relation, "the human being must be considered a thing, since he then becomes a product of relations in which he stands and falls, and is conditioned and calculated."[121] For Cohen the human being is neither a causal statistic nor an individuated hero of historical action. As a neo-Kantian, Cohen could only understand this problem as a return to Kant's antinomies, in which freedom is problematically presented as both an unconditioned cause and a determination of causal order.[122] Cohen's interpretation of the Kantian problematic seeks therefore to address the question of human action in the terms of these contemporary debates, focusing on the historical role of human agency in acting on ideal norms and concepts.[123]

Idealization is therefore an answer to the historical question of how ideas are related to human actions and institutions. For Cohen, no philosophical idea or question remains isolated in a historical moment or vacuum, nor is any question beyond the historical unfolding of science and reason.[124] Idealization is therefore an attempt to examine the temporal flexibility of an idea—of how ideas are revisited and remolded as the putty of human experience. The idea of a human being as a historical actor must therefore be idealized into these normative terms. The methodology of idealization gives the scholar a norm as well, since, as Cohen argues, *the historian should be a philosopher. The historian should not hesitate to place himself between the contending parties.*"[125] The historian *ought to* see her task as normative. And this normativity is not limited to the past.

Unlike Weber's, Schmoller's, and Rauscher's accounts, Cohen does not see the work of historical inquiry terminating at the determination of a historical law to help explain the past. Rather, for Cohen history is written for the sake of the future, for the sake of what ought to be. This understanding of the normative within the historical is more than historical hermeneutics; it is part of a unique conception of time altogether. As Cohen would later claim, the future represents the "purest form of idealization" because it represents the location of what ought to be to the exclusion of what is. It is a configuration through which "past and present sink into this time of the future. This return into time is the purest idealization."[126] History therefore transfigures the past into a norm for the future.[127] This kind of historical representation is what I mean by idealization. Cohen's methodology thus turns to the past with an eye to the future and the normative implications of ideas in that future.

Idealization is therefore a conceptual process of determining the historical origin of an idea, recognizing the idea as a source of judgment, and recognizing that the norm by which a judgment operates need not be invalidated by either the failure or success of actualizing that norm. Idealism, for Cohen, is therefore enchanted by ideas—and by the idea's future possibilities—since they transcend the particular determinations of historical happenings. This is why Cohen employs infinitesimal numbers as the model for judgments of reality,[128] for they represent very little, almost nothing, but not nothing. They are discursive projections of the value that thinking employs to make reality intelligible within the language of mathematical natural science. The reality of the "infinitely small although not nothing" helps Cohen concretize his account of concepts to make sense of what thinking does when it judges nature. However, when it comes to treating human beings, Cohen's logical classes of judgments give way to the more social shape of cognition and knowledge (*Erkenntnis*). Only knowledge that can differentiate the singularity of the human being from the logical class of conceptual unity, argues Cohen, can be considered ethical.[129] Human beings, after all, are not numbers. Ethical cognition treats the singularity of *this* human being as well as the recognition of the concept of *a* human being.[130] Social science, for Cohen, cannot be neutral.

While Weber's appeal to ideality is in service of preserving a neutral standpoint that would guard against the pseudoprophetic conflations of political, religious, and scientific values on the part of some of Weber's colleagues, it is significant that Cohen's idealism seeks to provide an explicit mechanism for ascertaining norms. The difference, it seems, lies in the accounts of normativity that they both provide. While Weber insists that the logical validity of ideal types is both the sole domain of natural and social science and somehow distinct from the generation of values themselves, Cohen insists that logical validity and necessity are indeed conceptual principles of logic, but that history, law, religion, and human sociality operate according to a different character of lawfulness and normativity. For Cohen, only a commitment to virtues such as truthfulness and justification, which emerge from ethics, guarantee that science will achieve its goal of rigor through self-reflexivity. Thus, Cohen turns to ethics as the science of norms that will help render historical meaning and preserve a record of the labor that was invested in reasoning the norm out of its particular moment. This idealization of the norm and idea is the work of critical idealism and is aimed at securing value judgments, normative assertions, and ethical judgments within the scope of the social sciences.

Why, we should ask, did a liberal Protestant like Weber turn toward a neutralizing method while a minor Protestant and Jew like Cohen turned to an explicit account of norm generation? In my next section, I aim to answer this question by showing how secularization ignited a debate over the historical origin of values and the possibilities of reenchanting knowledge. While Weber's work provides a beginning to the discussion surrounding secularization, his insistence on neutrality reveals the immanent turn in a liberalism that sought to cover over its minoritizing impulse. Rather than secure reasoning as a sphere of protest and democratization of knowledge independent but alongside institutional dogma, value neutrality shows how liberal rationality instead assumed the mantle of authority for itself. While Weber's attempt may have been to cut off the appeal to prophets in the war of the gods at the pass, the consequence might be said in fact to have helped erase the normative origin of liberal Protestantism itself. Cohen, as I will argue, therefore provides an antidote to this memory loss in his attempt to show how Jewish religion and the study of religious reasoning out of the historical sources of Judaism makes explicit the work that religion does within reasoning and thus provides a control on the secular war of the gods while preserving a method of public reasoning for religion.

SCIENCE AND SECULARIZATION

While the natural sciences achieved foundational status in Cohen's intellectual milieu with their appeal to facts and the concrete and immediate forms of natural life, the social sciences were similarly in pursuit of concrete human activities on which to base judgments about social change and economic motivation. What was the basis on which modern society functioned, sociologists and economists, historians and philosophers began to ask, and how might science account for the dramatic transformations of human industry and forms of thought in the nineteenth century?

The ideal of scientific knowledge thus stretched well beyond the confines of the natural sciences. If, as Weber worried, the role of religion was quickly receding in public life and newfound gods and prophecies were vying for equal hearing, how then should religion be understood in such a world? How should it be studied? Liberal Protestant theology had absorbed, for example, the scientific ideal of young Hegelianism, calling for tradition to submit to "the flames of criticism," as Bruno Bauer would write, thus drawing attention to the historical development of Christianity so as to better recast it in the shape of modernity. Therefore, German humanists in the nineteenth century were growing increasingly concerned with the tension between the truths gleaned from the past and those from the empirical present, which is what some scholars have referred to as the problem of historicism.[131]

Cohen's understanding of the relationship between history and idealism, as we have seen, was not only an attempt to make the history of scientific and social norms explicit but also a window into the broader issue of secularization, in part attributed to the role of historicism in the liberal theology of nineteenth-century Protestantism.[132] Liberal Protestant academics, for example, were becoming more acutely aware of the problem of legitimating values that had been made more transparent by reflecting on their historical past. In particular, Ernst Troeltsch was concerned that by individuating the ideas and traditions of the Christian past, historical criticism needed to guard against undermining the claims to validity of these historical sources. Attention to history, however, should demonstrate the lasting validity of religious ideas beyond their historical grounds and causes, the "power [of] which lies deeper than any historical formulation which it may have produced."[133] However, the risk of historicizing how contemporary culture and its institutions developed, it seemed, was that those same institutions might become unmoored from their validating ideas, and these validating ideas might themselves be left stranded in the ether of knowledge. Placing religious traditions under a historical microscope accentuated the apparently conditional nature of religious truths, their location in time and space, and their causal connection to external influences. In other words, historicizing religion expressed the ideology of self-assertion in a modern, materialist, and scientific epistemology. This, we might say, was the liberal character of cultural Protestantism.

But the question remained: could historical knowledge command the belief that transcendent revelation once did? Secularization therefore named outright the challenge that rationality and science posed to traditional values.[134] This, for example, motivated Weber, Ferdinand Tönnies, and Ernst Troeltsch to reshape a conversation among German social theorists, historians, and theologians about the degree to which historical institutions of moral and religious authority should either continue or fail to legitimate contemporary values and norms. In this sociology of concepts, the problem of historical consciousness and its effects on legitimacy remained the most glaring topic of debate about the dynamics of secularization.

For example, the problem of legitimacy was an implicit starting point of Weber's monumental *Protestant Ethic and the Spirit of Capitalism* and made fully explicit in his *Economy and Society* (1921–22). Weber noted that the increasing rationalization of religious life was a result of religion becoming an independent sphere that motivated, rather than saturated, social life.[135] With the differentiation of religion in the realm of public life, Weber's thesis therefore proposed that the disenchantment of modernity would continue to spark expressions of skepticism concerning traditional institutions of power and the myths that give legitimacy to those institutions.[136] Hence, the world would become more secular through an increase in crises of legitimacy.[137] And because legitimacy meant attachment to and justification through a connection to the past, questioning the truth of that past meant questioning the solidity of that connection. For his part, Weber therefore proposed a value-neutral methodology, as we saw above, in order to stymie the rush to fill the void amid such legitimation crises. Weber, after all, was wary of populism and false prophets.

Weber's arguments about rationalization and shifting standards for evaluating legitimacy were the root of a looming debate surrounding secularization and history. However, the relationship between secularization and legitimacy gains more political specificity in the argument of Carl Schmitt's now famous *Political Theology* (1922).[138] Schmitt claimed that modern political concepts are secularized theological concepts, revealing an incomplete translation that fails to legitimate modernity by dissociating historical ties to those concepts.[139] In Schmitt's account, the neutralization of politics occurs in the attempt to idealize and positivize concepts of law and state as though they were disconnected from their historical and mythic pasts. And as we will see in chapter 4, Schmitt leveraged this historical dilemma to insidious ends. For, although quite differently than Weber, Schmitt also believed liberalism and secularism were inextricably bound together.

Significant to both Weber's and Schmitt's accounts of secularization, however, is the emphatically historical dimension of this process. Legitimacy hinges on forgetting or remembering the sources out of which our concepts emerge. Moreover, by locating the secularization question on an expressly historical horizon, the methodological problem that secularization represents for liberalism is that of how to interpret disparate ideas in history and draw on them for the sake of a social and political present.

While Schmitt saw in political theology a basis for conceptual legitimacy in both knowledge and politics—as a historical trajectory beyond the synchronic legality of a positive legal order—later thinkers such as Hans Blumenberg debated Schmitt's claims and made the case for the legitimacy of modernity without recourse to political theology. Blumenberg defended the very institutions of the Enlightenment as the modern project of making self-assertion into a new form of legitimacy. That is, by creating a "principle of sufficient rationality," Blumenberg insisted that the Enlightenment represented a historically conscious *rational decision* to give itself a nontheological foundation by positing the nothing out of which to create itself.[140] This was neither an arbitrary choice nor an act of forgetting. Rather, Blumenberg's thesis retained a particular historical consciousness of the foundations of a foundationless legitimacy.

In his debate with Schmitt, Blumenberg also took issue with Karl Löwith's claim that modern philosophy of history was a secularization of eschatology. Löwith worried that the attempt to simply replace the contents of theological concepts with secular ones—particularly in the political sphere—risked legitimating the hubristic volition of the human being.[141] Blumenberg argued against this account of history and instead suggested that a kind of structural identity exists in the history of ideas. The "question positions" forged by theology's "world-description"[142] cannot simply be left aside or remain unoccupied on account of the rise of Enlightenment rationality. Rather, by understanding the history of those ideas and question positions, Blumenberg believed that secularization could be legitimated through a historical awareness that culminates in a "reoccupation of answer positions." With new answer positions to questions that the past no longer sufficed to answer,[143] Blumenberg believed he had demonstrated the legitimacy and authority of a self-assertive knowledge: namely, the hermeneutic continuity of historicizing and reoccupying question and answer positions; hence, the conceptual structure rather than any specific content of knowledge provided a legitimating function.[144] While similar to Cohen's thought, in that Blumenberg argues that concept formation has a lawfulness of its own, Blumenberg believed that modern philosophy had reoccupied the role and function of theology, thus conceding a line of argument Weber had begun: namely, that concept formation was a control on the assertion of values. Neutrality itself becomes something of a value, in such an account. Unlike Blumenberg, however, Cohen did not believe that simply deciding in favor of some norms would result in the complete renunciations of others. History might be forgotten, but it cannot be decided away.

From this very brief overview of secularization theories, we glimpse the core problem facing liberalism at its epistemological roots: while liberalism is a Protestant tradition that opened the space between faith and knowledge—between traditional dogmas and their reflection in the language of historical reasoning—the work of rationalization effected by the rise of the natural sciences effaced this historical link. Rather than admit openly that liberalism proceeds from the minority protest and democratizing impulse of this tradition, scholars from Weber to Blumenberg espouse the claim that rationality can serve as a self-authorizing worldview. This may be the case, but the foundationless posture openly called a *decision*, as Blumenberg insists, renders the historical source of that self-reflexivity increasingly opaque. The origins of liberalism's steady neutralization of values can be glimpsed therefore in this turn from minority protest to majority hegemony. Once scientific rationality *believed* itself sufficient, it ceased to be marked as a particular past and normative worldview. Instead, it simply claimed to be rational.

The dominant paradigm of secularization theories has therefore traced ideal types or historical causes of contemporary social logics and ideas of legitimacy, sovereignty, authority, power, force, and duty, among others, to Christian theological categories. However, the very vehicle of this analysis—the reasoning and methods of social science—has been whitewashed of its past. What is neutralized is the historical connection between liberalism and Protestantism. This should not prove surprising, however, since Christianity remains the majority past of European nation-states that we might characterize as liberal secularist states. Thus, the majority narrative of secularization—from Christianity to secular reason to natural science—also reveals its blind spot concerning the very premise of a liberal worldview: the self-reflexivity of historical consciousness. This demand for self-reflexivity and historical consciousness was felt ever more intensely by Jews, and Jewish minority experiences therefore show different trajectories in the encounter with secularization. Cohen's account of idealism—and his method of idealization—thus makes the particular history of liberalism explicit through its minority inflection.

A MINOR SECULARITY

The secularization thesis culminates in a crisis of legitimacy surrounding rationality and historicism. While the former occupied the sciences, the latter is often considered the epistemological foundation of liberal Protestantism. Thus, Schmitt and Blumenberg were continuing debates that had begun with late nineteenth-century cultural Protestantism (*Kulturprotestantismus*) wherein Protestant theologians argued that historicism had decisively transformed the way that Christian religion was studied as a source of and continued influence within modernity. Moreover, these theologians embraced historicism as part of their epistemological program. Yet, if Christianity was to become merely a historical remnant and a source—and thus no longer a norm-generating resource—what, then, was left to secure the footing on which social institutions and conceptions of selfhood should be based?

The turn to history framed moral and political values in distinctly nominalist terms,[145] embossing knowledge about how a religious text, practice, concept, or institution came to be in bolder relief than knowledge of why or what such a text, concept, or practice *should* mean. For this reason, Cohen characterized the historicism of his own time as yet another avenue for metaphysics to elevate the historical past to the level of causal occurrence rather than to treat history as a repository of possibilities for directing knowledge and cultural consciousness toward changing the world for the better. Nevertheless, historicism enshrined a new fundamental principle to reign over knowledge production: self-reflection.

While Cohen clearly endorses a notion of historical self-reflexivity, he also deems mere awareness (*Bewusstheit*) of the past insufficient. Awareness of the past is not enough to elevate an idea to its normative status. Merely recognizing the historical past as though it were a cause is insufficient. Thus, claiming religion is merely perfected by a higher organ of reason, or supplanted by a supposed awareness of what religion is *really about*, fails to demand the degree of historical reflexivity demanded by Cohen. This kind of *historische* (historic) thinking is not idealist. For Cohen, such "awareness (*Bewusstheit*) is myth," while only "consciousness (*Bewusstsein*) is science (*Wissenschaft*)."[146] Consciousness, by contrast to merely positing a historical precursor, is scientific because it is transparent and self-reflexive at the level of logical and ethical judgments. Concepts thus become reflexive. Consciousness can thereby be said to be lawful and remains a resource for future acts of reasoning and human actions through this historical reflexivity. Merely recollecting the past is the stuff of myth, but to have a *justification* for consciousness is methodological and continues to have salience beyond the specificities of a historical moment.

Cohen therefore insists that the humanities must remain vigilant about the historical basis on which to educate the nation about itself, its diverse sources of culture, and its pasts, both major and minor; furthermore, idealism must serve as the methodological lever of that endeavor. And perhaps most important for Cohen's attempt to articulate a space of Jewish religious reasoning in a German national identity was his claim that idealism must establish science, not myth, as the basis of the nation. That is, *religion* must remain a source of the nation since, as Cohen writes, "the modern concept of a people [*Volksbegriff*] is a cultural concept, and culture means the collectivity of consciousness's forces [*Bewusstseinskräfte*]." The collectivity of consciousness's forces, as Cohen saw it, must include Judaism as well as Christianity. Protestantism makes this understanding of religion explicit, as we saw in the previous chapter, and through idealist reasoning secures a place for the cultural significance of religion. The idealization of religion contributes to an ethical idea of a Fatherland through the "realization of the idea of a people [*Volksidee*] [which] is the content of the tasks of idealism."[147] Cohen's engagement with historical justification is therefore aimed at providing a deeper consciousness of the provenance of German public institutions and their moral culture.

Cohen's interest in the historical sources of ideas helped him negotiate between the immanent turn to materialism in organized secularism as well as the neutralizing liberal theoretical pattern of German academic social scientists. Cohen therefore insisted that a rigorous method of idealization and a commitment to the transcendence of ideas could provide the methodological clarity needed to translate the historical past into justifiable norms for the present. But Cohen's idealism, unlike the theories of secularization described above, does not focus exclusively on the majority experience of Christian history. That is, Cohen's account of idealization is more than a reoccupation of past question positions. It is an attempt to retrieve the historical status of minority that afforded Protestantism its revolutionary epistemological opening. Cohen's description of reasoning, whether scientific or religious, is therefore in the service of continuing the process of idealization—of continuing to remind ourselves of the historical provenance of our norms and social goods, of continuing to minoritize our reasonings.

Cohen's idealism helps reclaim an obscured perspective on secularization. Cohen's reading of Heine, for example, and the connection between Judaism and idealism, locates a forgotten step in the secularization of German Protestantism into German philosophy. This account of secularization no longer sees the past recede and give way to pantheism and materialism as new answer positions. This was only one consequence. Rather, as the previous chapter argued, in order for such questions to be possible, Protestantism must be interpreted as the opening up of freedom of thought—the freedom to distinguish between faith and knowledge. This distinction allows for historicizing and debate over the reasons provided for social and political goods. In this historical self-reflexivity of Protestantism, Cohen finds a place for Judaism as well. In what follows, I want to show how Cohen's turn to religion and to Judaism in particular helps make explicit the role of Protestant epistemology in opening up a space of reasoning for religion in the public sphere.

In his explicit discussions of Jewish religion, Cohen's insight into the necessity of historicizing concepts becomes a dominant theme. Cohen insists on the lawful and historical dimension of concepts and their justification, which provides ethical idealism with a normative connection to historical sources such as positive law and religious texts and concepts.[148] For example, in his posthumously published *Religion of Reason: Out of the Sources of Judaism* (1919), often considered one of the most important works of modern Jewish thought, Cohen sketches the methodological crux of his argument: the study of religion and the study of reason are both historical labors. In undertaking a study of Judaism, Cohen therefore begins with an explicit question about the very concept of religion. He writes,

> We do not shrink from the argument that reason must rule everywhere in history. However, history in itself does not determine the concept of religion. The concept is always a separate problem, which must serve as a presupposition for the problem of development.
>
> We find a similar methodological situation in the concept of Judaism, though the conflict with history is in this case less extreme. . . . Judaism has literary sources, and as much as these may differ in the objective value and literary clearness, the historical material is nevertheless narrowed down and limited in these sources. . . . It is impossible to develop a unifying concept of Judaism out of the literary sources unless the concept of Judaism itself is anticipated as an ideal project, in a manner methodologically analogous to the study of the organism.[149]

According to Cohen, religion is a concept that is at no time the same in history. This is because the study of religion must ask whether it is the study of a concept—one determined in advance and then deployed in the study of diverse historical phenomena—or the process of developing a rubric from the study of such historical phenomena. In other words, for Cohen the question concerns whether the study of religion is deductive or inductive: a study that begins with a concept or that seeks to produce one. In the case of religion, history does not simply amass materials that are then deduced to imply that a concept of religion should exist. Rather, as Cohen notes, "History does not determine the concept," but, as the example of Judaism demonstrates, the "concept of Judaism" must be "anticipated as an ideal project." In other words, the concept of religion—like all logical concepts in Cohen's idealism—is anticipatory and guides the investigation into historical sources. "Therefore," Cohen continues, "the objection that history in itself is in opposition to the objective value of the concept is removed. This objection is based on a misunderstanding. The concept, like everything spiritual, requires history for its own development. However, history by itself does not determine anything about the essence and peculiarity of the concept, which in the course of history up to now, may not yet have developed to its final realization."[150] The concept is both anticipatory and constellated from out of history; its content may in fact be unfinished. History cannot monopolize it, nor exhaust the concept through the historical happening of development. Rather, the concept must be "anticipated beforehand" and, as with the scientific "case of an organism," this concept must be tested against the literary and historical sources encountered. The study of religion is therefore the study of a conceptual problem—namely, the fact that, on the one hand, religion cannot be a ready-made and completed thing and yet, on the other hand, without such a concept we cannot begin the work of historical study. This is, Cohen claims,

> the fundamental question of all knowledge; it is the magic word that illuminates all the obscurities, all the difficulties, all the innermost depths of the theory of knowledge. Insofar as religion, insofar as Judaism presents a conceptual problem, and insofar as this problem has to be solved, if the literary sources are not forever to remain a book with seven seals, the disclosure and the depiction of these concepts—religion and Judaism— have to be obtained from the understanding of the respective concepts themselves. The worshipper of fire, not only the worshipper of the sun, might perhaps have the same single religion along with the prophets, with Judaism. However, even if I am referred to the literary sources of the prophets for the concept of religion, those sources remain mute and

blind if I do not approach them with a concept, which I myself lay out as a foundation in order to be instructed by them and not simply guided by their authority.[151]

According to Cohen, religion is neither sui generis nor the cumulative statement of historical contingencies. Rather, religion signifies a conceptual problem concerning the individual human being, the human community, and the transcendence of moral value. Religion therefore represents something particular about the moral worth of human existence, which is not solely determined by the sources, doctrines, or rituals of one or even all such instantiations. Thus, while it may be the case that practices of fire worship, considered polytheistic or idolatrous in the rabbinic sources of Judaism, are in fact part of the same religion as that of the prophets, such an equation or distinction is meaningless without a more general account of the conceptual work that religion does when we encounter such historical circumstances. "Hence," Cohen writes, "there is another source besides the merely literary one which gives me guidance in the use of literary sources."[152] This other source is the very same as that which permeates all concepts: reason.

In Cohen's account, therefore, religion is related to reason. That is to say, to the extent that "reason is the source of concepts,"[153] the meaning of a "religion of reason is opposed to the idea that religion is an invention of the people of a certain rank, whether priests or rulers or the privileged classes."[154] Religion is neither a preliminary form of science and philosophy nor contained in an underdeveloped form within the latter. Rather, "reason does not exhaust itself in science and philosophy,"[155] which is to say that a religion of reason is not a reduction of religion to some ready-made reason. Rather, if we recall Cohen's account of reason as a public canon of knowledge that develops and is tested in socially exchanged reasonings, we learn something else. He writes,

It is not possible to say that *consciousness* is to be thought of, and sought, as this other source. For consciousness is, properly speaking, only another expression for history. As all culture is developed *by* history, so also is it developed by consciousness; the only difference is that consciousness actualizes the narrower history of man. If consciousness, therefore, cannot be thought of as the other source, which besides and over and above history vouches for the legitimacy and value of religion, then the other source can be expressed only through the word "reason" as it appears in the title of our book. *The concept of religion should be discovered through the religion of reason.* The sources of Judaism should be shown and proven to be that material which in its historical self-development must engender and verify the problematic reason, the problematic religion of reason. Thus, history itself again becomes the literary touchstone for the creativity of reason; however, it is not merely life or instinctive production that is able to testify to the legitimacy of reason and its specific character. Reason itself is the problem that exists for every concept, for every possible knowledge of a concept, which consequently has to be presupposed and set up as a foundation for the concept of religion and for the concept of Judaism. Consequently, placing the concept of religion in a necessary relation to the problem of reason, we introduce the problem of religion into general philosophy.[156]

Reason is therefore the source that helps identify religion as a concept more universal than its particular manifestations in any one religion or any one people. While consciousness represents the history out of which culture develops, reason manifests in the sources of Judaism, in the *public body of knowledge*, represented by Judaism's literary sources of the Bible, the Mishnah, the Talmud, and commentaries.[157] As with the history of science, found in books, so too religions of reason are found in public, historical sources. The history of Judaism therefore occasions this inquiry into the problematic of reason and religion and shows how consciousness—which is "identical with the specific form of human spirit in science and philosophy"[158]—becomes human in the form of religion. That is, the public nature of reason, which the histories of science and philosophy demonstrate as a developing body of norms and ideas that are exchanged and reasoned about over time, extends to religion as well. But religion makes this kind of consciousness—this justification of reasons and norms, ideas and concepts—*human* through the expression of moral worth, concern for human suffering, and the commitment to believing that a moral world is possible.

By demonstrating that religion occupies a specific role in the cultural resources of human life, Cohen has broached the very problem facing the theorists of secularization, albeit in more explicit terms. Cohen does not locate the specificity of religion in an enchantment that is now increasingly isolated from human reasoning and sociality, or opposed to the contemporary scientific and philosophical culture that would style itself secular, material, universal by dint of its neutrality, and thus

dehistoricized. Rather, Cohen instead suggests that reason is by definition a historical canon and an also ideal and that religion actively contributes to the expansion of reason as well as being an instantiation of
reason. Religion is the humanization of the cultural consciousness of
various peoples as they negotiate between the spheres of morality and
science. In other words, making religion explicitly part of culture, Cohen
breaks down the barrier not only between science and moral normativity
but also between one people and another.

The social and political significance of Cohen's theory of religion
should be a bit clearer now: rather than hide the minority expression of
Protestant religion behind a veil of neutrality, Cohen calls direct attention
to Judaism as a set of particular historical sources that can now be articulated openly within reasoning. Judaism can now be treated as a concept
through which to show that the idealization of public morality is likewise
a democratizing process. In other words, Cohen demonstrates the self-
reflexivity of Protestant epistemology—of a historicized reasoning—at
work. So while Cohen's historical account of reason presents Judaism as
a determinate moment in the development of reason itself, this is not the
end of the line for Judaism. Indeed, it need not also be the end of the line
for Christianity. Yet Cohen recognizes that reason has a history dominated by exclusively majoritarian terms. For example, in his 1916 essay
entitled, "The Jew in Christian Culture," Cohen considers the problem
of Christian history for the Jew, which covers over Jewish contributions
to culture and the modern world. He writes,

> Here we have reached the point concerning the apparent authority of this
> appearance of strangeness that overtakes the Jew in the modern world,
> insofar as it is Christian: it appears as if this Christian world were an
> entirely independent creation of Christian ideas, in which the Jew had
> not significantly contributed as a creative subject. Yet there was [such a
> contribution] at the beginning. So it remained the same in the Middle
> Ages. And so was it yet again renewed at the beginning of the modern
> period and thus will it remain in the present day as long as this whole
> culture retains its religious and ethical framework.[159]

While we can interpret Cohen's remarks as an implicit rejection of a secularization thesis, since it hinges on the exclusivity of Christian ideas as the
source of the modern world, we can also see how he subverts this history.
Even if the presumed exclusivity of a Christian past persists in the modern

push forward in scientific, humanistic, and philosophical research, Cohen worries that this exclusion of the Jewish contribution to the Christian sources of the modern world has misconstrued the meaning of religion in modern thought. The *exclusively* Christian sources of this secularization suggest that the historical legitimacy of reason is either Christian or post-Christian. But Cohen's exhortation to intervene in such a past and retell its story opens the door for idealism to interrupt the thread of pantheism, the immanence of radical materialism, and humanism, which are all variations of this exclusively majoritarian history of Christianity. Cohen's anxiety over the secularization of idealism therefore explains his insistence on the Protestant dimension of idealism and modernity. Idealizing Judaism into the past as a norm for monotheistic transcendence and the lawfulness of morality supports a history and a future of reason in which Judaism is a contributor.

We might better understand the connection between the minor Protestantism I described in chapter 1 and this minoritizing idealism when we consider an example of Cohen's early commitment to a shared history and goal of moral culture. Early in Cohen's career when Lange asked whether Cohen's Judaism might impose a bias on his teaching at Marburg (an expression of the liberal calm before the anti-Semitic storm of the late 1870s and early 1880s), Cohen's response should be seen as a subtly subversive deflection when he retorted, "What you call Christianity, I call Prophetic Judaism."[160] As opposed to eliding the differences between Christian and Jewish eschatology that would preoccupy Cohen's philosophy of religion, this remark must be seen as a mutual idealization of these histories. What Lange sees in his Christianity—a scientific culture explicitly rooted in Protestantism—is what Cohen sees in Prophetic Judaism. This is not simply a liberal Jewish apologetics.[161] Rather, idealization provides the rubric of reasoning—of a common project of social and public reasoning under which to coordinate these two invocations of religion. Thus, Cohen would later remark that Judaism and Protestantism share the crucial aim of "ethicizing all human pursuits, which is in a certain sense joined to a secularization of the spiritual offices."[162] The secularizing of spiritual offices and vocations remains linked to Protestantism and Prophetic Judaism as forms of religion, but their spiritual labor does not cease. Both are bound to the "other basic concept of the Reformation" which, Cohen claims, is "justification."[163] For Cohen, the direction of this secularizing is toward a future in which both traditions become idioms of reasoning. Protestantism's contribution to understanding a religion of reason is its detachment from Christianity to become the figure of modern public religious reasoning. Protestantism therefore aids Judaism in articulating what it finds flawed in Christian eschatology and claims of supersessionism. The prophetic idealism of morality therefore aligns these traditions in the future of reason. Jewish religious reasoning in turn helps Protestantism assert its role as the root of liberalism by reminding us that such pursuits are ethicized when they are idealized and viewed from the perspective of the norm that motivates human action.

This idealizing project was certainly liberal in its orientation, although Cohen referred to it explicitly as an ethical socialism. Inflecting religious ideas through ethics as a resource for affirming social equality and freedom, this socialist dimension of Cohen's thought can be seen from his early writings to his final works.[164] Thus, elements of both Cohen's ethics and philosophy of religion were present in his work early on. Around the same time as his conversation with Lange about Prophetic Judaism and Christianity in 1872, Cohen claimed to have taken up (*mitgenommen*) the Kantian God-idea, a guarantor of morality, and would begin to develop his critical idealism in light of such a God in relation to morality.[165] Nevertheless, Cohen would come to express some ambivalence over the status of a "postulate of practical reason."[166] Could such a concession, as Franz Rosenzweig describes the Kantian God, support an idealist ethics? The relationship between a monotheistic God and social ethics thus remained a preoccupation for Cohen.

MONOTHEISM AND CULTURE

We can now better understand the role of monotheism in Cohen's thought, which I began to explore in chapter 1. Monotheism becomes the idealized concept that bridges religion and public morality by providing a cultural norm for a morality independent of Judaism or Christianity. Monotheism is implicitly idealism. God therefore becomes an epistemological norm, an idea that marks a common ground between distinct traditions of religious reasoning, such as Christianity and Judaism. Cohen's monotheism considered God not only a supreme ethical norm—a hypothesis of the guarantor of justice and the good as he would describe in his *Ethik*—but also the guarantor that truth could be predicated of knowledge.[167] God became an ideal, always beyond the immediacy of this world, and a basis on which ethical culture must critique politics. Insisting that such an idea of God was not an attempt to capitalize on and justify "exploiting a Jewish slogan,"[168] Cohen was therefore not concerned with justifying monotheism to Jews alone. Rather, Cohen claimed that the idea of a singular God for the whole world and for all humanity was a universal goal. This devotion to monotheism also provided the resources for a moral language beyond the divide of Jew or Christian. And since Protestant Christianity and Judaism both configure the idea of a monotheistic God prominently as a single and unique God of all, excluding all interceding forms of immanence, perhaps the future-oriented gaze in Judaism's prophetic God-idea and its promise of a messianic emancipation for all of humanity could provide conceptual support to the critical project of building a new cultural consciousness of true freedom and equality.[169] Centered on the figure of an ideal unity, monotheism relates these "confessions,"[170] while idealism normatively regulates this bond between Protestantism and Judaism.

Monotheism therefore extends the work of idealization from natural science to ethics to religion. This idealization of monotheism as a source of public morality thereby counters the dilemma of secularization by explaining the legitimating function of the most important Kantian and liberal inheritance of the modern world—namely, the moral law. The lawful nature of morality, Cohen claims, reflects the contribution of Jewish monotheism to *public morality*. In idealizing Jewish law, which is the foundation of monotheism, as a normative ground for ethical public law, Cohen saw a strategy for justifying Judaism in the light of reason and modernity. However, this idealization was also inherently historical since, as Cohen articulated, "[Jewish] law in its rigid strictness, as well as in its living flexibility, can only be understood in its historical significance, in which it is a model for the problem of cultural and historical influence in general. In this sense, it is namely the problem of the ideas or the ethical mores [*Sitten*] and its uses are the prevalent forces for preserving and developing spiritual phenomena."[171] Law exemplifies Judaism's ability to contribute to normative dimensions of general ethical discourse. But as a historically fluid and developing canon of knowledge, law also helps shape Judaism anew, "preserving and developing spiritual phenomena." Law is the key to idealizing and justifying Judaism as it navigates the secularization of the modern world. Yet in justifying Judaism through the use of an idealization, we see that Cohen is tracing a different account of public reasoning. Cohen claims the lawfulness of the moral law itself can be traced as Judaism's contribution to the history of reason. Hence, this kind of idealizing strategy allows Cohen to "forward a different root of the ancient world, rather what becomes even a root power of our German Idealism. And there will come the time when no contrast, much less a contradiction, is seen between the Jewish and Greek sources of modern religiousness, which both united in Christianity."[172] Cohen redefines the meaning of idealism through the contribution of Jewish monotheism. Monotheism within idealism creates a different public rationality. Thus, taking his historical cue from Hegel's notion of determinate religion, Cohen's narrative of reason turns to the form of ethical culture (*Sittlichkeit*) in order to demonstrate the possibility of monotheistic culture.

The historical scope of law occupies a significant role in Cohen's thought. In the prophetic description of Israel's election and the relationship between Israel and humanity, Cohen sees a precursor to his own attempt to employ the lawfulness of reason as the unity in difference. Hence, Cohen sees law as the vehicle for justifying Judaism both in terms of history and in light of his own contemporary encounter with the Jewish Question.[173] Against claims that a "purer form of Christianity" at the root of German national identity should exclude any link to Judaism,[174] Cohen envisions both an idealized Christianity and Judaism as the two pillars on which German culture had been nurtured. Hence, the monotheistic element of the law dictates that "the unique God [*einzige Gotte*] does not give particular commands for a particular people, but gives commandments that *ought to be* valid as *laws* for all peoples."[175] The law is a vehicle for translating commandment into law. In sharing monotheism as the root of their morality, Cohen claims, both Christian and Jewish Germans therefore find common ground in the idealism and transcendence of this monotheistic morality.[176] For Cohen, Jewish law must both be divorced from the Pauline polemic against legalism[177] and be philosophically translated as a normative idea of ethics, since "the law wants to be valued as the ground of the ethical world [*das Gesetz will als Grundgesetz der sittlichen Welt gelten*]."[178] Law has the capacity to traverse the historical spectrum between past and future norms. Thus, Cohen suggests that this idealization of Jewish law as morality is the work required by the duty of justification instilled in the German spirit by the Reformation. This is the work required by the idea of religion introduced by the Reformation, which enabled the independent pursuit of the "ethical side of religion."[179]

Idealism therefore becomes the method of public reasoning that negotiates social and political difference as well as shared history. Idealization both provides the basis for minoritizing what seem to be universals, such as religion or reason, and thereby shows where our ideas come from. While even the philological and philosophical bias of Christianity within the study of religion has led to a prejudice that "one's own religion more or less recognizes and specifies itself as absolute religion," the method of idealizing interpretation by contrast has the advantage of enabling one "to also idealize *other religions*, in that one simultaneously develops a distinction according to their conceptual determinations."[180] Idealization therefore recognizes the goal of a public moral culture and seeks to negotiate a way toward such a reality by taking seriously the plurality of religions.

Despite Cohen's insistence both on normativity within reasoning and on the project of democratizing reason and religion to recognize Judaism's contribution to moral culture, both public and intellectual perceptions of the transformations of secularization and rationalization varied dramatically from Cohen's minority account. While it was certain that natural scientific thought had established itself as the new barometer of objectivity, the metaphysical impulse to seek truth, meaning, and value in something more concrete than reason alone was gaining currency as well.

Weber warned, for example, that modern life was increasingly disaffecting the youth, who were striving for "idols whose cult today occupies a broad place on all street corners and in all periodicals. These idols are 'personality' and 'personal experience.'"[181] This, or something similar, Weber claimed, "is one of the fundamental watchwords one hears among the German youth, whose feelings are attuned to religion or who crave religious experiences. They crave not only religious experience but experience as such. The only thing that is strange is the method that is now followed: the spheres of the irrational, the only spheres that intellectualism has not yet touched, are now raised into consciousness and put under its lens."[182] The longing for something concrete to fill the void that religious experience once occupied, was lured into other domains. In the turn toward the concrete—toward life, experience, and the religiously infused meaning of this immediacy—the novelty of the irrational recast pleas for reasoning such as Cohen's as part of the larger disenchanting process. As we will see in the next section, Cohen worried about the irrational and mythic force of appeals to immediacy, because of its naive and yet very real immediacy. Indeed, liberalism—both past and present—most clearly fails to grapple with this appeal of irrationality on account of misunderstanding what animates this longing. By treating irrationality as beyond reason, liberalism ignores how the appeal to irrationality is an attempt to reenchant. Cohen worried both intellectually and politically—and it should continue to worry proponents of liberal rationality—that the enchantment of irrationality was not only real but also growing ever more palpable in German culture. We can therefore return to the question of why Cohen, as a member of a minority, would insist on this normative structure to knowledge and insist on its Protestant history. The answer is located primarily in the rise of a new secular worldview that was also animated by materialism, pantheism, and natural science: political anti-Semitism.

SECULARISM, METAPHYSICS, AND THE JEWISH QUESTION

In contrast to the metaphysical impulse of materialism, Cohen called direct attention to scientific reason as a discursive entity. He defined reason through practices of reasoning and understood reasoning as open to all who can access and read books and participate in this cultural education of *Bildung*. But as we saw above, the lure of materialism was its appeal to a directly accessible spiritual quality immanent within nature itself. Indeed, the failure to distinguish between materiality and the scientific language that represents material as a meaningful object represented an ideological blindness to the implicit value and valuation made by scientific discourse. Value-neutral science fared no better in assessing the role that such reenchantment plays, committing itself to a belief in science's neutrality. Thus, Cohen worried that without being self-reflexive about the labor of reasoning, scientific reason would be susceptible to uncritical and unjustified assertions of substitute absolutes as the bases for new worldviews. Whether this absolute took the shape of materialism and pantheism or the neutral, universal rationality of the liberal pattern of value-neutral science, Cohen saw a threat to public reasoning in culture.

Cohen was not merely expressing an abstract anxiety. As Weber articulated, Germany's intellectual crises were resonating with the larger public, who were yearning for meaning, experience, and value. This trend is illustrated in the growing influence of the nationalist *völkisch* movement, who advocated for a "return" to the concreteness of a *Volksgemeinschaft*, or folk-community, as in the imagined ancient Teutonic past.[183] This appeal to a mythic past as the concrete source of German identity was hardly a fringe movement; it gained institutional sanction, as evidenced in the public memorialization of ancient Germanic figures.[184] While Cohen insisted that religion is a concept that transcends historical and material particularities, the rise of *völkisch* political theology in the early 1900s represented an attempt to deduce a new spiritual movement in response to disenchantment.[185] In Cohen's view, the attempt to sanction moral and spiritual values by appealing to the material fact of a people expressed the growing metaphysical lure of pantheism and materialism. Moreover, while Cohen saw the state as a space in which Jews and Christians could critically examine their histories and cultivate a shared nation,[186] he observed an offshoot of the metaphysical materialism of monism alive in concepts of national spirit, linking blood, soil, and reason with the national ethos of a people.[187] The *völkisch* movement's designs on national identity thus imbued citizenship with a metaphysical texture. Hence, to be a German in this context would also require abiding by the metaphysical norms and justifications provided by a material, if not altogether biological stock (*Herkunft*).

In this climate, we can see why Cohen became increasingly anxious about pantheism and materialism. Representing a metaphysical reinvigoration of the Jewish Question, the elevated position of monism as a quasi-scientific and quasi-spiritual doctrine provided methodological cover for the spread of anti-Semitism. Indeed, Ernst Häckel's monism was in large part a rebellion against the values of Western civilization, claiming the latter, writes Daniel Gasman, "and especially Christianity, with its doctrines of weakness and submission, represented an intrusion into the functioning of nature and, as a consequence, had fatally disturbed the evolutionary balance between man and the natural world." Häckel's monism therefore also rejected the dualism "postulated by the Jews, as the creators of the monotheistic God,"[188] and the consequential projection of laws onto nature. As a prelude to later fascist ideologies, monism thus called "for the destruction of the values and historical consciousness of the West that had been shaped by transcendental religious and moral teachings." According to the monists, "there were deeper, more authentic, natural laws determining the nature of human existence—omnipresent Monist laws—and these had to be accorded free rein in defining the course of politics as well as all other domains of social and historical existence."[189] This appeal to lawfulness in nature inspired the *völkisch* movement and, viewed in light of the Materialism Controversy of the 1850s and 1860s, was more than political rabble-rousing. Instead, the methodology of the natural sciences was implicated in a debate over cultural and moral values, where materialist determinism and Darwinism began to shake the bedrock of traditional religion in Germany.[190] The academic debates of the late nineteenth century were thus spilling over into real life social and political movements, and the stakes were that much higher for Jews, who were only now mounting a politics aimed at negotiating secularization. However, secularizing the Jewish Question meant that Jews were no longer simply marked as a religious other; within such a scientific worldview, Jews were being racially categorized as others beyond the pale of public reasoning.

The significance of secularization within the frame of the Jewish Question is crucial to understanding both Cohen's approach to Judaism as a religion and his critique of science for the sake of public reasoning. The Jewish Question was first named as an implicit anxiety within the sphere of Enlightenment liberalism. With the publication of Christian Wilhelm von Dohm's *Über die bürgerliche Verbesserung der Juden* (1781), the rhetoric of Enlightenment civility, moral education, and *Bildung* led to a discussion of whether the Jews could exhibit such expressions of reason. Perhaps, with proper moral education, the state could ensure that the Jews be given "instruction . . . in the pure and holy truths of reason, and especially on the relationship of all citizens to the state and their duties to it."[191] Citizenship, as Mendelssohn would also agree, must consist of the state's refusal to coerce what could never have been given up in the social contract, the liberty of conscience. According to Mendelssohn, the state must distinguish between the moral education of persuasion and reasoning and the distinct sphere of religion. The latter must be

separable in order to guarantee the right of conscience.[192] By the time
Bruno Bauer authored his pamphlet, *The Jewish Question* (1843), to which
Marx famously responded, the Prussian bureaucracy had already been
steadily adapting to the major tenets of the Enlightenment, with education reform aimed at encouraging such civic development.[193]

However, if the Jewish Question really was a question, it was deliberately posed as one without an answer. Prussian Jews received equal
rights with their first, limited emancipation in 1812, but this did not settle
the matter. Indeed, to speak of *the* Jewish Question is quite misleading,
since there were multiple questions associated with the modern Jewish
Question. Could the Jews give up their corporate or national identity
to become members of the nations of Europe? Were the Jews capable of
moral autonomy, or were they bound to a revelation of statutes? Would
equality lead to conversion? While full emancipation was guaranteed with
German unification in 1871, one solution to the Jewish Question brought
many Wilhelmine Jews to recognize that the *modern* Jewish Question was
no longer really about equal political rights (*Gleichberechtigung*) but rather
about the Christian cultural character of the German national entity.[194]
Yet liberalism insisted that legal rights could be apportioned independent
of religion. Indeed, in the halcyon days of German liberal advances, between 1873 and 1890, no fewer than five hundred publications on the Jewish Question were printed.[195] At the apex of German liberal and national
prominence, the height of neo-Kantian philosophical influence as well,
anti-Semitism became a more defined ideological movement. Moreover,
these were the formative years of Cohen's career at the University of Marburg (an epicenter of the growing political anti-Semitism of the 1880s and
1890s), where his hiring was the result of a liberalizing shift in the universities and state institutions.[196] Thus, the purportedly Christian character of German identity imagined by the *völkisch* and later anti-Semitic
movements was not about an appeal to theological legitimacy. The Jewish Question was not solely about rights but also about the secularizing
discourse that placed religion, reason, and now biological racialization at
the focus of national identity in an increasingly liberal and secular society.

Cohen, like many German Jews, nevertheless held dear the ideals of the
Enlightenment, particularly the ideal of education as a path to citizenship
and equal rights (*Bildunsbürgertum*).[197] But Cohen's faith in the Enlightenment to navigate such issues also stemmed from his commitment to

transcendental idealism as a method of reasoning. Thus in 1881—the centenary year of Kant's first edition of the *Kritik der reinen Vernunft* (1781)—Cohen wrote a new foreword to Lange's highly influential *Geschichte des Materialismus*. In his foreword, Cohen provides a succinct defense of the Kantian form of reason as the "shibboleth of the present and the solution to the future."[198] Cohen's reinterpretation of Kant, which I explored briefly above and will return to in the following chapter, was influenced by Lange to a great degree, and Cohen's insistence that reason cannot be reduced to the psychological components of the human mind should be reconsidered in light of the dramatic social dislocation facing the Jews. For Cohen, reason cannot be found in race, biology, or peoplehood. Rather, as quoted earlier, Cohen claims that the "transcendental method does not proceed according to the principles of human reason, but rather according to the conditioned ground laid out for the sciences as scientifically valid."[199] Cohen insists that the liberal Protestant democratization of reasoning found in the Enlightenment and crystallized in Kantian critique defines science as knowledge that cannot be reduced to biological human reason. However, materialism would soon be mobilized toward justifying a contrary view amid the ascendant social Darwinism of the later nineteenth century.

In Cohen's view, materialism was therefore complicit in fueling the new racial anti-Semitism of the 1880s. Thus, science also had its perversions. Indeed, Cohen found himself in 1880, "in the nation of Kant," required to confess his position on the Jewish Question. Cohen's response to the German nationalist historian Heinrich von Treitschke's anti-Semitic indictment of Jewish chauvinism demonstrated the social and political value of Cohen's Kantian faith in the Enlightenment. In addressing a reply to Treitschke, Cohen claims he intends "to deal most notably with this *religious* point of view of the *Judenfrage*, not as a speaker on behalf of a Jewish party, rather as a representative of philosophy in a German institution of higher learning and one who confesses [*Bekenner*] Israelite monotheism."[200] From the beginning, Cohen identifies the degree to which religion displaces the racial question from dominating a discussion of citizenship and nation.[201] His self-identification is therefore telling, since Cohen wants to stress the *scientific* definition of religion as precisely the overlooked dimension of the Jewish Question. Moreover, in order to prove Treitschke's opinions are scientifically and philosophically bankrupt, Cohen makes an argument about the conceptual nature of religion. To this end, Cohen begins by arguing that, citing Kant, just as distinct historical types of faith corresponding to different religious texts are simply vehicles of the one religion of reason, so too the religious *books* shared by Jews and their Christian fellow citizens should bind them to the hope for a "purer form of religion."[202] That is, for Cohen, "in the scientific concept of religion it is not possible to recognize a difference between Israelite monotheism and Protestant Christianity."[203] With such an understanding of religion, the German nation can therefore become the site on which a new religious consciousness of civic nationalism can be built. Indeed, as Cohen claims, "it is a false liberal template, which unfortunately many Jews have adopted, that religious form is a matter of political indifference and that the state ought not to concern itself with it." By contrast, therefore, Cohen contends that

> the Church should in no way become appalled by the state; but the task is to produce [*herzustellen*] such a religious constitution that is fair and equal, obtaining in the cultural formation [*Bildung*] of the German state.
>   A nation that wants to establish and strengthen its civic-existence [*staatliches Dasein*] has to take care of its religious foundation. What belongs to a single people [*Einem Volke*] must have a share in this common religious ground. By this commonality, without harming the harmonious [*einmütigen*] national morality, confessional differences concerning historical tradition may yet be maintained, on account of having interpretations—the scientific as well as the pedagogic—that are reconcilable with a modern state, only so long as this can take place upon the site of such general religio-ethical foundations.[204]

Cohen sees the scientific concept of religion, of the cultural and philosophical construct of the moral foundations of a nation, as the basis for the construction of a new national identity. As late as 1917, Cohen would find himself again defending such a view of religion when discussing the national state (*Nationalstaat*).[205] Once again, Cohen focuses on religion as a way of negotiating the debated question of constitutional law, concerning whether the state or the nation is prior.[206] In both 1880–81 and 1917, Cohen rallied science to his side in order to explain how religion must be understood as an ideality, a position that Protestantism's epistemological revolution had first made possible. In other words, for Cohen the Jewish Question is the religion question.

Cohen's methodological arguments beginning in the 1880s are therefore ones that concern the social security of the Jews. But as Cohen would note in his more public writings, "Public polemic is not my affair. My business [*meine sache*] is *Wissenschaft*."[207] Science would therefore serve as the forum for Cohen's critical assessment of the German Jews. And yet, while Cohen's task may not have been public polemic, he nevertheless treated science as an *ideal* and *public* affair, since "the sciences are laid out for us in printed books" whereas "no methodological means is available for us to ever gain reliable exact scientific information about even the simplest constituents of our spiritual being."[208] Published and disseminated across time and space in the eyes of the critical public, science is thus subject to public scrutiny and a more justifiable venue for debating social and cultural contributions to advancing both knowledge and the nation. Hence, if for Cohen the key to Kant's transcendental idealism is its public form, then the crux of debating the place of Jews in the public sphere, as I began to suggest in chapter 1, is emphasizing the ideality of religion, citizenship, and nation.

While Kant's account of public reason served as an ideal guiding practical philosophy in the nineteenth century, this recognition and differentiation of religion in the public sphere did not guarantee that a cultural minority such as the Jews could be and should be treated as a religion (Judaism) rather than as a nation (Jewishness).[209] Yet these two inflections of Jewish identity—as religion and nation—are dialectically positioned to express the growing surge of liberalism and the consequent backlash of anti-Semitism.[210] Implicit in the public reason of Kant's account of enlightenment was a capacity for historical self-reflexivity that only Christians were believed to possess.

Thus, Treitschke's emphasis on Christian citizenship was hardly novel. But his view demonstrates the degree to which political anti-Semitism no longer needed to expend energy providing arguments for the metaphysics underlying the nation. Rather, materialism and historicism were now presupposed. For example, as early as 1844 the erstwhile young Hegelian Constantin Frantz articulated a similar view when he claimed that since a "*Volk* is shaped by the collective sharing of its God," the Jews could never be *citizens*. Rather, "they can form neither a people nor a state, nor can they decompose themselves through mixtures into the Christian peoples and states. ... Emancipation is an empty word. Not only is it inadmissible in itself; it would also be unsuccessful. Jews always remain Jews and are thereby in their innermost being excluded from Christian history."[211] Because the structure of history was Christian, the modern nation-state was grounded in the course of that history. Secularization was the hegemony of Christian history, and the Jews would remain outsiders in both Frantz and Treitschke's definitions of the *Volk*. Irreducibly other in this history, the Jews remained locked into their material and historical individuality. Hence, the very historicizing of modern institutions had self-reflexively placed its Christian heritage at the center of a secular self-assertion of truth-value. Insofar as religion is named by politics, recognizing its place within the state required that religion present itself as Christian.

CONCLUSION: RELIGION, NATION, AND SECULARITY

Cohen's idealization of both Protestantism and Judaism as inflections of a modern public religion—a religion subject to public reasoning—reveals the limits of liberalism's immanent turn to embrace secularization as the rule of neutral reason. By desecularizing the German nation, consciously reworking its national religion on the basis of the historical self-reflexivity of its Protestant epistemology, Cohen's account of public reasoning does not seek to eliminate difference and diversity. Rather, it seeks to expand reason—to broaden what counts as reasoning. For Cohen, the Jewish Question therefore reflects the consequence of neglecting the implicit role of politics, ethics, and religion in the shaping of science, as well as of public civic life and moral culture. If ethics should have any meaning, Cohen thought, then anti-Semitism cannot continue to "distract us from understanding the task of a truly open social policy." In Cohen's view, the legacy and remaining goal of the Reformation was to deepen the unity of all people with the unity of God. Without such a goal, all talk of social progress, indeed, "all ethics remains empty and insincere, and all attempts to deepen religion remain unsubstantiated and afloat in unhistorical air when the original source of the pure belief in God, the living people still guarding it today, are neglected, bypassed, tarnished, and inhibited. This poses the most severe damage to ethics and for culture the next greatest harm to religion."[212] So long as anti-Semitism continues to manifest in supposedly cultured intellectual milieus of German public discourse, Cohen warns, neither ethics nor religion can be said to participate in the public sphere. Ethics must become the entry point for religion, as the translation or "the *Aufnahme* of religion into ethics."[213] That is, if the social struggle for equality, recognition, and rights is to have any chance of negotiating both the historical and political prejudices of the modern state, then ethics must become a philosophical keystone that can place the idea of God in a public forum. By enabling religious individuals to be free persons capable of community with each other[214]—capable, that is, of an ethical socialism[215]—this shared norm of a monotheistic God would further democratize public reasoning. Only ethics is capable of reformulating public reasoning as the reasoning of those who seek to build a culture together.

But whereas Cohen envisioned such an ethical labor as a work of scientific rigor, it was likewise the pretense to scientific progress that parasitically harnessed the power of materialism and biologism in the natural sciences to fuel the growing racial inflection of the Jewish Question. As I argued, the attempt to stave off the rise of organized secularism led liberals like Weber to cordon off science as a neutral domain. But Cohen saw the threat of such an account of reason and science as hypostatized, neutral abstractions that granted claims to materiality and objectivity an air of sanctity; instead, his method of idealization sought to minoritize science and show where it came from. To do this, Judaism played an eminent role in his ethical idealism as an example of a public morality shaped through its critical engagement with the concept of a religion—a Protestant inheritance—that made possible the idealization of Judaism. Thus, monotheism, normativity, and a conception of moral culture helped push Cohen's idealism into the explicit work of making scientific reason self-reflexive and responsive to this minoritization. Ethical idealism thus became a vehicle for renegotiating the secular.

Emancipation, Cohen claimed, had definitively demonstrated the importance of religion for the modern state, since "a great principle of momentous significance for all questions of culture is established in this recognition of our religion within public law."[216] However, as Cohen noted, the problem with an established church is that it politicizes religion. Indeed, Cohen understands Christianity as opposed to the very idea of a racial nation or state, since its principle is universal. All the more so, the "principle of the Reformation contradicts just as much the notion of a Christian state."[217] Following this logic, Bismarck's attempt to legitimate the German Empire by giving the Protestant Church both an official and cultural-national status as a Prussian, "Christian State," therefore proved detrimental to Christianity.[218] Such a political Christianity leads to the secularization of religion as a state function, in Cohen's reading. This established religion is no longer Protestant, since citizens no longer exchange reasons with one another in the cultural sphere but are required to confess a legal obligation.

By contrast, the recognition of a freedom *from* state religion demonstrates the degree to which Judaism is indebted to Protestantism because of this creation of a public sphere in which justified knowledge is so central. For Cohen, idealism provides an answer to such questions about the legitimacy of values, institutions, and knowledge because it seeks to historically justify ideas that have future possibility. Religion becomes a resource for this kind of public reasoning by helping renew and idealize the concepts of law and state such that society "can be brought to a higher actuality, though one still in itself in need of a further improvement."[219] For Cohen, the need for justified reasoning, for a public reasoning that is democratized to include all voices but also contextualized as a canon with rules for such reasoning, serves to foster this new dimension of liberalism in a space between the state and the individual: namely, the "moral idea of society."[220]

NOTES

1. Jürgen Habermas, *Legitimation Crisis* (Boston: Beacon, 1975); Reinhart Koselleck, *Critique and Crisis: Enlightenment and the Pathogenesis of Modern Society* (Cambridge, MA: MIT Press, 1988).

2. Charles Taylor, *A Secular Age* (Cambridge, MA: Harvard University Press, 2008), 142.

3. Woodruff Smith, *Politics and the Sciences of Culture in Germany, 1840–1920* (New York: Oxford University Press, 1991), 9.

4. Smith, 22–24.

5. Kuno Fischer describes Fries as having developed an "anthropological" dimension to Kantianism, which interpreters have understood as Fries's "psychologist" reading of Kant. While Fischer stresses the antimetaphysical stance of Fries, in contrast he presents Herbart's psychology as a "metaphysics." Kuno Fischer, *Die beiden kantischen Schulen in Jena* (Stuttgart: Cota, 1862), 17–20, 10–13; cf. Frederick C. Beiser, *The Genesis of Neo-Kantianism, 1796–1880* (New York: Oxford University Press, 2014), 23n.

6. On the influence on the young Cohen and the southwestern neo-Kantian Wilhelm Windelband and the psychological interpretations of

Kantianism as a source of neo-Kantianism in the late 1790s, see Beiser, *Genesis of Neo-Kantianism*, 17–20.

7. On "sensualism and materialism" as scientific absolutes, see Klaus Christian Köhnke, *Entstehung und Aufstieg des Neukantianismus: Die deutsche Universitätsphilosophie zwischen Idealismus und Positivismus* (Frankfurt am Main: Surhkamp, 1986), 109; cf. Thomas Wiley, *Back to Kant: The Revival of Kant in German Social and Historical Thought* (Detroit: Wayne State University Press, 1978). Cf. Beiser's earlier dating of the origins of neo-Kantianism in Beiser, *Genesis of Neo-Kantianism*. See also Ulrich Sieg, *Aufstieg und Niedergang des Marburger Neukantianismus: Die Geschichte einer philosophischen Schulgemeinschaft* (Würzburg: Königshausen und Neumann, 1993).

8. On the growing emphasis on empiricism in the humanities, see Otto Gerhard Oexel, "Krise des Histrorismus, Krise der Wirklichkeit: Eine Problemgeshichte der Moderne," in *Krise des Historismus, Krise der Wirklichkeit, Wissenschaft, Kunst und Literatur 1880–1932* (Göttingen: Vendenhoeck & Ruprecht, 2007), 11–116.

9. Friedrich Adolf Trendelenburg and Hermann Lotze had been developing such a reworking of idealism from early in the 1830s and 1840s. See Frederich C. Beiser, *Late German Idealism: Trendelenburg and Lotze* (New York: Oxford University Press, 2013).

10. Köhnke, *Entstehung und Aufstieg*, 110.

11. Köhnke, 110.

12. Friedrich Adolf Trendelenburg, *Logische Untersuchungen*, 3rd ed. (Leipzig: S. Hirzel, 1870), 1:170.

13. Cf. Beiser, *Late German Idealism*, 28.

14. Beiser, 28.

15. Köhnke, *Entstehung und Aufstieg*, 109.

16. See for example Gillian Rose's critical comments on neo-Kantianism "logicism" and "method" as a new form of metaphysics in *Hegel Contra Sociology* (London: Althone, 1995), 13.

17. Charles Darwin, *The Origin of Species*, The Harvard Classics, ed. Charles W. Eliot (New York: P.F. Collier & Son, 1909), 9.

18. Beiser, *Late German Idealism*, 239–49.

19. Beiser, 242.

20. Rudolf Wagner, *Ueber Wissen und Glauben mit besonderer Beziehung zur Zukunft der Seele* (Göttingen: Georg H. Wigand, 1854), iii–iv.

21. Beiser, *After Hegel: German Philosophy, 1840–1900* (Princeton, NJ: Princeton University Press, 2014), 60.

22. Karl Vogt, *Köhlerglaube und Wissenschaft: Eine Streitschrift gegen Hofrath Wagner in Göttingen* (Gießen: Ricker, 1856), 121–22. Cf. Beiser, *Late German Idealism*, 243–44.

23. On the Materialism Controversy more generally, see Frederick Gregory, *Scientific Materialism in Nineteenth-Century Germany* (Dodrecht: Springer, 1977); Beiser, *After Hegel*, 53–96.

24. Ersnt Häckel, "Über die Entwicklungslehre Darwins" (1863), in *Gemeinverständlich Vorträge und Abhandlungen aus dem Gebiet der Entwicklungslehre*, 2nd ed. (Bonn: Emil Strauß, 1902). On Häckel's relationship with Darwin and his defense of Darwinism in Germany, see Robert Richards, *The Tragic Sense of Life: Ernst Haeckel and the Struggle over Evolutionary Thought* (Chicago: University of Chicago Press, 2008), 94–104. Cf. Beiser, *After Hegel*, 55–56.

25. See Marc D. Chapman, *Ernst Troeltsch and Liberal Theology: Religion and Cultural Synthesis in Wilhelmine Germany* (New York: Oxford University Press, 2001), 76.

26. Ernst Häckel, *Die Welträtsel*, 13th edition (Leipzig: Alfred Kröner Verlag, 1922), 229.

27. Häckel, *Welträtsel*, 309.

28. See Ernst Häckel, *Monism as Connection Religion and Science: The Confession of Faith of a Man of Science*, trans. J. Gilchrist (London: Adam and Charles Black, 1895).

29. On monism and pantheism in the popular scientific consciousness of mid-nineteenth-century Germany and its role in organized secularism see Todd H. Weir, *Secularism and Religion in Nineteenth-Century Germany: The Rise of the Fourth Confession* (New York: Cambridge University Press, 2014), 117–29. See also Horst Groschopp, *Dissidenten—Freidenkerei und Kultur in Deutschland* (Berlin: Dietz Verlag, 1997), 243–98.

30. Weir, *Secularism and Religion*, 192–95, 256–67.

31. Ernt Häckel, *Der Monistenbund: Thesen zur Organisation des Monismus* (Frankfurt am Main: Neue Frankfurt Verlag, 1905).

32. Groschopp, *Dissidenten*, 246–52.

33. Weir, *Secularism and Religion*, 100.

34. See for example the juxtaposition of religion and science as social forms, citing Häckel in particular, in B. Saphra "Staat und Kirche," *Ost und West* 19, nos. 5–6 (1919): 127–38, 130

35. Jürgen Habermas, "Conceptions of Modernity: A Look Back at Two Traditions" in *The Postnational Constellation: Political Essays*, trans. Max Pensky (Cambridge, MA: MIT Press, 2001), 130–56, 134. See also Reinhart Koselleck, *Critique and Crisis*.

36. Hermann Cohen, "Spinoza on Christianity and Judaism," in *Hermann Cohens Jüdischen Schriften*, vols. 1–3, ed. Bruno Strauss with an introduction by Franz Rosenzweig (Berlin: C. A. Schwetschke & Sohn/Verlagsbuchhandlung, 1924) (hereafter cited as *JS*), 3:363, 371, and *Hermann Cohens Werke*, ed. H. Holzhey, 17 vols. (New York: G. Olms, 1978–) (hereafter cited as *Werke*), 16:414, 424; Cohen, "Spinozas Verhältnis zum Judentum," *Werke* 15: *Hermann Cohens Werke, Kleinere Schriften*, vols. 12–17 of *Werke*, 6 vols. (hereafter cited as *KS*) 4, *1907–1912*, 347–88; see Franz Nauen, "Hermann Cohen's Perceptions of Spinoza: A Reappraisal," *AJS Review*, no. 4 (1979): 111–24, 118

37. Oexel, "Krise des Historismus," 11–116; Reinhart Koselleck, *Critique and Crisis*. I discuss the consequences of these debates for Cohen's philosophy in greater detail in chapter 2.

38. As Köhnke, *Entstehung und Aufstieg*, 264, and Beiser, *Genesis of Neo-Kantianism*, 3, have noted, Liebmann's comments were an echo of earlier declarations of an ongoing return to Kant. Liebmann's call highlighted the mistakes in Kant's reception history; see Otto Liebmann, *Kant und die Epigonen, Eine kritische Abhandlung* (Stuttgart: Carl Schober, 1865), 15. Thus, many neo-Kantians first established themselves as historians of philosophy; see Beiser, *Genesis of Neo-Kantianism*, 221–24, 283–327, 356–97.

39. Friedrich Albert Lange, *Geschichte des Materialismus und Kritik seiner Bedeutung*, 1st ed. (Leipzig: Iserlohn: J. Baedeker, 1866). See Beiser's discussion of the Materialismusstreit and the rise of Darwinism in *Genesis of Neo-Kantianism*, 422–54.

40. Lange, *Geschichte*, 550, excerpt translated in Sebastian Luft (ed.), *The Neo-Kantian Reader* (New York: Routledge, 2015), 63–78, 74.

41. Lange, *Geschichte*, 556, 77 (Eng.).

42. Lange, 71.

43. On the nuanced account of materialism in Lange and its influence upon later nineteenth century Jewish thinkers, see Eliyahu Stern, *Jewish Materialism: The Intellectual Revolution of the 1870s* (New Haven: Yale University Press, 2018)

44. Lange, *Geschichte*, 71.

45. See Cohen's comments in his biographical foreword to Lange, *Geschichte des Materialismus und seiner Bedeutung in der Gegenwart*, 2nd ed. (Iserlohn & Leipzig: J. Baedeker, 1887), xi (hereafter cited as "Vorwort," 1887)

46. Lange, *Geschichte*, 68 (Eng.).

47. For an overview of Lange's foray in the *Materialismusstreit*, see Beiser, *After Hegel*, 89–96. See also his discussion of Darwinism in Beiser, *Genesis of Neo-Kantianism*, 285.

48. Cohen, "Einleitung mit kritischem Nachtrag zu Langes Geschichte des Materialismus," in *Schriften zur Philosophie und Zeitgeschichte*, ed. Albert Görland and Ernst Cassirer (Berlin: Akademie Verlag, 1928), 2:199 (hereafter cited as *EkN*).

49. *EkN*, 201.

50. Hermann Cohen, *System der Philosophie, Zweiter Teil: Ethik des reinen Willens* (Berlin: Bruno Cassirer, 1904; repr. in *Werke* 7) (hereafter cited as *ErW*), 275 (1st ed.).

51. In addition to Häckel's own claim of Spinoza as a progenitor, there was no shortage of publications that sought to link monism and pantheism, especially for those animated by the spiritualizing tendencies of materialism. Consider the early example of Robert Wirth, *Ueber Monismus (Pantheismus) mit Berücksichtigung der "Philosophie des Unbewussten"* (Plauen i.V.: F.E.

Neupert, 1874); as well as the later influence on Jewish thinkers, as reviewed by J. Lewkowitz, "Häckels 'Welträtsel' und die Religion," *Monatschrift für Geschichte und Wissenschaft des Judentums* 48, new series, 12 (1904): 257–67; and, Isaac Rülf, *Wissenschaft des Einheits-Gedanken: System einer neuen Metaphysik, II:3, Wissenschaft der Gotteseinheit (Theo-Monismus)* (Leipzig: Hermann Haacke, 1903).

52. First published in 1899, Chamberlain's *Die Grundlagen des Neunzehnten Jahrhunderts* (München: Bruckmann, 1909) was in its fourteenth edition by 1922.

53. Hermann Cohen, "Der Jude in der christlichen Kultur," translated in Alan Mittleman, "'The Jew in Christian Culture' by Hermann Cohen: An Introduction and Translation," *Modern Judaism* 23, no. 1 (2003): 51–73, 67 (translation modified).

54. See, for example, Cohen, "Spinozas Verhältnis," 360–61.

55. Gregory, *Scientific Materialism*, 31–32.

56. Peter Harrison, *The Bible, Protestantism, and the Rise of Natural Science* (New York: Cambridge University Press, 1998), 4, 91, 107–8.

57. Beiser, *Genesis of Neo-Kantianism*, 182–84.

58. On philosophy's identity crisis, see Köhnke, *Entstehung und Aufstieg*, 23–57, 109; Beiser, *After Hegel*, 17.

59. Hermann Cohen, *System der Philosophie, Erster Teil: Logik der reinen Erkenntnis* (Berlin: Bruno Cassirer, 1902; repr. in *Werke* 6) (hereafter cited as *LrE*), 289–90; cf. Ernst Cassirer, *Substanzbegriff und Funktionsbegriff: Untersuchungen über die Grundfragen der Erkenntnistheorie* (Berlin: Bruno Cassirer, 1910).

60. See Hermann Lotze, *System der Philosophie: Erster Theil, Drei Bucher der Logik* (Leipzig: Hirzel, 1874), 1:465–97, cited in Frederick C. Beiser, *The German Historicist Tradition* (New York: Oxford University Press, 2011), 369. On Lotze in particular, see Beiser, *Late German Idealism*, 179–87.

61. See Guy Oakes, *Weber and Rickert: Concept Formation in the Cultural Sciences* (Cambridge, MA: MIT Press, 1990).

62. Cohen instead describes the thing-in-itself as a task (*Aufgabe*) and a law. See *Kants Begrundung der Ethik* (Berlin: F. Dümmler, 1877; repr. in *Werke* 2), 43–45 (hereafter cited as *KBE*).

63. Rickert therefore tries to account for an objective path that "leads us directly to a transcendent value. . . . Value and ought do not coincide. . . . Only the value which rests on itself and holds valid as value . . . is the transcendent object." Heinrich Rickert, *Der Gegenstand der Erkenntnis: Einführung in die Transzendentalphilosophie* (Tübingen und Leipzig: JCB Mohr, 1921), 242, quoted in Andrea Staiti, "Heinrich Rickert," in *Stanford Encyclopedia of Philosophy*, ed. Edward N. Zalta (Stanford, CA: Stanford University, summer 2013), http://plato.stanford.edu/entries/heinrich-rickert/.

64. Beatrice Centi, "The Validity of Norms in Neo-Kantian Ethics" in *New Approaches to Neo-Kantianism*, ed. Nicholas de Warren and Andrea Staiti (Cambridge: Cambridge University Press, 2015), 135–37.

65. Cf. Heinrich Rickert, *Die Grenzen der naturwissenschaftlichen Begriffsbildung: Eine logische Einleitung in die historische Wissenschaften*, 2nd ed. (Tübingen: Mohr, 1913). On the "ideographic" nature of historical science and the "nomothetic" natural sciences, see Wilhelm Windelband, "Geschichte und Naturwissenschaft" (1894) in *Präludien* (Tübingen: Moher, 1907), 2:149–51; cf. Wilhelm Windelband, "Normen und Naturgesetze" in *Präludien*, 2:59–98; Beiser, *The German Historicist Tradition*, 400–401.

66. Hermann Cohen, *Das Prinzip der Infinitesimal-Methode und seine Geschichte*, in *Schriften zur Philosophie und Zeitgeschichte, zweiter Band*, ed. Albert Görland und Ernst Cassirer (Berlin: Akademie Verlag, 1928), 6 para. 8, reprinted in *Werke* 5.

67. On the *hiatus irrationalis* in Emil Lask and Heinrich Rickert, see Guy Oakes, "Introduction: Rickert's Theory of Historical Knowledge," in Heinrich Rickert, *The Limits of Concept Formation in Natural Science: A Logical Introduction to the Historical Sciences*, trans. Guy Oakes (New York: Cambridge University Press, 1986), viii, xvi, xxiii; xxvii.

68. *ErW*, 428.

69. Like idealism, Cohen claims, metaphysics "occupies itself with thinking." However, "insofar as this thinking sits amidst the all-embracing concept of consciousness" this resemblance to idealism is but a "deceptive illusion." Metaphysics insists that consciousness is a principle relating thinking and sensibility (*Empfindung*), which attempts to unify what Kant described as heterogeneous sources of knowledge. Metaphysics therefore wavers between "sensualism, spiritualism, including even materialism." In other words, by uniting the abstraction of understanding with the substance of sensibility, consciousness becomes a hidden source of material essences. *ErW*, 429.

70. See *ErW*, 156, where Cohen specifically criticizes the physiological theory of Johannes Peter Müller, whose work closely resembled that of Ernst Häckel.

71. *ErW*, 253.

72. Hermann Cohen, *Kants Theorie der Erfahrung, Werke* 1.3 (New York: Georg Olms, 1987), 9–10.

73. See Beiser, *The German Historicist Tradition*, 273–74, 372–73.

74. Rickert and the southwestern school insisted that the validity of the claims made according to either method were delimited by their respective science, therefore reinstituting to knowledge a dualism of nature and human. See Heinrich Rickert, *Kulturwissenschaft und Naturwissenschaft: ein Vortrag* (Tübingen und Leipzig: JCB Mohr, 1899). Cf. Rickert, *Die Grenzen der naturwissenschaftliche Begriffsbildung*, 225: "We look for the science not in its concept of its object but conversely the concept of the object from the concept of the science that deals with it." Quoted in Beiser, *The German Historicist Tradition*, 400–401.

75. *LrE*, 424–26.

76. Cohen, "Vorwort" (1887), x.

77. Comparing Cohen and Weber, see Hermann Kantorowicz's review in *Archiv für Sozialwissenschaft und Sozialpolitik*, no. 31 (1910): 602–6, cited in Gesine Palmer, "Judaism as Method with Hermann Cohen and Franz Rosenzweig," *Hermann Cohen's* Ethics, ed. Robert Gibbs (Boston: Brill, 2006), 37–63, 42.

78. See Guy Oakes, introduction to Max Weber, *Critique of Stammler*, trans. Guy Oakes (New York: Free Press, 1977); Oakes, *Weber and Rickert*.

79. Max Weber, "Agrarvehältnisse im Alterthum" quoted in editor's introduction to Max Weber, *Economy and Society: An Outline of Interpretive Sociology*, 2 vols. (Berkeley: University of California Press, 1978), xxxviii.

80. Weber, *Economy and Society*, 1:9.

81. Weber, *Economy and Society*, 1:20.

82. Max Weber, "Science as Vocation," in *The Vocation Lectures*, ed. David Owen and Tracy B. Strong, trans. Rodney Livingstone (Indianapolis: Hackett, 2004), 142.

83. Weber, "Science as Vocation," 138–39.

84. Weber, "Science as Vocation," 149.

85. Max Weber, "Objectivity in Social Science and Social Policy," in *Methodology of Social Sciences*, trans. Edward A Shils and Henry A. Finch (1949; repr. New Brunswick, NJ: Transaction, 2011), 55.

86. Cf. Anthony Carroll, "The Importance of Protestantism in Max Weber's Theory of Secularisation," *Archives Européenes de Sociologie* 50, no.1 (2009): 61–95.

87. Hermann Lübbe, *Säkularisierung: Geschichte eines ideenpolitischen Begriffs*, 2nd ed. (Munich: Karl Alber, 1975), 71–72.

88. Weber, "Objectivity," 91–92.

89. Todd H. Weir, "Germany and the New Global History of Secularism: Questioning the Postcolonial Genealogy," *Germanic Review: Literature, Culture, Theory* 90, no. 1 (2015): 6–20, 15–16. Weir echoes Lübbe's thesis as well.

90. Weber's insistence on value neutrality was a response to the problematic coincidence of German nationalism and anti-Semitism being preached from the lecture hall. Weber variously identifies Gustav von Schmoller, Heinrich von Treitschke, and Theodor Mommsem (to whom I return below) as examples of over-determined scholarship with political valuations. See Max Weber, "Der Sinn der 'Wertfreiheit' der soziologischen und ökonomischen Wissenschaften," in *Logos* no. 7 (1917): 40–88, translated as "The Meaning of 'Ethical Neutrality' in Sociology and Economics," in Weber, *Methodology of Social Sciences*, 1–48.

91. On the specific modes of temporality in Cohen's logic, see Pierfrancesco Fiorato, *Geschichtliche Ewigkeit: Ursprung und Zeitlichkeit in der Philosophie Hermann Cohens* (Würzburg: Königshausen & Neumann, 1993).

92. *LrE*, 35–36.

93. Robert Gibbs, *Correlations in Rosenzweig and Levinas* (Princeton, NJ: Princeton University Press, 1992), 49.

94. *LrE*, 154, 123.

95. *LrE*, 83–84.

96. *LrE*, 79.

97. *LrE*, 15.

98. *LrE*, 15.

99. *LrE*, 35–36, 90–91.

100. *LrE*, 395–403.

101. *LrE*, 528.

102. See chapter 3.

103. *ErW*, 86.

104. *LrE*, 88. See also Hermann Cohen, *Charakteristik Ethik Maimunis, JS* 3:227; translated as *Ethics of Maimonides*, trans. Almut Sh. Bruckstein (Madison: University of Wisconsin Press, 2004), para. 18: "even the good cannot become more than idea, and hence hypothesis. However, the content of ethics distinguishes the idea of the good from anything that is in the heavens and on earth. And so by means of this distinction in value of this content, [the good] for its sake as hypothesis, is granted a privileged terminology."

105. *ErW*, 44.

106. *LrE*, 16–18; *ErW*, 96, 204–5.

107. *LrE*, 604.

108. *LrE*, 612.

109. *ErW*, 65.

110. *ErW*, 83–84.

111. *ErW*, 270.

112. *ErW*, 271.

113. *ErW*, 272–73.

114. *ErW*, 274–76.

115. See Roscher's opening comments to volume two of his *Ansichten der Volkwirthschaft aus dem geschichtlichem Standpunkte*, 2 vols., 3rd ed. (Leipzig: Winter'sche Verlagshandlung, 1878), 3. Roscher had already explicitly tied this theory of natural economic laws to his theory of the centralization of state administration over entrepreneurial activity as well as agricultural production as shaped by the "*volksthümliche Elemente.*" See Wilhelm Roscher, *System der Volkwirthschaft: Ein Hand- und Lesebuch für Geschäftsmänner und Studierende, zweiter band: die Nationalökonomie und Landwirthschaft enthaltend*, 8th ed. (Stuttgart: J.G. Gotta'schen Buchhandlung, 1875), 539.

116. Schmoller describes both the physical-material conditions of human life and culture as well as a sphere of "Geist" and "Sittlichkeit," only to distinguish his *Moralstatistik* from full-fledged materialism. See Gustav von Schmoller, *Ueber die Resultate der Bevölkerungs- und Moral-Statistik* (Berlin: C.B. Lüderitz'sche Verlagsbuchhandlung, 1871), 14–26.

117. In the 1880s and 1890s, Carl Menger and Schmoller attacked each other's methodological assumptions with similar claims. The debate concerned the methodological grounding of economics as a human and cultural science

yet prefigured much more. See Aliki Lavranu, "Deskription, Causalität und Te-
leologie: Gustav Schmollers methodologischen und wissenschaftstheoretischen
Positionen im Anschluß an den 'Methodenstreit,'" in Oexle, *Krise des Historismus*, 181–206.

118. Yuichi Shionoya, "A Methodological Appraisal of Schmoller's Research
Program," in *The Theory of Ethical Economy in the Historical School: Wilhelm
Roscher, Lorenz von Stein, Gustav Schmoller, Wilhelm Dilthey and Contemporary
Theory*, ed. Peter Koslowski (Berlin: Springer, 1995), 60–61.

119. For a detailed overview of the so-called *Methodenstreit*, see Jürgen Back-
haus and Reginald Hansen, "Methodenstreit in der Nationalökonomie," *Journal
for General Philosophy of Science* 31, no. 2 (2000), 307–36. See also Oakes, introduction to Weber, *Critique of Stammler*.

120. Weber, *Critique of Stammler*; Weber, *Economy and Society*.

121. *ErW*, 292.

122. 292–93.

123. See chapter 3.

124. Cohen explains that the logic of idealism must be both systematic and
historical. *LrE*, 595.

125. Quoted in Andrea Poma, *The Critical Philosophy of Hermann Cohen*,
trans. John Denton (Albany: State University of New York, 1997), 5.

126. Hermann Cohen, *Religion der Vernunft aus den Quellen des Judentums*
(Wiesbaden: Fourier Verlag, 1966), 291–92. Published in English as *Reason of
Reason: Out of the Sources of Judaism*, trans. Simon Kaplan (Atlanta: Scholars
Press, 1995), 249–50 (hereafter cited as *RoR*), translation slightly modified.

127. See Robert Gibbs, "Lines, Circles, Points: Messianic Epistemology in
Cohen, Rosenzweig and Benjamin," in *Toward the Millennium: Messianic Ex-
pectations from the Bible to Waco*, ed. Peter Schäfer and Marc R. Cohen (Leiden:
Brill, 1998), 365.

128. *LrE*, 139–40.

129. 141–42.

130. 496.

131. On historicism and the controversies of the 1920s, see Oexel, "Krise des
Historismus," 49–52. Specific to Protestant theology, see Friedrich Wilhelm Graf,
"Geschichte durch Übergeschichte überwinden. Antihistoristisches Geschichts-
denken in der protestantischen Theologie der 1920er Jahre," in *Geschichtsdiskurs
4: Krisenbewusstsein, Katastrophenerfahrungen und Innovationen 1880-1945*, ed.
Wolfgang Küttler, et al. (Frankfurt am Maim: Fischer Taschenbuch Verlag, 1997),
217–44; Dietrich Korsch, "Hermann Cohen und die protestantische Theologie
seiner Zeit," in *Zeitschrift für Neue Theologiegeschichte*, no. 1 (1994): 66–96. See also
David N. Myers, *Resisting History: Historicism and Its Discontents in German-Jewish
Thought* (Princeton, NJ: Princeton University Press, 2009), 35–42.

132. Cf. Karl Barth, "Evangelical Theology in the Nineteenth Century,"
in *The Humanity of God*, trans. Thomas Wieser (Louisville, KY: Westminster

John Knox, 1960), 14; Samuel Moyn, "From Existence to Law: Leo Strauss and the Weimar Crisis of the Philosophy of Religion," *History of European Ideas* 33 (2007): 174–94.

133. Ernst Troelscth, "The Dogmatic of the 'Religionsgeschichtliche Schule'" *American Journal of Theology* 17, no. 1 (1913): 1–21; 12, cited in Chapman, *Ernst Troeltsch*, 46.

134. Consider Hermann Lübbe's thesis that both Tönnies and Weber identified secularization as a way of critically resisting the assertion of a "tyranny of values" on the part of either radical secularists or conservatives. See Lübbe, *Säkularisierung*, 68–72. Cf. Weir, "Germany and the New Global History of Secularism."

135. Max Weber, *The Protestant Ethic and the Spirit of Capitalism*, trans. Talcott Parsons (London: Routledge, 1992).

136. See Peter L. Berger, *The Sacred Canopy: Elements of a Sociological Theory of Religion* (New York: Anchor Books, 1967). For Berger's more recent reconsideration of the secularization thesis, see Peter L. Berger, "The Desecularization of the World: A Global Overview," in *The Desecularization of the World: Resurgent Religion and World Politics*, ed. Peter L. Berger (Grand Rapids, MI: Wm. B. Erdmans, 1999).

137. Weber, *Economy and Society*, 874; see also, Peter Lassman, "The Rule of Man over Man: Politics, Power, and Legitimation," in *The Cambridge Companion to Max Weber*, ed. Stephen Turner (New York: Cambridge University Press, 2000), 83–98, 97.

138. Carl Schmitt, *Politisches Theologie: Vier Kapitel über den Begriff der Souveranität* (München und Leipzig: Duncker und Humblot, 1922). English translation as *Political Theology: Four Chapters on the Concept of Sovereignty*, trans. George Schwab (Chicago: University of Chicago Press, 2005).

139. Schmitt, *Political Theology*, 42.

140. Hans Blumenberg, *The Legitimacy of the Modern Age*, trans. Robert M. Wallace (Cambridge, MA: MIT Press, 1983), 98–99.

141. Karl Löwith, *Meaning in History: The Theological Implications of the Philosophy of History* (Chicago: University of Chicago Press, 1949), 158–59.

142. Blumenberg, *Legitimacy of the Modern Age*, 64.

143. Blumenberg, 65.

144. Blumenberg, 69.

145. Beiser, *The German Historicist Tradition*, 5–6, and with regard to Max Weber in particular, 512, 534.

146. *LrE*, 424; cf. *ErW*, 155.

147. *EkN*, 302.

148. Gesine Palmer, "Judaism as a Method with Hermann Cohen and Franz Rosenzweig," in *Journal of Jewish Thought and Philosophy*, no. 13 (2006): 37–63.

149. *RoR*, 3

150. *RoR*, 3.

151. *RoR*, 4

152. *RoR*, 4.

153. *RoR*, 5.

154. *RoR*, 7.

155. *RoR*, 7.

156. *RoR*, 5.

157. Cf. Daniel H. Weiss, *Paradox and the Prophets: Hermann Cohen and the Indirect Communication of Religion* (Oxford: Oxford University Press, 2012).

158. *RoR*, 7.

159. Hermann Cohen, "Der Jude in der christlichen Kultur" in *Werke* 17, *KS* 6, *1916–1918*, 423; Cohen, "The Jew in Christian Culture," 62.

160. *EkN*, 279–80.

161. See, for example, Christian Wiese, *Challenging Colonial Discourse: Jewish Studies and Protestant Theology in Wilhelmine Germany*, trans. Barbara Harshav and Christian Wiese (Brill: Leiden, 2005), 289–350.

162. Hermann Cohen, "Deutschtum und Judentum," parts 1 (originally published 1915) and 2 (originally published 1916) in *JS* 2:237–318; reprinted in *Werke*, part 1 in *Werke* 16: *KS* 5:465–560; part 2 in *Werke* 17, *KS* 6:109–32; published in English as "Germanism and Judaism," in *Reason and Hope: Selections from the Jewish Writings of Hermann Cohen*, trans. Eva Jospe (Cincinnati: Hebrew Union College, 1992) (hereafter cited as *DuJ* 1 or 2), 1:496.

163. *DuJ* 1:496.

164. See, for example, Cohen to Hermann Lewandowsky, September 28, 1870, and Cohen to Louis and Helene Lewandowsky, September 22, 1871, in *Briefe*, eds. Martha and Bruno Strauss (Berlin: Shocken, 1939), 25–28, 33–34.

165. See Cohen to Hermann Lewandowsky, 1872, in *Briefe*, 42. Cf. Wendell Dietrich, *Cohen and Troeltsch: Ethical Monotheistic Religion and Theory of Culture* (Providence, RI: Brown Judaic Studies, 1986). Dietrich sees much of Cohen's polemic against Troeltsch within his overall systematic goals when he claims, "Cohen is convinced that Judaic ethical monotheism, not Christianity, is the most appropriate religious basis for modern culture as a whole" (17).

166. See Cohen's ambivalent comments regarding the postulates of practical reason in *KBE*, 357–66.

167. *ErW*, 87.

168. Cf. Cohen to Louis and Helene Lewandoswky, 33–34. Cohen would later provide a scathing critique of Moritz Lazarus's *Ethik des Judentums* on precisely the ground that it provides superficial apologetics rather than an account rooted in Judaism's ethical and legal sources. See Cohen's review, "Das Problem der jüdischen Sittenlehre: Eine Kritik von Lazarus' Ethik des Judentums," in *Monatsschrift für die Wissenschaft und Geschichte des Judentums* (1899): 385–400, reprinted in *JS* 3:1–35.

169. The influence of *Völkerpsychologie* on Cohen, in which culture is best understood as *Geist*, or the symbolic dimension of human social existence,

is palpable. See Dieter Adelmann, "H. Steinthal und Hermann Cohen," in *Hermann Cohen's Philosophy of Religion: International Conference in Jerusalem, 1996*, eds. Stephane Moses and Hartwig Wiedebach (New York: Georg Olms, 1997), 1–34 as well as Dieter Adelmann, *"Reinige dein Denken": Über den Jüdische hintergrund der Philosophie von Hermann Cohen* (Würzburg: Könighausen & Neumann: 2010). For a critical review of this position, see George Y. Kohler's review in *Modern Judaism* 31, no. 1 (2011): 109–13. See chapter 3 for Cohen's critique of *Wissenschaft* historicism.

170. Hermann Cohen, "Emanzipation: Zur Hundertjahrfeier des Staatsbürgertums der preußischen Juden (März 11, 1912)," *JS* 2:221.

171. *RoR*, 342 (397 Ger.).

172. Hermann Cohen, "Der deutsche Idealismus und die Antike," *Werke* 17: *KS* 6:184–85.

173. On the Wilhelmine Jewish Question, see Peter Pulzer, *Jews and the German State: The Political History of a Minority, 1848–1933* (Detroit: Wayne State University Press, 2003).

174. Heinrich von Treitschke, "Noch einige Bemerkungen zur Judenfrage," in *Der Berliner Antisemitismusstreit*, ed. W. Boehlich (Frankfurt am Main: Insel Verlag, 1965), 87. See also Andrea Poma, "Hermann Cohen's Response to Anti-Judaism," in *Yearning for Form: Essays on the Thought of Hermann Cohen* (Dodrecht, Netherlands: Springer, 2006), 4; Michael A. Meyer, "Great Debate on Anti-Semitism: Jewish Reaction to New Hostility in Germany, 1879/81" in *Leo Baeck Institute Year Book*, no. 11 (1966): 137–70.

175. *RoR*, 338 (Ger., 393), translation modified.

176. *DuJ* 1:477–78.

177. *DuJ* 1:481; *ErW* (1st ed.), 253; Cohen, *Religion der Vernunft*, 399.

178. Cohen, *Religion der Vernunft*, 393 (Eng., 338).

179. *DuJ* 1:476.

180. Hermann Cohen, "Die religiösen Bewegungen der Gegenwart," *JS* 1:36–65, 41–42.

181. Weber, "Science as Vocation," 137.

182. Weber, 143.

183. Raphael Gross, *Carl Schmitt and the Jews: The "Jewish Question," the Holocaust, and German Legal Theory*, trans. Joel Golb (Madison: University of Wisconsin Press, 2007), 54–59

184. Thus, the more public memorials of the *Kaiserreich* invoked Germanic pasts, such as the Hermannsdenkmal and the Vercingetorix monument. See Charlotte Tacke, *Denkmal im sozialen Raum. Eine vergleichende Regionalstudie nationaler Denkmalbewegungen in Deutschland und Frankreich in 19. Jahrhunderts* (Göttingen: Vandenhoeck & Ruprecht, 1995), cited in Geoff Eley, "Making a Place in the Nation," in *Wilhelminism and Its Legacies: German Modernities, Imperialism, and the Meanings of Reform, 1890–1930; Essays for Hartmut Pogge von Strandmann*, ed. Geoff Eley and James Retallack (Berghahn Books, 2003), 16–33; 22–23.

185. See Gesine Palmer, "The Case of Paul De Lagarde," in *Antisemtismus, Paganismus, Völkische Religion* (München: K.G. Saur, 2004), 37–54; Ulrich Sieg, *Germany's Prophet: Paul de Lagarde and the Origin of Modern Antisemitism* (Waltham, MA: Brandeis University Press, 2013). On *Volksnomos* theology in the 1920s and 1930s, see Gross, *Carl Schmitt and the Jews*.

186. *ErW*, 496–97.

187. *ErW*, 255; *DuJ* 2:118.

188. Daniel Gasman, *Haeckel's Monism and the Birth of Fascist Ideology* (New York: Peter Lang, 1998), 26.

189. Gasman, *Haeckel's Monism*, 23–24.

190. On the relationship between the occult and the rise of social Darwinist racial theories, see Helmut Zander, "Sozialdarwinistische Rassentheorie aus dem okkulten Untergrund des Kaiserreichs," in *Handbuch zur Völkischen Bewegung, 1871–1918* (München: K.G. Saur, 1999), 224–51.

191. Christian Wilhelm von Dohm, "On the Civil Improvement of the Jews," in *The Jew in the Modern World*, ed. Paul Mendes-Flohr and Jehuda Reinharz, 3rd ed. (New York: Oxford University Press, 2011), 32.

192. Moses Mendelssohn, *Jerusalem or on Religious Power and Judaism*, trans. Allan Arkush (Lebanon, NH: Brandeis University Press and University Press of New England, 1983), 40–41; 44–45. Mendelssohn was not advocating a kind of protosecularist policy, however, insofar as the state can never be fully distinguished from the church that manifests in terms of *Bildung*. Religion is therefore axiologically bound to the state as the sphere of eternal felicity that *ought to* condition temporal felicity. Cf. Willi Goetschel, *Spinoza's Modernity: Mendelssohn, Lessing, and Heine* (Madison: University of Wisconsin Press, 2004), 155–56; Bruce Rosenstock, *Philosophy and the Jewish Question* (New York: Fordham University Press, 2010), 13.

193. Pulzer, *Jews and the German State*, 31.

194. Sigbert Feuchtwanger, "Grundsätzliches zur deutschen Judenfrage," *Neue jüdische Monatshefte*, no. 19 (1917): 543–50, 544–45.

195. Pulzer, *Jews and the German State*, 31. See also Hans-Ulrich Wehler, *The German Empire, 1871–1918*, trans. Kim Traynor (New York: Berg, 1985), 106.

196. See Brett Fairbain, "Membership, Organization, and Wilhelmine Modernism: Constructing Economic Democracy through Cooperation," in *Wilhelminism and Its Legacies: German Modernities, Imperialism, and the Meanings of Reform, 1890–1930*, ed. Geoff Eley and James Retallack (New York: Berghahn Books, 2004), 34–50, 40.

197. Shulamit Volkov, "The 'Verbürgerlichung' of the Jews as a Paradigm," in *Bourgeois Society in Nineteenth-Century Europe*, ed. Jürgen Kocka and Allan Mitchell (Oxford: Berg, 1993), 367–91; George L. Mosse, *German Jews Beyond Judaism* (Cincinnati, OH: Hebrew Union College Press, 1997).

198. Cohen, "Vorwort" (1887), ix.

199. Cohen, x.

200. Hermann Cohen, "Ein Bekenntnis in der Judenfrage," *JS* 2:74.

201. Cohen, "Ein Bekenntnis," 75.

202. Cohen, 75.

203. Cohen, 75.

204. Cohen, 78.

205. See chapter 4.

206. Hermann Cohen, "Beträchtungen über Schmollers Angriff," *Werke* 17: *KS* 6:400.

207. Hermann Cohen, "Zionismus und Religion: Ein Wort an meine Kommilitonen jüdischen Glaubens," in *K-C Blätter*, no. 11 (May-June 1916): 643. Reprinted in *Werke* 17: KS 6.

208. Cohen, "Vorwort" (1887), x.

209. See, for example, Mendelssohn's remark that "Michaelis never speaks of Christians and Jews, but always of *Germans* and *Jews*," in Moses Mendelsohn, "Anmerkung zu des Ritters Michaelis Beurtheilung des ersten Theils von Dohm, ueber die buergerliche Verbesserung der Juden" (1783), trans. J. Hessing, in Mendes-Flohr and Reinharz, *The Jew in the Modern World*, 41.

210. On the ebb and flow of liberalism in the 1860s and early 1870s and the rise of conservative Germanism in relation to the Jewish question, see Reinhard Rürup, "Emanzipation und Krise—Zur Geschichte der 'Judenfrage' in Deutschland vor 1890," in *Juden in Wilhelminischen Deutschland, 1890–1914* (Tübingen: Mohr & Siebeck, 1976), 1–56.

211. Constantin Frantz, *Ahasverus oder die Judenfrage* (Berlin, 1844), 16, 27, quoted in *Revolutionary Antisemitism in Germany From Kant to Wagner* (Princeton, NJ: Princeton University Press, 1990), 344–45.

212. *EkN*, 280.

213. *EkN*, 282.

214. *EkN*, 285.

215. *EkN*, 280.

216. Cohen, "Emanzipation," 221.

217. *EkN*, 296–97.

218. Todd Weir notes how Stahl's philosophy of law influenced antisecularizing legislation in Friedrich Wilhelm IV's "dissident law" of 1847 permitting Prussian citizens to leave the corporate rights of the established churches (Catholic and Protestant) and simultaneously sought to quell the liberal Free Religious aim of achieving confessional status alongside those established churches. See Weir, *Secularism and Religion*, 29–30, 59–61.

219. *EkN*, 294.

220. *EkN*, 294.

THREE

—꼰—

RIGHTS, RELIGION, AND RACE

Cohen's Ethical Socialism and the Specter
of Anti-Semitism

THE LAST DECADE OF COHEN's life coincided with the centenary of
the first, limited emancipation of German Jews in 1812. In that time, many
German Jews learned the strengths and weaknesses of appealing to civic
rights and individual freedoms to seek recognition in German public institutions. On the one hand, these liberal principles of freedom, equality,
duty, and obligation to the rational legal state (*Rechtsstaat*), gave German
Jews a sense of belonging in the German Fatherland. These ideals helped
prop up an image of the rights-bearing citizen as a guide for articulating
a new Jewish identity. But on the other hand, as we saw in the previous
chapter, the Jewish Question was also increasingly framed as a problem
implicit in the developing scientific and philosophical discourses surrounding liberalism and secularization. Thus, the two paths of Protestant
liberalism and its dialectic of enchantment and reenchantment explored
in the previous chapters had a direct impact on the struggles of the German Jews. However, to the extent that liberalism symbolized a historical
and critical reflection on the past, it could also be construed as intimating
a degree of distance and even subversion. Hence, the combined political
and epistemological dialectic of enchantment left the Jews as symbolic
targets for a growing anxiety over both political and moral values legitimated by the kaiser and the church(es). And so, despite the ebb and flow
of liberal political successes, the Jews nevertheless served as a reminder
of the most basic liberal achievement: the right to citizenship without the
necessity of baptism.

Implicit in the liberal emphasis on civic identity independent of religious membership, therefore, is the root of the German-Jewish Question. And Cohen's idealism sought to respond to this question by providing German Jews (and majority Protestant Christians) a way to articulate values and norms in a self-reflexive manner. Cohen's idealism both referred to this public reasoning about law, self, and society as ethics and wagered that Jews could develop an ethical practice of reasoning their way to a new German-Jewish identity. Ethical idealism therefore presented the fruits of a democratization of the public sphere, allowing for a new socializing space between the individual and the state.

Nevertheless, if democratizing knowledge had opened up German identity and allowed Jews to negotiate their own identities anew, it was conversely perceived as a moment of great identity crisis for Germans who sensed this as a secularizing shift in society. To some, this meant that Wilhelmine Germany's public institutions faced a looming crisis of legitimacy. After all, granting civic recognition of religious difference and social equality to the Jews was one major goal of German liberalism.[1] Liberalism's great achievement was thus to shine some light between the legal regime of rights and duties of the citizen and the broader moral and theological history of Christianity in the structuring of the modern state. To do this, liberalism apparently required this separation of law from morality.

The German Jews openly expressed their commitment to the rights-based dimension of liberalism. Insofar as they did, however, their minority expression and endorsement of the Protestant liberalism that made this possible left in question the absoluteness and exclusivity—the limits and extent—of Protestantism and Germanism as cultural and religious worldviews. However, did Jewish self-understanding of liberalism and of a German identity freed from religious establishment really mean the same thing as an endorsement of the separation of law from morality?

In this chapter, I turn to the public and political stakes of Cohen's critique of knowledge to consider both how he sought to present a model for Jews in Wilhelmine Germany to negotiate national and civic identity as well as the anti-Semitic backlash against this appeal to state law and civic rights that had rendered Jewish claims audible in public. To demonstrate Cohen's vision for religion in civil society and public culture, I begin with Cohen's critical appraisal of Jewish advocacy for freedom of conscience, particularly Samson Raphael Hirsch's secessionist Orthodoxy, which sought a path toward a privatized religious freedom. As we saw in the previous chapter, Cohen worried that a secularist reasoning—a metaphysical worldview of self-legitimation—and the alleged disenchantment of value, identity, and legitimacy were endemic to such attempts to cede religion to the private realm. The Kantian legacy of erecting a boundary between law and morality therefore solidified the creation of a more legally equal public sphere but saddled liberalism with this problematic separation. Therefore, I next explore just what Kantian liberalism might have advocated. Regardless of intentions, the secularism of Kantianism gave credence to the criticisms fomenting the antiliberalism for which Carl Schmitt would later provide greater conceptual clarity in the early 1920s.

I next consider the anti-Semitic critique of liberalism that implicated the Jews as proponents of the neutralizations that insisted on the separation of law from morality and citizenship from blood, spirit, and *Volk*. Many of these antiliberal arguments turned on the legacy of Kant, who, as the father of enlightenment subjectivity and its model for the public use of reason, made the distinction between positive law and inner morality the principle of his liberalism. Whether or not this meant that Kantian, and especially neo-Kantian, philosophy had secured an opening for Jews to become German citizens, this philosophical legacy was translated into a concrete polemical front for both German Jews and German antiliberal nationalists and anti-Semites.

Cohen's position as a Jew in the philosophical and cultural landscape— and in arguments over Kant's legacy especially—is therefore illuminating. His neo-Kantian epistemology sought to provide German-Jewish liberalism, which we can now better define as public reasoning, with a secular idiom without falling into a politically secularist ideology that separates legality from religious morality. Rather, as I suggest, Cohen sought to retain a robust morality of law and was keenly aware of the need to critique the insidious conflations of civic participation with questions of race, theology, and identity in imperial Germany. Thus, in his own reworking of Kantian philosophy, Cohen outlines the possibilities for liberal religion between the poles of disenchanted neutrality and mythic reenchantment, or between what I will explore in the following chapter as politically liberal secularism and political theology, respectively. That is to say, Cohen negotiates the possibilities for liberal religion between the political definition of partisan goods as exclusive norms of a majority tradition on the one hand and, on the other, the state and legal requirement that the Jewish religious minority appear only as ghosts of themselves, masking the potential compatibility of a liberal *and* religious civil society.

Hence, Cohen's neo-Kantian idealism presents an alternative pathway for religious minority and difference by theorizing an implicit morality of law, a critical renegotiation of state law through the work of ethical reasoning about religion, morality, and history. In other words, Cohen radicalizes the liberal separation of the state and society to show why this does not mean the same thing as a separation of law and morality. Public reasoning about the morality of law, Cohen imagines, releases the ethical potential for religion to reshape the law and does so first at the level of society, not the state. As a newly articulated possibility both for Jews to become citizens and for Judaism to contribute to the reshaping of the morality of law itself, Cohen imagines a theory of consensus that pushes past politically irreconcilable difference and navigates majority and minority goods and needs at the level of sociality. This is what he refers to as a theory of ethical socialism.[2]

RELIGION AND PUBLIC LAW

One of the more vexed public debates surrounding Wilhelmine liberalism, as I have mentioned, was that regarding the secular tensions engendered by the Jewish Question. In the years following German unification, Jews were gaining unprecedented access to a sphere of social activity, economic adaptability, and the basic materials of modern society. Their commercial successes were beginning to earn them recognition as contributors—for better and for worse—to the transformations of German society.[3] Jews now had a seat at the table. But Jewish access to the materials of society should not be considered solely in commercial terms. As Cohen's philosophy shows us, the stuff of German civil society also includes the public, political, and communicable goods that we might devise for the traffic and interaction of sociality understood as a whole. Beyond a market-oriented society, Cohen saw Jewish religious life playing a crucial role in providing both access to these materials and a norm to guide their use. Hardly idle observers of the broader transformations of German society, the Jews of Germany were invested in the health of the public sphere first and foremost because they were now participants.

Much like the majority culture in which they now found themselves immersed, Jewish social life underwent a dramatic reorganization as well. Despite recognizing individual Jews as citizens, German law in the *Kaiserreich* did not recognize Judaism as a distinct religion benefiting either from state-appointed and compensated clergy or established spaces of worship.[4] Rather, in Germany's confessional order, Catholicism and Protestantism were recognized as established religions, while Judaism was primarily considered a public association able to administer taxes.[5] Judaism lacked a politically established structure as a confession.[6] This tense atmosphere of bourgeois rights within a rapidly socializing state thus presented an opportunity to create new possibilities of collective identity[7]—as a nation or a people, a religious community or a trade union— and it was against this backdrop that many Jews first *publicly* participated in debates in the German political landscape.

Amid this precarious position between religion and a social estate, the metaphysics of secularism presented Jews with an alternative to traditional religion. As we saw in chapter 2, popular monism and pantheism afforded the scientific imagination a redeemed enchantment, a way of creating spiritualistic science and modernizing religion for Germans seeking to consolidate their proud intellectualist roots. But these metaphysical shifts in the public sphere extended beyond popular ideas. They also gave rise to new associations and organizations, and Jews were implicated in this development of alternative religions. Their belonging to these new alternative associations therefore solidified just what Cohen had feared. It was a fear—triggered by Spinoza—that metaphysical assimilation was the only way to ensure full social participation. Scientific materialism, pantheism, and monism may have provided Jews with entry tickets, but Jews were also expected to participate in this scientific eclipse of traditional religion, including Judaism. Indeed, the synonymy of a popular scientific worldview and modern identity gained a proximity sufficient to warrant B. Saphra's (Binjamin Segel) tongue-in-cheek critique of religious freedom in Germany. He claimed, "'Thou shalt be modern: thou shalt cry out loudly in agreement with each catchword of the day, all the same, whether it is to your benefit or your detriment!' This would appear to be the unwritten eleventh commandment we Jews pride ourselves to unconditionally follow."[8] Segel was criticizing the liberal Jewish penchant for joining such alternative popular organizations as a pathway to acculturation. Indeed, it was because so many believed the quest to enter modernity was beholden to scientific commitment that Segel, like Cohen, worried Jews were too quick to follow the trends of the time. Indeed, because Cohen suspected that the replacement of religion with metaphysics was the favored worldview of many Jews who identified with liberal political parties in Germany,[9] he maintained that Spinoza's legacy was a double-edged sword. The liberalism that had made it possible for Jews to participate in society was becoming a rationale for leaving Judaism altogether.

If Jewish communal identity remained interwoven with the liberal theoretical pattern permeating German society, this was because Judaism differed dramatically from other popular associations, lodges, and charitable associations formed under the aegis of the Catholic or Protestant Churches.[10] The Jews, after all, held a corporate identity that predated the nation-state, and this public recognition helped some German Jews negotiate the intersection of civic and religious identities without experiencing a compromise between them. Jews now had a choice: there was no longer a need to convert to Christianity to become German. And if we follow Cohen, this is because modern Jews had already succeeded in becoming Protestants. With a guaranteed right to citizenship independent of religious affiliation, where religion primarily meant Christianity, German Jews therefore saw the private freedom of conscience granted to them in imperial Germany as the basis on which to identify as true citizens of the Fatherland—citizens who did not need a common religion in order to find commonality with the ideal of the German nation.

Therefore, Jewish organizations such as the largest, nondenominational Centralverein deutscher Staatsbürger jüdischen Glaubens (Central Organization of German Citizens of the Jewish Faith, or C.V.) emphasized the constitutional definition of citizenship and affirmed the right to an equal treatment under the law as part of their advocacy against anti-Semitic attacks and public defamations.[11] To secure the freedom and guarantee of continued participation in the public sphere, many Jews in the C.V. championed the nineteenth-century German *Rechtsstaat* as a social end in itself. Rather than mirror the social-democratic appeals for greater socialization of the state, the C.V. focused its advocacy around the minimal guarantee of individual rights secured by public law, undertaking legal advocacy in some instances for Jews as a class rather than as a race or even a religious organization.[12] By protecting the rights that establish individual citizens as Germans, a particularly private faith could remain unthreatening to the civic consciousness of Germanness afforded by legal rights. This expression of a rights-based liberalism meant to many Jews, however, that belief in the law meant a belief in Germanness. Being Jewish was not contradictory to such a belief because being German meant believing in the legal recognition of citizenship as a path to Germanness.

Nevertheless, the Christian confessional structure meant that many conservative Germans saw the separation of citizenship and religion as a symptom of a more sinister attempt to neutralize and secularize civic identity. Whereas the C.V. understood Germans to be defined by law and not by religious affiliation or by any other historical interest, the legal and civic definitions of citizenship were often cited amid the growing anxiety over national identity in which even the academic elite began questioning whether such citizenship represented a neutralization of the historical identity of Germany and its Christian heritage.

It was this separation of citizenship from religion that the anti-Semitic political movement saw as the crux of modern Judaism's irreligious power,[13] a power often cited as the design of an insidious Western liberalism that was foreign to German soil.[14] Because Cohen, like Eugen Fuchs and his colleagues in the C.V., insisted that his legal advocacy on behalf of the German Jews was not an attempt to establish their legal rights as a return to being medieval *Schutzjuden* or "protected Jews" but, rather, German *citizens*,[15] he stressed a legal articulation of moral psychology as a model for civic identity. The fact that Jews such as Cohen, Fuchs, and the German-Jewish community continued to emphasize the constitutional definition of citizenship, however, further provoked the claim that the liberal distinction between state and society should be broken into even further partitions. Individual and community, conservatives bemoaned, were being strictly separated by a regime of self-serving positive law that assumed for itself a legitimacy superseding the historical norms of Christian or Teutonic communal identity.[16] Thus, as the foremost German-Jewish public intellectual, Cohen set himself the task of publicly accounting for the relationship between Judaism as a public religion and the confessional structure of Germany. In order to reframe the relationship between individual and society, Cohen therefore pushed back against conservative critiques of liberalism and Jewish civic emancipation. However, Cohen also sought to revise how Jews ought to present their religious identity and social engagement within the scope of German culture. In order to do so, he suggested that religion and public law must be seen as epistemologically interwoven sites of value formation and historical identity.

Cohen's defense of civic equality and the right to religious difference became increasingly public and ever more frequent amid the deepening spiritual crisis in Germany during the First World War. In a public response to the question of what unites the confessions, Cohen notes how foreign such a designation is for Judaism. He writes, "By 'confession' German state law only understands the two main church bodies, which are united under the name of Christianity. Judaism, however, is in this official sense not a confession at all but its own religion."[17] Cohen invokes religion in the sense of a lived religious tradition with ritual practices and communal obligations; Judaism is therefore not subsumable under the rubric of Christian religion as a confession. Yet this exclusion of Judaism from the designation of an official confession of an established church under Prussian state law presents an opportunity for Cohen. This legal classification reveals the process of historicization implicit in the law whereby the state "fulfills the concentration of cultural consciousness," which refers to a more general spiritual conception of norms and values, by providing "religious communities with not merely political security, but also freedom of conscience."[18] By protecting conscience in addition to confession, Cohen sees the beginning of a legal protection of a space of reasoning through which to reconcile different religions under a single public culture. As we saw in the previous chapter, the conceptual structure of such a space of reasoning, Cohen claims, is located in the conceptual structure of law and judgment. The state provides the institutional framework for recognizing the questions and answers developed by society. In other words, law represents *the sociality of reasoning* as the dialectical *origin* of the state, rather than the will of the *political sovereign*, whose own religious denomination once reigned supreme as a norm for civic identity (*cuius regio, eius religio*). Law becomes a site of public reasoning through which the formation of the citizen occurs. This is because, Cohen articulates,

the state never stands alone, although it is the focus of all cultural aspirations; rather, let us consider that to its side stands equally as driver,
assistant, consoler: society. While the state assumes the fiction of inertia
[*Beharrung*], since it embodies the law, which as that which is extant must
always vouch for the prevailing condition, society on the other hand,
concerns the principle of development, hence also the self-dissolution
of persisting rigidity in the state. From the concept of society arises not
only socialism, but all social reform policy as well, which seeks to develop civil law, to redeem the principle of property of its rigidity, and to
reconcile with the principles of ethics. Thus it can seem as though the
principle of society would be preferably the concern of ethics, and yet,
even the state cannot be uprooted from the concern of ethics. Ensuring
that this uprooting does not become actual is the principle of society,
which therefore confronts that of the state, not in order to conquer the
latter, but rather to continually free it of the necessary fiction of rigidity
in order to preserve its truthful vitality and to incessantly rejuvenate.
This relation between society and state exists in politics. Should it not
also exist for religion?

Thus it is now extremely surprising how society seems almost entirely
to fail to realize the principle of the freedom of conscience, as compared
with its political realization. And yet society is here more than anything
else not a latent potency, but the allegedly dominant power of public
opinion. About which questions might the public sphere [*Öffentlichkeit*]
be called upon to judge, if not about the care of freedom of conscience,
this most important bulwark of public morality?[19]

Society (*Gesellschaft*) stands in contrast to the state as the background
against which the *Rechtsstaat* achieves its articulation of public norms.
But society shows the state how dynamic it really is. Society's fluidity
rejuvenates the state's rigidity. Thus, politics remains a vehicle not unlike
religion, navigating the narrow if yet abyssal strait separating society and
state. This is why spiritual culture must begin with the sociality of law
in Cohen's account.[20] But as Cohen notes, ethics would seem to be distinguished from politics by focusing on society instead of state. Because
society fails to uphold freedom of conscience if it merely outsources this
right to the state and preserves for itself private discriminatory prejudices
against religious difference, ethics is needed to reorient the public sphere
and public morality. Cohen's understanding of ethics therefore prioritizes
the sociality of law as a dynamic power of reasoning prior to the political
because the idealization of difference (the work of ethics) exists prior to
the judgments of conflict and political partisanship.

As the space of public opinion and public reasoning, society must be called on as the site of ethical critique and ethical labor where state law can be reshaped. Hence, the freedom of conscience and religion ought to be seen as another passage between society and state, capable of rejuvenating the rigidity of state law. Confession or religion must not be hypostatized as an attribute of the rigid state structure. So, too, the right to religion must not encode difference merely as a private affair of belief and conscience, isolating that set of reasons, beliefs, and practices from public scrutiny. Rather, the freedom of conscience fundamental to the liberal constitutional regime, Cohen believes, must not limit religion in terms of private conscience. This obscures the *socioethical* potential of religion in the modern *Rechtsstaat*: a spirit of culture *between* state and society. If society confines the right of religion to private conscience, then it fails to both capitalize on this ethical differentiation of legal and social belonging and integrate religion into the public reasoning that rejuvenates the state with a practice of critical justification and, if need be, a revision of law from the vantage point of social rather than strictly political goods. Conscience and religion ought to secure a right to public reasoning.

Cohen's articulation of the sociality of law and the recognition of religion in public also represents a normative response to the social transformations of his time. For example, in the continued debates over the secession controversy, in which German-Jewish Orthodoxy successfully lobbied to secede from mandatory taxation and belonging in the larger Jewish community, Samson Raphael Hirsch argued that the constitutionally defined freedom of conscience required the government to treat Judaism as a religion with its own confessions and denominations, a matter of private conscience. This was not due to a belief that Judaism was indeed a religion subject to such parsing out, but rather, as Mordechai Breuer notes, because "the state, in fact, force[d] him into this position. He could win the ear of a Prussian deputy for the law of secession . . . only by using terms current among politicians and civil servants trained in the laws of church and state, and by applying such terms to the religious and political situation in the Jewish communities."[21] Compulsory membership in the Jewish community, Hirsch argued, required membership in political rather than religious entities, and "because this is the chief argument in favor of Jewish political and civil equality, one would expect that [the law of secession] would have been welcomed by all Jews, be they Orthodox or Reformist."²² In other words, Hirsch cited the political classification of Judaism as a separate civil caste as justification to convert Jewish religion into a denominational or confessional model. For Hirsch, freedom of conscience was precisely the key phrase that would convince Prussian civil servants of his political plea. In contrast to Cohen's description above, therefore, Hirsch began with a state law as the source for his argument about the social role of religion.

Cohen objects to this maneuvering of regnant political definitions of religion, not to the term *religion* itself. Turning the basis of Hirsch's argument on its head, Cohen claims that such an account of freedom of conscience is willfully misunderstood as a right to privacy, such that, when dealing with Jewish religion, a Jew invoking the freedom of conscience presents himself or herself as something other than first a member of a social group. Thus, he writes,

> The withdrawal from the community enacts opposition to the continuation of the Jewish religion, although apparently done in deception. And this opposition is said to be an act of freedom, freedom of conscience, faithful conviction. With such arguments one gives oneself an escape from the difficulties that arise for the individual in all matters of state-oriented, social, and historical existence, as compared with those of collective existence, out of which the individual itself commences, and in which alone it can assert itself. With his subjective freedom, the individual believes himself to possess a right to detach himself from the community that above all else is reliant on his assistance.²³

By claiming this private right of conscience as existing prior to the communal and social order of norms, including the public status of a religious community such as the Jewish community, Cohen claims that secessionist Orthodoxy misunderstands the sociality of law in which the "I" of the individual originates. Hence, as Cohen claims in his *Ethik*, "There is no individual in the ethical sense without legal community (*Rechtsgemeinschaft*)."²⁴ This is because, as we saw in Cohen's logic, the *I* can only be thought of by means of its relative nothing, the *not-I*. In other words, because the *I* is not the sum total of all there is, the *I* is grounded in a broader concept of the human being (*Mensch*), which is implicitly a concept of a plurality of human beings.²⁵ Therefore, to claim a right to freedom of conscience prior to the recognition of a self as already part of a plurality of selves misunderstands what it means to be an *I* in the first place. Cohen therefore criticizes this individualist understanding of conscience, effectively labeling Hirsch as a neutralizing liberal. Thus, in order to better understand Cohen's critique of both this account of a freedom of conscience and this version of liberal individualism,[26] I want to explore his account of self-consciousness, which helps explain his appeal to sociality and objectivity.

In Cohen's systematic philosophy, consciousness is complexly defined as a "union of the other with the one [that] generates self-consciousness as the self-consciousness of the pure will."[27] Consciousness is plural, and its plurality is facilitated by what Cohen calls pure will or the motor driving an idea to become embodied as action. There is always more than one action and more than one will. Law therefore constellates plurality through the legal unit of an action, such that the ethical notion of consciousness is always a consciousness *of* something other. That is, "self-consciousness is first and foremost conditioned by consciousness of the Other."[28] Moreover, the legal community out of which the individual first emerges is objectified as pure will, or the will that is identical with law.[29] Self-consciousness is therefore a product of plurality, of the legal community, that is always prior to my individuated consciousness.[30] Yet self-consciousness is not simply an abstract principle of cognition for theoretical reason; rather, Cohen sees it as something practical, manifesting in objective actions; self-consciousness must be *willed* into action. Consciousness therefore takes up the objectively recognizable norm, the self, where the self is a task or a goal claimed by the existence of actions outside myself.[31] The objectivity of law is achieved through a will to act that is at the same time a will to legislate, and thus these actions accrue as legal norms, as actions now required by law. These are not actions that I first author by myself, but rather actions that originate in an other.[32] In other words, the legal self is *otherwise than*. That is, the legal self is someone foreign to *me* as the individual agent *willing* this self in accordance with the law.

The law, as Cohen writes, is thus my origin. He states,

> The law is cognized as the groundlaying [*Grundlegung*], which is laid in self-consciousness. The task of self-consciousness is indeed but a hypothesis of self-consciousness. And it signifies nothing other than the task of the self, the summons [*Aufforderung*] to the self. Thus, the task of self-consciousness becomes the law of self-consciousness, because it becomes the groundlaying of self-consciousness. Thus, no foreign [*auswärtige*]

task can be the issue; it is rather the innermost development of the basic idea of the hypothesis, which is carried out in the claim of the law. And it is simultaneously the clearest and most natural deviation from all egoistic, transitory, fungibility of the isolated individual that is pursued and carried out by the law. Just as I cannot find my self in the "I", but rather in the "You" and "We," so too is it only by means of the task, which occurs for me in the first stirring of the will, being carried out in action that I cognize self-consciousness as a law, as I have come to know it in the state.

The concept of law must remain the guiding star of my self-consciousness . . . for the law here means precisely the individual law [*das einzelne Gesetz*], and yet should also represent the concept of law [*den Begriff des Gesetzes*] without contradiction. This goes beyond the authority of a natural law, which rules out pathological exceptions. Here, however, the individual law, in all its baseness, nevertheless should be a symbol of eternal and true law. Thus one can see from this that the concept of law, as the individual law, is necessary and irreplaceable for the pure will and self-consciousness.[33]

The individual law—and not the liberal individual—is the origin of my own enactment of the *I* because the law represents the objectivity of the pure will united with its subject, the willing agent of law.[34] It is only in an action that I recognize my self as acting in accordance with the law. The law calls *me* to act in accordance with a normative action, in accordance with the hypothesis that this *I* could be my own. This I becomes a task to be achieved. It is a ground on which to underlay my actions with the claim that they are moral. This *I* is an ideal toward which we strive. Hence, the legality of this individualizing law, which is first other to me, is the grounding of self-consciousness and indeed of all ethics. It is ethical because I become conscious of my self through actions that I *ought to do*. I am therefore never isolated, because my action originates with the task of becoming self-conscious. I must bring myself out of mythic awareness of my individuality and, rather, recognize my self in legal community.

This is why Cohen turns to the idea of the state since the law as I recognize it in state law provides a location in which to act. But the individual law that calls me to act is only an occasion for me to perform and generate [*erzeugen*] my self in action; only once I have generated my self as acting can I witness [*bezeugen*] my self. If this self-legislation is not predicated of a self-sufficient I, then it is always the law that is prior. Within the law, I find an implicit other within me, who always accompanies my *I* as a legal concept relative to other *I*s that are generated in action.[35] Consciousness of the self is therefore no longer a principle of the self-conscious *I* but the principle of law itself. This is how Cohen understands the meaning of autonomy (*autos nomos*): "autonomy itself is concerned with the origin of the law. The law is what makes action action; not the person, not the *I*."[36] By becoming the law, autonomy now means the objectification of the objects of ethical cognition prior to the production of the subject. Self-consciousness is therefore achieved only through actions; my moral action based on law. It is therefore not the actual state laws that generate the morality of my actions and my selfhood but the concept of law as an ideal normative order that produces the subject who is first objectivized by the law itself. In other words, self-consciousness does not produce its own law but is itself generated from "a seemingly foreign one."[37]

Judith Butler's theory of performativity provides a helpful analog here. Like Cohen, Butler insists that the performativity of the *I* of subjectivity is a product of subjectivization.[38] For Butler, the matrix of possibility for this *I* is traced by discursive power, or the normative possibilities that are preassigned to the *I*. *I* can be a man; *I* can be a woman. *I* can perform the subject position even if it deviates from its expected, normative performance and thereby subvert the presumption of an ontology to that *I*.[39] For Jacques Lacan, upon whom Butler draws, this means that the *I* associated with my own self-representation is already attached to an agent position in language before I inhabit that self. Hence, for Butler, subversion becomes a possibility inscribed into the structural fabric of the *I*, since my *I* must be performed, and each and every performance that (re)iterates this *I* performs new attributes: *I* am young; *I* am dying. Each attribute modifies the specificity of the preassigned agent and performs the subversive shifting in discursive meaning. Through performance, the *I* adopts new representational baggage, connotation.

Similarly, Cohen proposes a self that is mandated by law, which must be inhabited. Like Butler, Cohen also insists that the *I* that is performed conditions the kind of ethical self that the *I* aims to be. Unlike natural law, however, the law underlying consciousness and the state—the origin of the *I* in the law—is not a set of eternal norms. It is not a predetermined doctrine or a statute-based collection of authorized rules. Rather, law signifies the *unique* law, the individual law. This means that the law is the conceptual origin of the individual; the concept of law is a law *for* self-consciousness and not the conscious production of any one law of the state or any one individual person. Law is therefore a generative concept. It generates my *I* because the law legislates that I ought to be and what I ought to be. If the law legislates, however, that I ought to be a moral self, a self that dutifully strives for humanity in my person, then, Cohen claims, the meaning of moral autonomy must be redefined as the legislation of the moral self. This is the separate and unique character of law.

Because of his insistence on the priority of the law as a meaningful conceptual structure and not the priority of the individual as a self-sufficient being, we can see the extent to which Cohen is not a typical liberal. Hence, returning to Cohen's critique of Hirsch, we see more clearly both how Cohen is working with a socially constituted understanding of the self and that legal rights are always predicated of this sociality. The objectivity of legal rights, according to Cohen, is based on the community of legal persons, before any right can be claimed as an individual right. Secessionist Orthodoxy's use of private conscience to invoke a right to private conscience as though it were a confession in fact attempts to maneuver Prussian state law to redefine Judaism as a politically determined religion. Hirsch effectively privatizes Jewish conscience and makes Judaism irrelevant in the public sphere. Cohen's critique is thus primarily philosophical in that it insists that a private individual is something recognizable only to a community. But it is also a social critique, since withdrawal from the community is understood as a *political action* that has less to do with religious belief than with partisan and secular politics. Despite Hirsch's claim to sustain religion by appealing to a political classification of conscience as prior to sociality, Cohen objects precisely to the introduction of a privatized conception of religion. Ironically, while Hirsch appears to be more of a liberal with this individualist emphasis on a private sphere, Cohen subverts the notion of an atomized individual in favor of a self formed through sociality.

By contrast to Hirsch's invocation of private conscience, Cohen believed that the legal recognition of conscience enables a different potential for religion in the modern legal state, a potential we might describe as the birth of modern public religion. The freedom of conscience not only is a *right to religion* but also represents the separation of religion from the requirements of citizenship.[40] It is a freedom *from* state religion.[41] Religion therefore becomes part of public culture but not a condition of legal rights. Thus, in his commemoration of the centenary of Jewish emancipation in Prussia in 1912, Cohen describes his understanding of religious freedom. The public recognition of Jews as worthy of citizenship, he maintains, gives religion a new meaning. He writes,

> A great principle of momentous significance for all questions of culture is established in this constitutional recognition of our religion. The concept of the *modern* state, which consists in and rests in the *ethically intrinsic right [sittlichen Eigenrecht]* of the state, is confirmed and made certain by this expansion of the religious horizon. The religion of the one unique God, the ur-religion of monotheism is thus recognized as equal to the confession of Christianity under the law of the state. The concept of the *Christian State,* which in any case contradicts the *Protestant state concept,* is thereby uprooted. The state and the Jewish religion have now become regular members of a legal relation.[42]

The legal relation in which Judaism now stands with the state is not an equal relation. Cohen knows this. Rather, the state remains a legal output, while the Jewish religion is placed within a triangulated relationship with Christian religion as a source of moral input for the law. Although the relation is not an equal one, it is nevertheless a dynamic one, because monotheism becomes a term that secures a step beyond confessional distinction.

Cohen is not advocating that, in becoming a publicly recognized religion, Judaism becomes a political religion. Instead, that legal recognition places Judaism and the state in a relation of *legal idealization.* Judaism is now part of the dynamic fluidity of society that helps articulate social and ethical goods. Thus, if religion is a legal right and conscience can be reframed as the right to help critique and rejuvenate the rigidity of state law with the resources of religion, then it is the sociality of law that enables this relation.

The modern state, on this reading of Cohen, can now be understood as instituting a legal secularity, if we understand the freedom to offer religious reasoning in the public sphere as a kind of social practice. But this does not require the secularization of Judaism. This is why Cohen relies on monotheism as the cultural thread of society. And because the religious confessions of Christianity recognized by state law are now juxtaposed with the term *religion* as something explicitly social and not simply an internal distinction between Christian groupings, the concept of the one, unique God becomes a borderline concept between a plurality of religions in the state.

If God becomes a legal norm, then the state is no longer the Christian state imagined by conservative Protestants like Bismarck but a state united under the idea of God. Law, as the purest idealization of culture, becomes the normative form in which the content of Protestant and Jewish cultural concepts can be debated, justified, judged, and acted on in order to bring about a more just state—a state in which legal norms help consolidate the history of our reasons and norms. This designation of religion as something that is dynamically shaped in the social sphere, rather than an explicitly established state institution, therefore reshapes the meaning of the right of conscience. Conscience now becomes a public concept and vehicle for the performance of social *citizenship* compatible with, yet irreducible to, membership in a *public religion*. In other words, conscience becomes a resource in society for the work of public reasoning.

Yet Cohen knew that Germanism (*Deutschtum*) remained indelibly Protestant; its institutions were only nominally free of the influence of dogmatism, and pleas for dialogue between Christian confessions were often met with ridicule and accusation while the authoritarian state of Kaiser Wilhelm II discriminated against the Jews in both civic and military office. To therefore pretend that the freedom of conscience secured complete equality is naive, to say the least. Cohen was thus critical of this illusory claim to legal protection. Rather, the significance of this legal right was that the public good that it secured, and that had been laboriously outfitted to suit Protestant and Catholic confessions, might be reshaped as a way for Jews to be Jewish Germans.[43] The right of religion and conscience articulated a right to religious reasoning, in Cohen's view. And in the hands of a minority, such an abstract principle of private equality before the law vis-à-vis the more expressly public confessional structure presented an opening for Jews to participate in public reasoning and the social rejuvenation of state law.

Cohen's turn to law as the source of idealization of individuals and citizens therefore represents a rigorous attempt to develop a theory of civic recognition and belonging. As Cohen understood the problem, citizenship and national belonging first required a critique of any metaphysical presuppositions undergirding a would-be theory of cultural values, knowledge, or social normativity. This is because the social rejuvenation of state law must take place as both a conceptual and an ethical labor of critique. Thus, the various philosophical and scientific worldviews I discussed in the previous chapters, including pantheism, materialism, social Darwinism, myth, *Volk*, blood, and so on, presented epistemological foils for Cohen's account of law and civic identity. As worldviews that challenged the presumption of received moral and cultural norms of knowledge in traditional Christianity, they nevertheless sought to establish a public culture for the national state.

Such a search for a mythic basis of German national identity was longstanding. Since the eighteenth century, the search for a national identity had led many thinkers to seek out folk customs, practices, and oral traditions, such as the brothers Grimm, the Schlegels, and many others.[44] In addition to such mythic conceptions of national identity, the rise of German philology also deployed Aryan and Semitic myths as ways of characterizing notions of national cultures.[45] Heinrich von Treitschke's controversial description of German national identity in 1880, along with his defense of growing popular anti-Semitism, also invoked the mythic notions of Semitic and Occidental spirits as distinct historical identities.[46] Hence, in the steady development of imperial German national identity, to the extent that religion was increasingly relegated to the background of intellectual and scientific discourse, myth played the part of a new *public* liturgy, ritual, and religion.[47] According to Cohen, however, such worldviews were unjustifiable because they presented themselves as the basis for a public culture without demonstrating what Cohen and other Kantian-inspired intellectuals believed to be fundamental to this principle of German liberalism: namely, the fact that myths do not rely on the types of reasoning necessary for publicity, such as justification and evidence. Myths are instead assertions of intuition, imagination, and metaphysics. And while the enchantment of myth certainly represents a moment in the dialectic I discussed in chapter 2, without justification, historicity, and the transparency of a public argument, myth cannot be a basis for public law. Cohen therefore sought a more compelling model of objective-practical norms for an account of public culture and sociality. In idealism he found the necessary force to mitigate the pretense of myth. Without idealism, however, "myth within religion remains the enemy of science and culture."[48]

A public ethic based on science and culture—hence, public reasoning—could only be developed, Cohen believed, according to the model of a critique of knowledge (*Erkenntniskritik*). As I suggested in the previous chapter, Cohen's idealist philosophy was therefore the root of both a theoretical critique of science as well as a social-practical critique of politics. Moreover, his idealism was consistent with the vision of Jewish civic equality he shared with Jewish communal leaders of his time.

For example, Eugen Fuchs, the cofounder of the *Centralverein* with whom Cohen coedited the *Neue jüdischen Monatshefte*, shared Cohen's commitment to philosophical idealism as a blueprint for advocating a harmonization of German and Jewish culture, which many have ridiculed as naive optimism.[49] Fuchs, along with many other leaders of the C.V., saw Cohen's systematic philosophy and its advocacy of neo-Kantian idealism as part of their own struggle to articulate a liberal vision for German citizenship.[50] But what these leading German-Jewish intellectuals may have failed to acknowledge was how Cohen's engagement with Kant served as a critical revision of the liberalism that many in the C.V. championed wholesale.

Cohen's distance from liberal individualism, which we can find in his account of religion in public law, is philosophically elaborated in his account of legal form and moral content in a revised Kantian categorical imperative—a demand to respect the ideal of humanity as the lawful basis for the very conception of an ethical self. With this philosophical basis, Cohen therefore sought to define ethical self-consciousness as the product of a constitutional order of civic rights and national identity. Because the ethical self-consciousness that emerged from that legal I was no longer the natural person who would claim to be isolated as a self-conscious being, however, Cohen recognized the potential objection to his thinking as positivist and even neutralizing. Cohen therefore sought in the Kantian idea of humanity both a way to correlate the plural definition of self with others under law and a norm for ordering a collectivity. Emphasizing the juridical fiction of the legal person and legal community that grounds it, Cohen therefore went about revising Kant's original statement on the relationship between abstract legal personality and moral law. For Cohen, the task was thus to prove how the person can be presupposed neither as a natural self nor as having an ontology or substance that is not itself posited by the judgment of a plurality—such as the law—as giving the self rights. As Cohen writes, "The legal subject is the citizen; the legal subject is as such intellectually and morally equivalent."[51] Acknowledging the citizen-subject as a legal fiction—as an ideal, not an empty abstraction—Cohen therefore theorizes a socially responsive selfhood that is distinct from liberal individualism.

KANTIAN SECULARISM: THE SEPARATION
OF LAW AND MORALITY

As we have seen in the previous chapters, Wilhelmine philosophy and natural science were deeply interwoven with the public discourse of the day, including the social and political tensions described above. As self-styled measuring rods for arguments about moral and political values in the public sphere, the Kantian ideals of publicity and critique provided the epistemological roots of the German public sphere.[52] And as the bearer of Kant's legacy, the professional academic professoriate, dominated by neo-Kantianism, therefore played a crucial role in the shaping of public opinion.[53] Indeed, the younger generation of Weimar thinkers who followed in their footsteps often disparaged the values and crises of Wilhelmine Germany as identical with those of the neo-Kantians.[54]

Yet there were significant political differences between various neo-Kantian schools and individual philosophers, and although the shared questions of the day concerning methodology and the relationship between natural and cultural sciences were the backbone of public debate, more than Kant's philosophy was at stake: Marburg neo-Kantianism in particular represented a significant moment in the history of the German academy in which Jews had achieved previously unknown social and professional successes. Together with the move of many Jewish students and colleagues toward Marburg neo-Kantianism, a demographic shift in philosophy occurred. But, at base, the social question of who was a German citizen was reflected in philosophical debates over *who* was permitted to interpret Kant and *how* their interpretations affected the nation of Kant.[55]

Cohen's neo-Kantianism was emphatically idealist and sought to wrench ideas away from both metaphysical speculation and their reduction to the physiological. But Cohen also placed a great deal of emphasis on scientific knowledge as a model of conceptual clarity and justification.[56] With Cohen as the head of the Marburg school, this emphasis on the ideal standpoint and the methodological paradigm of science in neo-Kantianism more generally became the subject of both philosophical and political dispute, especially in light of the growing influence of social Darwinism and racial science. The perception of Cohen's philosophy as a leveling and positivist theory was thus widespread.[57] However, as we can see from reading Cohen's account of ethics and normativity, this reading was due more to Cohen's success as an unbaptized Jew in the face of academic and popular anti-Semitism than to his actual philosophy. Cohen made explicit what had already been a longstanding Jewish veneration of Kantian philosophy, valued especially for promoting an account of *Bildung* or cultural formation that was accessible equally to all.[58] Yet this same veneration led to the suspicion that Jews were willfully misreading Kant for their own purposes. Hence, parallel to the discrimination Jews faced over their citizenship and belonging, Cohen faced similar challenges in the professional realm of philosophy on account of his interpretation of Kant.

Indeed, it was the contested legacy of Kant that obliquely figured in the 1879–80 public condemnations of the liberal Jewish intelligentsia by the historian Heinrich von Treitschke, who mockingly invoked the image of the nation of Kant[59]—a nation of enlightenment and moral education (*Bildung*)—as the shibboleth against any proper Jewish integration.[60] As an indictment that forced Cohen to publicly defend the legitimate right of all Germans to invoke this Kantian legacy, whether Jewish or Christian, Treitschke's attack also indirectly drew attention to a substantive philosophical problem: namely, the question of whether Kantian idealism was inherently normed by a genealogical link to a particular German stock of values of thinking and thus restricted to certain members of a historically constituted critical acumen—"real" Germans. How might a Kantian define a German?

Neo-Kantians translated this question into a debate over Kant's idealism. Was Kantianism, they asked, rooted in some kind of sensible intuition of natural stock or historical-tribal connection or a pure idealism and critique of reason—including a critique of culture—according to a priori principles independent of either nature or empirical perceptions? In other words, did Kant envision a form of objective knowledge open to all?[61] Should the nation and the citizen be defined in vulgar materialist terms or in ideal ones? Philosophically, this framing stemmed from a

longstanding debate in the history of Kant's reception over the relationship between the seemingly dual spheres of knowledge—namely, sensibility and understanding, or intuition and concept—which interpreters
had struggled to reconcile since the publication of the first edition of the
Critique of Pure Reason in 1781.[62] It was also a problem that beset interpreters of Kant's practical philosophy, which had decisively shaped German
political and legal thought in the nineteenth century.[63] For Cohen, these
questions of Kantian idealism were of the utmost importance, for Cohen
believed that they held a rigorous answer to the problems of civic identity
and religious difference. So before turning to Cohen's account, we must
better understand both Kant's original separation of law and morality
and why the moral law and the categorical imperative might provide opportunities for reworking that separation and, more broadly, a notion of
liberalism.

At the root of Kant's theory of practical reason are perhaps the most
well-known concepts of his moral philosophy: namely, the moral law and
the categorical imperative. While a line of Protestant thinkers including Philip Melancthon, Hugo Grotius, Samuel von Pufendorff, Gottfried
Wilhelm Leibniz, and Christian Thomasius had all variously argued that
reason was a legislative faculty—a source of laws governing human actions, will, and desire—Kant's philosophy changed how positive, hu-
manly legislated law was understood. His insight began with an attempt
to ground knowledge of positive and moral law in a priori judgments, or
rationally determined moral principles whose validity depends on neither
empirical factors such as desire and emotion nor the fact of tradition, custom, and command. Moral autonomy expressed the view of enlightened
freedom, or an individual's emergence from self-imposed immaturity in
order to think for one's self.[64] Moral autonomy was thus a basis on which
to theorize the modern individual as an agent of what Kant called practical reason.

Because of its rational basis and a priori status, Kant argues, the moral
law is a law to the extent that it represents formally self-authorized duty.
The moral law is therefore an ideal motivation and the origin of the freedom of will, "the possibility of which we *know* a priori, though without
having insight into it, because it is the condition of the moral law, which
we do know."[65] We know freedom, therefore, as a transcendental fact.[66]
That is to say, while the moral law is the condition for knowing we are free,

both freedom and moral law remain what Kant calls noumenal concepts. Put differently, these concepts are unknowable except as ideal grounds on which to base practical actions. This emphasis on the a priori status of both freedom and moral law is the root of Kant's conception of the moral individual.

Kant thus casts the a priori validity of freedom and the moral law as the basis for "laws of a causality of pure reason." Moreover, Kant's insistence on pure reason as a cause of moral actions leads to a foundational distinction that explains how actions are autonomously willed rather than externally motivated and commanded: namely, the distinction between legality and morality.[67] For Kant, the moral autonomy of the individual must be isolated from the values that are socially constituted and shared in an empirical social world. The state and its laws, which consist of legislative acts of institutions and are thus heteronomous, are considered under a different rubric than that of pure moral laws. Actions mandated by statute laws, Kant claims, are juridical or legal. Acting in accordance with such laws, however, is not in itself moral. Rather, morality concerns actions that conform to laws that "also require that they (the laws) themselves be the determining grounds of actions." In other words, such laws require moral autonomy to incorporate the principle behind that law into decision-making, or choice. Only such laws, Kant claims, "are *ethical* laws, and then one says that conformity with ethical laws is its *morality*."[68]

Kant seems to have in mind a distinction between laws such as observing a speed limit or stop sign and laws forbidding murder. Kant therefore distinguishes between laws with no rationale beyond the conformity of actions to those laws and other laws that appear to point to a deeper moral value. The morality of a law should lie in its capacity to become an independently motivating principle for autonomous moral individuals to behave accordingly. However, as a result Kant leaves the legitimacy of juridical laws susceptible to doubt. And because it remains unclear how moral law as a pure causality within reason alone relates this autonomous self to the social world of human beings—including the state—where moral actions dovetail again with the juridical laws, Kant casts positive law as rather precarious in its abstraction and formalism. It is, therefore, also unclear how or why a principle should motivate an autonomous moral individual at the same time that it is sanctioned as a juridical law. What is the relationship between legality and morality?

In order to explain how juridical and moral laws interact, Kant appeals to his distinction between the empirical and a priori grounds of action—between nature and ideal. While Kant understands the moral individual as a noumenal self set against the empirical world of social relations, he claims that this individual is caught in a paradoxical asocial sociality, or an antagonism between the individual's desire to be "more than the developed form of his natural capacities" and the correlative longing to master nature and the world around him.[69] The individual is therefore suspended between nature and ideal. Thus, oppositions surround this paradoxical individual, especially in the social sphere. In Kant's account of sociality, therefore, the individual is tamed only by a pure conceptual construction of reason: legal rights.

Right is an analytic or ideal concept, for Kant, that pertains to individual freedom. Because of its pure a priori status, Kant describes individual freedom as a universal law, such that the freedom of everyone is implicit in the concept of equal rights (along with coercion as a limit to each and every coordinated freedom).[70] Kant's theory of legal right is thus constructed "in pure intuition a priori, by analogy with presenting the possibility of bodies moving freely under the law of the *equality of action and reaction.*" That is to say, Kant tries to develop a theory of positive right that is analytical and not premised on empirical nature of the state or sociality. Rather, in an analogy to mathematics, Kant claims that "just as a purely formal concept of pure mathematics (e.g., of geometry) underlies this dynamical concept [the equality of action and reaction], reason has taken care to furnish the understanding as far as possible with a priori intuitions for constructing the concept of right."[71] While the definition of legal right and equality may prove logically compelling in this ideal sphere where they can be constructed as if circles and points, the legitimacy of such a law remains unclear, as well as how we move between ideal and real.

What guarantee exists for the morality of such an account of positive law? Kant's answer is that a theory of legal right is primarily a formal definition of law. And claiming that legal right is based on freedom, a fixture of reason, presupposes that reason is a timeless faculty that stands above the historical details of human action, legislation, and social relationships. Moral legitimacy is thus an extension of what Kant deems a purely rational legitimacy. But what happens when reason changes? Indeed, what happens when the purity of reason gives way to a more immanent and even potentially material basis for lawfulness? Kant's definition of law is thus susceptible to the intellectual and scientific transformations that I have been discussing. Understanding Cohen's rereading of Kant therefore relies on understanding the broader context in which he was working.

As Cohen points out, the *moral law* should be the systematic key to justifying positive law as nevertheless *moral*. With a view to this concern of locating value in law, Cohen believes Kant's understanding of legality is fundamentally flawed and needs to be revised.[72] Presuming that a juridical law or pure legality simply requires an abstract account of an external action that conforms to law, Kant's separation of law and morality leads to a serious problem: how does the duty to law become a moral principle that helps legitimate positive state laws? Why should moral individuals, acting in purely autonomous fashion, need positive laws at all, and how would such autonomous individuals remain part of any social relation? Indeed, how could a Jew, for example, now legitimated by a pure morality, be expected to abide by the specificities of German law, including the historical attributes of national identity underlying such a historical body of laws? A lurking atomization of moral autonomy lies beneath this pillar of Kantian liberalism, and an answer to these questions capable of quelling such suspicions of Jewish subversion, Cohen believes, requires more than the strength of Kant's logical analogies and formalism.

In order to rescue what he sees as the conceptual strength of Kant's original formulation of the moral law, Cohen therefore turns to the categorical imperative. As the principle with which Kant defines the moral law, the categorical imperative provides a mechanism for translating the principle or maxim of an individual's moral will into a potentially universal law.[73] The ferrying between the individual and universal, Cohen believes, is crucial. The appeal to an idea of "all rational beings" and "humanity in one's person" as the image of a universal audience, Cohen claims, alters the nature of moral autonomy. The appeal to humanity, as it were, becomes the content generated from the form of the moral law. In this formulation, Cohen sees a proper deduction of freedom and thus a defense of citizenship and duty as cultivations of an objective morality. Law and morality must be related if the ideas of moral freedom and of ethical action are to have any real historical and civic significance. Between the positive law of the state and the moral law of the autonomous Kantian subject, Cohen claims the structure of law is implicitly social. Thus, the importance of law, in Cohen's interpretation, is that it provides a norm for developing freedom. The law sets out the goal and task (*Aufgabe*) of cultivating the self.

If we recall Cohen's understanding of ethics as a science in its own right, then we can better understand the object of ethical cognition as the will—the lawful will. For Cohen, we can only discuss consciousness of the will through recognizing the actions that are willed. The law-abiding will, as the formal and analytic concept of law (*Gesetz*), has its form as a universal lawgiving without depending on any object. However, this does not mean its form is based in an abstraction from all ethical content.[74] Rather, the formal character of universal legislation in Kant's categorical imperative points to its content as the ought and its requirement of action: legislation is an activity of embodying pure will.

The ethical dimension of objectivity, Cohen claims, can be found in Kant's claim that the categorical imperative takes the form of universal legislation. However, Cohen takes issue with Kant's description in the *Typic of Practical Judgment* of the moral law taking a form similar to that of a law of nature.[75] For Kant, an action based on the moral law can be described as both moral and physical because both share the same formal representation of law. This type of law that can apply to concrete actions is modeled on a law of nature. However, Cohen claims this typology of law leads to Kant's flawed distinction between legality and morality.

The *form* of a law of nature suggests that the necessity and universality of a law is based on the categorical form of causal necessitation.[76] This framing of legality therefore emphasizes a quality of inevitability or a wholly dependent relation in which all effects are bound to their causes, which are heteronomous or outside the self-contained effect. Using this type of lawfulness, Kant therefore nests his entire account of moral law within a formal analogy to a law of nature.[77] Can causal necessity, however, account for the transformations of the state, society, and public morality that I have been describing throughout these chapters? Kant's description of the a priori status of the moral law—a law free from empirical determination[78]—now seems somewhat toothless, since it is really a watered down version of a law of nature. What, then, should we make of Kant's account of the individual agent of such a moral action? Is such an individual conceivable as anything more than a type itself?

As we saw in the previous chapter, Cohen considers necessity to be a logical concept while ethics operates in a modally different form. Thus, the form of lawfulness that gives the moral law its structural integrity and validity as a categorical imperative must be refocused. For Cohen, Kant had already gestured toward such an understanding of law in his criterion of universalization: *that a maxim must be universalizable for all of humanity—all rational beings—and that this universality of a community of rational beings provides the content of the moral law.*[79] This is a maxim's categorical function.

While the criterion of universal legislation provides the formal expression of legality, Cohen believes Kant originally had provided a point of access to legal content as well, thus circumventing Kant's later problem. This content, Cohen asserts, is found in what he referred to as Kant's great socialist insight: namely, the idea of *humanity* as an *end in itself.*[80] The idea of humanity, claims Cohen, both explicitly distinguishes moral law *"from the nature of experience"* and proposes another nature, a rational nature. Rational nature emerges from the formal expression of the law that the idea of humanity is an end in itself.[81] The idea of humanity is the *purpose* (*Zweck*) of law. As Kant writes in the first formulation of the categorical imperative: "Act only in accordance with that maxim through which you can at the same time will that it become a universal law." In the *Groundwork*, Kant adds to this formulation and writes, "Act as if the maxim of your action were to become by your will a *law of nature.*"[82] This is the formal criterion of legislation itself, that a law of nature represents the universal and necessary binding quality of law. But Kant coordinates this formulation with the following one: "So act that you use humanity, whether in your own person or in the person of any other, always at the same time as an end, never merely as a means."[83] As an end that is set for the will, *rational nature* becomes the determining ground of the moral law. Furthermore, because of its purposive character, the idea of humanity—rational nature—is what provides "the sovereign limiting condition of all subjective ends."[84] The idea of humanity therefore provides an objective end in itself for the individual; which is to say, the idea of humanity is the condition of possibility for moral autonomy. As a regulative ideal—a noumenal goal—Cohen understands the concept of freedom that is grounded in humanity as the basis for thinking the ethical a priori of a legitimate lawfulness (*Gesetzemäßigkeit*).[85] In humanity, subjective and objective ends merge. I act so as to help embody humanity; if my action cannot help to advance this idea, then my action is neither moral nor lawful. Because this account of freedom is the goal of law, it is not an isolated, individuated freedom. Rather, the idea of freedom is implicit in the idea of *all* humanity. This is the social dimension of practical reason that Cohen credits to Kant.

If we understand the content of the moral law to be generated by the categorical imperative, then we can better understand Cohen's theory that all laws are ethical laws, or subject to ethical cognition. This is not the same as saying that all actual laws are just but rather that all laws aim to cultivate the subject of an action as the goal of that law. Each law provides an action as its content. Hence, if we make explicit this relationship between humanity and the moral self in the figure of pure will, then the action mandated by law *should* always have as its goal the ethical rejuvenation of state law through the development of *moral selves* striving to become part of humanity.

This relationship between humanity and the moral self cannot be the mandate of partitioned communities of morality alone, nor imposed from above by the nation-state. Rather, the way that law conceptually expresses the *I* of a moral action through the performance of that action means that this relationship between the moral self and the idea of humanity is primarily social. The ethical relationship between cultivating a self and cultivating humanity is the *labor* of public reasoning. Thus, with a revised concept of law as moral law, Cohen finds in individual law a call to the self; the concept of the individualizing law is the call to the self to be moral and to act for the sake of humanity.

By insisting on the separation of law and morality, Kant was attempting to provide the ideal foundations for a theory of public law. Cohen, for his part, showed why the gap need not exist in the first place.[86] Understanding his criticisms of Kant helps us understand Cohen's account of the law as the origin of the individual and the citizen. This sociality of law provided an answer to antiliberal attacks on Kantian thought. However, as we will see, many conservative and antiliberal thinkers believed the gap between law and morality was implicit in liberalism and could only be sutured with a turn toward an essential freedom grounded in a more concrete value such as the shared existence of a religiously *and* naturally grounded people. Thus, it was this suspicion of a lingering dualism in Kantian philosophy that Cohen feared would lead to a certain curtailment of critical and justified accounts of moral norms and, worse, the exclusion of many from partaking in the work of reasoning.

SECULARIZATION OR JEWISH DISENCHANTMENT?

The Kantian separation of legality and morality was in large part the basis for a particular tradition of German liberalism. Inspired by Kant's articulation of a priori legal rights, many legal theorists actively theorized how law could be extricated from the influence of morality and politics.[87] Apace with the rationalizing tendencies of the sciences I explored in chapter 2, the pretense to scientific neutrality therefore exerted a great deal of influence on constitutional theory in imperial Germany,[88] especially public law, where it would have a lasting impression on both Hugo Preuss and Max Weber (more informally) as consultants in the drafting of the Weimar constitution.[89] The concern for political and moral neutrality of positive law stemmed in large part from a theory of public law that deemed the state a legal personality independent of any moral personality, a theme introduced by Wilhelm Eduard Albrecht in an essay appearing in 1837[90] and elaborated as an explicitly nonmetaphysical basis for Paul Laband's famed treatment of the Prussian constitution of 1871.[91] The rationalization of positive law was therefore a major contributor to the anxieties that gripped Wilhelmine society as a whole, and informed Weber's description of this age of disenchantment and rationalization that saw the retreat of the "most sublime values" from public life.[92]

Related to the separation of legality and morality, therefore, was the perceived separation of civic and religious identity. Predicated on a pure or a priori construction of legal personality, this problematic redefinition of civic and national identity in legal terms struck many conservatives as a neutralization of German identity. Unification of the German Empire both brought about a transition from corporate identities to mass culture and a market-oriented civil society and, as Weber himself characterized his own context, transformed how customs and mores such as honor were articulated as social values. Honor and duty served as justifications for membership in privileged classes and estates that gave way to the rationalized membership in a market-society in which a person's "relation to production" was recognized instead.[93] As Ann Goldberg writes of imperial Germany, "On the one hand there was the continuation of traditional corporate notions of identity and honor and sharp class distinctions. On the other hand, industrial capitalism and the democratization of German society were undermining paternalistic and deferential relations that had been the basis of a hierarchical society."[94] Indeed, the cultural emphasis on German honor and identity in the Kaiserreich was so strong that the courts became sites of heated litigation over charges of defamation and libel. In these venues of newly articulated legal rights, Germans were negotiating their traditional cultural mores within a shifting juridical regime. However, the fact that Jews were such keen interpreters of Kantian philosophy and actively engaged in pursuing such defamation suits and using these newfound rights against libel in the courts and in the press only further instigated the charge of growing disenchantment and the claim that Judaism, secularism, and liberalism were interchangeable.[95]

Antiliberals and anti-Semites perceived the disenchantment of liberalism that accompanied this new legal regime as the design and orchestration of a uniquely Jewish secularism. This was because the liberalizing emphasis on rights and equality was purported to sail under false colors when it valorizes reasoned discussion and consensus as capable of evaluating different opinions and recognizing opposing viewpoints. Whether in religious thinking or in political argument, as the young Leo Strauss describes, liberalism leads to "but one tendency, which is the political-apologetic tendency."[96] The worst form of such liberalism, Strauss describes, paraphrasing the radical conservative and anti-Semitic thinker Paul de Lagarde, was to be found in the work of Jewish writers. Their apologetic invocation of an abstract monotheism, tolerance, and the eschewal of dogmas, as purportedly liberal political goals just so happen to be of particular benefit to the Jews. This subterfuge is, Strauss comments, "A sign of a lack of seriousness; [since] every religion is exclusive." In other words, self-reflexivity and the attempt to critically justify public arguments with conceptual transparency struck conservative thinkers of Wilhelmine Germany as vacuous. But, according to Lagarde, this was a ploy on the part of liberalism to conceal whom its equality and positive definition of citizenship benefited most: the Jews. As Strauss writes, according to conservatives like Lagarde, "Liberalism is nothing but secularized Judaism."[97]

From the vantage point of conservative thinkers like Lagarde, against whom Cohen argued in an affidavit during the Marburg Talmud Trial of 1888, this equating of liberalism with Judaism was evidence that more than religious freedom or the freedom of conscience was at stake. By emphasizing the individual citizen as the bearer of rights, Kantian formalism and its separation of legality and morality had helped erect a legal definition of citizenship and transformed national identity into a positive assertion on the part of a pure, empty formalism. The problem facing the German nation-state was thus a question of not only the values that would inform law but also the *essence* of national identity. What benefited the Jews, certainly, was that this distinction between religious collectivity and national collectivity opened up the space of law in which to reason their way into German civic belonging. However, the charge of apologetics targeted how this distinction between religious corporatism and national belonging effectively prioritized individuals over their social and communal locales. This path of liberal neutralization left conservatives disenchanted. And in its worst manifestation, the disenchantment of citizenship and national identity opened up a space for conservative thinkers such as Eugen Dühring to employ the notion of a racial community of blood in order to reenchant the national community.[98]

The "racial distinction," as the Jewish, National Liberal politician, Ludwig Bamberger noted already at the time of the Berlin anti-Semitism dispute in 1879-80, "was adopted only when inequality of right could no longer be justified with reference to religious denomination."[99] That is to say, Bamberger recognized that the secularization of the public sphere left religion an insufficient ground on which to model scientifically and politically credible values. Liberalism was therefore caught between a rock and hard place. On the one hand, the legal equality granted to Jews independent of religious identity enabled new forms of social and political participation; on the other hand, the claim that this equality had chipped away at the foundation of the state left Jews to face yet another charge of outsider status. As Wendy Brown notes, "The racialization of the Jew circumvented the difficulties in submitting Jewishness to a construal of religion as a belief community."[100] The rise of political anti-Semitism should be, consequently, considered in the context of the secularization of the German public sphere.

With the erosion of a Christian Germany, a search for a new solution to liberal disenchantment beyond religious identity alone emerged.
This was just the tone telegraphed in Wilhelm Marr's infamous tract,
"The Conquest of Jewishness over Germanness: Considered from a *Nonconfessional* Standpoint," in which he coined the term *anti-Semitism*.[101]
Thus, liberalism's treatment of religion as a private concern allowed for a
reconfigured Jewish otherness at the level of the scientific and the political. Blood provided a supplement with which to fill in the gap between
the individual and the state—between legality and morality.[102] No longer
an issue of religious difference, this racialized Jewishness in politics, philosophy, and society represented a different kind of neutralization, and
the mythic quality of racial difference, in turn, helped fuel a newfound
enchantment for Germans. The Jews were considered purveyors of an
opposing *worldview* to that of Germans; that is, the Jews were seen as
carriers of an opposing *Weltanschauung*.[103]

To suture the gap between legality and morality, antiliberals sought
out new spiritual avenues of enchantment, and many of them presented
worldviews that were emphatically scientific and philosophical. Using the
model of a hermeneutic worldview,[104] the rising Nazi philosopher and son
of Wilhelm Wundt, Max Wundt (1879–1963), for example, appealed to the
forces of myth and the occultism of a blood-consciousness to bind the
nation—and Kantian dualism—together. This conflated spiritual ethos
and historical meaning—biological race and empirical human life—in
one immanent spiritual-material whole. For example, Wundt pleaded
for Germans to

> establish the connection, which for other peoples becomes the highest vo-
> cation of their people's spiritual life such as the Greeks or the Hindus: the
> connection between their Mythos and their religion and their philosophy.
> We must establish this connection in new and artistic manners, since they
> were so fully torn up from the natural development of our history. From
> the spirit of Germanic myth must we clarify for ourselves the conceptual
> world of our great thinkers, from the spirit of Germanic myth must we
> understand their work. When we succeed in this, we will have fastened
> together our entire spiritual inheritance, which is ancestrally stamped in
> our blood and is inherited in our history, into one great unity.[105]

Wundt claimed that the consciousness of blood *as* history and the symbolic worldview of Germanic myth would reorient the entire structure

of the state, saving it from liberalism. Law and culture would be refit, their legitimacy drawn from the immanence of blood and history, in the "glory days [*Blütezeiten*] . . . in which the inner and outer life of a collective people achieves for itself the highest reign [*Reichtum*]." All aspects of life and culture, "economy and state are powerfully and all-encompassingly constituted and serve as the ground for a complete Spirit, in which all branches in equal measure come together in their best form, in art and poetry, in religion and science."[106]

Wundt considered himself an idealist, despite the biological material of blood figuring so prominently in his language of myth. It is therefore helpful to consider the anti-Semitic rhetoric on which Wundt built his interpretation of the "German Spirit's self-forged weapon" against the foreign threat of liberalism to Germany's spiritualist worldview. Indeed, there is a palpable influence of theosophical spiritualism in the anti-Semitic attack on Jewish materialism and commercialism.[107] Moreover, Wundt aims that spiritual weaponry against the "un-German effects of the new framing of the world brought about through the assumption of foreignness," a foreignness of Spirit that had dissolved the "inner connection between the individual and the communal." Having forgotten the goal of a "folk-consciousness [*Volksbewusstsein*]," the foreign spirit of liberalism and modernism leads these "individuals, on self-stitched together grounds, [to] elect freely assembled groups" who in their atomized existence "are amply prepared to forget the health of the state in exchange for the health of the party."[108] Through legal protection of free associations, a legal privilege almost unknown in the early Kaiserreich, people were positing themselves as groups without legitimacy, claims Wundt. The state, he continues, "is now nothing but a machine," a tool and instrument of the individual.[109] The individual is nothing but a piston or cog in the machine of the state. Such technology, Wundt believed, best served liberalism's separation of state and the individual and, thus, armed the "bankers and businessmen" with the weaponry necessary to mutiny against the state. Recognizing only the machinations of individual and state, liberalism was to blame for blurring borders in service of foreign investment interests, since "gold is bound by no national-borders."[110] Lest there be any doubt as to which foreigners Wundt has in mind, we need only look at the *völkisch* press for confirmation that these bankers and businessmen, the Rothschilds and the Rathenaus, are Jews.

Wundt's criticisms were primarily inspired by the upheavals that brought the Weimar constitution into place, although such debates were not unique to Weimar. In Wilhelmine debates, the rational legal structure of the *Rechtsstaat* was often attacked for guaranteeing the rights of the individual at the expense of the communal or the national community. It was this emphasis on the *Rechtsstaat*, the positivity of law, and the security of private rights over and against the public institutions of the state, that fueled the antiliberal and antimodernist critique boiling over on the political right and in the anti-Semitic parties of the *Kaiserreich*. Wundt's suspicions over this positive legal identity therefore centered on the dissolution of a folk consciousness and its replacement with individual rights. In this social state of legal rights all that remained, to invoke Bismarck's own policy, was a machine made of iron and drained of its blood. Wundt was therefore giving voice to anxieties that had beset the German public sphere well before the war.

This rhetoric surrounding the technologized state and the critique of individual protections was a focal point for political conservatives in their critique of the liberal distinction between law and morality—between individual and state-community. While Christianity dominated the public memory and remained the historic source of the Christian German State, the imperial court chaplain Adolf Stoecker (1835–1909) insisted that modernizing forces of secularization, stoked and spurred by the liberal Jewish press's war against religion, were responsible for its demise, since Judaism was not simply a religious other. Rather, in Stoecker's account, "modern Judaism is, all things considered, an irreligious power [*irreligiöse Macht*]; a power that bitterly struggles against Christianity, in the nations [*Völkern*] that are rooted in Christian faith just as much as in national feeling, and as a replacement seeks nothing other than the idolatrous worship [*abgöttisch Verehrung*] of Judaism just as it is, which has no other content than its own self-love."[111] For Stoecker, Judaism represents the attempt to desiccate the state of religion. Judaism seeks to insert, in the place of the organic relationship between individual and state-community, its idolatry in the form of a redefined national entity. Securing for itself the recognition of a historical tradition and for its members recognition as individual rights-holders independent of religious belonging, Stoecker and Wundt's characterizations of Judaism hold it in contempt as a force of neutralization. Modern liberal culture, Stoecker suspected, was therefore built on the technological power of modern Judaism as an irreligious power. It is the power of a neutral and positive state that has replaced religion with the liberal *Rechtsstaat*, or a veneration of legal rights that both mechanizes and disenchants the relationship between individual and the state. The power of this liberal tendency was yet another product of a "century of steam and electricity, of the railways and the machines."[112] This technology, Stoecker intimates, was one expression of the power of liberalism, which pitted enchantment and machine against one another in battle. Law and morality were camped across front lines.

Between Stoecker's context of imperial Germany and Wundt's later Empire and Weimar Republic, the anti-Semitic chorus of voices similarly understood the separation of law from the legitimating force of Christian moral religion as the decay of German national identity. Viewed together, the budding German youth movements, the *völkisch* movement of the 1880s and 1890s, and the growing legitimacy of the anti-Semitic parties in reconstituting a Christian Germany has led Shulamit Volkov to characterize anti-Semitism in the *Kaiserreich* as a cultural code.[113] Following the work of Clifford Geertz, Volkov's description attempts to provide an anthropological dimension to the rhetoric of the anti-Semitic parties, which cast all aspects of culture and everyday life in the symbolic discourse of an overall revitalization project of re-Christianizing and re-Germanizing the state.[114] Such a cultural code of Germanism attempted to induce "moods and motivations," as Geertz describes religious culture,[115] with Christianity understood as something more than confessional difference. Christianness, as opposed to any one confession, was fuel for a new conception of an enchanted culture, a code in which the symbolic power of blood and spirit prevailed. This mythic Christianness, turning away from the machine of liberal rationalism, dressed the metaphysics of secularism in new clothes.[116]

In sum, the goal of the *völkisch* movement was to reoccupy legal validity with new moral value, to create a complete code with which to reshape German life. Kant's separation, the bedrock of liberalism, left philosophy and culture with a crisis: how should law be legitimated if not from some authentic source of moral value? For many *völkisch* and antiliberal thinkers like Paul de Lagarde, Houston Stewart Chamberlain, and the young Wundt, the answer lay in the unity of "the Germanic world, through [which] racial blood and spiritual disposition"[117] might bring a new national religion to fruition. Only the "belief in the unmediated unity of spirit and actuality [*Geist und Wirklichkeit*], universal and particular" might reenchant German national identity. Only in such an identity would liberalism be defeated by the "one spirit [that] lives in the individual and the collective."[118] In so doing, the idealist spirit of a folk consciousness, united with the materiality of blood and soil, might finally overcome the liberal separation of law and morality and give new legitimacy to authority. Hence, as the Weimar-era, antiliberal thinker Hermann Meyer described, the *völkisch* movement's rejoinder to the Kantian separation of law and morality was, quite simply, power. Meyer writes, "Law extracts its force of value, not from moral law [*Sittengesetz*] rather from out of its own essence, this is called power, which can command, which can coerce. . . . Law is power."[119] Only power can confront power; only the weapons of blood and sprit can combat the neutralized machine. In the language of the *Völkischer Beobachter*, the periodical organ of the early Nazi movement, the highest expression of this spiritual warfare is in law as power, for only law can expel definitively the external inferiority of a foreign spirit; only law can make transparent the opacity of blood.[120] In this respect, the law becomes an embodiment of the nation, of the law within the blood and soil of a people, or what Wundt's professional patron, the neo-Kantian philosopher Bruno Bauch (1877–1942) referred to as the basis for *Mitgeborenen*, the native-born fraternity of those whom are "blood of my blood."[121]

BLOOD, HISTORY, AND UNITY

In the rhetoric of antiliberalism, blood had become a spiritualized material, an enchanted source of norms and history.[122] But only if we acknowledge the status of blood as both a scientific and a metaphysical concept—much as monism and materialism represented in chapter 2—can we better understand the extent to which a blood-spirit nexus created new forms of enchantment. The positive distinction between law and morality, the eminently Kantian form of liberalism, had been united in a new value system. But the stakes of Kantian philosophy were no mere addendum to this public shift in worldviews. Rather, Kantianism was the emphatic stage on which such debates were given the greatest intellectual credibility. And in leaving open the door to model moral law on the empirical law of causal necessity, Kant also left a legacy of perceived dualism, which was used by some to justify the appeal to empirical intuition in the formation of moral values. How to unite the two spheres of law and morality, material and ideal, was now a point of philosophical and political contention.

For example, in 1917, Bruno Bauch's appeal to the "blood of my blood" would transform the pages of the eminent journal *Kant-Studien*, one of the most respected philosophical journals of the twentieth century, into what amounted to an appendix of the *Völkischer Beobachter*. In his "Vom Begriff der Nation (Ein Kapitel zur Geschichtsphilosophie)," Bauch argues that we must distinguish between the "nation considered as a natural groundwork for the people's unity (*völkischer Einheit*) on the one hand and the historical unity of the people (*Volkseinheit*) on the other."[123] This distinction, however, does not imply that the historical unity of a people could completely reorient the meaning of natural unity to the point of becoming neutralized. To the contrary, Bauch argues that it is the historical "labor of those born-in-common (*Mitgeborenen*) that sanctifies the [natural] land of the *Vaterland* and *Heimat*."[124] In other words, the natural and historical meanings of national unity are inflections of a dialectic played out by historical actors' unifying labor, shared language, and the blood and soil of that people whose spiritual purpose takes shapes as ethical ideals carried by the nation. Bauch was not speaking strictly as a materialist, however. His description of how natural unity is sanctified by history and has its unity transposed into a higher octave indicates just how predominant ideas still are. But Bauch insists on an irreducible practical life or intuition of a natural fact of the people and their labor; life and intuition gain their own value, even if only as irreducible remainders left in the wake of idealization. It is this remainder of a natural value or intuitive bond between real and ideal that exposes the degree to which Bauch's thought exploits a problem in Kantian philosophy and introduces a philosophy of racialized nationalism.

The most charitable reading of Bauch's argument must assume that he is repurposing the Kantian division between sensibility and understanding or intuition and concept. In Bauch's hands, this dualism serves as motivation for a theory of value cognition that negotiates between nature and history. These latter concepts set the parameters for what we take as true. For example, in his previous publications in *Kant-Studien* dealing with natural science, Bauch argues that there should be no confusion between sensation and experience; to confuse them is to rely on "naive intuition, in the worst sense of the word."[125] Rather, much like Cohen and Ernst Cassirer, Bauch insists that natural experience and sensibility are based on the lawful cognition of substance. In other words, a judgment is like a mathematical function that generates a map of the cognitive mess it encounters. In turn, the determination of how things are described in qualitative terms (color, shape, texture, environment) is mapped onto a quantitative series of objects and helps gird those cognitions together.[126] All cognition is of what Bauch claims to be relation (*Beziehung*).[127] Yet, despite claiming that there is "no graspability of nature without conceptuality [*keine Begreiflichkeit der Natur ohne Begrifflichkeit*]," Bauch nevertheless retains a notion of intuition, or intuitability [*Anschaulichkeit*], as the necessary index of the indivisible remainder.[128] In other words, Bauch maintains that the function-like cognition of material or sensible experience is the cognition of something [*Etwas*] like a series that extends over time, and that the cognitive function of a series is to provide the *intuition* of change over time with unity. Cognition therefore reproduces the real series as a sequentially divided set of attributes of what we call experience.[129] However, in emphasizing its unity and lawfulness, Bauch also describes cognition as simultaneous with the moment of intuition. In other words, although the gap between sense and understanding, intuition and concept, is sutured, it nevertheless remains a gap.

The relationship between intuition and concept is therefore crucial to Bauch's conception of natural and historical unity in his arguments about the concept of the nation. When considering the intuition of natural unity, Bauch's argument culminates in a theory of representation or recognition of categories such as blood, soil, and language—the bedrocks of romantic nationalism—as the intuited series. However, Bauch seeks to idealize these natural elements while indexing their unification into a manifold of cognition. Thus, the natural unity of the nation (*völkischer Einheit*) persists as an index of the value of historical unity (*Volkseinheit*). The value assigned in the historical sphere is therefore essentially related to the intuition of natural unity.

While the relationship between nature and history suggested by Bauch might not seem like an expressly racialized account, the motivations for Bauch's more polished philosophical argument can be found in a 1916 open letter published in *Der Panther*. While Bauch's essay on the nation outlined a more technical Kantian argument, in this letter he explicitly charges that Cohen could not understand Kant because Jews were merely guests in the German nation, and the difference between national spirits precluded a proper interpretation by a foreigner.[130] As a direct challenge to the very school of neo-Kantianism to which one of the previous issues of *Kant-Studien* was dedicated, Bauch implied that no degree of acculturation or of idealized performance of language or culture could establish the veracity of national belonging. The connection between the two arguments hung on his insistence that Kant and German identity were indissolubly linked by the kind of natural unity that he described in his essay on the nation. He writes,

> Corporeal, just as spiritual, communal origin of the "born-in-common" [*Mitgeborenen*] however, finds its expression in the community of language. It is the decisive expression of the relationship of the nation. The folkish alien may live through generations among us and speak no other language more capably, than ours. Nevertheless, his language is not ours. From physical sound to the most delicate shading in the expression of the inner experiences that pour into the language, there remains something alien between him and us. Much evidence is palpable, from the jargon of the street to the most famous poems. Only where blood of our blood in language also pulses us forward, only there can the appeal from our lips strive: "O sweet voice! Much perfect sound / the mother tongue!"[131]

Kant and German identity are bound together by language. And, although not explicitly named, there was little doubt that Cohen was the target of this indictment. Bauch's selection of this issue of *Kant-Studien* for his essay was no coincidence: a recent issue of the journal had been almost entirely dedicated to Cohen's neo-Kantianism. All who read these words knew what was at stake.[132] Bauch had indicted the movement stemming from Marburg, and if any doubt remained as to Bauch's intensions, there was ample precedent for the sentiment. Indeed, Bauch was making explicit what many had already claimed was implicit in Kantian liberalism. For example, in an article appearing in the eminent *Preußische Jahrbücher,* Max Hildebert Boehm criticized Cohen's idealization of Deutschtum und Judentum as nothing more than Kantian moral-formalism, a critique that met with great praise among members of the Zionist youth movement, Bar Kochba.[133] Bauch's argument divided the editorial board of the Kant Gesellschaft and led to Cassirer eventually stepping down in protest.[134]

The politics of Kantianism were about more than the interpretations of philosophy; they were about Kantian philosophy as the basis for German identity, first and foremost.

The significance of the event must be understood yet again through the lens of the history and intellectual debates I have been discussing throughout this text. In pursuit of an enchantment based in the explicitly scientific thrust of neo-Kantian philosophy, Bauch pursued values that could be retrofitted to serve material interests. To many, only a blood-spirit of language and ideas—a language of spirit-as-blood-as-history—could account for the truly *scientific* sources of the nation. Only such a properly grounded science could reunite the spheres of form and matter, spirit and history, in a nation. The quest to overcome the separation between legality and morality, which was liberalism's great coup, was more than a technical philosophical problem; it represented a politics of cultural reform surrounding the so-called crisis of modernism and the secularization of the public sphere.[135] But rather than historically clarifying the conceptual problem of legality and morality being separated in practical reason, the haste to unify them in a new metaphysical mixture of spirit and matter was propped up with mythic grandeur. For if science and the state were to have remained enchanted, and if pantheism, materialism, and the metaphysics of secularism might all have continued to feed off of the concept of value, then law and morality would indeed have been unified.

Yet, as Cohen noted in his affidavit for the Marburg Trial, "where racial hatred and defamation rage, there govern stereotypes (*Phrase*). Stereotypes and prejudices effect an epidemic and even infect the strict work of *Wissenschaft* with misunderstanding."[136] In other words, the pretense to scientific justification and reasoning and the pursuit of mythic enchantment are incommensurable. It had been such an infection that intensified the thirst for enchantment in antiliberal thinkers and led them to brew their own theoretical elixirs with which to overcome the rationalization of imperial Germany. Cohen recognized the vicissitudes of the search for reenchantment and therefore sought answers of a different kind, which he believed could be held up to a public and scientific standard.

Anticipating this crisis of disenchantment, Cohen worried that a liberalism both forgetful of its own past and construed solely as the sum of its abstract legal parts would leave a secularized human reason stranded on a path of what I am calling metaphysical secularism. The dialectic of enchantment and disenchantment therefore played out along two distinct paths: one neutralizing and the other metaphysical. As we have seen, this dialectic also led legal and moral values along similar trajectories, and Cohen thus went about revising Kantian principles in order to resist both the appeal to an abstract liberal and secular individualism as well as the claim that the values of honor, identity, and paternalism were the only legitimate foundations of rights, culture, society, and nation.[137]

Therefore, Cohen's revision of Kantian legal and moral thought should also be understood as connected to his critique of materialism. Together, both provide a trenchant critique of the scientific presuppositions of materialism and social Darwinism, as well as their deployment in a social and political discourse about the legal and moral unity of a people rooted in some pregiven patchwork identity of traditional class distinctions and discriminations. Cohen suspected that if reason were held to model its laws on natural causality or necessity, then reason would remain fixated on a pregiven datum, such as the materiality of blood and history. Hence, we ought to examine how and why Cohen agreed that the separation of law from morality needed a principle with which to overcome the gap between legitimate moral law and positive legal statute, as well as how the divergent approaches taken by antiliberals and Cohen reflect the divisive paths of the dialectic of enchantment.

HUMANITY AND THE NATION

We are now better equipped to understand Cohen's multifaceted concerns with the Kantian separation of legality and morality. Unlike Kant and Bauch, Cohen refused to admit nature or natural causality as having any value for the structure of moral judgment. The problem in Kant's account stemmed from his reliance on causal lawfulness as the model of law, which Cohen maintained would not suffice for ethics because the kind of universality of a moral law does not determine actions in a physically causal manner. Indeed, no one would claim, even in a formal sense, that his or her actions were *necessitated* by a moral law or duty. For example, if I act out of a sense of duty to a moral law, my sense of duty cannot be said to coerce my action, such as the laws of gravity might be said to force a rock to fall to the ground at a determinable velocity. Rather, the law that conditions my will can be the origin of my action but not the cause of my action. The relation between action and ideal—the world described by natural scientific models of experience and the world viewed through ethical ideas, including laws, rights, and their actualization—cannot be collapsed into one single form of lawfulness. Laws of nature ascribe necessity and universality to their objects of knowledge, but this is so only through a causal modality that describes how things came to be. Ethical laws, by contrast, are oriented toward the *purpose* of action, thus describing how things *ought to be*. Hence, true moral freedom would have to be detached from such a formal model of natural or causal legality.

We can see how Cohen's critique of the Kantian dualism between sensibility and understanding led him to revise the meaning of law in the coupling of law and morality. While Cohen, in his *Logik*, rejected sensibility for the infinitesimal for reasons that had to do with natural scientific cognition, his ethical philosophy presents a rearguard action against the kind of materialism and spiritualism of the *völkisch* movement—and particularly of a thinker like Bauch—that might seize on the use of nature to model moral law and value.

By contrast to Bauch, for example, Cohen insists that the very concept of law within ethics must be understood as an ideal that points toward the *end of law*, the idea of a universal, of humanity. There is no intuition and no lingering sensibility that anchors the values of history. Rather, Cohen insists that concepts provide the schematization of universality as the content of the ideal law itself. Akin to Hegel's critique of Kant, Cohen insists both that the relationship between ideality and actuality, between law and morality, must be dialectically strengthened and that the gaps must be filled in. *Morality* needs *Sittlichkeit*, or a conception of ethical culture including history and positive legal institutions.[138] Law is not only a systematic concern, for it resonates on a cultural-symbolic level as well. However, *Sittlichkeit* must be reinterpreted as lawful to the extent that it is neither a natural law nor a law in our members. Law cannot rely on intuition. Ethical culture represents the sphere of opinion, and Cohen writes, "Opinion [*Meinung*] is, as the Hegelian expression goes, 'my own' [*die Meinige*]."[139] However, the method of ethics is nevertheless a science of sociality. The legal dimension of ethical culture is therefore not the subject of metaphysics or naturalism—it is not the study of my own laws or the natural person—but what Cohen describes as analogous to mathematics, namely, the idealization of culture and society according to a priori principles.[140] But human actions are dynamic and developing and the ethical sociality of human action is what conditions law. Thus, Cohen writes,

> [Kant's] concept of the law finds its greatest difficulty emerge on the very site upon which it has its deepest ground. Kant made law [Gesetz] a focal point of ethics. And yet, he *distinguished legality [Legalität] from morality.* Morality is rooted in the law [Gesetz], but it is not legality [Legalität]. One immediately sees from this, though it is invalid, the suspicion as though the law undermines ethics, making ethics insufficient unto itself and unfree. That would be the suspicion concerning legality; it is not with morality. *It is precisely law that distinguishes morality from legality.* However, before we try to illuminate and make full use of this meaning of "law," we ask above all for the sense of "legality."[141]

For Cohen, Kant's distinction between legality and morality is animated by an antiquated suspicion concerning legalism in morality. This flawed understanding is associated with the kind of moral theology that had feared the deterministic reduction of free will and moral agency. This suspicion about legalism does not originate with Kant but, rather, "with Paul's polemic against the Mosaic teaching, which he designated and recognized as 'law' [Gesetz]."[142] It is on account of this prejudice against law, which Cohen intimates as a prejudice against Jewish legalism, that Kant seems to fear any mixture of ethics and law. And yet, because of Kant's fear of legalism, his philosophy of law ended up reifying a causal model of physical law all the same. For Cohen, the notion that morality is rooted in law means that the moral content of the law must be located in the form of law itself, in the conceptual structure of normativity. Thus, the scientific mandate of ethics must be to discover what makes law possible.

In order to provide ethics with the fundamental principle with which to begin this construction of an ethical culture, therefore, Cohen must reinterpret the meaning of intelligibility and the moral good. Cohen does this by refocusing the relationship between action and ethical ideals in temporal terms. That is, the law must be understood as that which provides action with purposiveness. In accordance with his revised account of the categorical imperative, whereby the idea of humanity in my person gives me an objective norm for enacting the self or a subjective end, Cohen's emphasis on the purpose of law provides him with critical leverage for his theory of citizenship and national identity. He therefore offers a critique of Kant's *Typic*, an account of archetypal and ectypal natures, which I briefly discussed above, and shifts the emphasis toward a purposiveness of the law. By enacting humanity, Cohen believes he has found a model for producing an action from rational grounds without modeling law on any kind of natural event, cause, or essence. Rather, "the intelligible character [of ethics] does not mean an intelligible cause, but only an intelligible purpose, the purposive end [*Endzweck*], which forms the ethical being [*sittliche Wesen*]. But in what kind of being [*Sein*] is this purposive goal realized? In the ought [*Sollen*]. And what is the meaning of being of this ought apart from the being of the task [*Aufgabe*]? In what relation does it stand to the being of nature?"[143] The origin of an action is the idea and norm. But although actions may appear to be effects produced by causes, Cohen is interested in how a purposive determination of action attributes the action with meaning. Ethical norms provide actions with a *Sollen*, or "ought," as opposed to an ontological *Sein* or "is." Or, as Cohen puts it, "the being of what ought to be [*das Sein des Sollens*]."[144] Cohen therefore reinterprets the is/ought distinction, the Humean catalyst for Kant's transcendental idealism as a whole, and its role as the basic problem of legal and ethical philosophy. Cohen claims that the ought has its own being: as the purposive end that is intelligible to ethics and that distinguishes itself from the being of nature.

In contrast to Bauch's division between nature and history, Cohen's idealist ethics represents thinking and willing as modalities. Both are ideal; thinking concerns what is, and willing concerns what ought to be. For Cohen, modality expresses the particularly important relationship between logic and ethics, which he refers to as the "basic law of truth."[145] Insofar as truth is a concept that ethics generates out of its relationship to logical necessity and universality, as we saw in chapter 2, logic provides the underlying conceptual fabric permeating the entire system of philosophy. But, without ethics, the being of nature could not be properly idealized into the normative dimension that human actions require.

Cohen therefore does not take issue with Kant's claim that logic and ethics both share the cognition of experience as their focus. However, the natural world and the object of pure cognition cannot be schematized in the same way as an ethical ideal. Thus, Cohen refers to his method as one of purity, which is to say the pure *idealization* of these two worlds and two models of temporality that originate in thinking: for logic it is nature, while for ethics it is law and history.[146] While thinking anticipates the being of an object, or nature, the will anticipates a different kind of being. As Cohen claims, in ethics "the pure will wants eternity. It wants nothing other than the eternal. And only the pure will can generate the eternal."[147] In ethics, the illusion[148] of a suspended present in the abstraction of logical judgment is overcome through an act of judging and volition (*Wollen*), a decision to will an object on the basis of the future correlation of ideality and actuality. In so doing, eternity—which is merely abstract for thinking—is brought into being. Thus, ethics makes it possible for us to speak of the being of the ought, or "the being of the law; rather, the being of the ideal; this is the being of the pure will."[149]

By opposing the idea of any given object and the insistence on its pure production, Cohen emphasizes the practical focus of his critical idealism.[150] But in intuition—even pure intuition, which Cohen attributes to Kant's modeling of experience such as in mathematics—Cohen sees an attempt both to locate a source outside of thinking, a given being, and to seize hold of this illusory source as though it were eternally present for logical judgment.[151] But for Cohen, time is anticipatory and in ethics it is emphatically futural, even when it considers history. Thus in contrast to Bauch's description of a racialized natural unity and intuition of a series, Cohen claims that a series can only be modeled on anticipation. In logic, that is because what is in the past, such as the unity claimed by Bauch, "does not come first, rather what comes first is the future, from which the past is drawn out (*abhebt*). In light of the not-yet emerges the no-longer. Both moments commence in the future, which the series frames."[152] The relationship between the logic of pure cognition and the ethics of pure willing, Cohen claims, is established in the figure of futurity, which is to say the concept of an object comes first by anticipating its object.[153]

While both nature and history are idealized by logic and ethics, according to Cohen, no ontological separation exists between the natural and pure thinking or willing. Rather, because Cohen does not appeal to the intuitions of space and time, his focus is on "infinitesimal reality." As an infinite origin in thinking itself, the model of the infinitesimal "is therefore the presupposition for the concept of law, which the term function now designates."[154] That is to say, in contrast to Bauch's description of a quantitative series, Cohen claims that, in the lawful cognition of nature, law must be understood as a function, as a necessitation rule that applies infinitesimally. Thinking is an act of judgment rather than an act of representation, which is the work of intuition. Thinking therefore begins with the idea of quantity—the idea of an object rather than no object—and generates the value of that object as the output of cognition. Physical laws *necessitate* their described events only to the extent that as mathematical laws they anticipate the reality with which they are concerned. A triangle, for example, anticipates the possibility of angular measurement but does not represent something located in the world corresponding to which the sum of three angles equaling 180 degrees serves as its representation.

Ethics, by contrast, consists of more than just logical concepts; ethics also consists of ethical *ideas* (*sittliche Ideen*), which are coordinated as ends. Rather than describe an experience in retrospect, ethical law prescribes what *should* be the case, even if that which ought to be does not occur. Ethical judgments aim at a task or goal, and this goal provides an account of the logical concepts and a justification for their use. In Cohen's words, "Ethical ideas are distinguished from theoretical concepts; but this distinction may not permit their kinship to be their sublation."[155] The intimate relationship between logic and ethics, concepts and ideas, implies that ethics presupposes logic as its methodological skeleton. However, the conditions of all ethical ideas must not be sought in the historical and positive institutions of natural anthropological human being. In deliberately mimicking Hegelian language, Cohen insists that these *ideas* (*Ideen*) cannot be sublated (*aufgehoben*) into *concepts* (*Begriffe*). Ethics is a method, in the sense of a plan or a blueprint, to bring about the ethical ideal. It is not enough just to know the law; we must justify it with purposive action.

By refocusing lawfulness on the purpose of ethical judgment and the pure will—on the ought, rather than causality—Cohen reorients the Kantian problem of relating the ideal and the real. According to Cohen, the will originates action on the model of an idealized, temporalized lawfulness, a law that brings us into the future. This is why Cohen's account of moral autonomy is primarily concerned with how law legislates the self. The future to which action aspires is one in which a moral self has helped bring about the idea of humanity. Thus, a lawful will helps provide a nexus between thinking and willing. Just as thinking must schematize the norms of knowledge with possible experiences, so too the will must relate to the actualization of the norms of the law that mandate its actions. For Cohen, this is the problem of relating logic to ethics, of relating thinking to willing. And it is a problem that Kant was attempting to solve in the *Typic of Practical Judgment*.[156] The difference between the *Typic* and Kant's description of schematism, however, lies in what Cohen claims to be the incompleteness of an action. "Ethical concepts," he writes, "do not have their methodological nature [*Charakter*] according to this relationship to scientific sensibility or the scientific representation of actuality [*Wirklichkeit*]."[157] The task of moral law, or freedom, is never actual. Freedom is only intelligible because, in Cohen's eyes, it remains a task, a goal, and a purpose that orients all action. And as an end or goal (*Endzweck*), the idea of freedom is also an origin, a beginning of action as the *ought* of freedom.

By emphasizing the purposiveness of moral law, Cohen is able to distinguish pure cognition of nature as the judgment of space and time constructed through the system of principles from ethics, in which space is not a factor. Whereas Bauch mischaracterized the relationship between schematism and intuition by emphasizing an irreducible element of natural unity as determining what conceptual unity will look like, Cohen emphasizes the temporal dimension of the ethical ought as the origin of values. Hence, the values that Bauch seeks to undergird his national unity, Cohen claims, are only ever the result of a lawfulness of morality itself, a mandate of what the nation ought to be. The future therefore becomes the proper domain of ethical action. Legality now achieves a noumenal status as a kind of temporal mode, to the extent that the law idealizes nature as a rational nature.

The social ramifications of Cohen's critique may be apparent by now. If a law of nature is the determining form of all lawfulness, then it remains possible to reduce legitimate law to a natural force or power emanating from a people, from material fact, or even biological elements such as blood. If law is caused by something else, we lose the normative justification of the law and are left only with the necessity of law. Laws cannot be changed if they can remain valid or necessary only in the way we have inherited them. If law is merely the form of causality, then the content of the law can be justified by appeal to the successive past. But history is not the same as the causal past. Like ethics, as we saw in chapter 2, history identifies the norm that animates the past. History is a normative enterprise. Therefore, the history of law must be analyzed transcendentally by examining the conditions that made historical actions possible. This is already an idealization, and law therefore expresses this rational nature of ethics and history. Rational nature is the idealized content of law. From this law neither one people's past nor another's is sufficient to explain the logic of legislation, to explain what citizenship or nation means. Whereas the mythic past described by *völkisch* thinkers like Wundt and Bauch relies on this model of fate or necessity, the scientific and reasoned account presented by Cohen insists on the ideal and on the future.

THE PEOPLE AND THE STATE

While Cohen advocated for a constitutional model of citizenship, his goal was to reinscribe the importance of moral law in the legislation of positive law. Citizenship and ethical agency were thus inseparable in his eyes and served as a critical distancing from the kind of abstract individualism that some of his liberal contemporaries held dear. Nevertheless, the anti-Semitic press saw this appeal to law as more than a demand for equal recognition under German law. Instead, they feared that citizenship was being tailored like a one-size-fits-all suit—free of historical attachment to land and tribal values—to accommodate Jewish citizenship. The basic element in developing an anti-Semitic cultural code was therefore a mythological claim to ownership of German identity. In this sense, Cohen's project, along with that of the C.V., represented a kind of secular project opposed to the anti-Semitic cultural code, which, as we saw above, articulated a distinct kind of German secularism, or national religion. Both Cohen's advocacy for Jewish inclusion and the antiliberal backlash were attempts at reenchantment. For if Todd Weir's recent assertion is correct—that the developing German secularist organizations, having identified a set of common values and norms aligned with German confessionalism, were not anticlerical in scope—then the anti-Semitic movement must also be considered part of this confessional marketplace. In fact, we could even say that anti-Semitism was an attempt to bisect the identity of Jews by drawing attention to their abstract right to citizenship as legally recognized *individuals*, whose lack of recognized religion somehow made their citizenship implicitly other than religious. Jewishness was consequently perceived as a kind of neutralizing force that advocated that all individuals be detached from any religion implicit in their citizenship.

The boundaries between religious othering and secularist, racial othering were somewhat blurry. For example, in 1916 the famed social economist Gustav Schmoller published a review of Hugo Preuss's *Das deutsche Volk und die Politik*. In his review, Schmoller describes Preuss's arguments in favor of a democratic and social state—a state that recognizes its people in all their forms as the basis for a common legislative state will—as the bias of "one of the chief representatives of the Berliner-communal freethinkers, who, on the basis of the social and Semitic millionaire, more or less rule our capital city."[158] Schmoller interestingly conflates in his description of Preuss the image of a liberal, nonconfessional "freethinker" and a secular "Semite." This sentiment, for which Schmoller came under intense criticism in the liberal press and which provoked a stern response from Cohen himself, no doubt stemmed from Preuss's explicitly secular vision of a modern state in which the identity of people and state enables legal equality of citizenship that does not depend on "lineage or religious confession [*Abstammung oder religiöse Bekenntnis*]."[159] Preuss, seeking to identify the people with the laws of the state, noted that "there is hardly any other modern state, whose identity with its people has the effect of hindering its unification into a state-determined definition of peoplehood [*Staatsvolks*] because of its combination of state and church in the masses, as is the case in Germany."[160] Germany needed to forego the attachment to Christianity, particularly the Evangelical Protestant Church, as a condition limiting social and legal equality. But it is significant that Schmoller indicts Preuss's vision as a religiously neutral national belonging. While Preuss insisted on a legal definition of citizenship, Schmoller's criticisms focused on the effect such a vision has on the nature of political authority. Schmoller assailed the idea that the Jews were a minority in need of legal equality since the Jews of imperial Germany had already demonstrated their predominance in positions of power, the press, medicine, and education.[161] Schmoller accused Preuss of harboring an agenda within his rhetoric of collective sovereignty and people's rights, secretly favoring the particular dominance of a Jewish minority. Thus, he half-heartedly acknowledges the truth of Preuss's claim of injustice of authoritarian prejudice before the law by claiming Preuss is really interested in providing "unbaptized Jewish candidates who do not yet have access to public office" the very opportunity to gain admission.[162] Schmoller's comments therefore revealed something much deeper than criticism of liberal tolerance.

While Schmoller insists that Jews had achieved a degree of participation in the German public sphere, he simultaneously insists that religious preference for Christians is simply part of the German national identity. By contrast, Schmoller invokes race in order to highlight this conflict as a political tension between peoples. Schmoller insists that the threat of neutrality or secularization is the most significant concern of Jewish integration, since he believes Jews could assimilate—convert to Christianity—by marriage. In other words, the incoherence of anti-Semitic rhetoric, which Schmoller here represents, lies in the claim that Jews seek to neutralize the state of religious and national values, disestablishing Christianity as a state religion. However, he simultaneously implies that their route to assimilation through marriage will not efface but only reorient their racial differences. Thus, the natural and conceptual dimensions are blurred.

Cohen recognized the muddled conceptualism at work. Basing his argument on racial difference, Schmoller had both politically abstracted religious differences from the fold of confessionalism—a difference of Christian degree rather than non-Christian kind—and replaced Jewish religious difference with racial difference. In other words, while Schmoller implied that Jewish religious difference is the catalyst for secularization of the nation, Cohen accused Schmoller of complicity in the secularization and politicization of religion by trying to collapse race and religion.

In his response, Cohen calls Schmoller to account for his weak reasoning, charging that

> all discussion is disingenuous, superficial, and of deceptive conscientiousness when circling around this point and always speaking only of race, while keeping silent about religion. You really are not against race at all, because you just want to assimilate it. And primarily for this purpose have you calculated your statistics about the increase in intermarriages. But you know that it is no longer appropriate to openly wage a struggle against a religion—the "freedom of conscience" has become a similar keyword, just as "brotherly love"—, so you prefer to hold on to race, dealing with the Jewish Question from this point of view, which from this point of view can only become a political problem, while the real political problem is truly no less than to consider the religious question and the role of the Jewish religion in the development of a pure religion of culture [*reine Kulturreligion*].[163]

According to Cohen, Schmoller muddles race and religion through his politicization of the very values that articulate religion as a historical spirit. In other words, Schmoller's willingness to accept assimilation as a solution to the Jewish Question points to the straw-man appeal to nature or race. Schmoller implicitly acknowledges his anxiety over the erosion of religion as the basic value grounding citizenship. Judaism is therefore synonymous with the threat of secularization. As a political problem, this version of the Jewish Question presents the Jews as a foreign nation, unable to become German without first being converted to the nation and its folk consciousness (*Volksbewusstsein*) of religion. This is the real source of Schmoller's attack, which fails to address the question raised by Preuss and Cohen—namely, of the national state as a *social question* of law, the most idealist of social spheres.

If indeed Schmoller's reasoning had been an appeal to race as a cover for his antiliberalism, perhaps Cohen would have levied a different set of criticisms. But the real issue named by the Jewish Question, Cohen claims, is whether modern culture can be built on a morality that is not exclusively Christian. This should be of concern to more than just Jews, as the intellectual history I have examined suggests. Yet by replacing this question of secular morality with the racial emphasis of Jewish difference, Schmoller fails to address the very point of Preuss's argument.

For his own part, Cohen would continue to deny the philosophical admissibility of any arguments from natural fact as though such a theory of cognition could be justified as the basis for legal and moral values. Socially, Cohen articulated this position in his response to anti-Semitic attacks such as Schmoller's by demonstrating the idealizing history that law presents and insisting on the legal source of national belonging. Noting that Jewish participation in the German war effort was strong,[164] Cohen argues that the war had revealed something instructive about the unity of a national state and a federal state (*den nationalen Einheitstaat und für den Bundesstaat*): namely, that differences of nationality, of *religion*, do nothing to hinder the full-fledged duty of citizens to their national state. Although he understands patriotism and civic spirit as the explicitly *ideal* sources of national unity, Cohen, wary of the kind of *Volksbewusstsein* with which Schmoller seeks to affirm the authority of Christian identity to dictate civil belonging, does not endorse Preuss's view of the *Volkstaat*. However, because Cohen does not seek metaphysical or political answers to the Jewish Question but rather an answer demonstrating how ethics are expressed in *law*, Cohen insists that the state's legal recognition of Judaism in the freedom of conscience clears a space in which a cultural spirit surpasses the political machinations of authority and power.

While Schmoller decries a hybridized "minority of race and of faith" that he claims has risen to political dominance, he also conflates the authority of the state with a German *Volksbewusstsein* that is both religious and racialized. By contrast, Cohen argues that the distinction between Jews and Germans becomes a false construct of politicized argumentation when law is taken as the norm prior to collective unity. But he nevertheless suggests that the law of the state is the source of national belonging because "it is not *Volkbewusstsein* that may limit and constrict authority, but rather authority that has to educate the people and to enlighten *Volksbewusstsein* with the *spirit of law*."[165] For Cohen, the role of ethical socialism is not simply to hand over the legitimate authority of the state to the *Volksbewusstsein*, because this kind of mass democratization results in populist acclamation of *political* maneuvers in which the relative communities of the state are fused into parties. Such suspicion makes good sense in the era of populist advocacy for anti-Semitic *Volkstum*. Cohen insists that the state must maintain a legitimate authority in the form of cultural education, of *Bildung* and *Wissenschaft*.[166] However, national consciousness is a product—and not the origin—of the state. Yet, it nevertheless remains the *spirit of law* that legitimates the state's authority and the national consciousness that the state cultivates. This is because the law is the space of reasoning wherein the performance of citizenship—including that of German citizens of the Jewish *religion*—can deepen the pure religion of culture. Law must educate *all* citizens to be disciplined and dutiful selves—ethical citizens who honor the *idea of* law rather than the *fact* of authority or belonging. Duty to the law and the spirit of the law must be performed by each and every citizen if the state is to function, if its authority is to be legitimate, and if its people are to be constituted by this duty. Cohen claims that a religion of culture (*Kulturreligion*), oriented around the idea of a law for all—a law of humanity—might just help negotiate between the poles of neutralization and mythologization.

Law is therefore the cornerstone of the project of idealizing religion and nation as correlated concepts. As a legal construct, citizenship, like all ethical ideas in Cohen's thought, is not merely an idea. Rather, ethical ideas are intimately related to logical concepts, as we saw in chapter 2. The legal construction based on an ethical idea is therefore a historical praxis, since at the heart of Cohen's theory of law is a theory of action (*Handlung*) in which "all action is reaction, process, redress [*alle Handlung ist Behandlung*]."[167] The legal process is a relationship between past norms, present judgments, and future actions. The significance of this basic concept of legal cognition is that, viewed through the law, an action is always a historical constellation. In this respect, Cohen's insistence that Judaism is a religion of reason that can be justified in modernity stems from this conception of legal action. Moreover, in following from the conception of science and the transcendental method that I discussed in chapter 2, action becomes the basic scientific fact of legal rights, a construct that must transpire in *public*.[168] Action is the counterpart of the norm. Law therefore represents the process by which ethical ideas ground historically and socially actualized actions; and through this transition from ideal norm to actualization (an action striving to actualize an ideal), positive legislation in the state thereby constructs a *nation*.

As we have seen, Cohen is not advocating a form of legal positivism whereby the legitimacy of the state and the spiritual bond of the nation are rent apart. Rather, Cohen insists on the ideal relationship between morality and legality—the spheres Kant separated—as the means by which *sittliche Geist*, ethical spirit and the bedrock of culture, is actualized. And insofar as he understands Judaism to have experienced an autoidealization of its positive ritual law, Cohen can revise Kantian practical philosophy so that the moral law becomes a common normative framework for both Christians and Jews to secure *public law* as the true expression of *Bildung*. This is Cohen's vision of ethical idealism as a theory of normativity and a socially justified expression of ethical judgment. Justification and normativity therefore provide the resources for a modesty in reasoning, since, as Cohen claims, "a democratization of the 'I' needs modesty."[169] Thus, Cohen's response to the Jewish Question is based on the law as the foundation of an ethical and national self-consciousness.

CONCLUSION

If Cohen was able to ground Kantian morality on a more robust foundation, both bringing Kant's theory of law into more precise logical articulation and demonstrating the purposive emphasis of ethical law, a question nevertheless remains: is law but a technical instrument, a means to this greater end? If so, what remains of the legitimacy of law to the citizen? How should a people take shape if the law is a pure construction? And should a citizen merely follow every law?

We have seen how the antiliberal critique of positive law centered on a particularly secular anxiety about the source of values and identity for a changing German nation. What Cohen's account of law presents is a critique of liberal individualism that avoids the private/public distinction usually attributed to liberalism and articulates law as a space between state and individual. Indeed, the entirety of ethical law is public, constructed in reasoning according to judgments about the history of our positive laws and the attempt to recognize the flaws in the logical structure of our judgments. By recognizing the universality of legislation as the purpose of law, Cohen therefore derived the most important content from his theory of law: its public and social nature. Law becomes the ethical *spirit* of the state and "the state becomes the world of spirits."[170] Law is what conditions our political existence; law is the basis of our citizenship. This is the social content of the moral law, and Cohen thus has no need of a sovereign to arbitrarily decide which miracle requires belief or which affirmation of private belief should be voiced. We must believe in law because the scientific norm that grounds all public law is found within the moral law: humanity is the norm of ethical law. This is the universality of the moral law. This is the purpose of law, and this is why public reasoning about the law is a duty.

If we move away from historical contextualization and try to philosophically describe Cohen's account, however, we begin to see that the critique of this separation of legality and morality was not only a Weimar preoccupation but also a clear battle line drawn between liberals and conservatives in the *Kaiserreich*. We can now better understand how Cohen's ethical idealism and revision of Kantian morality, despite mischaracterizations, were concerned with correcting this Kantian formalism. Thus, to account for the crisis of legitimacy—this theologico-political predicament of Wilhelmine Germany surrounding this separation of law and morality—we must understand it through the lens of the dialectic of enchantment and disenchantment.

The attempt to reunify legality and morality on the basis of a cultural code of blood, *Volk*, and nation reifies the structural description of secularization articulated by Hans Blumenberg, which we saw in chapter 2. In this sense, the answer positions that blood and Volk reoccupy seek to hold back the perceived neutrality and disenchantment of legal and national identity. But the use of blood and myth as a "reoccupation of answer positions"[171] to questions that the past no longer sufficed to answer shows the degree to which the debates surrounding neo-Kantianism should be understood as part of a larger polemic against the modernizing changes implicit in cosmopolitan bourgeois culture, which had benefited the Jews and yet was perceived as the epitome of imperial German social tensions. Did the nation—did citizenship—have a historical origin, or should this question too be treated in abstract, disenchanted terms? Anti-Semitism, *völkisch* philosophies, and antiliberalism therefore provided other answer positions. But the lingering question remains: can there be a theory of consensus about public morality, a culture of secular reasoning, that does not fall prey to the vicissitudes of disenchantment? How might a religious reasoning avoid falling into either a privatization of reasons or an alternative politicization of its theological aspirations?

NOTES

1. See chapter 1. Cf. Gangolf Hübinger, *Kulturprotestantismus und Politik: Zum Verhältnis von Liberalismus und Protestantismus im wilhelminischen Deutschland* (Tübingen: Mohr Siebeck, 1994), 170, 266–67. See also Shulamit Volkov, "The 'Verbürgerlichung' of the Jews as a Paradigm," in *Bourgeois Society in Nineteenth-Century Europe*, ed. Jürgen Kocka and Allan Mitchell (Providence, RI: Berg, 1993)

2. Hermann Cohen, "Biographical Introduction" to *Geschichte des Materialismus*, viii. Cohen had employed this term already in 1887. On the term *ethical socialism* as a pejorative description of Bernstein's "revisionism" on the part of Rose Luxembourg, see Henry Tudor, introduction to Eduard Bernstein, *The Preconditions of Socialism*, trans. H. Tudor (New York: Cambridge University Press, 1993), xxx–xxxvi.

3. Paul Lerner, *The Consuming Temple: Jews, Department Stores, and the Consumer Revolution in Germany, 1880–1940* (Ithaca, NY: Cornell University Press, 2015).

4. On the lack of equal recognition of Jewish religion and the Christian confessions, see Marjorie Lamberti "The Jewish Struggle for Legal Equality of Religions in Imperial Germany," *Leo Baeck Institute Year Book* 23 (1978): 101–16. Established churches represented politically thick sources of value for determining political goods in Wilhelmine Germany. Consider the example of intra-Catholic tensions around 1900, when German Catholics also participated in popular organizations and associations, albeit as dissident manifestations of an established church. See Thomas Nipperdey, "Religion und Gesellschaft: Deutschland um 1900," *Historische Zeitschrift* 246, no. 1 (1988): 291–616, 594.

5. Lamberti, "The Jewish Struggle for Legal Equality," 102; Marjorie Lamberti, *Jewish Activism in Imperial Germany* (New Haven, CT: Yale University Press, 1978).

6. Cf. Todd H. Weir, *Secularism and Religion in Nineteenth-Century Germany: The Rise of the Fourth Confession* (New York: Cambridge University Press, 2014), where he attempts to place Judaism within the confessional structure of Germany. To the extent that his argument is aimed at introducing organized secularism as a confession, the model works heuristically for Judaism, however, the fact remains that, in a state with established religions, the language of confessionalism expressed a desideratum at best for Judaism.

7. In contrast to the antisocialist laws, Bismarck had conceded to a number of policies securing worker's benefits, a ten-hour workday and other social welfare laws.

8. B. Saphra (Binjamin Segel), "Staat und Kirche," *Ost und West* 19, no. 5–6 (1919): 127–38, 128.

9. See for example R. Dr. Julius Lewkowitz, "Judentum und Monistenbund," in *Ost und West: Illustrierte Monatsschrift für das Gesamte Judentum* 21, no. ½ (1921): 1–6; Segel also juxtaposes religion and science as social forms, citing Häckel in particular; see "Staat und Kirche," 130.

10. While Jews certainly presented themselves as a confession, the legal realities were much more complex and have often been overlooked by historians. Cf. Weir, *Religion and Secularism and Religion in Ninenteenth-Century Germany*, where *confessionalism* describes the religious plurality of the German public sphere; the secession controversy ignited within organized Judaism a shift from merely communal association toward something much more akin to the Protestant conception of religion as a faith-based private experience. See Breuer's references to R. Samson Raphael Hirsch's political realism as an example; Mordechai Breuer, *Modernity within Tradition: The Social History of Orthodox Jewry in Imperial Germany* (New York: Columbia University Press, 1992), 296–97. Cf. Leora Batnitzky, *How Judaism Became a Religion: An Introduction to Modern Jewish Thought* (Princeton, NJ: Princeton University Press, 2011), 42.

11. Avraham Barkai, *Wehr Dich! Der Centralverein deutscher Staatsbürger jüdischen Glaubens, 1893–1938* (München: C. H. Beck, 2002).

12. Reflecting on the Weimar constitution's recognition of freedom of association and religious distinctions, see Erich Eyck, "Die Stellung der Rechtspflege zu Juden und Judentum," in *Deutsches Judentum und Rechtskrisis*, ed. Jacques Stern, Erich Eyck, and Bruno Weil (Berlin: Philo Verlag, 1926), 31–66, 41. By contrast, Barkai notes the increasingly religious self-representation the C.V. inspired during the Weimar period. See Barkai, *Wehr Dich!*

13. Adolf Stoecker, *Das moderne Judenthum in Deutschland, besonders in Berlin, Zwei Reden in der christlich-socialen Arbeiterpartei* (Berlin: Verlag von Wiegandt und Grieben, 1880), 12. See also Todd H. Weir, "The Specter of 'Godless Jewry': Secularism and the 'Jewish Question' in Late Nineteenth-Century Germany," *Central European History* 46, no. 4 (2013): 815–49.

14. The association of liberalism and the West developed primarily during WWI and became a mainstay of Weimar-era polemic; however, the association of Jews with liberalism was longstanding, and key to Heinrich von Treitschke's argument in the Berlin Anti-Semitism dispute was his insinuation of this "foreign" element. For primary source documents in the dispute, see *Der "Berliner Antisemitismusstreit" 1879–1881—eine Kontroverse um die Zugehörigkeit der deutschen Juden zur Nation: kommentierte Quellenedition*, ed. Karsten Krieger, 2 vols. (München: K.G. Saur, 2004) as well as Marcel Stoetzler, *The State, the Nation, and the Jews: Liberalism and the Antisemitism Dispute in Bismarck's Germany* (Lincoln: University of Nebraska Press, 2008), 35.

15. Eugen Fuchs, "Bestrebung und Ziele. Ansprache gehalten in der Delegierten Versammlung am 6. Oktober 1895," in *Um Deutschtum und Judentum. Gesammelte Reden und Aufsätze (1894–1919)* (Frankfurt am Main: J. Kaufmann, 1919, 56), cited in Inbal Steinitz, *Der Kampf jüdischer Anwälte gegen den Antisemitismus: Die strafrechtlich Rechtsschutzarbeit des Centralvereins deutscher Staatsbürger jüdischen Glaubens (1893–1933)* (Berlin: Metropol Verlag, 2008), 13.

16. See Stoetzler, *The State, the Nation, and the Jews*, 38.

17. Cohen, "Was einigt die Konfessionen?," 455.

18. Cohen, 456.

19. Cohen, 461–62.

20. See chapter 2.

21. Breuer, *Modernity within Tradition*, 296.

22. Cited in Breuer, *Modernity within Tradition*, 297.

23. Hermann Cohen, "Die Zugehörigkeit zur Gemeinde," in *Hermann Cohens Werke*, ed. H. Holzhey, 17 vols. (New York: G. Olms, 1978–) (hereafter cited as *Werke*) 17: *Hermann Cohens Werke, Kleinere Schriften*, vols. 12–17 of *Werke*, 6 vols. (hereafter cited as *KS*) 6:282–83.

24. Hermann Cohen, *System der Philosophie, Zweiter Teil: Ethik des reinen Willens* (Berlin: Bruno Cassirer, 1904; repr. in *Werke* 7) (hereafter cited as *ErW*), 225; Michael Zank, *The Idea of Atonement in the Philosophy of Hermann Cohen* (Providence, RI: Brown University Press, 2000), 280.

25. *ErW*, 209; cf. Zank, *The Idea of Atonement*, 285.

26. Cf. Harry Van Linden, *Kantian Ethics and Socialism* (Indianapolis: Hackett, 1988).

27. *ErW*, 213.

28. *ErW*, 213.

29. *ErW*, 265.

30. *ErW*, 212.

31. I will return to this sociality of the moral law below.

32. *ErW*, 212.

33. *ErW*, 266–67.

34. As Michael Zank puts it: "Law presupposes a notion of unity of legal subjects that can be taken to include all human beings." Zank, *The Idea of Atonement*, 280.

35. Zank, 293–302.

36. *ErW*, 319; cf. Andrea Poma, *The Critical Philosophy of Hermann Cohen*, trans. John Denton (Albany: State University of New York, 1997), 112.

37. *ErW*, 266.

38. Butler also invokes the *asubjettisement* that Lacan describes in the imago encounter and then subsequently in the law of the father as a critical model. Judith Butler, *Bodies That Matter: On the Discursive Limits of "Sex"* (New York: Routledge, 1993). Cf. Jacques Lacan, *The Seminars of Jacques Lacan: Book II: The Ego in Freud's Theory and in the Technique of Psychoanalysis, 1954–1955*, ed. Jacques-Allain Miller, trans. Sylvanna Tomaselli (New York: Cambridge University Press, 1988).

39. Butler writes, concerning the gendered *I*: "This suggests that 'sexed positions' are not localities but, rather, citational practices instituted within a juridical domain—a domain of constitutive constraints. The embodying of sex would be a kind of 'citing' of the law, neither sex nor the law can be said to preexist their various embodyings and citings. Where the law appears to predate its citation, that is where a given citation has become established as 'the law.'" And further on, "Insofar as any *position* is secured through differentiation, none of these positions would exist in simple opposition to normative heterosexuality. On the contrary, they would refigure, redistribute, and resignify the constituents of that symbolic and, in this sense, constitute a subversive rearticulation of that symbolic." Butler, *Bodies That Matter*, 108, 109.

40. Consider the Prussian constitution of 1850 article 12 on freedom of conscience and citizenship not being dependent on religion and article 14 stating that the Christian religion is the basis of all religious institutions. See Lamberti, "The Jewish Struggle for Legal Equality," 102.

41. Compare with Cohen's comments in "Der Religionswechsel in der neuen Ära des Antisemitismus," in *Hermann Cohens Jüdischen Schriften*, ed. Bruno Strauss with an introduction by Franz Rosenzweig, vols. 1–3 (Berlin: C. A. Schwetschke & Sohn/Verlagsbuchhandlung, 1924) (hereafter cited as *JS*) 2:342–45.

42. Cohen, "Emanzipation," *JS* 2:221.

43. Cf. George L. Mosse, *German Jews Beyond Judaism* (Cincinnati, OH: Hebrew Union College Press, 1997), 18–19.

44. Cf. Wilfried van der Will, "The Functions of '*Volkskultur*,' Mass Culture, and Alternative Culture," in *The Cambridge Companion to Modern German Culture*, ed. Eva Kolinsky and Wilfried van der Will (New York: Cambridge University Press, 1998); George S. Williamson, *The Longing for Myth in Germany: Religion and Aesthetic Culture from Romanticism to Nietzsche* (Chicago: University of Chicago Press, 2004).

45. Bruce Lincoln, *Theorizing Myth: Narrative, Ideology, and Scholarship* (Chicago: University of Chicago Press, 1999), 67–68.

46. Heinrich von Treitschke, *Ein Wort über unser Judenthum, Separatabdruck aus dem 44. und 45. Bande der Preußichen Jahrbücher*, 3rd ed. (Berlin: Reimer, 1880), 5.

47. Williamson, *The Longing for Myth*, 12.

48. Hermann Cohen, *System der Philosophie, Erster Teil: Logik der reinen Erkenntnis* (Berlin: Bruno Cassirer, 1902; repr. in *Werke 6*) (hereafter cited as *LrE*), 424.

49. For two examples, compare the very negative view of Michah Brumlik, "1915: In *Deutschtum und Judentum* Hermann Cohen Applies Neo-Kantian Philosophy to the German Jewish Question," in *Yale Companion to Jewish Thought and Writing in German Culture, 1096–1996*, ed. Sander Gilman and Jack Zipes (New Haven, CT: Yale University Press, 1997), 336–42, and Edward Skidelsky, *Ernst Cassirer: The Last Philosopher of Culture* (Princeton, NJ: Princeton University Press, 2008), 38.

50. For a more positive assessment of Cohen's claims, see Steven S. Schwarzschild, "'Germanism and Judaism'—Hermann Cohen's Normative Paradigm of the German-Jewish Symbiosis," in *Jews and Germans from 1860 to 1933: The Problematic Symbiosis*, ed. David Bronsen (Heidelberg: Winter, 1979), 129–72.

51. Cohen, "Das allgemeine, gleiche und direkte Wahlrecht" (1904) in *Ethische Kultur*, reprinted in Schriften zur Philosophie und Zeitgeschichte, ed. Albert Görland and Ernst Cassirer, vol. 2. (Berlin: Akademie Verlag, 1928), 331–34, 333.

52. Jürgen Habermas, *Structural Transformations of the Public Sphere: An Inquiry into a Category of Bourgeois Society*, trans. Thomas Burger (Cambridge, MA: MIT Press, 1991).

53. See also editorial introduction to Sebastian Luft, ed., *The Neo-Kantianism Reader* (London: Routledge, 2015).

54. Peter E. Gordon, *Continental Divide: Heidegger, Cassirer, Davos* (Cambridge, MA: Harvard University Press, 2010), 22, 60–69.

55. Treitschke, *Ein Wort über unser Judenthum*, 3.

56. Cohen's Kantianism, as invested in ideas as it was, was nevertheless concerned with historical, public experiences. Science is the canon of know-

ledge about such experiences considered in the natural world, while ethics is the canon pertaining to sociohistorical experiences.

57. See Heidegger's comments cited in Peter E. Gordon, "Neo-Kantianism and the Politics of Enlightenment," *Philosophical Forum* 39, no. 2 (2008): 223–38, 236.

58. George L. Mosse, "Jewish Emancipation: Between Bildung and Respectability," in *The Jewish Response to German Culture: From the Enlightenment to the Second World War*, ed. Jehuda Reinharz and Walter Schatzberg (Hanover, NH: University Press of New England, 1985), 1–16.

59. See Zank, *The Idea of Atonement*, 77–79, 458–60.

60. Heinrich von Treitschke, "Noch einige Bemerkungen zur Judenfrage," in *Der Berliner Antisemitismusstreit*, ed. W. Boehlich (Frankfurt am Main: Insel Verlag, 1965), 87. See also Andrea Poma, "Hermann Cohen's Response to Anti-Judaism," in *Yearning for Form: Essays on the Thought of Hermann Cohen* (Dodrecht, Netherlands: Springer, 2006), 4; Michael A. Meyer, "Great Debate on Anti-Semitism: Jewish Reaction to New Hostility in Germany, 1879/81," in *Leo Baeck Institute Year Book* 11 (1966): 137–70; Jehuda Reinharz, *Fatherland or Promised Land? The Dilemma of the German Jew, 1893–1914* (Ann Arbor: University of Michigan Press, 1975), 16–30.

61. Sebastian Luft, *The Space of Culture: Towards a Neo-Kantian Philosophy of Culture (Cohen, Natorp, and Cassirer)* (New York: Oxford University Press, 2015), 3, quoting Ernst Cassirer's *The Philosophy of Symbolic Forms*.

62. On this reception history and the search for variously dualistic and monistic solutions to Kant's epistemological project, see Paul W. Franks, *All or Nothing: Systematicity, Transcendental Arguments, and Skepticism in German Idealism* (Cambridge, MA: Harvard University Press, 2005).

63. For an overview of the legal theory of this period and its relation to the philosophical worldview of materialism and psychologism, see Chris Thornhill, *German Political Philosophy: The Metaphysics of Law* (New York: Routledge, 2007), chaps 7 and 8; Peter. C. Caldwell, *Popular Sovereignty and the Crisis of German Constitutional Law: The Theory and Practice of Weimar Constitutionalism* (Durham, NC: Duke University Press, 1997); for an overview of neo-Kantian jurisprudence in particular, see Deniz Coskun, *Law as Symbolic Form: Ernst Cassirer and the Anthropocentric View of Law* (A.A. Dodrecht, Netherlands: Springer, 2007), chap. 9 in particular.

64. Immanuel Kant, "An Answer to the Question, 'What Is Enlightenment?,'" in *Practical Philosophy* in *The Cambridge Edition of the Works of Immanuel Kant*, trans. Mary Gregor, ed. Paul Guyer and Allan Wood (New York: Cambridge University Press, 1996), 11–22.

65. Immanuel Kant, *Groundwork of the Metaphysics of Morals*, in *The Cambridge Edition of the Works of Immanuel Kant*, 37–108; Kant, *Gesammelte Schriften*, ed. Royal Prussian (later German) Academy of Sciences (references to Kant will be hereafter cited following the Academy volume and pagination,

which the Cambridge Edition includes. Citations will be abbreviated as *Ak.*),
Ak. 4:397. Freedom and the moral law are known a priori only to the extent that
they are interdependent conditions of each other, where "freedom is the *ratio
essendi* of the moral law, the moral law is the *ratio cognoscendi* of freedom"; *Critique of Practical Reason*, in *The Cambridge Edition*, 133–272; *Ak.* 5:5n.

66. Thus, Kant claims in his second *Critique*, "consciousness of this fundamental law may be called a fact of reason because one cannot reason it out from
antecedent data of reason, for example, from consciousness of freedom (since
this is not antecedently given to us) and because it instead forces itself on us of
itself as a synthetic a priori proposition that is not based on any intuition, either
pure or empirical, although it would be analytic if the freedom of the will were
presupposed; but for this, as a positive concept, an intellectual intuition would
be required, which certainly cannot be assumed here. However, in order to
avoid misinterpretation in regarding this law as *given*, it must be noted carefully
that it is not an empirical fact but the sole fact of pure reason which, by it, announces itself as originally lawgiving (*sic vollo, sic jubeo*)"; *Critique of Practical
Reason, Ak.* 5:31.

67. Kant therefore refers in his moral philosophy to a sphere of "outer freedom" and the "positive use of freedom" through which, "the concept of freedom
proves its reality by practical principles, which are laws of a causality of pure
reason for determining choice independently of any empirical conditions (of
sensibility generally) and prove a pure will in us, in which moral concepts and
laws have their source"; *Metaphysics of Morals, Ak.* 6:221. Kant considers the observance of laws as a dual-pronged affair: on one side, we have the external action,
and, on the other, we have the internal, private duty to the moral law and the virtues predicated on it. Although both positive law and moral law are a priori, they
are nevertheless considered distinctly determinative for human action.

68. As Kant writes, "In contrast to laws of nature, these laws of freedom are
moral laws. As directed merely to the external actions and their conformity to
law they are called *juridical* laws; but if they also require that they (the laws)
themselves be the determining grounds of actions, they are *ethical* laws, and
then one says that conformity with ethical laws is its *morality*. The freedom to
which the former laws refer can only be freedom in the *external* use of choice,
but the freedom to which the latter refer is freedom in both the external and
internal use of choice, insofar as it is determined by laws of reason"; Kant, *The
Metaphysics of Morals, Ak.* 6:214.

69. Kant, "Idea for a Universal History with a Cosmopolitan Aim," in
Anthropology, History, and Education, The Cambridge Edition, Ak. 8:21, fourth
proposition.

70. On the "analytic" definition of right and its relation to coercion, see
Arthur Ripstein, *Force and Freedom: Kant's Legal and Political Philosophy*
(Cambridge, MA: Harvard University Press, 2009), 52–56.

71. Kant, *Metaphysics of Morals, Ak.* 6:232–33.

72. *ErW*, 267.

73. As I discussed in the previous chapter, Cohen both emphasizes the lawfulness of cognition within a set framework of the categories of understanding and explains the transcendental method as an inquiry into the conditions that make a scientific canon possible. In the case of practical philosophy, the conditions that make the basic unit of legal cognition or "action" possible must also be the laws of judgment that apply to the autonomous will rather than to pure thinking alone. As the expression of practical reason, the will must also be understood as pure action.

74. Hermann Cohen, *Kants Begrundung der Ethik* (Berlin: F. Dümmler, 1877; repr. in *Werke* 2) (hereafter cited as *KBE*), 212–13.

75. Kant wants us to think of nature as running a parallel track to that of the supersensible world of the understanding. The latter has its own form, which by virtue of being *formal* need not interrupt the "mechanism" of natural causality. Yet Kant also assigns the idea of natural causality to the function of the understanding in its ability to prescribe the form of laws. Hence, the two tracks run parallel in the same domain—namely, that of the understanding. This is the source of the confusion. The *natura archetypa* is a kind of paradigm of pure autonomous determination of the will under the moral law. It is the world of the moral good, which means action purely produced according to the moral law. However, the *natura ectypa* would be the world of sensible experience in which the action actually transpires. As Kant says, the archetypal nature is a form that we transfer to the ectypal nature, and in so doing we assign a form of a whole of rational beings to the sensible world. The moral good therefore becomes a *formal* assignment from the one world to the other. And, because neither the moral law nor the moral good derive from empirical determinations but are ideal, the understanding puts before reason the idea of law. Kant writes, "such a law, however, as can be presented *in concreto* in objects of the sense and hence a law of nature, though only as to its form; this law is what the understanding can put under an idea of reason on behalf of judgment, and we can, accordingly, call it the type of the moral law"; *Critique of Practical Reason, Ak.* 5:69.

76. In the *Critique of Practical Reason*, Kant initially tried to distinguish between the laws of nature, which are causal, and the law of practical reason. Practical judgment concerns the action brought into being on the basis of a practical principle. Nevertheless, the action, once determined, transpires in nature and so must be considered from the perspective of laws of nature as well. See *Critique of Practical Reason, Ak.* 5:43.

77. Kant therefore problematically models law on the very causally described nature from which it is supposed to be *free*. This account of law and freedom would appear to be aporetic at best. As a debate largely sparked by Cohen's interpretation in his *Kants Begrundung der Ethik*, scholars continue to question whether Kant abandoned the search for a transcendental a priori of ethics. Cohen believed the open question of Kantian freedom was, Where is

the ought? Where is the *Sollen*, of freedom? See Werner Busch, *Die Enstehung der Kritisch Rechtsphilosophie Kants 1762–1780. Kant-Studien-Ergänzungshefte* (New York: Walter de Gruyter, 1979), n110. On the abandoned deduction, see Dieter Henrich, "The Deduction of the Moral Law: The Reasons for the Obscurity of the Final Section of Kant's *Groundwork of the Metaphysics of Morals*," in *Kant's "Groundwork of the Metaphysics of Morals": Critical Essays*, ed. Paul Guyer (New York: Rowman & Littlefield, 1998), 303–41. G. W. F. Hegel, *Faith and Knowledge*, trans. Walter Cerf and H. S. Harris (Albany: State University of New York Press, 1977), 68, 71, 80; Hegel, *The Difference Between Fichte's and Schelling's System of Philosophy*, trans. H. S. Harris and Walter Cerf (Albany: State University of New York Press, 1977). Cf. G. W. F. Hegel, *Phenomenology of Spirit*, trans. A. V. Miller (New York: Oxford University Press, 1977), paras. 600–631.

78. The Kantian individual is surrounded by conditions and states of opposition such that this isolated individual is trying to map autonomy over and against nature and other people. Hence, empirical determinations for action might take shape, for example, as a willingness to jump off of a bike because the brakes do not work, or a willingness to fix the electric circuit in an apartment building because the heater is no longer working. In other words, when acting in direct response to another empirical state of affairs, rather than acting based on a principle, or the representation of a principle, such an action is determined by those conditions. But if I jump off of my bike because I am trying to save someone about to be hit by a car, or I fix the circuit breaker in my building because the power is out and I want to help the older folks in my community who do not have heat, although empirical conditions may be cited as stimulus for my decision, I am acting based on principles. My goal is to save a life in need and to help vulnerable people. But as Kant suggests, to the extent that action occurs in the natural world, all possible actions must in some sense be ascribed to the laws of nature, which stand on the other side of a barrier that encloses the morally autonomous individual. So, in citing other natural causes as the reason for acting, am I not also excluding any idea of the moral good as the reason for acting? After all, Kant theorizes the idea of the moral good as supersensible, or something that cannot be experienced and has no correlate in "sensible intuition."

79. *KBE*, 223, 26–27.

80. See Steven S. Schwarzschild, "The Democratic Socialism of Hermann Cohen," *Hebrew Union College Annual* 28 (1956): 417–38. Cf. Van Linden, *Kantian Ethics and Socialism*.

81. *KBE*, 222–23, 265–87. Cf. Kant, *Groundwork*, Ak. 4:421–29.

82. Kant, *Groundwork*, Ak. 4:421.

83. Kant, 4:429.

84. Citing Kant, *KBE*, 224.

85. *KBE*, 214.

86. *ErW*, 66.

87. Such was the positivism of Carl Friedrich von Gerber (1823–91), who influenced the entire generation of jurists to follow. See his *System des Deutschen Privatrechts*, 2nd ed. (Jena: F. Mauke, 1850). See Michael Stolleis, *Public Law in Germany, 1800–1914* (New York: Berghahn Books, 2001), 255.

88. See Caldwell, *Popular Sovereignty*.

89. Dana Villa, "The Legacy of Max Weber in Weimar Political and Social Theory," in *Weimar Thought: A Contested Legacy*, ed. Peter E. Gordon and John P. McCormick (Princeton, NJ: Princeton University Press, 2013), 73–100, 78.

90. The legal person of the state replaced any discussion of the *persona moralis*, which intimated private law categories such as those articulated in Georg Friedrich Puchta's Pandects and in some of the early organicists of German law. See Stolleis, *Public Law in Germany*, 321. Cf. Horst Denzer, "Die Ursprung der Lehre von der juristichen Person (*persona moralis*) in Deutschland und ihre Bedeutung für die Vorstellung von der Staatspersönlichkeit," in *La Formazione Storica Del Diritto Moderno In Europa, Atti del terzo Congresso internazionale dell Societa italiana di Storia Del Diritto*, vol. 3 (Florence, 1977), 1189–1202.

91. Peter. C. Caldwell, *Popular Sovereignty*, 19; Michael Stolleis, *Public Law in Germany*, 323.

92. Max Weber, "Science as Vocation," in *The Vocation Lectures*, ed. David Owen and Tracy B. Strong, trans. Rodney Livingstone (Indianapolis: Hackett, 2004), 30.

93. Max Weber, *Wirtschaft und Gesellschaft*, 2 vols. (Tübingen: J. C. B. Mohr, 1956), 538; cited in Ann Goldberg, *Honor, Politics, and the Law in Imperial Germany, 1871–1914* (New York: Cambridge University Press, 2010), 6.

94. Goldberg, *Honor, Politics, and the Law*, 10.

95. Goldberg, 164; cf. Lamberti, *Jewish Activism in Imperial Germany*.

96. Leo Strauss, "Paul de Lagarde," in *Der Jude: Eine Monatsschrift* (Berlin) 8, no. 1 (Jan. 1924): 8–15; reprinted, edited, and translated by Michael Zank in *Leo Strauss: The Early Writings, 1921–1932* (Albany: State University of New York, 2002), 90–101.

97. Strauss, "Paul de Lagarde," 94 (Eng.).

98. Eugen Dühring, *Die Judenfrage als Racen-, Sitten-, und Culturfrage, mit einer weltgeshichtlichen Antwort* (Leipzig: H. Reuther, 1881).

99. Cited in Stoetzler, *The State, the Nation, and the Jews*, 99.

100. Wendy Brown, *Regulating Aversion: Tolerance in the Age of Empire* (Princeton, NJ: Princeton University Press, 2006), 55. While I agree with Brown on the relationship between racialization and the obstacles of construing Judaism in terms familiar to intra-Christian definitions of religion, I find her attention to the relationship between Jewish ethnonational identity and ritual and communal life less compelling.

101. Wilhelm Marr, *Der Sieg des Judenthums über Germanenthum: vom* nicht confessionellen *Standpunkt* (Bern: Constenople, 1879).

102. Mitchell Hart, for example, cites Werner Sombart's *Jews and Modern Capitalism*, in which the latter linked the Jewish "spirit" to the anthropological or racial continuity of the Jews. See Mitchell Hart, *Social Science and the Politics of Modern Jewish Identity* (Stanford, CA: Stanford University Press, 2000), 174.

103. Cf. David Patterson, *Anti-Semitism and Its Metaphysical Origins* (New York: Cambridge University Press, 2015), 146–47.

104. By the 1920s, Wilhelm Dilthey's hermeneutic conception of a philosophy of *Weltanschauungen* as one attempt to forge a greater philosophical link between natural science and the humanities had become a constructive site for reworking values and validity, a related concern of neo-Kantian philosophy. See Rudolf A. Makkreel, "Wilhelm Dilthey and the Neo-Kantians: On the Conceptual Distinctions between *Geisteswissenschaften* and *Kulturwissenschaften*," in *Neo-Kantianism in Contemporary Philosophy*, ed. Rudolf A. Makkreel and Sebastian Luft (Bloomington: Indiana University Press, 2010), 253–71. The promotion of a "worldview" was even considered a constitutionally recognized basis for religious corporations in Weimar. In the late imperial period, "worldviews" were often code for classifying associations affiliated with the free religious movement such as the Monist's League and the Ethical Culture Society as "religious groups." See Todd Weir, *Secularism and Religion*, 66–67. Cf. Kurt Nowak, *Geschichte des Christentums in Deutschland— Religion, Politik und Gesellschaft* (München: C.H. Beck, 1995), 181–85, 207–11.

105. Max Wundt, *Deutsche Weltanschauung: Grundzüge völkischen Denkens* (München: J.F. Lehmann, 1926), 52, emphasis is my own; cited in Jacques Stern, "Völkische Rechts- und Staatsphilosophie," in Stern, Eyck, and Weil, *Deutsches Judentum und Rechtskrisis*, 12.

106. Max Wundt, *Vom Geist unserer Zeit* (München: J. F. Lehmann, 1922), 17.

107. Consider Madame Helena Petrovna Blavatsky's subordination of the Semitic to the Aryan "basic races" in her spiritualist doctrine. See H.P. Blavatsky, *The Secret Doctrine: The Synthesis of Science, Religion, and Philosophy*, vol. 2, *Anthropogenesis* (London: Theosophical Publishing Company, 1888), 266, 128, 241, 507, 538.

108. Wundt, *Vom Geist unserer Zeit*, 38; though he shared with Cohen an interpretation of Platonic philosophy as the birth of idealism, Wundt's perversion of idealism with racial categories led him into conflict with Cohen's longtime colleague in Marburg, Paul Natorp. On Cassirer's relationship to Bauer and the broader context of the controversy, see Ulrich Sieg, "Deutsche Kulturgeschichte und jüdischer Geist: Ernst Cassirers Auseinandersetzung mit der völkischen Philosophie Bruno Bauchs. Ein unbekanntes Manuskript," *Bulletin des Leo Baeck Instituts* 34 (1991): 59–91.

109. Wundt, *Vom Geist unserer Zeit*, 120.

110. Wundt, 38–39.

111. Adolf Stoecker, *Das moderne Judenthum in Deutschland, besonders in Berlin, Zwei Reden in der christlich-socialen Arbeiterpartei* (Berlin: Verlag von Wiegandt und Grieben, 1880), 12.

112. Cited in Günter Brakelmann, Martin Greschat, and Werner Jochmann, *Protestantismus und Politik: Werk und Wirkung Adolf Stoeckers* (Hamburg: Hans Christians Verlag, 1982), 124.

113. Shulamit Volkov, *Antisemitismus als Kulterelle Kode: Zehn Essays*, 2nd ed. (München: C.H. Beck, 2000).

114. For a sampling of organizations dedicated to just this re-Germanization, see Ludwig Holländer, *Zeitfragen: Eine Broschürensammlung des Centralvereins deutscher Staatsbürger jüdischen Glaubens* (Berlin: Gabriel Riesser Verlag, 1919), 4.

115. Clifford Geertz, "Religion as a Culture System," in *The Interpretation of Cultures: Selected Essays* (New York: Basic Books, 1973), 87.

116. On the role of supernaturalism in nineteenth-century popular scientific imagination and secularist sensibilities, see John Lardas Modern, *Secularism in Antebellum America* (Chicago: University of Chicago Press, 2011), 178; cf. Pamela Klassen, *Spirits of Protestantism: Medicine, Healing, and Liberal Christianity* (Berkeley: University of California Press, 2011), 100.

117. Cited in Hübinger, *Kulturprotestantismus und Politik*, 127.

118. Wundt, *Vom Geist unserer Zeit*, 107.

119. Hermann Meyer, *Der deutsche Mensch*, 2 vols. (Munich: J.F. Lehmanns, 1925), 2:23, 32. Quoted in Jacques Stern, "Völkisch Rechts- und Staatsphilosophie," 27.

120. See Ludwig Holländer's collection of citations from the anti-Semitic press in the late Kaiserreich, in Holländer, *Zeitfragen*, 7–9.

121. Bruno Bauch, "Vom Begriff der Nation," *Kant-Studien* 21 (1917): 139–62, 144–45.

122. The myth of blood would dominate national socialist language in the years following Cohen's death. See Alfred Rosenberg, *Der Mythus des Zwanzigsten Jahrhunderts: Eine Wertung der seelischen-geistigen Gestaltenkämpfe unserer Zeit* (Munich: Hoheneichen Verlag, 1930).

123. Bauch, "Vom Begriff der Nation," 144–45.

124. Bauch, 147.

125. Bruno Bauch, *Studien zur philosophie der exakten Wissenschaften* (Heidelberg: Carl Winter's Universitätsbuchhandlung, 1911), 101. Collected essays previously published in *Kant-Studien*.

126. Bauch, 103.

127. Bauch, 65.

128. Bauch, 73.

129. Bauch, 80.

130. Bruno Bauch, "Offener Brief vom 22. Mai 1916," published with the title, "Nochmals ‚Ein Briefwechsel,'" *Der Panther*, no. 4 (1916): 741–45. On Bauch's attacks on Cohen, see Matthias Schöning, "Bruno Bauchs kulturphilosophische Radikalisierung des Kriegsnationalismus: Ein Bruchstück zum Verständnis der Ideenwerde von 1916," *Kant-Studien* 98 (2008): 200–219.

131. Bauch, "Vom Begriff der Nation," 144.

132. Max Wundt had cofounded the Deutschen Philosophische Gesellschaft as a reaction to the "Jewishness" in Kantian philosophy and the founding of which Bauch's essay had been a catalyst. Wundt would later publish an essay recording his own criticisms, See Sieg, "Deutsche Kulturgeschichte und jüdischer Geist."

133. Max Hildebert Boehm, "Vom deutsch-jüdischen Geist," *Preußisches Jahrbuch* 162 (1915): 404–20, 419. Cf. Ulrich Sieg, "Bekenntnis zu nationalen und universalen Werten. Jüdische Philosophen im Deutschen Kaiserreich," *Historisches Zeitschrift* 263 (1996): 609–39, 627; cited in Peter Hoeres, *Krieg der Philosophen: Deutsche und britische Philosophie im Ersten Weltkrieg* (Paderborn: Schoeningh, 2004), 235. See also Ulrich Sieg, *Jüdische Intellektuelle im Ersten Weltkrieg: Kriegserfahrungen, weltanschauliche Debatten und kulturelle Neuentwürfe* (Berlin: Akademie Verlag, 2001), 236–39.

134. Sieg, "Deutsche Kulturgeschichte und jüdischer Geist," 76.

135. Sieg, *Jüdische Intellektuelle im Ertsen Weltkrieg*, 236–29.

136. Cohen, "Die Nächstenliebe im Talmud als ein Gutachten dem Königlichen Landgerichts zu Marburg erstattet," *JS* 1:145–74, 174, 35.

137. *ErW*, 238–40.

138. Hegel, *Phenomenology*, paras. 437–43.

139. *ErW*, 98–100.

140. *ErW*, 65–66.

141. *ErW*, 267.

142. *ErW*, 268. Leora Batnitzky notes that Cohen's criticism of Kant concerns the Pauline polemic and that this critique likewise demonstrates the Protestant categories of Cohen's own envisaging of Judaism. See *How Judaism Became a Religion*, 55. I will return to this point in chapter 5.

143. *ErW*, 392.

144. *ErW*, 13, 21–25.

145. *ErW*, 395–96: "We recognize, however, a new difficulty within our problem. The actuality of morality must be based on nothing other than nature and history. But at the same time, nature and history may not constitute the model of our desired actuality. *The basic law of truth makes the claim of a correspondence between the two problems in the methodologically basic concepts of knowledge. But at the same time, it also preserves the distinction between them in the scope of this basic idea.*"

146. Hence, Cohen writes, "nature and history inevitably form the presuppositions of [the method of] purity. It is not only the fundamental law of truth that places the ideal and nature in correlation; rather, it is the very first natural

presupposition, from which the method of purity starts. The natural will is not the pure will. The natural man is not the pure man. The empirical I is not the pure I. But if there were no natural man with natural will and natural self-consciousness, then the method of purity could not begin; it would have absolutely no meaning." *ErW*, 436–37.

147. *ErW*, 408.

148. *LrE*, 62.

149. *ErW*, 427.

150. See *LrE*, 88; see also, Helmut Holzhey, *Cohen und Natorp*, 2 vols. (Basel: Schwabe, 1986), 1:145; cf. Pierfrancesco Fiorato, *Geschichtliche Ewigkeit: Ursprung und Zeitlichkeit in der Philosophie Hermann Cohens* (Würzburg: Königshausen & Neumann, 1993), 72.

151. *LrE*, 12–13.

152. *LrE*, 154–55, 63.

153. See *LrE*, 154–55; cf. Fiorato, *Geschichtliche Ewigkeit*, 87. See also Pierfrancesco Fiorato, ed., *Vereinung, Andersheit und Unendlichkeit im Neukantianismus* (Würzburg: Königshausen & Neumann, 2008), 80.

154. *LrE*, 277. Ernst Cassirer would develop Cohen's theory of science in his *Substanzbegriff und Funktionsbegriff: Untersuchungen über die Grundfragen der Erkenntniskritik* (1910; repr., Hamburg: Felix Meiner Verlag, 2000); For the influence of this kind positivism on state law theory in the imperial period, see Georg Jellinek, *Allgemeine Staatslehre (Das Recht des modernen Staates)* (Berlin: Verlag von O. Häring, 1900), 1:153. For a general overview of the use of the terms *substance* and *function* in the idealistic philosophical milieu, see Rudolf Eisler, *Wörterbuch der philosophischen Begriffe* (Berlin: Ernst Sigfried Mittle und Sohn, 1910), 3:1456f.

155. *ErW*, 38.

156. Cohen writes:

> One should also here note a sharpness in Kantian terminology, which has cast strong shadows in this primordial light. Kant dealt with our problem under the title of the typic of practical reason. The typic is distinguished from the schematism. In nature, the categories are realized. Kant describes this realization under the expression of schematization. The schema is the pure form, rather the pure configuration. This is possible in nature. Since space and time are the pliable areas in which the terms can be arranged. All requirement and every measure of reality is given here and provided. The terms are as pure forms, configuring forms. This is the concise sense of the schematism. (*ErW*, 392)

157. *ErW*, 393.

158. Gustav von Schmoller, "Obrigkeitsstaat und Volkstaat: Ein missverständlicher Gegensatz," *Schmollers Jahrbuch* 40, no. 4 (1916): 2031–42 / 423–34, 424, 2032.

159. Hugo Preuss, *Das deutsche Volk und die Politik* (Jena: Eugen Diedrichs, 1915), 194.

160. Preuss, 195.

161. Peter Pulzer, "Why Was There a Jewish Question in Imperial Germany?" in *Leo Baeck Institute Yearbook* 25 (1980): 133–46. Erik Grimmer-Solem, "'Every True Friend of the Fatherland': Gustav Schmoller and the 'Jewish Question' 1916–1917," in *Leo Baeck Institute Yearbook* 52 (2007): 149–63. See Gustav Schmoller, "Die heutige deutsche Judenfrage," *Tägliche Rundschau*, Jan. 16, 1917, repr. in *Schmollers Jahrbuch* 41 (1917): 563–67.

162. Schmoller, "Obrigkeitsstaat und Volkstaat," 2033/425.

163. Cohen, "Betrachtungen über Schmollers Angriff," *Werke* 17: *KS* 6: 397/*JS* 2:384–397.

164. According to Oppenheimer's *Judenzählung*, a hundred thousand Jews served as comrades in arms with their fellow Germans; twelve thousand of which shed their blood and died for their country. See also Werner T. Angress, "The German Army's '*Judenzählung*' of 1916," in *Leo Baeck Institute Yearbook* 23 (1978): 117–35.

165. Cohen, "Betrachtungen über Schmollers Angriff," 410.

166. Cf. Wiedebach's different reading in Hartwig Wiedebach, *The National Element in Hermann Cohen's Philosophy and Religion*, trans. William Templer (Boston: Brill, 2012), 112–16. Wiedebach does not address the question of the political versus the social but examines Cohen's claim concerning education as a problematic form of liberalism.

167. *ErW*, 65.

168. The first chairman of the *Centralverein*, Martin Mendelssohn, emphatically declared, "The very principle upon which our entire organization is built is that of publicity ... [and the] goal of the organization to be the advocacy on behalf of Jewish Germans." Martin Mendelssohn, *Die Pflicht der Selbsverteidigung: Jahresbericht des Vorsitzenden in der ersten ordentlichen Generalsversammlung des Centralvereins deutscher Staatsbürger jüdischen Glaubens* (Berlin: n.p., 1894), 18.

169. *ErW*, 543.

170. *ErW*, 246.

171. Hans Blumenberg, *The Legitimacy of the Modern Age*, trans. Robert M. Wallace (Cambridge, MA: MIT Press, 1983), 65.

FOUR

ENCHANTED REASONING

Self-Reflexive Religion and Minority

HAD HE LIVED TO SEE it, Cohen would have marveled at the rise of the supranational project of the European Union. And he most certainly would have had much to say about what appear to be the tremors of its imminent decline.

The possibility that both public law and constitutional norms would lead a union of nations toward a single ideal represents the ethical thrust of his idealism and his advocacy for a system of law to provide the foundation for a cultural worldview. However, the forces of nationalism are once again resurgent along with the blatant disregard for truthfulness, reasoned exchange, and the belief in consensus in public discourse. These threats, which were as pernicious at the beginning of the twentieth century as they are at the outset of the twenty-first, would have certainly given him pause. The struggle for recognition and the ability to reason openly and transparently has been so crucial to the world's recovery from colonialism, genocide, and total war. Yet, even a passing familiarity with contemporary politics would suggest that this very form of public reasoning is increasingly liable to pass into the annals of history. Identities are growing ever more incommensurate, partisanship ever more entrenched, and the consequences of enmity ever more fatal, all while the lessons of the past seem to go unheeded.

In the story I have been telling, Cohen's philosophy has presented a sibylline vision both of the threats of encroaching materialism, essentialism, and racism and of the solutions that could be found to these threats in idealistic philosophy. To that end, Cohen philosophically positioned Judaism alongside Protestant Christianity as a historical source and origin of norms and reasons for modern culture.[1] Caught in the headwinds of secularization in the nineteenth century, Cohen therefore sought to navigate between the lure of metaphysical pantheism and materialism, as well as the ideological attempts to reoccupy the values and ideals of the public sphere with blunt assertions of power. Ethics, therefore, became a scientific enterprise for Cohen and, having culminated in a theory of law and state, ethics provided a method for idealizing religion. Cohen's account of Judaism in historical consciousness therefore presented one avenue for envisioning the morality of law without imposing religion on the state. This implicit recognition of what Leo Strauss would later describe as the "theologico-political predicament" of Wilhelmine Germany gives credence to the view I have been advocating from the outset: namely, that Cohen recognized the threat of antiliberal and anti-Semitic forces afoot in Germany, which asserted an uncritical mythic awareness (*Bewusstheit*) of their identity, values, and Christian past as a newfound possibility within the epistemological vacuum of a neutralizing secularism. It has been my goal to suggest that Cohen's idealism—his refusal to give into the forces of materialism and essentialism—also provides an alternative model for a liberal worldview to retain its enchantment and move forward.

In contrast to the decline of justified thinking that has once again emerged in the form of demagogy, Cohen's ethics must be seen as an appeal to *justified reasoning*, a consciousness (*Bewusstsein*) of cultural history[2]—a history of law and state—with which he believed Jews and Christians could identify a broader constellation of common belonging than that afforded by the intra-Christian rights of the *ius reformandi* in shaping recognition of religious difference. The latter remains a political construct of the sovereign, which began as an intra-Christian language of identity and difference—conflict and resolution—and remains a problematic framing of how social consensus is often imagined. But as a socio-legal justification of cultural consciousness, Cohen's affirmative support for the liberal constitutional recognition of religion discussed in the previous chapter suggests that idealized historical goods could be articulated within a new standard of cultural consensus—namely, that of public law. Differing conceptions of lived religion therefore need not preclude the ethically reasoned and justified goods or truths articulated by the method of idealization. In Cohen's case, this normative agreement configures Jewish and Christian *religions* as the *sources* of legal and moral values for a public culture rather than increasingly incommensurable identities that provide only mythic affirmation of party politics or confession. And in this spirit of ethical culture, different religions should be understood as always already idealizing social rather than political goods; and as *public religions*, they should be understood as idealizing themselves in the process. This is the dialectic of enchantment that is developed from the minority history of German Judaism and from Cohen's epistemological secularity as a reflection of that history.

Throughout these chapters, I have presented Cohen's account of ethics as a labor of philosophically negotiating space for Judaism in the cultural modernity of German Protestantism. Chapter 1 introduced the transformations of Protestant liberalism, in which an epistemological revolution allowed for philosophical and scientific reasoning to make space between dogma and knowledge. Protestantism therefore provided Cohen with a historical source for articulating the value of scientific reflexivity—critique and justification. Following Heine's narrative of German philosophy, Cohen introduced Judaism into the history of idealism in order to justify Judaism within modern Protestant culture. Against the image of Spinoza's metaphysical assimilation, Cohen's idealism mapped the ways in which philosophy's relationship to the public nature of science helped Jews negotiate the secularization of the German public sphere, which was not only newly accessible to but also ideally shaped by the historical encounter with Judaism. The two paths of Protestantism—one into neutralizing secularism and metaphysics and the other into secularity and religious reasoning—became explicit in chapter 2, which sought to sketch the historical problem of justifying norms and values of religion and morality amid the rise of natural science as a new dogma. The struggle between materialism and religion therefore provoked new philosophical challenges, in response to which Cohen examined both Kantian idealism and a theory of ethical monotheism as the basis for a new public reasoning. As the method for this reasoning, I suggested that Cohen's account of idealization of religious and moral norms and values proves key to his later thought. This was hardly a claim that the Jewish cultural struggle for modernity, for the right to belong and to be recognized as different, had employed science as a neutral method for the aims of one particularity among others. Rather, Cohen saw the intellectual developments of biology and physics, history and the science of law, and knowledge of the natural and the human, as normative sources in the history of reason, understood as a developing canon of knowledge. History is crucial to understanding our norms. Thus, as I concluded in chapter 3, reason becomes *public*, an evolving archive of values that are integrated into a canon of knowledge and rules. Reason becomes a practice of reasoning and knowledge itself can be characterized akin to Alasdair MacIntyre's description of tradition, namely, as "a theory of knowledge according to which each particular theory or set of moral or scientific beliefs is intelligible and justifiable—insofar as it is justifiable—only as a member of an historical series."[3] For Cohen, I have suggested, this historical series is reason.

Reason is both public and transparent, an ideal that must remain unchanged in its regulative function as the symbol of intelligibility, but natural science is not the only sphere of human reason. Chapter 3 therefore focused on ethical reasoning as it developed the practical consequences of engaging the Kantian worldview of critique and justification as an epistemology of secularity. By juxtaposing the problems of Kantian liberalism's separation of law and morality with the anti-Semitic union of blood and spirit, we saw how Cohen developed the distinction between the world of natural science and that of ethics into a neo-Kantian justification of a priori ideas, thus resisting the lure of materialism and pantheism as metaphysical foundations for racism and nationalism. Instead, Cohen understands the practice of reason—of *reasoning*—as the process of historically idealizing norms and then demonstrating justified ideals that can be held in common. Reasoning is therefore normed by the sociality of law that implicitly links logic and ethics as much as it reconnects legality and morality, and Cohen provided a reformulation of Kant's categorical imperative as a vehicle for performing citizenship and achieving equal civic recognition without reducing religion to a private affair.

As a theory of conceptual justification and of the reflexivity of ideas as publicly constituted, debated, and shared, idealism can therefore be understood as a theory of self-reflexive public reasoning. Widening this perspective, in this chapter I want to look at how Cohen views law as a mediating structure between ethics and religion. While it is certainly the case that the relationship between ethics and religion in Cohen's thought has been debated a great deal,[4] my goal is not to retell the ebb and flow of Cohen's attitude toward religion in the purview of his philosophy. In fact, my interests are less with Cohen's posthumous *Religion of Reason* than with his many statements on the social recognition of religion and the way ethics can help articulate norms for that recognition. In this respect, Cohen's account of religion within the public sphere is consistently articulated as an issue of public reasoning.

I therefore take up the question of public reasoning by surveying two particularly prominent and pervasive attempts to negotiate the problem of secularization and legitimation with epistemological weight: the political theology of Carl Schmitt and the political liberalism of John Rawls. After tracing their various critiques and proposals for public reasoning, whether liberal or antiliberal, I then turn to Cohen's own approach, wherein idealization provides a religious community with the epistemological means to argue for public goods by reasoning from out of the sources of its religion. However, Cohen does this by developing a theory of epistemic self-reflexivity, a theory of justified reasoning and conceptual transparency about norms idealized out of the Jewish religious tradition. Thus, using as a symbolic model of religious minority the Noahide—the figure imagined by the Talmudic sages as a non-Jewish resident alien in a Jewish polity—I conclude by indicating how Cohen draws upon rabbinic legal thinking to develop a model of minoritizing public reasoning, or a reasoning that seeks to idealize and provincialize would-be claims to absolute value.

JEWISH DEPOLITICIZATION AND THE PROBLEM OF LIBERALISM

In 1938, at the height of National-Socialist rule, Carl Schmitt penned his most explicitly anti-Jewish work (though later claimed as evidence for his critical distancing from the Nazi party), *Leviathan in der Staatslehre des Thomas Hobbes*, in which the relationship between Jewish religious difference, liberal neutralization, and secularization all come to the fore. In *Leviathan*, Schmitt interpolates the Jewish Question—in all but name— as the very problem of liberalism: the problem of citizens maintaining a private faith beyond the state's grasp. Couched within his polemic against the Jewish proclivity for liberalism, however, is what amounts to Schmitt's most succinct exposition of the problem of secularization, or what he refers to as the neutralization of politics. Schmitt describes the historical development of the liberal state as a machinelike apparatus "independent of every political goal and conviction" that "assumes a value-and-truth neutrality of a technological instrument. It is in this manner that the neutralization process has taken place since the seventeenth century, a logical process that culminates in a general technologization."[5]

This neutralization of the state, Schmitt continues, begins with Hobbes's Leviathan, the mortal god who determines the political reality of religion by mandating public confession of belief, marking the sovereign power to constitute the public sphere on the basis of a political mythology. This mythology is consciously distinct from Christian dogma. It is, rather, the result of the sovereign's legitimate ecclesiastical authority to enforce a bargain between confessions, but on behalf of Christian culture itself. The mythos of the Leviathan is precisely not a fiction. It is the work of a political craft that is not reducible to the technological patchwork of a liberal consensus-based society.[6] The sovereign creates truth.

For Schmitt, the ideal of mechanical artisanship in Hobbes's early modern conception must be understood as a craft, as the ideal of art and scientific creation merging together in an organic whole.[7] Thus, Schmitt describes Leviathan's machinelike public sphere as nevertheless constituted by the declaration of what is and is not miracle, a fundamental religious norm. Miracles are politically sanctioned in order to guarantee political authority over ecclesiastical power. This secures the authority of the sovereign. But the potency of a political myth, which is what miracles become under the aegis of the Leviathan, derives its power from theological symbols and principles. While the Leviathan converts miracle into a publicly recognized religion and a *civic* commitment, individual, private faith nevertheless remains beyond the reach of the sovereign.[8] Yet, the declaration of faith, the public confession of miracle, belongs to the sovereign. This is the basis of a state's legitimacy.

In Schmitt's reading, the Leviathan is a machine that combines the social differences among potential enemies in the state of nature into a compact. This machine is not yet the technological positivity of an automaton or bureaucratically haunted entity; it is not the state as we have come to know it in statute-positivist terms. No, the state is a work of art, and its mythos is its ethos. The state is to be believed in; it is still enchanted.

This power within the ideal of the total state, claims Schmitt, is what the Leviathan has lost to the neutralizing liberalism of the Jews.

According to Schmitt, it is this space between private and public that "the liberal Jew, Spinoza" exploits. Spinoza's liberalism consists in inverting the sovereign power to determine public confession and placing the internal freedom of individual belief front and center; in other words, the inner takes precedence over the outer, the individual over the sovereign. Private right of belief, the baseline of emancipatory hopes for early modern Jews, thus determines the birth of classical liberalism. And if Spinoza noticed the crack left over, Schmitt maintains, Mendelssohn pried it wide open. Mendelssohn, he claims, employed the "Jewish tactic of drawing distinctions," which separated "between inner and outer, morality and right, inner disposition and outer performance and demanded from the state freedom of thought."[9] For Schmitt, Mendelssohn's attempt to distinguish dogma from revealed legislation delivers a fatal blow to the power of the mortal god, Leviathan, by decaying the legitimacy of political myth required by the sovereign state. But we see here the clear invocation of the image of liberalism as a technology of drawing distinctions. While Kant remains unnamed in this attack, it is clear from Schmitt's many remarks in *Leviathan* and in his other works that Kant's thought is equally responsible for the "age of neutralization" that has culminated in a machinelike use of public reason—Kant and the Jews, that is.

The Jews are singled out because, in Schmitt's eyes, they are not an enchanted people. The overall disenchantment of the modern liberal *Rechtsstaat* consists in the dualistic requirement, of which the Jews would seem to be the most notable continued benefactors, of a separation between citizenship and nationality—between legality and morality—and the reduction of religion, considered as a mythos of social existence, to a private realm free of the state. No longer the work of art that brings together the nation through public affirmation of miracle, the technological state of the Jews prioritizes the privacy of individual rights as the basic algorithm of calculation and neutralization of the state. This mortal god, Schmitt suggests, is now left clawing away at the walls of its technological grave, condemned to a hauntological condition of positive rights that linger as apparitions of legitimacy but nothing more.[10] In Schmitt's account, the Jewish Question remains the specter of the secularization question.

Fundamental to, yet not explicit in, Schmitt's discussion of public and private is the notion that liberalism originates with both a fundamentally Protestant and a fundamentally Jewish Question. Historical conflict between Protestantism and Catholicism led Hobbes to conclude that the *Christian* sovereign must decide what is publicly affirmed as miracle, beyond confessional difference, such that all Christians could join together as *citizens* and affirm that "Jesus is the Christ."[11] This becomes the basic norm of a Hobbesian public reason, in Schmitt's view. Since they cannot affirm this miracle of political theology as civic religion,[12] the Jews supplant the religious power of political myth with the neutrality of the state and its ensuing value-free attitude toward private belief. Only when the state stops enforcing lip service can the Jews be free, and then, Schmitt fears, is when the state reaches its most vulnerably neutralized point. The Jewish Question is distinct, because only the Jews are unable to affirm, even publicly, the miracles of Christianity.

The indirect target of Schmitt's political theology, however, is the modern condition of self-reflexivity left open by Protestantism. While Schmitt's political Catholicism has been debated a great deal, it is evident from *Leviathan* that his disdain for Protestantism stems from this recognition of a *liberal* compact between Jews and Protestants. If liberalism first sets out to overcome the problem of Protestantism by creating a Christian public sphere, Judaism undermines the homogeneity of a national culture as a religious culture altogether, since religion becomes, if not a private affair, then at least a *nonpublic* one. For, according to Schmitt, the Jews do not seek to infuse the state with their religious myths but rather opt out of the publicly affirmed miracle. Rather than engage the norms of this public reasoning, they neutralize them. Not surprisingly then, Schmitt, a Catholic, sees the legitimating myth of Christ's incarnation into the world of history and mankind as precisely the myth that sets Judaism apart, just as Augustine famously described the Jews as bearing unwilling witness to the truth of Christian revelation.[13] The political myth of the incarnate messiah shapes the form of sovereign power that the Jews simply cannot help legitimate since, "as concerning the gospel," Paul writes in Rom. 11:28, "they are enemies for your sake." However, the problem of modernity, of secular liberalism, is that the separation of law from morality in order to accommodate religions that cannot affirm this miracle calls the legitimacy of state-law into question. Without avowing

Christianity as the public mythos of the state, Judaism, it would seem, faces the dilemma of proposing an alternative conception of legitimacy for the modern state. Are constitutional rights enough to secure a spirit of public life, a spirit of social ethos on par with mythos? Can law in itself become an ethos of the state?

The problem Schmitt helps identify with a theory of public reason lies in the dynamics of majority and minority. Is it possible for a minority to accept the terms of debate when they are simply antithetical to the public existence of the minority? Schmitt provides a clear demonstration of how these major and minor dynamics of secularization are fundamental to the Jewish Question by asking what the normative basis of the legitimate state might be if it is not to be found in civic religion. If other religions are recognized by the state, how does this legal recognition affect the definition of the national whole? Is the whole made up of pieces? Can these pieces be united by something else, by an ethos if not a common mythos?

Here we should recontextualize Schmitt's anxiety over the depoliticization of the Leviathan as an account of secularization. Because the sovereign declaration of publicly affirmed miracles is a political decision regarding the values of a relative community, this decision elevates partisanship over publicity. As a consequence, the Jews represent a dissenting attempt to neutralize public religion. Sharing a common belief and requiring its profession by the public provides a regulatory check on the partisanship that fueled confessional conflict, forcing such beliefs inward and into the private sphere. Refusing to publicly confess this belief, however, undermines the civil compact, in Schmitt's mind. Thus, Protestantism's catalyzing effect of creating a rift between public and private is exploited by what Schmitt calls the Jewish tactic of drawing distinctions. The Jews represent the odd ones out; their foreign customs and ritual practices index what is no longer just a privately held belief but a public expression of dissent that the civic myth of religion—and, thus, of the sovereign state—is not their own. How, then, should the law regulate the Jews? This paradoxical experience of secularizing political religion—of affirming private belief so as to secure public, civic religion—leaves open a back door to the public sphere and slowly neutralizes the public requirement of confession from within. This is how Schmitt imagines the social and political paradox of the Jewish Question.

What Schmitt deems a paradox of civil religion for the Jews is, as I suggested in chapter 3, described by Cohen as the result of a politicization of religion—the result of the process of secularization. Unlike Schmitt, Cohen therefore avoided the assertion of an exclusive past of Christian or Jewish moral revelation; rather, for Cohen the basis for a liberal cultural consensus, as between Judaism and Protestantism, must be found in the method of reasoning about history itself. The self-reflexivity of any norm requires *history* to be idealized in order to negotiate the norms of the public sphere. In other words, Schmitt's conception of sovereign power over religion, which creates public myth, is limited to the assertion of a good derived from a partisan past. But Schmitt's account helps name the dilemma of secularization: namely, that the sovereign's declaration is always already an abstraction from Christianity, and the lowest common denominator between the confessions, or "Jesus's kin,"[14] is emblematically encapsulated in the affirmation that "Jesus is the Christ." Schmitt therefore represents the *political* articulation of religious norms. What Cohen's attempt to harness this distinction between political religion and the sociality of reasoning provides, by contrast, is an attempt to help us recognize which norms are worth endorsing and continuing to commit to in our public expressions of religion and which norms simply exclude others from participating in such reasoning.

But as we saw in the previous chapter, the minority life of the German Jews in the late nineteenth and early twentieth century was indeed marked by struggle with this paradox of private conscience as the expression of public belonging. Thus, Cohen's criticism of secessionist Orthodoxy, Kant's formalism, and antiliberal essentialism focused on the performance of citizenship. This ritualizing power of public law, to borrow a phrase from Catherine Bell, configured legal rights and the sociality of law as the objective context in which the moral self is cultivated. Thus, the civic duty performed in law became the effective performance of citizenship. In other words, the ritual performance of the law does not simply communicate an abstract duty to the citizen but provides a purposive context in which observance and performance of duty actually creates a dutiful citizen.[15] Hence, in contrast to Schmitt, Cohen's emphasis on the law's idealization of religion, history, and morality critically articulates how the legal fiction of a private right to conscience provides an opening for the sociality of public reasoning. But this same right is the product of a public conflict between confessions of a now sovereign-declared political religion. Hence, private conscience originates as a subset of public, political religion. But Cohen's account of law demonstrates how public law, the sociality of reason par excellence, secures private conscience as an unexpected path for the Jews to access reasoning in the public sphere. In Cohen's account, the modern development of the state places law in a structurally anterior position to recognized religion. The law thereby idealizes the values and moral norms generated by different religions as recognized norms and reasons. In this way, these norms and reasons become *public*.

SECULARISM AND PUBLIC REASON

What, then, is the relationship between this modern entanglement of Protestantism and Judaism and the minority experience of secularization, if we understand secularization as the process both by which public law and civic rights were detached from institutional membership in the Christian churches and by which religion became a political category?[16] To answer this question, we must first address the idea of secular public reason and understand what expectations are placed on a minority religion in the face of a majoritarian secularism. It is important to note that, by Cohen's standard, Schmitt's account of political religion—the sovereign declaration of public miracle—is still a form of secularism since it reshapes a majoritarian religious past into a majoritarian politics. It is just not liberal secularism. Liberal secularism, as we will see, seeks to neutralize both the partisan pasts as well as historical norms, leading to another set of problems concerning liberalism's epistemic origins. What, then, might the German-Jewish experience of secularity teach us about the metaphysical presuppositions of contemporary secularisms? How might the minority history of Judaism within a liberal and Protestant context reframe the terms of discussion surrounding religion in the public sphere? For we are certainly asking a question about political policy with regard to how the laws of the state should be structured. Are religious exemptions from certain laws the only manifestations of public religions? Or do secularisms pose a more fundamental epistemological question to the minority religions they confront?

A theory of secularism, as compared with the historical and social process of secularization, cannot help but advance a subtle yet tacit approval of some value doctrine, despite protest to the contrary.

Historically, secularism is tied to the liberal political tradition and shares along with it the assumption that tradition and custom are terms to be contrasted to liberty and freedom.[17] Throughout political liberalism's classical iterations, this contrast in the nineteenth-century nation-state project has contoured discussion surrounding the state's relationship to religion, in which the values of freedom and equality are abstracted from historical circumstance to provide basic norms for a conception of society and justice. But the epistemic building blocks of secularism—freedom and equality—are metaphysically colored by the genealogy of scientific and equalizing pantheism, moral will, law, and decision, all of which I have been exploring in relation to Cohen's thought. These same building blocks therefore represent a majority narrative within the genealogy of the secular, in which the Christian sources of modern society remain the formal index of the question positions of secularism.[18]

Insofar as I have suggested that the Jewish Question reveals the intra-Christian dynamic of the public/private distinction, we can see how secularism presents a position vis-à-vis religion. In the wake of European attempts to negotiate the relationship between majoritarian policies and minoritarian backlashes, the contemporary iteration of secularism has been met with a great deal of criticism. Thus, Akeel Bilgrami notes, "secularism has come to be seen as too blunt since it was not merely taking a stand against religious majoritarian domination but equally against religious minoritarian backlashes opposing that domination. It was a stand, therefore, against *all* religious practices—whether that of a minority or that of a majority—placing those practices second whenever they clashed with the nation's laws."[19] This imposition of a homogeneous political category of religion serves to compel a new public myth of secular neutrality toward different religions.[20] But, as we have seen, the minority history of the secular revealed by the Jewish Question is a minoritarian dynamic that presents not a backlash but rather a performance of the norms of secular law, in which the publicity of reasoning becomes a new source of religious culture. What, then, is the source of secularism's insistence on a political doctrine of liberalism for its epistemological neutrality? Moreover, can secularism make sense of this hybrid of religious and cultural norms that we find in Cohen's negotiation of the Jewish Question?

It may help to first clarify what I mean by a politically liberal doctrine of secularism. By such a doctrine, I understand secularism to insist on two crucial points. (1) The doctrine of secularism is a neutral policy with regard to different religions; and (2) the neutrality of the policy itself is presented as based on no specific set of values. By values, however, I mean the kinds of ritualized behaviors and beliefs that are encoded in law. Secularism presents its face to the world as a policy of fair and equal terms on which to adjudicate the goods of a just society, but implicit to this doctrine is a set of fundamental questions, such as in what foundational documents or events are these values found, and how or why do we hold them dear in common? In what sense of shared good do we hold firm in our associations? Why does the validity of a constitutional separation of religion and state persist if the people for whom these institutions are separated are not members of a homogeneous social sphere of Christianity?

The answer of political liberalism is that secular values, as the values for which a politically liberal society lives and dies, must be worked out in common. But such questions of course remind that society of the values and rituals—the beliefs and actions—that are *not* held in common, though they might be values for which others may be willing to live and die. These are the values deemed foreign rather than minoritarian. How, then, should a new majority be established? Is there a determined quantity of support for the values established in common so as to claim that laws have qualitative and decisive reasons to support them? And are these decisive reasons exclusive, exceptionless norms?[21]

From the vantage point of secularism, the answer to both these questions must be yes, because this appearance of an exceptionless norm enables the *political* deployment of law as if it were a structural determination of the method of public and political reasoning. As a political doctrine, therefore, secularism is beholden to the parliamentary or at least republican ideal of representation, seeking to translate and construct a voice of the people into decisive laws representing a majority. Yet the implicit political decision regarding which values become basic while claiming neutrality toward religion obscures the conceptual work done by this last vestige of Westphalian sovereignty: namely, that religion is a political category. That is to say, religion is the reminder of a regulatory and disciplinary arm of a majority, which imposes one political doctrine, secularism, on the perpetual conflict encountered when differences with minority religious practices and values emerge.

For many contemporary theorists of secularism, this is why a theory of public reason is so important; there must be a standard by which to adjudicate between competing and conflicting norms and claims on the good of society. But many contemporary secular legal tests for the freedom of religion adopt a conception of private belief and conscience without indexing how this definition of private conscience is itself derived from and determined by a set of majoritarian public norms of cultural reasoning.[22] That is to say, the specific religious history of Christian confessional conflict underlying the concept of private conscience renders such a standard of adjudication of religion implicitly political. This secularist public reason, therefore, remains a majoritarian set of values.

Philosophically, however, this pursuit of a *political doctrine* that might neutrally adjudicate between competing visions of political goods remains a liberal inheritance with which we must grapple. The most prominent and thoughtful version of such neutrality is found in the work of John Rawls. For Rawls, the question of toleration implicit in a liberal model of secularism is the consequence of historical conflict. The move away from a society in which there might be little or no doubt about the nature of the highest good, to one, after the seventeenth-century European wars of religion, where there is such doubt requires the development of a theory of "reasonable pluralism."[23] Out of this skepticism about the good, Rawls's political liberalism seeks to identify an objective and determinate standard, an epistemology, by which to judge reasons beyond their religious comprehensiveness (a comprehensive doctrine) in service of an agreement known as an overlapping consensus on the public good.

Explicitly acknowledging Kant as a guide, Rawls describes his constructivist method for seeking neutrality as an objective structure aimed at determining possible agreements between members of a society based on fair terms for the value and shape of justice of that society. As a political constructivism, the goal is to provide a "public basis of justification."[24] Indeed, Rawls insists that constructivism is only concerned with what ought to be and, even then, only with what *can* be. It is therefore a theory of practical reason that provides a method capable of maneuvering and avoiding the evaluation of truth claims. Rawls claims that the values of society ought to be constructed within the frame of what he refers to as the original position, a neutral stage at which collaborators derive the norms of justice while presuming an equal standing of difference and advantage between agents.[25] Rawls therefore aims to bracket or suspend judgment concerning truth and falsity of moral values since his standard is the reasonableness of a conception of justice, which is to say a "standard of correctness, and given its political aims, it need not go beyond that."[26]

The political aims of political liberalism are to avoid truth claims, and this neutrality makes the doctrine optimally compatible with other comprehensive doctrines, since "constructivism tries to avoid opposing any comprehensive doctrine."[27] Constructivism only seeks to lay the foundation for a political epistemology.[28] Instead of evaluating truth and falsity, Rawls seeks a method for identifying an overlapping consensus between doctrines. Such an image of consensus, however, is primarily concerned with the "principles of practical reason in union with conceptions of society and person." When this standard of reasonableness overlaps with a comprehensive doctrine, then the claims put forward as a result are those that might help achieve a consensus. Reasonableness is thus our standard of public and social objectivity.

Public reason therefore represents the standard of "appropriate reasons [which] rest on such ideas as publicity and reciprocity."[29] Hence,

> public reason is characteristic of a democratic people: it is the reason of its citizens, of those sharing the status of equal citizenship. The subject of their reason is the good of the public: what the political conception of justice requires of society's basic structure of institutions, and of the purposes and ends they are to serve. Public reason, then, is public in three ways: as the reason of citizens as such, it is the reason of the public; its subject is the good of the public and matters of fundamental justice; and its nature and content is public, being given by the ideals and principles expressed by society's conception of political justice, and conducted open to view on that basis.[30]

In this characterization of public reason, to be public is to be political. That is, the publicity of reason presupposes both that the citizens making use of this reason are already constituted according to a view of "society and person" and, accordingly, that they share that conditional epistemological structure and subject of their reasoning in common. The goal of reaching an overlapping consensus, therefore, assumes that a political unity can be achieved on the basis of a political use of this formalized public reason. The problem of an overlapping consensus, however, only begins once we assume that the ones reasoning about their comprehensive doctrines are citizens—citizens who have been constructed by that very same neutral reasoning.

While Rawls's ideal of overlapping consensus is singular in its philosophical depth, it nevertheless represents a political doctrine, and public reason's claim to neutrality therefore masks the majoritarian history of that epistemology. To Rawls's great credit, this hegemony of secular reason was something he worried about greatly and continued to address in his later work.[31] But a generally prominent feature of social-contract theorists in conversation with Rawls is this emphasis on secularism, if not public reason, as a state-sanctioned political discourse.[32] By assuming that public reason is a common tongue and set of secular principles, rather than itself a translation of a Christian morality,[33] Rawls fails to recognize that a pursuit of universal, rational principles nevertheless relies on the exclusiveness of a search for political unity or consensus. Thus, even the most careful critics of Rawls,[34] still conflate public reasoning with a particular liberal democratic political doctrine.[35] But constructivism is a political doctrine. It is the result of a specifically political liberalism. And by taking confessional differences as the catalyst for his theory,[36] Rawls's model of justice admittedly corresponds to the political use of public reason. As Ronald Beiner asks, can such a "view of society that is robustly egalitarian, 'civicist,' (committed to a shared doctrine of shared citizenship), and basically secular be 'impartial between comprehensive doctrines' in that way that Rawls suggests?"[37] As a political doctrine in search of such a robust secular democratic definition of justice, the question remains therefore: where and when was the decision made to mark *these* liberal democratic reasons as neutral? And who decided?

The historical context of Cohen's Wilhelmine Germany begs us to ask further: where and when was it decided that this citizen and not that one was reasonable? In other words, when was it decided that this one's religion was reasonable and not that one's? Recognizing the Wars of Religion as the reason why "we are condemned to live an overlapping consensus,"[38] the implicit virtue of Rawls's thought is its attempt to develop a political theory out of religious conflict. However, his reliance on Kantianism to forge a theory of public reason and his attempt to downplay the role of specifically Christian values in informing his theory[39] remain subject to the inherited criticism voiced by Schmitt as well as Cohen: that is, the separation of legality and morality obfuscates the effective basis for any account of legitimacy to public law. But the emphasis on overlapping consensus in Rawls's theory of public reason reveals what I believe is a crucial principle for any theory of secularity: that consensus must be built out of conceptions of society and person as well as through the deployment of a public reason. Cohen's idealism, therefore, provides a helpful corrective to the political focus of Rawls's theory by committing to an epistemological and historical self-reflexivity in the construction of conceptions of society and person. In other words, Cohen's sociality of law demonstrates a public *reasoning* that pluralizes reason.

ETHICS AS THE WILL OF PUBLIC REASONING

I would like to return to the reasons why Cohen is helpful in articulating this larger constellation of contemporary concerns. When we reflect on the political and social history in which Cohen composed his *Ethics of Pure Will* and his *Religion of Reason*, we begin to understand the broader context in which he envisioned his ethics and philosophy of law to function. But the theoretical edifice also reflects a poignant criticism of the politicization of religion in modernity.

For Cohen, the relationship between political religion and the state stems from the classical conception of the cultus, or the sacrificial cult at the center of civic life that the ancient Romans believed to regulate fate and lend legitimacy to the state.[40] The cultus, in which Hegel claimed "revering God turns into the reverence proper to humanity itself,"[41] is the sphere in which spirit materializes through honoring the gods with eating, drinking, and imbibing. It is a sphere of ritual performance. Yet Cohen claims that this aesthetic dimension of spirit is fundamentally transformed by the modern political creation of the state, in which the drive (*Trieb*) for power utilizes the state as an artwork to instrumentalize the aesthetics of cultic religious service and unify the particularity of a state and people around a mythic projection of the efficacy of that service.[42] The poetic hero is divinized by political lyric. Hence, political religion presents itself as the unifying bond between people and state, sovereign hero and spirit. In this aestheticization of the power symbolized by the gods "art binds itself to political power" and tries to capture the enchantment of the gods within the artistic representation itself. "So it is with religion in the *cultus* in such a union," claims Cohen. However, "in the religion of the *cultus* . . . the politicization of divinity is the least damage done by this connection."[43] Rather, the politicization of divinity is not merely a claim that divine power is an ally but the invocation of that power for humanity. Thus, a modern sovereign-established church, according to Cohen, exemplifies the political construction of religion and culminates in what Cohen refers to as a political theocracy.[44] Thus, Cohen continues, "the deeper, more unholy crime lies in [the church] imitating the state, by forming an independently consolidated community of faith following the image of the state."[45] The assertion of political unity in an established religious cultus carves an idol out of divine power and asserts it on behalf of the political whole.

By contrast, ethics addresses the universality of people not in terms of governance or power but rather in terms of spirituality and culture. As a critique of the politics of power, Cohen's ethics is an ethics of pure will: the will claimed in contract and obligation, the will that brings *you* and *I* together in legal relation. While the aesthetics of power claims for itself the divine image of unity and decisive force, the will is a scientific category of ethical judgment that is deliberately reflected into a plurality and thus not a claim to exclusive unity. The pure will is a law unto itself, a law-abiding will that correlates the class of singularity and totality (*Allheit*)—the latter again as a unity; that is, the singularity of the person must be fulfilled in the unity of all human beings as humanity.[46] Dissolving the connection between religion and state, the ethics of pure will carves spirit out of the stone of law. Tearing down the idol of the cultus, law erects a new "relationship between ethics and the theory of the state."[47] By evaluating the state as a locus of both ethical and unethical actions in human history, ethics presents a science of law to help justify how "values must become rights."[48] And because rights must be actionable if they are to be rights at all, the creation of rights establishes the ethical will as the origin and goal of sociality.

We can therefore describe Cohen's account of the ethical will as a logic of public reasoning, a practical logic of a science of spirit.[49] Consequently, the ethical ideal of humanity supplants the myth of particular peoples garnering particular rights through their mythic bond,[50] where the rights of some exclude the rights of others, and articulates a theory of right as a duty to respect the law of humanity, or the idea of law as such. Employing the legal model of the corporate collective (*Genossenschaft*), or social plurality in which each member is responsible for the well-being of the whole in a way specific to each,[51] Cohen articulates a different understanding of how the right to religious freedom or conscience might articulate different goods differently. The corporate collective is a space of rights that are apportioned according to need. With such a model, Cohen dispenses with political religion as the vehicle of myth in favor of the social particularity of religion as a cultural resource for public morality. Religions thus play distinct roles in the collective and contribute differently to the whole of morality.

Viewed from the perspective of the sociality of law, we can therefore better distinguish how a theory of secularism falls under the rubric of the political, presenting its decisive set of norms and values as a universal blueprint when it in fact represents the values of a relative community, of a majority relative to a minority. Even the structure of public reason on which Rawlsian political liberalism bases its overlapping consensus is but one layer of such a collective political structure.[52] That is because the myth of neutral rationality presupposes an already constituted citizenship or an equalization of reason givers as the criterion of reasoning. Concealing the historical origin of majoritarian values as timeless principles, such an account of public reasoning requires reasoners to accept a mythic version of reason: impartial, neutral, and ahistorical. Such a universalization of a particular history is structurally no different than the politicization of the cult, described by Cohen. The form of divine power is simply transmuted into public reason; the dialectic of enchantment unfolds at another stage. By contrast, Cohen's idealization of historically recognized norms out of Christian and Jewish sources sketches a public ethic in which reason gains an explicit history, and its majoritarian claims are presented as just that, claims of a majority community.

Therefore, Cohen's ethics demonstrates the difference between a political religion and the idealization of religion, or the translation of religion into ethics or public reasoning. Tied to politics, religion imposes the conditions of belief on citizenship, divides plural social groups into friends with shared beliefs and enemies with opposing ones, and presents a deceptive image of neutral, universal reason to solicit passive awareness of the reasons for belonging. Ethical idealism, however, understands religion as a scientifically meaningful history, one that is conceptually articulated and justified according to its form and content when ethics clarifies the norms, goods, and claims made on persons within as well as between communities. Idealization provides the hermeneutic mechanism for finding the necessary historical parallels and trajectories of normative agreement, and by recognizing these norms, customs, and practices as actionable, idealization utilizes the social function of law to translate these norms.

For example, if a religious community seeks to impose a norm on society it must make a claim not only on the future this community wishes to secure for its particular interests but also make a claim on the future of all human beings in the society as whole. As a political claim, the particular interests of the relative community become majoritarian as soon as they impose those interests on society as whole, as if they were universal. However, following Cohen's model of public reasoning, if the community articulates its interests self-reflexively as particular to its goals as a social collectivity, then this recognition is implicitly coordinated within a larger framework of multiple communities. This corporate model sews into the very fabric of public reasoning an implicit pluralism of social interests. Hence, by making religious reasoning explicit in society, the pitfalls of liberalism's attempt to forget its past are avoided; that is, even the ersatz political religion of neutrality in liberalism can be minoritized by this sociality. Recognizing each community as a minority within society therefore inscribes in the nature of public reasoning a principle of judgment that is consistent with Cohen's description of the categorical imperative: only laws that recognize the plurality of communities and their very real differences can pursue the content of the ethical will, namely, the idea of humanity within the form of that judgment.

Hence, the principle of continuity that interrelates the possible recipients of that normative claim is the ideal will that judges. Will becomes the legal representative within all publicly constituted communities and in all modern public religions. This is the will that claims, acts, and reacts to the social and public action of history. Such an ideal ethical will is the spirit of law and the sociality of reasoning. And, because all actors in a social world must will their actions according to one norm or another, ethics provides the account of that will and the source of a critique of such actions.

Philosophically, one way to understand Cohen's corrective to the liberal separation of law and morality is to recognize in Cohen's notion of ethical will a revision of Kantian ethics with the help of Hegelian spirit.

That is to say, like Hegel, Cohen criticizes Kant's account of moral will as enclosing autonomy within an abstraction and, thus, leaving the passage to sociality obstructed.[53] Like Hegel, Cohen therefore insists that sociality, or spirit, is manifested in law. For Cohen, however, "Spirit (*Geist*) has to signify more than merely the limited expression of intelligence [*Intelligenz*]."[54] In its relationship with logic, ethical, practical spirit—the will—articulates the justified past as a normative future. *Geist*, or spirit, therefore becomes the space of reasoning, where logic and ethics interrelate and give expression to social recognition of reasons and persons. Thus, Cohen writes, "*Geist*, however, has theoretical culture as its indispensable and irreplaceable presupposition. The ethical character and power [*Art und Macht*] of *Geist* first arises on the basis of theoretical culture. This is the claim made by the basic law of truth [that logic and ethics are fundamentally correlated]. And so it now also has a positive effect on the content of the state-concept. Thus, the fiction of the juristic person becomes the hypothesis of the subject in its highest expression as *Geist*."[55] Ethical spirit opens up a space of reasoning in which the subject of ethics and the idea of humanity are related in ideas. That is, as ethical ideas, the moral self is grounded in the legal fiction or task of performing an *I* that has humanity as its purpose. Thus, Cohen describes the subjectivity of ethics as hypothetical, or a ground on which to strive for the ideal. The *ought* that grounds an action, as a law, provides social objectivity. This is why the state becomes the culmination of the legal actions for both Cohen and Hegel: when legal actions are claimed as rights, they are no longer simply customs or practices accumulated ad hoc. Rather, these actions are logically justified as lawful because they pursue the goal of attaining humanity. The state therefore consolidates the sociality of law as its spirit. And, while Cohen acknowledges Hegel's fundamental insight—that *Geist* is built on theoretical culture, or the objective determination of the Idea in its mediated expression—Cohen nevertheless sees spirit advance beyond the theoretical and into this notion of legal will.[56]

Instead of a personified will, Cohen's ethical idealism insists on a pure, ideal will, or spirit—both a theoretical and a moral spirit. This ethical will is both normative and critical reasoning. This means that the conditions of public law must take account of the historical context in which such norms first emerge as claims made by and on the pure will. Hence spirit represents the historical chain between past, present, and future, in which these enchanted ideas still serve as norms. Retaining that historical index to their minority or majority origin, however, is correlated to the unifying goal of humanity. The balance struck between the historical origin of the norm and the ideal of humanity provides the public reasoning of ethical will with its justificatory parameters. But the idea of humanity cannot assume such a structurally important role without a higher justification. If moral culture were based solely on the ideal human being, then there would be no horizon on which to strive after the ideal, and no greater justice than what is. However, the work of spirit is to point toward the internal purposiveness of reasoning neither as a projection of forces beyond our control nor as a given for cognition. That is, the work of spirit is neither a work of fate nor an eschaton but rather a unity announced as a purposive goal of moral spirit.

Cohen's theory of spirit therefore arrives at a new conception of consensus that is suited to its Protestant and Jewish sources: namely, the monotheistic God-idea, who is spirit. That is, as we saw in Cohen's reading of Heine, the importance of spirit for idealism culminates in monotheism. "If," Cohen writes, "the God-idea signifies the unity of nature and morality, then this must not be confused with identity in a pantheistic manner. Rather, it signifies unity for nature and morality as a coalition [*Vereinigung*], a harmonization of nature and morality. There can be no contradiction left open between morality and nature, nor can there be a contradiction between the claim [*Forderung*] and its fulfillment, when each is dependent on the other. This harmonizing unity forms its own proper content, which no identity can occupy; that is, the content of the God-idea."[57] The God-idea represents the harmonizing unity of an idea, in which the potential contradiction between nature and ethics is redirected into a temporalized unity, a norm of the future in which the God-idea sustains the continued idealization of moral labor. Cohen feared that liberal Christianity had embraced a pantheistic identity of thinking and being in the incarnate divinity in man. The God of monotheism, by contrast, assures the unity of a single transcendent ethical goal of human striving for the good. As Cohen claims, "The singular and unique God is not so much configured in opposition to many gods, as much as against the many peoples and nations. The sense of Israelite monotheism lies foremost in messianism. . . . The unity of God signifies from the beginning nothing other than the unity of humanity."[58] The God of Jewish monotheism is therefore a God of justification and reconciliation, a guarantee that humanity can be brought about. God is therefore a cultural norm, an index of the future of humanity, and "The unity of God signifies first and foremost nothing other than the unity of humanity."[59] This future unity, in Cohen's thought is the enchanted purpose of ethical ideas.

MINORITY, MONOTHEISM, AND CONSENSUS

If we recall Schmitt's reading of *Leviathan*, we find a Christological coloring to his description of both the public confession of belief in miracles and the establishment of law as emanating from that principle of authority. Thus, we can further project Cohen's critique onto this account of the sovereign's unification of law and morality. Similarly, Paul de Lagarde's and Max Wundt's images of force, power, and blood consciousness of the *Volksgemeinschaft* all secularized this principle of the aesthetics of power, politicizing religion with the spiritual-material will and the moral force of a divinely sanctioned people. As attempts to suture the gap between law and morality, these attempts to spiritualize materiality and reenchant fall short of an actual justification of law with morality. Rather, this unification of nature and morality projects a natural morality, in which "the members of a *Volk* have a consciousness of one and the same God," from which "there arise among them, equally collectively, moral convictions and conditions, government and law."[60] In the historicized and secularized sphere of citizenship and national belonging, we therefore see how the materiality of the *Volksgemeinschaft* is predicated on the historically specific Christological model of law and morality. Neither Catholicism nor Protestantism but rather the mortal god sewn from both of these garments together becomes the organic machine of the Leviathan, the sovereign. To the extent that citizens once affirmed Jesus as the Christ, they can now affirm the autonomy of their will and the legislation of their law as their own common principle of moral culture.

As a critical response to the secularization of religion into political categories, Cohen's ethics provides a theory of consensus that seeks to consciously trace the dialectic between the social and the political. But Cohen derives this method of navigating between religious and political claims by appealing to a specific normative argument about the structure of judgment—a norm in itself that emerges from the minority history of secularization. Therefore, I want to consider how the model of ethical idealization as a form of public reasoning develops a view of normative consensus out of a minority history.

Consensus begins with a norm that recognizes, orders, and justifies other norms. As we have seen so far, in Cohen's thought this role is played by the God-idea. God is the ideal of unity, truth, futurity, and purpose. And because for Cohen the structure of judgment is a structure of reconciliation, of sustaining difference according to a temporal differentiation of origin and goal, God is a norm of judgment that idealizes difference—the difference between transcendence and immanence. Because God represents the infinite divide between the world of human action and the scope of possible ideas about that world as a norm, God limits the pretense of political decisions by promising more than what any state, any law, or any government could secure for human life. Similar to Descartes's "idea of the infinite," God represents the ideal impossibility of sameness between human and divine and so also of the impossibility of a single decision or act of human will becoming final or hegemonic. There will always be an idea that differs from such a decision. This difference is necessary for determining any one judgment from another; hence, God minoritizes all other ideas, norms, and reasons by pointing to this infinite difference.

Just as God idealizes difference, in order for the idea of humanity to have an identity and meaning, God must always be correlated to humanity as the unique God of a uniquely human collectivity. Hence, no majority exists without being minor in relation to another class, namely, humanity. And humanity is minoritized in relation to God, or the idea of unlimited differentiation between ideas, decisions, and groups. As a model for a norm of consensus, the God-idea therefore secures the ideal of future unity to humanity, the messianic dimension of the idea of humanity, as the limit to majoritarian reasoning.

Monotheism becomes a crucial dimension of public reasoning as imagined in Cohen's ethics. This is because ethics is a science of law that critically publicizes the structure of law, as I argued above. However, religion is distinct from ethics, which is the method of idealizing religion. By tracing the origin of the concepts of action, person, community, society, and the state back to the sources of family, tribe, people, as well as the other, the foreigner, and the neighbor, ethics clarifies the conceptual significance of these concepts for purposive action. While such concepts and practices might have originated in religious customs, translated into a law as the language of public reasoning, particularistic norms find recognition as rights or claims to rights.[61] Law adjudicates the cultural normativity of those practices and customs according to its structural orientation to the future as the site of possible consensus. In this manner, consensus seeks to justify what might first appear in the history of a community as a mythic basis for minority norms.

The idea of God as the idea of unity and truth is more than a minority norm, however. Although such an idea might not be universal, the idea of God presented Cohen with the closest thing to a possible norm of consensus between Christianity and Judaism, despite the dramatic neo-Marcionite denials of such a shared conception by some scholars in his day.[62] For example, in the midst of an explosion in scholarly use of the types of monotheism to characterize Biblical and Hellenic antiquity, nineteenth-century philologists such as Paul de Lagarde employed monotheism as a means of both abstracting an idea from the historical trappings of Israelite religion and solidifying the national identity of the Jews in opposition to that of the Germans.[63] This national inflection of philology was not uncommon. Indeed, Ernest Renan had first referred to monotheism precisely in order to describe the inheritance of the Semitic race, which includes Jews, Christians, and Muslims as distinct nations.[64] Thus, the identification of an ancient Semitic idea of divinity with their national community was an accepted premise for Lagarde. On this basis, he could claim that the Jews' emphasis on their chosenness, together with their "papier-mâchés-monotheism,"[65] created the conditions for modern Jewish exclusivism, the national enemy of modern Germany.[66] For Lagarde, Germans were locked in a spiritual battle with this enemy. Thus, Lagarde claims, Germany must remain committed as "antisemitic and not Jew-haters, because in the midst of a Christian world, the Jews are Asiatic heathens. Circumcision and the dietary laws of the Jews are atavistic. The monotheism of the Jews is based on [what seems like] a unit-stage within the report of a commissariat-commanded sergeant, for whom existence only references a single exemplary among several objects: one God, two tablets, three Fathers, four Mothers."[67] For Lagarde, monotheism is nothing more than a placeholder for a foreign and Asiatic religion or nation. Therefore, monotheism is the source of a particularism and exclusivism that will never lead to proper integration of Jews and Europeans yet alone Germans. Together with the "social-democrats and the Jesuits, [the Jews] stand on the same level: they are Fatherland-less."[68] But unlike these other partisan movements, the internationalism of the Jews is rooted, for Largarde, in their national and racial independence, which makes them not only foreign to his mythic Indo-Germanic people but likewise "the enemy of every European nation."[69] Both particularistic and too universalistic, Jewish monotheism fails to accomplish the political goal of unifying a modern people together in anything other than its own self-aggrandizement. The exclusive unity of monotheism, in other words, created the conditions of enmity between the Jews and the nations.

Lagarde turns the transcendent principle of one God for one (all) people into a principle of chauvinism: one God for one people means one God for the Jews alone. By emphasizing its exclusivism, Lagarde interprets the unity of God to mean a unity amid plurality; one people becomes one nation. But Lagarde's philosophical capacity for dialectical thinking was not his strong suit.[70] Cohen's God-idea, by contrast, represents the dialectical articulation of unity; that is to say, Cohen's God-idea presents not a unit or one among many but a *unique* God, whose uniqueness corresponds to the oneness of inclusion, of all people who collectively belong to humanity. Thus, Cohen turns to the God-idea of monotheism, as a principle of unity, to help negotiate precisely this kind of opposition between friends and enemies. As Cohen claims, it is not for us to decide between friends and enemies as a principle of social difference, since

> the nations are the enemy of the unique God and therefore the enemy of the unique nation. Were it to remain now with this antagonism, between the nation of Israel and the nations of the world, then the concept of monotheism would fail and in it at the same time the member of the correlation, which arises in the fellowman in plurality of nations, would fail. We will see how this antagonism, which hinges upon the utter fate of monotheism, is resolved through a relational-concept [*Verbindungsbegriff*], whose meaning is all the greater as through it, the plurality of fellowmen, is transformed and upwardly sublated [*emporgehoben*] into totality.[71]

Far from particularizing the Jews, in Cohen's mind, this focus on uniqueness provides a metanorm with which to negotiate opposition, to resolve antagonism between units. Indeed, the historical idealization of the nations and Israel mobilized a relational concept to transform the antagonism of friends and enemies into an ethical and legal relation. But there is certainly a potential tension. As Robert Erlewine writes, "On the one hand, with their idea of the unique God, the Jews bequeath to the world the correlation between God and human beings" or the irreducible relationship between these radically different members of the relation. "On the other hand, to embed this idea in history, Jews must radically oppose and negate other conceptions of the divine as idolatry, and must work toward eliminating them."[72] The resolution to this tension lies in the idealization of God as the God of humanity. Indeed, when a community within the plurality of sociality claims itself as a majority, as having access to truth or reason that excludes all others, then this claim becomes idolatry. This, as Erlewine notes, is "the great danger of pluralities masquerading as totalities . . . they distract and conceal the truth."[73] Monotheistic unity is therefore correlated to plurality but limits the pretense of any one claim to truth. Thus, in order to mediate between the practices of reason that would otherwise lead to exclusive claims over truth, Cohen believes that monotheism secures the relationship between different groupings, such as that between Israel and humanity. What kind of relational concept could accomplish this idealization?

Before exploring this relational concept, we must first understand how the monotheistic God described by Cohen is a God of correlation. That is, as I noted above, God represents the idealization of difference, and this correlation between the human and God creates a vision of messianic humanity, of a world in which all people are united under law and God. This is what God means in Cohenian terms. But, rather than a soft theocratic account of public law, Cohen's vision is methodological; it is yet again an idealization and the source of further idealizations. Rather than particularizing the Jews, Cohen sees the idea of God providing a normative language with which to address the possibility of disagreement and argument, opposition and conflict. Hence, our correlation to God manifests in spirit, in the possibility of acting morally in such a way as would befit holiness. The idea of correlation as the logical form that gives voice to God (correlated with the human being) becomes the logic of judgment that drives all decision about conflict and reconciliation. This, Cohen claims, is because "the holy spirit can be neither God alone nor man alone, but neither can it be God and man at the same time; it is an attribute of both concepts, or rather the bringing-together of both.

Spirit is nothing else but the link that brings together the correlation, and holiness is in the first place nothing other than the means [*Vollzugsmittel*] by which the correlation is carried out: how could the holy spirit be anything other than that function signified by correlation?"[74] The monotheistic theory of creation, for Cohen, takes on an ethical significance in distinguishing the immanent metaphysical God of pantheism from the transcendent God of creation. While God transcends creation, God is nevertheless related to this creation. This distinction stems from Cohen's claim that his idealism pursues "instead of immanence, correlation."[75] Similarly, instead of a God in all, Cohen's is a God *of all*. In the moral sphere, therefore, the spirit of holiness transforms the *decision* from an expression of majoritarian exclusivity into a *merger*,[76] in which correlation describes the inextricable logical relationship between two distinct components while each term nevertheless preserves its independent existence.[77] Because correlation idealizes changing terms as they react to one another with an account of their formal connection, correlation also describes the idealization of otherness within law. Correlation between human and God is therefore a normative basis for further idealizations, and as a spirit of idealized difference, correlation also relates human beings with fellow human beings.

As the *logic* of holy spirit—a logic of ethics—correlation idealizes moral action prior to decision. That is, correlation emphasizes the purposive orientation of a relationship. Correlation signals the time over which norms emerge. Hence, even the metanorm of God signifies a temporalized difference, which Cohen claims to have learned from Moses Maimonides's (1135–1204) description of the attributes of action, the only knowable characteristics of the monotheistic God.[78] In Cohen's reconstruction, God's action consists in thinking other beings as an eternal overflow that Maimonides claims is like "a gift that can never be returned."[79] For Cohen, this gift is the spirit of holiness, which means that "if God is the God of ethics, then He must be the inhabitation of the relation to man."[80] Or, as the Talmud seeks to describe this correlation, God is the space, the place (*ha-maqom*) of the world.[81] As the space of reasoning for a new kind of consensus, God becomes the site of ethics. This is not to suggest any physical dimension to God but rather the *spirit* of God as moral reasoning. Hence, this space of reasoning is more of a temporal dimension that transforms the act of cognition and thinking in God. God's thinking represents ethical thinking, a thinking that is perpetually generative and for the sake of something *other*. Thus, when God thinks,

> in that he thinks himself, He is for Maimonides not only thinking thought itself. This self-sufficiency, from which the world of human beings is excluded, suits the God of Aristotle; it becomes nonsensical for the God of Judaism. The God of Judaism must think of mankind when He thinks of Himself; but certainly He must think of mankind from out of Himself, never out of the essence [*Wesen*] of mankind.
>
> Thus from here it becomes understandable that Maimonides posits an equivalence between will and cognition.[82]

Cohen interprets the God of Maimonides with a view to the idealization of humanity. God generates the idea of humanity out of God's thinking God's self.[83] That is, the God-idea represents the implicitly idealized difference, the infinitesimal difference, between the concepts of God and human. By placing the essence of the human within God, Cohen stresses the indeterminate ideal of humanity, an idea that cannot be generated by self-consciousness but must be located in otherness, in the otherness of the correlation between God and human. This is the God of the prophets, the God who thinks of humanity when God thinks of God's self. And since humanity becomes the *action* of God's thinking, we can discern that God's essence is this ethical idea of humanity *as spirit*. God becomes the spirit of human morality, a spirit of idealized difference and a spirit of trust in the possibility of consensus. On this model of holy spirit, the action of ethical reasoning ought to be the performance of a similar kind of self-cultivation: human beings ought to act on behalf of the idea of humanity. The enchantment of such reasoning lies in our commitment to recognize such divine actions as normative and to strive to embody such actions as the path to becoming moral selves.

But can we realistically speak about God in politics? God is a norm for morality, religion, and even law, but God is not a norm for politics. In this sense, appealing to the God-idea as the metanorm for a secularity of culture is certainly counterintuitive, but, as I hope to show in conclusion, because the sociality of law conditions the possibility of the state and of rights, this sociality structurally allows for norms to be revised. In this sense, God signifies the hypothesis, as Cohen would have it, for the possibility of justice. As the structural condition for a normative correlation between minor and major, however, Cohen maintains that the idealization of difference in monotheism also enabled a transition from particular pluralities to a totality or class predicated of humanity alone. Thus, we can now return to the relational concept Cohen believes to negotiate between antagonisms—most readily discernible in the political sphere. This religious norm that articulates the self-reflexivity of public reasoning is found in the theory of the Noahide.[84]

The rabbinic concept of the Noahide is the imagined figure of a resident alien, a non-Jew living among the Israelite community. The rabbis of the Talmud endeavored to enumerate a set of laws pertaining to this resident without requiring conversion to Judaism as the condition for citizenship.[85] Hence, as a figure of minority and foreignness, Cohen reimagines the Noahide as a concept that is implicit in ethical monotheism and its method of idealization. The Noahide laws consequently provide an idealization of a minority moral culture within the larger structure of public law, a model of spirit and trust in the institutions of law despite the looming politics of identity.

SELF-REFLEXIVE MINORITY: THE NOAHIDE AND THE DEPOLITICIZATION OF CONSENSUS

We can now better assess Cohen's God-idea as a moral norm with which to establish epistemological recognition between Jews and Christians in the public sphere. As a public norm, the God-idea enables Jews to provide a reason shared with non-Jews as the basis for constructing a moral culture. Cohen defended this idea when in 1888 he submitted an affidavit to a Marburg court that was trying the case of a primary school teacher, Ferdinand Fenner, accused of defaming the Jewish *Religionsgesellschaft* by suggesting that the Talmud mandates that Jews treat Christians according to a moral double standard.[86] The implication was that Jews were immoral and chauvinistic in their treatment of Christians, thus justifying anti-Semitism in its own right. Cohen's affidavit took up the implicit question of whether Jews shared a common morality with Christians.[87] Emphasizing that Jewish monotheism provides recognition of the stranger, Cohen introduces the Noahide as an articulation of a norm with which to assess truth and sincerity in public discourse. But the figure of the Noahide would also become a foundational concept in Cohen's later philosophy of religion. In what follows, I want to suggest that the Noahide demonstrates the continuity of Cohen's thought, addressing the parameters of public religious reasoning.

The Noahide is represented in the Talmud as someone wishing to live with the Israelite and later Jewish community (and thus is bound to seven laws given to the sons of Noah), whom the rabbis depict as a kind of minority resident.[88] Thus, the Noahide provides a concept of citizenship that is independent of religious belief. But the relationship between the Noahide as a socially recognized agent of morality and the God-idea as the epistemological bridge from one social group to another is crucially dependent on a concept of a scientifically grounded and conceptually reflexive account of religion. Cohen's interpretation of the Noahide therefore traces a site of self-reflexivity in rabbinic Judaism. That is, to the extent that the Noahide represents the minority in an imagined Jewish majority society, Cohen sees the rabbis describing a self-reflexive concept not unlike Cohen's own neo-Kantian idealization of ethical reason giving. The Noahide provides a historical idealization of ethical agency and thus helps Cohen articulate an epistemologically secular moral agency.

According to Cohen, the Biblical sources of the Noahide already reveal the kind of idealization that Cohen links to prophetic monotheism.[89] By transforming natural fact into the stimulus for new social norms, the prophetic critique of society operates as a kind of idealism wherein the poor, the widow, and the foreigner *ought to have* their factual and natural suffering relieved; hence, they provide transcendental facts or problems whose existence issues new ethical demands. According to Cohen, the prophets therefore stress futurity and a justice that is not yet present; their religious vision is for a radically new kind of ethical culture (*Sittlichkeit*) that is a critique of the past.[90] For Cohen, the prophet's vision is by definition idealist, for it idealizes natural facts, affiliations, and determinations of social well-being and ill in pursuit of the higher norm of God's goodness. This, Cohen maintains, leads to the idealization of culture, since "the prophet rises above the level of primitive belief, which blindly assumes a correspondence between the good and well-being, the malicious or evil and woe. This correspondence would like to pass off as if well-being and woe were only subjectively distinguished. The social distinctions, however, must be entirely recognized as objective; otherwise the concept of the human for the tasks of ethical culture becomes endangered and risks being unraveled."[91] We remain blinded by mythic thought when we deem wealth and poverty as either subjectively distinguished or the results of goodness and evil; rather, the prophets recognized that social relations and distinctions are objective and thus subject to critique and revision. Put differently, the prophets treated the normative order as a social construct and thus believed that by altering social norms one might alter material well-being. If good and bad are considered only according to material success or failure, then eating of the tree of knowledge of good and evil in the Garden of Eden would result in *being* good or evil. This conflation of morality and empirical situation is the root of idolatry. Thus, Cohen insists in his affidavit that idolatry is the other against which the Talmud polemicizes and not Christianity. Idolatry is therefore the kind of mythic thinking that does not demand a reflexive consciousness of its own historical and critical shifts and adjustments. Only reflexive concepts that allow for their justification, critique, and revision can be the scientific basis for culture.

The prophetic idealization described by Cohen provides the basis for a critique of social relations, of which the Noahide is a crucial figure.[92] When we consider the distinction between Israel and the nations, out of which the Noahide first emerges as the figure of a foreigner, we find that this distinction is not a moral or theological judgment derived from natural facts. Rather, the Noahide idealizes a *legal* space between Israelite and non-Israelite. The rabbis recognize that minorities would no doubt dwell within any land over which Jews would gain halakhic (legal) sovereignty. Thus, between native and foreign born, the Bible identifies a mediating concept of the *ger toshav*, or stranger-sojourner. Cohen describes this as a concept premised on law or a set of objective norms rather than national identity. To trace this legal idealization, Cohen points to the textual sources of the concept of the *ger*, which he interprets to begin with the recognition of the other, of the fellow, *re'a*. As a neighbor or a fellow, this other is subject to certain restrictions but also to certain norms: "You shall love your fellow as yourself" (Lev. 19:18). Already, Cohen understands the biblical verses to establish a normative relationship between the other and the self. Love is the connecting tissue; the relationship between the self and the other is transformed from a question of numeric value, premised on "a concept which grasps man . . . as a unit in a series: one man next to other men, just *the next man*,"[93] and turns this question into one about the other as someone proximate, near, close. The *re'a* implies familiarity, which is then to be contrasted with the *ger*—the stranger, whose residency amid the Israelite polity is recognized in advance. The foreigner is not simply an unexpected other, an intruder. Rather, the foreigner is a concept already idealized according to the same relation as the *re'a*: "And love the stranger, for you were strangers in Egypt" (Deut. 10:19). Both the stranger and the fellow, the foreign and the familiar, are placed within the ideal relation of love.

The *ger*—the stranger, the guest, the one who dwells among the people—stands as a reminder to the children of Israel that they too were foreigners and strangers in Egypt. The *ger* both reflects the foreignness of the people of Israel and turns this concept of foreignness into a norm enjoined by the God of humanity for the purposes of reflecting Israel's past into its moral agency. The *ger* therefore mediates between political myth—Israel's chosenness—and the idealization of Israel's past suffering as strangers in a foreign land. But this mediation neither reduces the *ger*'s difference nor homogenizes the identity of the Israelite. Rather, the *ger toshav* begins as a political concept of an irreducible foreignness of the Israelite; however, this self-reflexivity of foreignness as Israel's recognition of the other dissolves the political altogether, since "God gives also to the stranger his share in the law of the land, although he does not profess the one God."[94] The Noahide is therefore the idealization of the minority.

As an idealization, Cohen connects the *ger* and the Noahide through the legal relationship established between foreigner and citizen. Through Biblical civil law, the *re'a* is specified as a citizen (*ezrah*), and the *ger* is specified as both a stranger as well as a foreigner, a member of another nation. The text therefore enjoins Israel that "one law shall be for you, as for the foreigner so for the citizen it shall be, for I am the Lord your God" (Lev. 24:22). This recognition of different status and yet single law places foreigner and citizen in a common relation under God. At the same time, it also places Israelite and foreigner under the jurisdiction of law,[95] since as Cohen writes, "Israel became a state, and in the concept of a *citizen* of a state an opposition arises between the native and the foreigner."[96] It is a normative relationship to the extent that it is commanded by God, who dictates that "You shall love." That is, because I am told I *ought to* love my fellow, the citizen as well as the foreigner, I have a norm of relation. I must *love* my other because the other is already cited within the norm itself. This is the first stage of idealized alterity.

But the Noahide becomes the legal representation of the *ger*, of the stranger that Maimonides recognizes as one of the "pious of the nations" who recognize a moral religion. The Noahide represents the legal status of minority as the idealization of foreignness under law. Thus, in the Biblical narrative Noah encounters the divine power of God's will and God's judgment of creation. Whereas creation was willed as good, Noah witnesses God's rescinded judgment of that norm. The preestablished good of creation does not overrule God's judgment of humanity. The flood, which drowns rather than bloodies (to invoke Benjamin's image of divine violence), submerges the fact of creation in favor of the norm of humanity. Hence, the manifestation of God's will is demythologized in the process of becoming a norm of humanity above the good of mere life, of mere creation. Noah is the recipient of this law of humanity, of the moral law that must withstand mythic manifestation. Law, in this sense, must be reoriented as justice, the law of God, not the law of nature or of human institutions. The sons of Noah therefore inherit this idealization of the good—not the good of creation but the good of a covenant with humanity.

Neither friend nor enemy but one accorded rights, the Noahide presents us with a concept of self-reflexivity: the Noahide is not only a borderline concept between native and foreign but also "unequivocally a borderline concept between religion and ethical culture."[97] As a borderline concept (*Grenzbegriff*) between religion and ethical culture, the Noahide represents the hermeneutic border between self and other, native and foreign, that reflects both sides of the divide. As Cohen writes, "The 'Israelite' also contains a further ambivalence [*Zweideutigkeit*], insofar as it signifies, out of a difference of religion, also a political distinction. For Israel became a state and the concept of the citizen of the state [*Begriffe des Staatsbürgers*] contains an antagonism between the native-born and the foreigner. We will see that through a relational concept [*Verbindungsbegriff*] the opposition is reconciled and overcome, not only eradicating the hostility, but even the indifference to the Foreigner."[98] Although the Noahide represents the encounter between the foreigner and native, as a legal concept, it marks the border between citizen and foreigner within the state. As a legal concept, the Noahide dissolves this distinction by reaffirming the ideality of rights. Thus, the Noahide represents the legal subject par excellence, since with such a concept "humanity [*Humanität*] begins, namely, in the law and in the state." The Noahide thus represents a concept of citizenship that is not reducible to nationality, since the Noahide is not required to affirm religious or mythic knowledge and need not believe in the declared public miracle of the sovereign.[99] The Noahide represents the *ideal* of humanity. As an idealization out of the sources of Judaism, this position between morality and religion—between ethics and politics—reveals the Noahide as a political concept whose relational role cannot reduce citizenship to friendship or enmity.

By contrast, for Schmitt such a conception of nationality and peoplehood is anathema to the very idea of the state and the concept of the political. But this is due, once again, to the priority Schmitt gives to *political representation*, which he defines as an existential relationship that generates the state; thus "representation is not a normative event, a process, and a procedure. It is, rather, something *existential*. To represent means to make an invisible being visible and present through a publicly present one. . . . The idea of representation rests on a people existing as a political unity, as having a type of being that is higher, further enhanced, and more intense in comparison to the natural existence of some human group living together."[100] Representation makes an invisible being, presumably the nation, *manifest* as a *public* sovereign. But what Schmitt means by this manifestation of an enhanced being beyond the "natural existence of living together" should not be mistaken for an idealization. Rather, representation occurs politically prior to the state, and it existentially enhances the bare life of political friendship, which here appears as the intensification of a sensible intuition of proximity between people. While more than the natural existence of a human group living together, what Schmitt's theory of representation manifests is a metaphysics of peoplehood that bolsters a secularist account of political consciousness. This is because Schmitt claims "the state as political unity rests on the connection of two opposing formative principles. The first is the principle of identity (specifically, the self-identity of then existing people as a political unity [i.e., the nation]), if, by virtue of its own political consciousness and national will, it has the capacity to distinguish friend and enemy, and the other is the principle of representation through which the government represents the political unity [i.e., sovereign decision in the personal will of the ruler]."[101] Friends and enemies are therefore determined by a political will and representation of unity that constitutes the public sovereign. Friends share the identity of a unit, which Schmitt simply believes the concept of humanity cannot maintain. For him, humanity has no political significance: "the concept of humanity cannot wage war because it has no enemy . . . there are no wars of humanity as such. Humanity is not a political concept, and no political entity or society and no status corresponds to it."[102] By placing humanity in a separate category than friends and enemies, Schmitt's definition of unity is premised on the identity that determines difference. He attempts to cordon off the political decision about who is a friend and who is an enemy as though it were a *logic* of decision. However, such a formalism merely claims to be driven by an existential intensity that identifies proximity as unity and enmity as foreign difference.

And yet, because Schmitt does not recognize humanity as a political concept, the Noahide must begin as a political concept that leads us back to the sociality of law. This is due to the fact that the Noahide marks the border between citizen and foreigner and then recognizes the rule of law as the condition of this difference. Hence, the unity implied by the law is the unity that links the Noahide as foreigner to the unity of humanity. In this sense, Schmitt's notion of political unity stands is sharp contrast to the idealization of difference within Cohen's monotheism. Moreover, Cohen's idea of humanity, as we saw in chapter 3, is an ideal; that is, humanity is the content generated by the form of law itself, the temporality of law as a purpose-driven judgment. Cohen's ethical socialism predicated on his ethics is therefore not a politics or policy in the first place. Rather, Cohen believes that humanity must remain a regulative ideal of the ethical culture (*Sittlichkeit*) of the state. Correlated to an idea of God as the grounding truth of a state built on law, the idea of humanity legitimates the more general category of human belonging as a purpose for the state to work toward. Humanity therefore becomes a norm that depoliticizes the Noahide by making the latter a concept of legal recognition of minority status. But the Noahide nevertheless represents the possibility of difference being recognized within the structure of law, whereby the majoritarian dynamic of humanity is infinitely generated in the social life of reasoning. And if humanity can become the figure of unity that links the particularity of the Noahide with the infinite universality of the God-idea, then we can begin to see how Cohen's notion of consensus in public reasoning is indeed enchanted.

Like God, humanity is therefore not a myth. Humanity is not one group of friends among the nations or peoples. As Cohen writes in a short 1913 essay entitled *Das Gottesreich,*

> A further opposition is that between *the peoples (die Völker)* and human-ity (*die Menschheit*), and it is apparently still exacerbated: Israel carries *election* as its vocation of professing belief in God. A single nation places itself in opposition to the whole of humanity. But this opposition ought to lead only toward unity. This unique people ought to become humanity, insofar as it fulfills its vocation: to spread the unity of God to the whole of humanity. Humanity, which confesses the one and only God, ought to be the *Vaterland* of the singular people chosen to spread the faith in God.[103]

Humanity is thus dialectically positioned as what carries the nationality of the Jews out of its stateless suffering, yet neither at the level of statehood per se nor at the level of a particular identity of a national unity. Rather, the unity of humanity is the predicate of Jewish nationality, since their sovereign remains God, the norm of norms for all law as such. Cohen sees the holiness of Jewish nationality in the Jews being unique in their devo-tion to the monotheistic God *for the sake of humanity,* in order to *become* humanity [*Dies einzige Volk soll zur Menschheit werden*].[104] Within the very concept of correlation between humanity and the various peoples— between the God of Israel and the God of humanity—Cohen therefore transforms the meaning of unity into the basis of social reasoning, the law. In order to reside within the land, therefore, the Noahide must pledge to abide by the authority of law, yet not the entirety of biblical or rabbinic law. Rather, the Noahide must pledge to abide by only seven laws, six of which are prohibitions:[105] to refrain from murder, theft, idolatry, denial of God, the eating of live animals, and sexual immorality. One is phrased as a positive requirement: to establish courts and a legal system to ensure social concord. And although disagreement exists as to the specifics of each commandment, both within the Talmud and in the commentators, there is no positive injunction to believe in God.

By contrast to both Hobbes and Spinoza's conceptions of ecclesiastical power, in Cohen's account one need not even pay lip service to God. The Noahide need not address the question of God or even belief at all but merely acknowledge these as the laws of the land in which he or she choses to live: "The Noahide is therefore not a believer and yet nevertheless a citizen (*Staatsbürger*), insofar as he is a stranger-sojourner. The Noahide is the precursor of natural law for the state and for the freedom of conscience."[106] The Noahide gains legal status as a citizen and falls under the civil jurisdiction of the state, but the state makes no claim on the privacy of the citizen. Belief is therefore not a condition of citizenship. By not requiring belief or even a public affirmation of belief, only an abstention from undermining the monotheistic belief affirmed by the state—which is to say, the belief that truthfulness and the idealism of reasoning govern public discourse—the Noahide is treated entirely as a national citizen, a foreigner who has become naturalized to the extent that this nature is a legal construct. Hence, this abstention from undermining the public morality of the state leads Cohen back to his original concern with ethical culture; he claims, "The Noahide provides the evidence of the true meaning of the *theocratic* constitution: that it is not built on the unity of state and religion, but on the unity of state and ethical culture [*Sittlichkeit*]."[107] The Noahide participates in the public morality of the state by acknowledging the idea of culture, and such a moral theocracy ends up looking like an enchanted liberal democratic constitutionalism.

Beyond the binary of friends and enemies, therefore, Cohen seeks the transcendental *fact* of the human being. Idealizing this fact of the human being, the figure of the foreigner emerges because this ethical and relational concept recognizes otherness, idealizes difference in the law, and exemplifies the idealism Cohen derives from monotheism. Thus, the Israelite is a "son of Noah before he is a son of Abraham," a human being before he is a Jew. Noah represents the past and the future of humanity as a norm of the law, prior to the particularization of law according to native and foreign born. Moreover, Noah represents the correlation between God and humanity as the ideal unity of law. In the relationship between the native-born and the foreigner, the native is not a natural fact. The conditions of nativity are not to be found in biological birth. Rather, once one is born, they then enter into class and status. To be a native means to fall under legal jurisdiction, for the law is what distinguishes native and foreigner. And the observance of law falls under the question of residency, of the sojourner or resident alien who enters the jurisdiction of the land. This is why the Bible enjoins legal parity, a correlation of sorts, since law "has to be uniform for all who live in the country and do not merely pass through it. . . . Law does not have its origin in human statutes but comes from God. Therefore God gives also to the stranger his share in the law of the land."[108] It is the status of residency, of being within the parameters of civil authority and residing in the land, that establishes legal recognition.

CONCLUSION: CONSCIENCE, BELIEF, AND EDUCATION IN SPIRIT

This discussion of a self-reflexive concept of minority therefore returns us to the question of freedom of conscience as a space in which to create a secular culture distinct from the role of religion. By limiting the scope of legal recognition to the status of a citizen, Cohen's Noahide explicitly dissolves the bind both between religious identity and belonging and between civic identity and belonging. The Noahide represents the possibility of nonbelief and of transforming public law into a ritualized cultural code without demanding a replication of the entirety of norms governing any one relative community. The corporate model of the state, in which each relative community is recognized as a legal entity with a public, fictive persona, stands in the background here. That is to say, the state represents the collective fiction of a self-consciousness capable of building on the norms and institutions of these relative communities.[109] And, having consolidated the fiction of an ethical self in legal form, the state recognizes a social difference that transcends political divisions; there will always be foreigners until there is only humanity. The task of public law is to recognize the foreigner as the origin of a broader concept of humanity. Hence, the Noahide represents the objective rights of the foreigner within the structure of public law without condensing this legal status into the form of the private citizen-subject. That is, the Noahide is anything but a private person; rather, the Noahide is the recognition of the foreigner as *legally entitled to rights*. For Cohen, the *Noahide is the idealization of minority within an already minoritized form of public reasoning.*

We can now better understand how and why Cohen turns to the freedom of conscience and the public morality of law as the dimensions best able to represent both Judaism as a public religion and liberalism as an enchanted worldview. As a minor expression of Protestant, modern, public religion, Judaism can utilize public law to ensure its religious morality is protected and even encourage its flourishing in the state. But in Cohen's description of a liberal society, this is done through culture rather than through politics. That is to say, Cohen is not interested in advocating for a political Judaism, such as he detects in Zionism, since the state must not become a religious administration overseeing the appointment of religious offices and institutions as well as dogma and beliefs. The state must not recognize religions as political entities, representing their communal norms and goals, since this recognition leads to a politicization of religious communities as confessional parties born of conflict. Rather, by limiting the state's ethical persona to the objective recognition of the social differences in law, the legal state guarantees the freedom of public religions to be public on their own terms. Believing or not believing in the dogma of religion therefore becomes immaterial to the moral actions that citizens are required to perform as rights bearers under public law. How these citizens may choose to advocate for their political articulations of social goods will not be determined by their membership in a politically organized religion but, rather, will presuppose that their vision of social goods is shaped by and simultaneously reshapes their religious norms. While culture becomes the space of public reasoning, the law must strive to embody the spirit of consensus in the face of political conflicts, limiting the partisan designs of legislation with the necessary standard and test of recognizing difference within the law.

But the state will inevitably insist on certain norms as foundational. And the political conflicts of partisan debate will not be eliminated by this identification of religion in the social sphere. This was the original source of the problem of neutrality in political secularism: namely, the advocacy of public reason as a neutral position between religions that are considered political. In the case of the monotheistic polity—in the enchanted liberalism imagined by Cohen—there is a norm above all norms and beyond neutrality. There is one God, the unique God. This cultural norm, however, does not impose political demands on the Noahide. By choosing to abide by the public laws of that polity, the Noahide tacitly agrees that God is a norm governing the rule of law but also that no individual affirmation of this norm is required. It is not a norm that claims the Noahide's personal conviction, only her agreement both to abide by the norms of the state as a legal order and to make explicit this commitment to reasoning about those norms. Hence, the Noahide can adopt contrarian beliefs, which have no effect on one's legal status. But the Noahide ought not to undermine the spirit of truthfulness and faithfulness in the project of creating a dynamic justice within culture. Such a perversion of ethical culture is the idolatry from which the Noahide must abstain. That is to say, since God represents the spirit of truth—of the harmonizing of logic and ethics, disciplined thought and disciplined action—any attempt to furtively contravene the norms of truthful and sincere reasoning, the epistemological structure of public law, represents a crime against humanity. That is, within the ideal structure of law, such a crime is not met with sanction, because it represents an attack on the future of humanity. It is a crime that is publicized as such and must be met with public rebuttal.

Dissimulation in public reasoning cannot be permitted, and this is why the Noahide is prohibited from denying God, which is phrased as blasphemy or idolatry. The Noahide, like any citizen, is not permitted to dissemble the spirit of good faith, of negotiating and reasoning in good faith and trust. Hence, the spirit of this secularity is really concerned with civility. To blaspheme is to deny God, just as deception and dissimulation mock the very spirit of civic conviction and concord. It undermines the sociality of our contractual relationships as human beings, as people exchanging reasons. The Noahide is therefore not a monotheist by default but rather a citizen that abides by the spirit of trust, truthfulness, and respect that is foundational to the idealized culture of monotheism. Consensus can only be built on our mutual consent to certain limits on our actions. Trying to build a normative discourse through the use of libel, slander, or violence undermines the very structure of legitimate normativity, which is the possibility of ratification and agreement.

If we recall Cohen's critique of Spinoza in chapter 2, this fear of unjustified and mythic claim making in public discourse was the reason that Cohen sought to ground a public *Bildung*, a scientific education for all citizens of the state in law. Consigning popular religion to the experience of the masses, Spinoza turned "True Religion" into a guild-bound esotericism, a metaphysically assimilated core of political beliefs that led to an aristocratic account of religion and undermined the liberal spirit of culture.[110] Cohen's 1915 critique of Spinoza, fueled by a great degree of personal polemic and a sense of betrayal, therefore culminates in the observation of Spinoza's fundamental blindness to the meaning of the legal freedom of conscience: namely, to believe and to practice norms that are not instituted by the state but that contribute to making the laws of the state ethical. Private belief cannot remain a vehicle with which to deceive the masses but must become the expression of a spirit of honest disagreement *for the sake* of the public. Since the state has neither the right to compel belief nor any claim on the individual's use of her own reason, then only public law can enable civic concord. This is the educative role of law.

Here Schmitt and Cohen are in agreement that Spinoza's model will not suffice but for radically different reasons. For Schmitt, as we have seen, only a political decision concerning unity and identity can vest an authoritative belief with legitimacy for a people. The decision between friend and enemy, for example, requires us to believe that the sovereign has the legitimate use of force, since we must also believe that without the sovereign other people would threaten us with violence. The sovereign must provide the parameters for that agreement of consent and trust, and the sovereign does so by commanding belief in public miracles, rituals, and practices. But Cohen's conception of the state and of public law does not require us to begin with privacy, for no such principle or right could exist were it not for the law that already claims multiple public and private spheres at once. For Cohen, it is not the sovereign that decides on the common belief. It is not even belief that is held as sovereign. Rather, the nature of public law is such that we need not believe in the partisan engagements of a particularism *as though it were* universal where the possibility of conflict remains implicit. Rather, when we always already have an idealization of what a legal relation looks like—a contractual model of encounter between legal persons— this creates the possibility of both conflict and resolution as a matter of normative form. That is to say, an ethics of law must educate citizens in the virtues of law. Indeed, the virtue of public reasoning is its spirit of honestly pursuing justice for all and of committing ourselves to ritualize that practice in our lives.

Cohen therefore offers a broader conception of the freedom of conscience as the basis on which to idealize a new *Bildung* in the figure of the Noahide. As a principle of difference within the very structure of law, the Noahide represents the freedom to believe in *spirit* without requiring belief in God. That is, although Cohen considers God the spirit of moral action and the norm for humanity, this normative meaning of moral law makes a claim on the state as a legal entity; the legal status of the Noahide makes no demands that the norm be affirmed by individual belief. Rather, such a belief remains implicit in the order of public law without becoming a rule.[111] This is why God remains a norm for the state but not for the legal subject.

This idealization of a minority status in the law is all the more intelligible when we reconsider Cohen's response to the Jewish Question with a turn to a socialized legal order, addressing Jewish minority status as a social rather than a political problem. The Jews are minorities in need of recognition, not political opponents of any other German party. Thus, the idealized Noahide translates the minority "out of the sources of Judaism" to address the question of religious difference as a social question rather than a political one. The depoliticization of the Noahide represents the minority secularity of the German Jews, providing an alternative model of the overlapping consensus necessary for a spirit of secularity. Taken as a method of public reasoning, Cohen's understanding of ethics therefore suspends political interest in religion.[112] Belief and conscience become the basis of a new civic education, a new spirit of *Bildung*, in which good faith, trust, and loyalty become virtues of reasoning.

Rawls's idea of an overlapping consensus is likewise heuristically useful insofar as it provides a methodological description of how differing sets of values compete for recognition in the public sphere. Charles Taylor has recently defended this overlapping consensus in an attempt to describe how minoritarian positions must be acknowledged, rather than precluded, according to Rawls's conception of the original position, wherein no "comprehensive doctrines," whether moral theories or religions, should be brought to bear on how the basic values are negotiated.[113] While Rawls's model may not account for its own genealogical impositions of certain values within the structure of public reason, it is nevertheless a model that Taylor believes can be refined. It is also a helpful reminder of the goal of public reasoning: namely, to acknowledge difference, recognize competing claims, and identify points of contact for agreement or at least comparative critique. Such an ethic of public reasoning constitutes the self-reflexivity demanded by Cohen.

In this respect, Cohen is advocating for a new, legally grounded conception of civic virtue. Virtue also articulates the relationship between logic and ethics, thinking and willing, and legality and morality, because virtue is primarily a collision between extremes—between the excessive and the deficient—and stresses the notion of skill and knowledge (*phronesis*) as both implicit to the habitus of virtue. Like ritual and the ritualization of law, virtue is a practice, both as a normative routine as well as an activity of repetition. Virtue is likewise the attempt to educate, to learn, and to advocate. This is why the ritualization of law becomes a path of virtue, an acculturation and education in morality. As a form of knowledge, virtue also describes both theoretical and practical spirit, a disciplined thinking that will lead to morally disciplined action, where "truthfulness does not allow the slightest trace of a solution in which well-being is considered as the reward and ill-fatedness as the punishment for the moral, for the religious behavior of a human being. The human being's relation to God may remain a mystery; his conduct to other people is not permitted to be considered such. With regard to the human, one has to judge and then decide. For the decision about good and bad is connected with this decision. The distinction between good and bad comes to nothing if it coincides with the distinction of well-being and ill."[114] One must judge and then decide. The sequence of the words is not arbitrary: for Cohen, the ethical judgment is prior to the political action. The idealized action grounds the historico-political action. Hence, decision presupposes the structure of judgment, and the natural facts of well-being and ill should be considered neither categories of decision nor facts toward which I may express indifference. I must idealize their facticity and transform them through critique. They indicate neither good nor bad, for as such they would be mere manifestations. They are not the result of mythic fate but, instead, must be decided on. As values that must be judged and decided on, they are irrevocably bound to my action toward other people. God therefore represents the discipline of thinking beyond facts to achieve normative results. As the idealization of a morality beyond material reality, God becomes the spirit of moral action, of judgment prior to decision, and a necessary spirit of secular reasoning.

But the meaning of morality, of the ideality of good and bad, and the refusal to reduce moral terms to natural facts, is that good and bad must be *decided on*. As a decision, a judgment, we therefore risk succumbing to Schmitt's logic, since he also affirms that "the concept of the state presupposes the concept of the political,"[115] and that "the specific political distinction to which political actions and motives can be reduced is that between friend and enemy."[116] The distinction between friend and enemy conditions the need for decision, for the sovereign will that can decide on the exception to a normative structure. However, as I argued above, Cohen refuses to acknowledge the material distinction between friend and foe, native and foreigner, as a normative source. For Cohen, moral decisions already assume the self and the other have been idealized as the components of the law, and the legal action presupposes the contractual relationship in which a foreign law has first claimed me. Hence, if the legal action is the decision par excellence, then it must be the figure of the *merger*.[117] The merger is the idealized contract, the agreement that foregrounds the norm.

But if the law presupposes this idealization of difference, and if God is always correlated to humanity, one might very well ask whether Cohen has simply imposed a different homogeneity of public reasoning on a collective of believers. Must all of humanity be friends, or must we accept that, as Schmitt claims, "humanity is not strictly speaking a political concept" and, in doing so, prioritize the political? The God-idea as a norm of the state leads us to question whether Cohen envisions anything like a secular state. How can all citizens be bound by this norm? Must they believe? Must all citizens be monotheists? Or does the limit of the state's grasp on belief result in the technological state that Schmitt feared?

While Cohen's affirmation of the monotheistic God as a basic norm of public law may appear to belie the possibility of secularity altogether, I want to suggest that Cohen's insistence on the messianic inflection of God into politics—of the prophetic vision of political history in which the state is eclipsed in the messianic era—provides a model of depoliticization that does not neutralize normativity. Rather, this ethical suspension of the political clears space for the possibility of a secular culture in which the method of ethics can provide an autocritique of this possible majoritarianism of monotheism.

For Cohen, the unity of virtue is what grounds political decisions based on the priority of ethical judgment. Because political decisions enact *actions* that are grounded in cultural practices and the securing of protections for such practices, virtue provides a bridge from the action of law as an ethical norm to the practice of law as a political argument. Hence, the ultimate civic virtues that ought to be cultivated within political discourse and driven by ethical public reasoning are embodied as principles of legal spirit. In this respect, Cohen offers a critical correction to Rawls's public reason: reasoning, Cohen claims, must be a practice of virtue in itself. Hence, the virtue of truthfulness is paramount to all civic practices. This virtue demands fidelity to the ethical norms of culture while advocating for specific protections and rights. But the virtues of truthfulness and good faith remain sovereign over all because they demand our commitment to logically grounding our practices of education and cultural participation in such a way that our ethical practices are based in a shared respect for truth amid differences in reasoning.

From truthfulness and good faith, Cohen believes, we can therefore trace the depoliticization of law back to the ethics of law, the scientific correlation of thinking and willing. Virtue stands as the norm extracted from legal form that sets political practice in motion, tempering the excesses of partisanship. Thus, the virtue of modesty becomes the virtue of critique,[118] which tempers our claims to either excessive skepticism or hubristic certainty.[119] The virtue of courage—to work and labor on behalf of justice, to struggle for change—becomes the eminently political virtue.[120] This conception of virtue therefore ties together the related virtues of what Cohen deems the true meaning of patriotism to the "national state, however in the sense of the legal state": the virtue of faithfulness or loyalty, which holds fast to the belief in change and that our world can be better; the virtue of justice, of the pursuit of greater sensitivity to demands of the downtrodden and poor, the equalizing of law as the benefit of all; the virtue of humanitarianism, of pledging our faith in the human community itself, the messianic people of humanity.[121]

With this set of virtues, although not an exhaustive list, Cohen concludes his *Ethik*, at which point we discover that the relationship between law and virtue is one of action and practice, of increasing steadfastness in the general culture of the state. Politics is therefore not abolished, for this messianic prerogative remains our burden. But we do gain a methodological distinction between law and politics, between sociality and partisanship. In this process of idealization, the virtues outline how the depoliticizing Noahide represents a new form of secularity, one in which religion continues to play the crucial role of the lever of idealization itself. Because politics remains our burden, religion remains the reminder that virtue is the necessary translation from ethical public reasoning into the realm of debate and discussion that conditions political discourse. In other words, we cannot operate under the assumption that a public ethic has been actualized and taken hold of the modern world, fulfilling and supplanting the ethical demands of religious traditions of the past. Rather,

> this maturity of culture is to be regarded only methodologically as having dawned; the overall condition and course of the world is reluctant and stands in opposition to it. It is already lacking in the implementation of theoretical culture, as truthfulness demands. Therefore it is practically impossible to dispense with the surrogate of religion. And so there is nothing left but for religion to be used as a cultural medium, and to make itself more and more useful for a clear purpose: that religion itself must bring culture to its completion. Religion must be used as a means to prepare the conversion of ethics into general culture.[122]

Because the spirit of secularity requires a spirit of truthfulness and good faith in which you and I share our honest assessments of what is needed to make our world better, there is no room for the kind of positivistic and exclusivist self-valorization that partisanship demands. Rather, we must humble ourselves before the ideal of culture in which we remain steadfast in our ethical faith that the world can be and ought to be better than it is. Religion too remains a necessary vehicle of critique, always reminding us of the cultural norm of justice, of God as the symbol of unity and reconciliation for all humanity.

But this role of religion in culture is not a defense of special pleading. Rather, as Cohen's account of the freedom of conscience demonstrates, religious traditions have the added responsibility of remaining *truthful* and *faithful* to the very public culture they are building. Idealization makes no room for dissimulation. Cohen writes,

> Faithfulness [*die Treue*] thus can carry out important services. It is the duty and naturally the right of faithfulness *to work incessantly on the idealization of religion*. Religions are fraught with mythology; and *metaphysics* does not stop them from reviving these rudiments again. The idealization

of religion on the other hand always proceeds out of the failures of myth, purifying them; and the ethical motives that lie dormant in them, and which are alive in them, are brought forward into clarity and integrated into a purer fruitfulness. This is an ethical labor from which practical as well as theoretical culture stands to benefit.

Faithfulness makes the right to this idealization into a duty. *In every religion, its ethical motives can be analyzed and developed.* Faithfulness is the signpost that points in this direction. It is convenient to raise oneself to the standpoint of the pure ethicist, and to abandon the religions to their own fate; while one must yet say that this position of the ethicist means a Robinson Crusoe-like abandonment, where one abandons not only religion, but at the same time politics itself, whose most intimate fates are linked to religion. Faithfulness, by contrast, urges us to never tire in the struggle *to improve* religion. . . . If idealization is only undertaken, as is required by truthfulness, in the scientific spirit, and is led by it, then this idealization of religion is a labor for the spiritual and ethical [*geistliche und sittliche*] progress of culture.[123]

The process of idealization is therefore a two-way street: culture must continue to draw on the conceptual resources of religions, the virtues and norms that can be idealized out of religions, such as the Noahide. At the same time, culture must continue to hope that this dialectic will improve religions as vehicles of critique, truthfulness, honor, loyalty, courage, justice and humanitarianism. Virtue presents a merger of these paths, where the idealization of common virtues that ought to be found in both religion and culture enables the process of public reasoning to transpire with a view to this correlation, this process of mutual refinement. We must never tire of trying to bring religions and general culture into greater expressions of themselves.

The lesson of this secularity is instructive; religious traditions are always reshaping their norms dialectically with public morality and culture. But the political powers of the secular-modern are not hegemonic, despite the narrative that shrouds its own logic in this myth. Rather, religions are shaping and being shaped in a dynamic process. The question of how we undertake this ethical labor without imposing power on one another, without the implicit coercion of a minoritarian tradition under the guise of the majority, returns us to the example of the Noahide. Once again, the Noahide helps us allay this concern by providing a model of a state that does not require conversion or even belief in God from its citizens. The state obligates the Noahide's trust but not belief in any one religion.

But the historical and spiritual roles of religion continue to generate norms at the level of ethical culture. By adopting a scientific posture, we therefore refuse to let religion slide into myth. Instead, we seize this category as a space in which to begin the work of depoliticization, of taking back the meaning of moral concepts and virtues and transforming them into practices that we may cultivate in a social practice of critique. We must never tire of working to identify the normative structures that enable conversations to take place. We must never cease to identify the norms shared between religious traditions and modern legal culture. And more broadly, we must continue to pursue the spirits of good faith, moral action, and trust. These are the spirits of secularity, but their enchantment can only be sustained by reasoning them into existence.

NOTES

1. See, for example, Cohen's comments in "Religiöse Postulate" (1907/1909), in *Hermann Cohens Werke*, ed. H. Holzhey, 17 vols. (New York: G. Olms, 1978–) (hereafter cited as *Werke*) 15: *Hermann Cohens Werke, Kleinere Schriften*, vols. 12–17 of *Werke*, 6 vols. (hereafter cited as *KS*) 4, *1907–1912*, 133–60, 140.

2. On the distinction between *Bewusstheit* and *Bewusstsein* as the difference between mythic and justified historical knowledge, see chapter 3.

3. Alasdair MacIntyre, *After Virtue: A Study in Moral Theory* (New York: Bloomsbury Academic, 2007), 171–72. MacIntyre continues: "the past is never something merely to be discarded, but rather that the present is intelligible only as a commentary on and response to the past in which the past, if necessary and if possible, is corrected and transcended." This definition of tradition is also similar to how Robert Brandom has set about interpreting Hegel and bears a strong resemblance to Cohen's account of reasoning. See Robert B. Brandom, *Tales of the Mighty Dead: Historical Essays in the Metaphysics of Intentionality* (Cambridge, MA: Harvard University Press, 2002).

4. See introduction, note 26.

5. Carl Schmitt, *The Leviathan in the State Theory of Thomas Hobbes*, trans. George Schwab (Chicago: University of Chicago Press, 2008), 42.

6. John P. McCormick, *Carl Schmitt's Critique of Liberalism: Against Politics as Technology* (New York: Cambridge University Press, 1997), 271

7. Wundt similarly associates the machinelike Leviathan with the Jews. Max Wundt, *Vom Geist unserer Zeit* (München: J. F. Lehmann, 1922), 120.

8. See Paul E. Nahme, "Law, Principle, and the Theologico-Political History of Sovereignty" in *Political Theology* 14, no. 4 (2013): 432–79.

9. Schmitt, *Leviathan*, 60.

10. Jacques Derrida, *Specters of Marx: The State of the Debt, the Work of Mourning, and the New International* (London: Routledge, 1994), 10, 63.

11. A point Hobbes made primarily in the context of ecclesiastical power, as the ultimate article worthy of martyrdom, but that Schmitt deployed as a principle legitimating civic belief. Cf. Thomas Hobbes, *Leviathan*, ed. Edwin Curley (Indianapolis: Hackett, 1994), 42, 13, 340.

12. Cf. Erik Voegelin's critique of political theology in light of Roman civic religion in Erik Voegelin, *The New Science of Politics* (1952; repr., Chicago: University of Chicago Press, 2012).

13. On the role of Augustine in the *Adversus Iudaeos* tradition, see Jeremy Cohen, *Living Letters of the Law: Ideas of the Jews in Medieval Christianity* (Berkeley: University of California Press, 1999).

14. Gil Anidjar, *Blood: A Critique of Christianity* (New York: Columbia University Press, 2014), 34.

15. Catherine Bell, *Ritual Theory, Ritual Practice* (New York: Oxford University Press, 1992), 100.

16. On the rise of free religious associations and freethinker societies that were not always aligned with anticlerical movements, see Todd H. Weir, *Secularism and Religion in Nineteenth-Century Germany: The Rise of the Fourth Confession* (New York: Cambridge University Press, 2014).

17. Owen Chadwick, *The Secularization of the European Mind in the Nineteenth Century* (New York: Cambridge University Press, 1975).

18. See my discussion of Blumenberg and question positions and answer positions in chapter 3. Cf. Charles Taylor, "Why We Need a Radical Redefinition of Secularism," in *The Power of Religion in the Public Sphere* (New York: Columbia University Press, 2011), 34–59.

19. Akeel Bilgrami, *Secularism, Identity, and Enchantment* (Cambridge, MA: Harvard University Press, 2014), 59.

20. Taylor notes that the "myth of Enlightenment" is fundamental to this vision of neutral "mere reason." Taylor, "Why We Need a Radical Redefinition of Secularism," 52.

21. Bilgrami, *Secularism*, 62, citing Brian Barry, *Culture and Equality: An Egalitarian Critique of Multiculturalism* (Cambridge: Polity, 2013).

22. See Winnifred Fallers Sullivan, *The Impossibility of Religious Freedom* (Princeton, NJ: Princeton University Press, 2011). Examining the difference between group and individual rights to religion in a Canadian context see, Syndicate Northcrest v. Amselem, [2004] S.C.J. 46, [2004] 2 S.C.R. 551. Cf. Richard Moon, "Religious Commitment and Identity: Syndicat Northcrest v. Amselem" in *Supreme Court Law Review* 29 (2005): 201–20. Cf. Brauna Doidge, "Finding Room for Religious Voices in Court and Public Discourse," unpublished talk

at delivered at Centre for Jewish Studies Graduate Conference, University of Toronto, 2010.

23. John Rawls, *Political Liberalism, Expanded Edition* (hereafter cited as *PL*) (New York: Columbia University Press, 2005), 21. On the condensed genealogy of liberalism as it relates to the late Rawls's vision of citizenship and society as more "ecumenical" if not actually part of a subtle account of "civil religion," see Ronald Beiner, *Civil Religion: A Dialogue in the History of Political Philosophy* (New York: Cambridge University Press, 2011), 283–300.

24. Rawls, *PL*, 99: we follow a "procedure of construction . . . based essentially on practical reason and not on theoretical reason." Cf. Rawls, 93 on theoretical vs. practical reason.

25. Rawls, 15–17.

26. Rawls, 127.

27. Rawls, 95.

28. The constructivist form of what Rawls calls "doctrinal autonomy," or a political view seeking "the order of political values as based on principles of practical reason in union with the appropriate political conceptions of society and person . . . the order of moral and political values must be made, or itself constituted by the principles and conceptions of practical reason" (Rawls, 99). Such a political view must be internally coherent in the ordering of the values and conceptions that it originates for its constructions.

29. John Rawls, *Justice as Fairness: A Restatement*, ed. Erin Kelly (Cambridge, MA: Harvard University Press, 2001), xvii.

30. Rawls, *PL*, 213.

31. Rawls, "The Idea of Public Reason Revisited," *The Law of Peoples* (Cambridge, MA: Harvard University Press, 2002), 143.

32. See for example, Andrew F. March, *Islam and Liberal Citizenship: The Search for an Overlapping Consensus* (New York: Oxford University Press, 2008), 101, notwithstanding March's acknowledged "ethics of conjecture"; Martha C. Nussbaum, *Frontiers of Justice: Disability, Nationality, Species Membership* (Cambridge, MA: Harvard University Press, 2009); David Novak, *The Jewish Social Contract* (Princeton, NJ: Princeton University Press, 2005). Habermas's discourse ethics is an exception, since it presents a moral theory that has what he calls "pre-political" and social dimensions. However, his robust account of norm and rule following is more of a doctrinal application of rules than Cohen's attempt to identify the structural futurity implicit to the generation of social norms and judgments. See Habermas, *Between Facts and Norms: Toward a Discourse Theory of Law* (Cambridge, MA: MIT Press, 2005); cf. Habermas, *Justification and Application: Remarks on Discourse Ethics* (Cambridge, MA: MIT Press, 1994). For an overview of the missed opportunity in the Habermas-Rawls debate, see the introduction to James Gordon Finlayson and Fabian Reyenhagen, eds., *Habermas and Rawls: Debating the Political* (New York: Routledge, 2011). Thomas Scanlon is the exception to this rule, insisting

on an "ethical contractualism"; see T. M. Scanlon, *What We Owe Each Other* (Cambridge, MA: Harvard University Press, 1998).

33. Rawls nevertheless displayed moments in his career—both early and late—where the explicitly Protestant contours of his discussion of political liberalism became explicit. However, this is not the dominant narrative of his larger body of work, nor the received interpretation influencing contemporary Rawlsian theory. On the former, see Eric Gregory, "Before the Original Position: The Neo-Orthodox Theology of the Young John Rawls," *Journal of Religious Ethics* 35, no. 2 (2007): 179–206.

34. Eric Gregory, for example, notes that Rawlsian theorists favor public reason over the "difference principle," which obscures the place of virtue in politics. See Eric Gregory, *Politics and the Order of Love: An Augustinian Ethic of Democratic Citizenship* (Chicago: University of Chicago Press, 2008), 72.

35. Such as those proposing a capabilities model of justice like Martha Nussbaum or Amartya Sen, who focus on the difference principle, Rawls's most normative detail in his otherwise neutral theory. Cf. Amartya Sen, *The Idea of Justice* (Cambridge, MA: Harvard University Press, 2009); Sen, "Equality of What?" in Sterling M. McMurrin, ed., *Tanner Lectures on Human Values* (Cambridge: Cambridge University Press, 1980). Martha Nussbaum, *Frontiers of Justice*; Nussbaum, *Creating Capabilities* (Cambridge, MA: Harvard University Press, 2011), 88–89.

36. Rawls, *PL*, 148.

37. Beiner, *Civil Religion*, 295.

38. Taylor, "Why We Need a Radical Redefinition of Secularism," 48.

39. On the role of Rawls's relationship to religion in his developing thought, see Gregory, "Before the Original Position," 179–206; see John Rawls, *A Brief Inquiry into the Meaning of Sin and Faith*, ed. Thomas Nagel (Cambridge, MA: Harvard University Press, 2009).

40. Cf. Voegelin, *New Science of Politics*, 76–106.

41. G. W. F. Hegel, *Lectures on the Philosophy of Religion, One-Volume Edition, The Lectures of 1827*, ed. Peter C. Hodgson (New York: Oxford University Press, 1988), Part 2: Determinate Religion, 351.

42. Hermann Cohen, *System der Philosophie, Zweiter Teil: Ethik des reinen Willens* (Berlin: Bruno Cassirer, 1904; repr. in *Werke* 7) (hereafter cited as *ErW*), 61–63.

43. *ErW*, 61.

44. *ErW*, 61. Cf. Cohen, "Spinoza über Staat und Religion," *Werke* 16: *KS* 5, 1913–1915, 319–426, 389, 406–67.

45. *ErW*, 61.

46. *ErW*, 62–63.

47. *ErW*, 63.

48. *ErW*, 63.

49. *ErW*, 65: "Ethics should be treated as the logic of the human sciences (*Geisteswissenschaften*)."

50. It is therefore interesting to note that one Houston Stewart Chamberlain's pseudoscientific attacks on Judaism dealt with the ancient Hebraic transformation of all myth into historical chronicles, the "decoloring" of myth, as Wellhausen put it. See *Die Grundlage des Neunzehnten Jahrhunderts* (Munich: F. Bruckmann, 1912), Part 1: 471, 470–73.

51. *ErW*, 229–30.

52. One might say the same of Habermas's discourse theory of communicative reason underlying deliberative democracy (see the introduction to this volume). Robert Erlewine claims that Cohen's account of monotheism also attempts to circumvent the vicissitudes of Habermas's theory; see Robert Erlewine, *Monotheism and Tolerance: Recovering a Religion of Reason* (Bloomington: Indiana University Press, 2010).

53. Thus, Hegel propose the state as the culmination of the objectivity of the law and the reunification of morality and legality (*Moralität* and *Sittlichkeit*). As Hegel writes, "The State is the actuality of the ethical [*sittlichen Idee*] Idea—ethical spirit [*sittliche Geist*], as the *manifest* and articulated-to-itself substantial will, that thinks and knows itself and what it knows in so far as it knows it, is that which carries it out. In *custom*, the state has its unmediated existence, and in *self-consciousness* of individuals, in their very knowledge and facticity [*Tätigkeit*], it has its mediated existence [*Existenz*], just as by means of the disposition within the state, self-consciousness has, as for its essence, purpose and product of its facticity [*Wesen, Zweck und Produkte der Tätigkeit*] its own *substantial freedom*." Georg Wilhelm Friedrich Hegel, *Grundlinien der Philosophie des Rechts oder Naturrecht und Staatswissenschaft, mit Hegels eigenhändigen Notizen und dem mündlichen Zusätzen, Werke 7* (Frankfurt am Main: Suhrkamp, 1986), 398; published in English as *Elements of the Philosophy of Right*, ed. Allan Wood (New York: Cambridge University Press, 1991), sec. 257.

54. *ErW*, 246.

55. *ErW*, 246–47.

56. That is, in contrast to Hegel, Cohen claims that the relationship between theoretical and ethical spirit rests within the ideality of the state as the expression of the "pure will" when it culminates in a purposive, action-oriented self-consciousness.

57. *ErW*, 462–63.

58. *ErW*, 214.

59. *ErW*, 214; cf. Cohen, *Der Begriff der Religion im System der Philosophie, Werke* 10:23. The cultural contribution of Jewish monotheism is therefore not just the concept of unity, which idealism takes to heart as a principle of identity, but, as Cohen writes, while there is "a bias toward emphasizing the importance of monotheism to lie in unity" what is really crucial to monotheism "lies in being, in the uniqueness of being, which constitutes the being of God" (23). The uniqueness of being, which is to say, the uniqueness of the being of an idea,

establishes monotheism as a principle within the history of philosophical idealism as the meaning of truth (26).

60. Constantin Frantz, *Ahashverus oder die Judenfrage* (Berlin: W. Hermes, 1844), 36; quoted in Paul Lawrence Rose, *Revolutionary Antisemitism in Germany: From Kant to Wagner* (Princeton, NJ: Princeton University Press, 1990), 344.

61. Erlewine also presents Cohen's monotheism as capable of idealizing otherness; see Erlewine, *Monotheism and Tolerance*, 174.

62. On the lure of Marcionism, a gnostic philosophy premised on a dualistic model of divinity that subjects the God of the Hebrew Bible to the role of world denier and demiurge, which was popularized through the work of Adolf von Harnack, see Jacob Taubes, *From Cult to Culture: Fragments Toward a Critique of Historical Reason*, ed. Charlotte Elisheva Fonrobert and Amir Engel (Stanford, CA: Stanford University Press, 2010); cf. Benjamin Pollock, *Franz Rosenzweig's Conversions: World Denial and World Redemption* (Bloomington: Indiana University Press, 2014), chapter 1, 19–24 in particular.

63. Ulrich Sieg, *Deutschlands Prophet. Paul de Lagarde und die Ursprünge des modernen Antisemitismus* (München: Carl Hanser 2007); Stern, *The Politics of Cultural Despair: A Study in the Rise of the Germanic Ideology* (Berkeley: University of California Press, 1961), 3–96.

64. Ernest Renan, *Nouvelles considerations sur la character Générale des Peuples Sémitiques, et en particulier, sur leur tendance au monothéisme* (Paris: Imprimerie Imperiale, 1855), 1–3.

65. Paul de Lagarde, "Juden und Indogermanen: Eine Studie nach dem Leben," in *Mittheilungen, Zweiter Band* (Göttingen: Dietkrichsche Universitätsbuchhandlung, 1887), 339.

66. Lagarde, "Juden und Indogermanen," 350.

67. Lagarde, 330.

68. Lagarde, 335.

69. Lagarde, 335.

70. See Sieg, *Deutschlands Prophet* for the many contradictions in Lagarde's vision of national religion.

71. Hermann Cohen, *Religion of Reason: Out of the Sources of Judaism*, trans. Simon Kaplan (Atlanta, GA: Scholars' Press, 1995) (hereafter cited as *RoR*), 115. Originally published as Hermann Cohen, *Religion der Vernunft: aus den Quellen des Judentums* (Wiesbaden: Fourier Verlag, 1978), 134.

72. Erlewine, *Monotheism and Tolerance*, 154.

73. Erlewine, 156.

74. *RoR*, 102.

75. *LrW*, 236.

76. *ErW*, 231.

77. See Reinier Munk, "Alterity in Hermann Cohen's Critical Idealism," *Journal of Jewish Thought and Philosophy* 9, 2 (2000): 251–65, 253–54.

78. On Cohen's idealized reading of Maimonides and the historical context in which such a reading yielded interesting philosophical conclusions as compared with contemporary Jewish thinkers, see George Y. Kohler, *Reading Maimonides in 19th Century Germany: The Guide to Religious Reform* (Dodrecht, Netherlands: Springer, 2012), 249–307.

79. Maimonides, *Guide of the Perplexed*, trans. Shlomo Pines (Chicago: University of Chicago Press, 1963), 1:58.

80. *RoR*, 257.

81. Bereishit Rabba *Va-yetsei*, par. 68, to Genesis 28:11 (Jerusalem: Vagshal, 2005), 1:349. Cf. Ephraim Urbach, *Hazal: Emunot ve-De'ot* (Jerusalem: Magnes Press, 1969), 53–68. Amos Funkenstein notes that "*maqom*" connotes divine immanence; see Funkenstein, *Theology and the Scientific Imagination: From the Middle Ages to the seventeenth century* (Princeton, NJ: Princeton University Press, 1986), 47.

82. Hermann Cohen, *Charakteristik Ethik Maimunis* (hereafter cited as *EM*), *JS* 3:253; English translation as Cohen, *Ethics of Maimonides*, trans. Almut Bruckstein (Madison: University of Wisconsin Press, 2004). Cf. Kenneth Seeskin, *Jewish Messianic Thoughts in an Age of Despair* (New York: Cambridge University Press, 2012), 199. Seeskin argues that this is part of Cohen's misreading of Maimonidean attribution, in which Cohen asserts a *docta ignorantia* verging on metaphysics.

83. Cohen maintains that this is the difference between Maimonides and Aristotle on "thought thinking itself." *EM*, *JS* 3:234; cf., Cohen, *Ethics of Maimonides*, 32.

84. Throughout, I will render the concept of the *ben noaḥ* or the agent of the *sheva'ah mitsvot benei noaḥ*, the seven commandments given to the sons of Noah, as "Noahide."

85. For an overview of the Talmudic sources of the Noahide, as well as a philosophical analysis of the Noahide laws in Jewish ethics, see David Novak and Matthew Lagrone, *The Image of the Non-Jew in Judaism: The Idea of Noahide Law*, 2nd rev. ed. (Oxford: Littman Library of Jewish Civilization, 2011).

86. On the Marburg trial, see Ulrich Sieg, "'Der Wissenschaft und dem Leben tut dasselbe not: Ehrfurcht vor der Wahrheit,' Hermann Cohen Gutachten im Marburger Antisemitismusprozeß 1888," in *Philosophisches Denken—Politisches Wirken, Hermann-Cohen-Kolloquium Marburg 1992*, ed. Reinhard Brandt and Franz Orlik (Hildesheim: Olms, 1993), 222–49; Ulrich Sieg, *Paul de Lagarde and the Origins of Modern Antisemitism* (Waltham, MA: Brandeis University Press, 2013), 202–14. On Cohen's philosophical argument in the affidavit, see Dana Hollander, "Ethical-Political Universality out of the Sources of Judaism: Reading Hermann Cohen's 1888 Affidavit in and out of Context," in *New Directions in Jewish Philosophy*, ed. Aaron Hughes and Elliot Wolfson (Bloomington: Indiana University Press, 2009), 229–52.

87. Cohen later published the testimony under the title *Die Nächstenliebe im Talmud. Ein Gutachten dem königlichen Landgerichte zu Marburg erstattet* (Marburg: Elwerth'sche Verlagsbuchhandlung, 1888), 8; reprinted in *Jüdischen Schriften* I (Berlin: Schwetschke, 1924).

88. On the rabbinic interpretation of the Noahide more generally, see "Ben Noah," *Entsiqlopedyah Talmudit* (Jerusalem: Mosad Ha-Rav Kook, 1947–), 3:348–62. Novak and Lagrone, *The Image of the Non-Jew in Judaism*; J. David Bleich, "Mishpath Mavet be-Dinei Benei Noah," in *Jubilee Volume in Honor of Moreinu Hagaon Rabbi Joseph B. Soloveitchik*, ed. S. Ysirachi, N. Lamm, and Y. Rafael (Jerusalem: Mosad Ha-Rav Kook, 1984), 193–208; Aharon Lichtenstein, *The Seven Laws of Noah*, 2nd ed. (New York: Rabbi Jacob Joseph School, 1986).

89. Not only is Cohen's interpretation admittedly rabbinic, he also employs a number of philosophical elaborations of these sources. On the figure of the stranger in biblical sources, see Saul Olyan, *Rites and Rank: Hierarchy in Biblical Representations of Cult* (Princeton, NJ: Princeton University Press, 2000).

90. *ErW*, 406–67.

91. *RoR*, 133.

92. See Dana Hollander, "Love-of-Neighbor and Ethics out of Law in the Philosophy of Hermann Cohen," in *German-Jewish Thought Between Religion and Politics: Festschrift in Honor of Paul Mendes-Flohr on the Occasion of His Seventieth Birthday*, ed. Christian Wiese and Martina Urban (Boston: Walter de Gruyter, 2012), 83–114. While David Novak has argued for a consistent account of natural law in the vein of the "new natural law" theorists, his attempt to outline Cohen's own arguments as those of a natural law account require greater scrutiny in their own context. See Novak, "Das Noachidische Naturrecht bei Hermann Cohen," in *Religion der Vernunft aus den Quellen des Judentums—Tradition und Ursprungsdenken in Hermann Cohens Spätwerk*, ed. Helmut Holzhey, Gabriel Motzkin, and Hartwig Wiedebach (Hildesheim: Georg Olms, 2000), 225–43, 231. For various engagements with the ambivalent and ambiguous concept of natural law in Cohen's thought compare Christoph Schulte, "Noachidische Gebote und Naturrecht," in *"Religion der Vernunft aus den Quellen des Judentums," "Tradition und Usprungsdenken in Hermann Cohens Spätwerk*, ed. Helmut Holzhey, G. Motzkin, and H. Wiedebach (Hildesheim: Olms, 2000); Cf. Peter Schmid, "Das Naturrecht in der Rechtsethik Hermann Cohens," *Zeitschrift für philosophische Forschung* 47, no. 3 (1993): 408–21. By contrast, Steven Schwarzschild argues that Cohen's must be seen as a problematization of natural law, see Schwarzschild, "Do Noachites Have to Believe in Revelation? A Passage in Dispute between Maimonies, Spinoza, Mendelssohn, and Hermann Cohen: A Contribution to a Jewish View of Natural Law," in *The Pursuit of the Ideal: Jewish Writings of Steven Schwarzschild*, ed. Menachem Kellner (Albany: State University of New York Press, 1990), 29–59.

93. *RoR*, 114.

94. *RoR*, 121.

95. Cf. Novak, *The Image of the Non-Jew in Judaism*, 36–52.

96. *RoR*, 115.

97. *RoR*, 122.

98. *RoR*, 115.

99. *RoR*, 332.

100. Schmitt, *Constitutional Theory*, trans. Jeffrey Selzer (Durham, NC: Duke University Press, 2008), 243

101. Schmitt, 247–48.

102. Schmitt, *The Concept of the Political*, trans. George Schwab (Chicago: University of Chicago Press, 2007), 54–55.

103. Cohen, "Das Gottesreich," reprinted in *Werke* 16: *KS* 5, *1913–1915*, 39–50, 46.

104. Cohen writes:

> "Finally, another opposition arises for man, as the fellowman [*Mitmenschen*], which emerges out of the meaning of plurality. The fellowman is a member of a nation [*Volk*], firstly, of the nation of Israel. But Israel is surrounded by other Nations, making war with them and concluding compacts with them. Opposition to states repeats itself, but it does not remain the same. For the concept of the nation [*Volk*] was altered through the national task of monotheism [*die nationale Aufgabe des Monotheismus*]. Invariably, a Singularity of one's own nation steps into force. This singularity [*Singularität*] is demanded of monotheism, whose fulfillment depends on the national oppositions to other nations." (*RoR*, 115)

105. There is significant debate over the exact number and the nature of prohibitions or commands, beginning in the Talmudic sources themselves. See Novak, *The Image of the Non-Jew in Judaism*, 11–35.

106. *RoR*, 123.

107. *RoR*, 123.

108. *RoR*, 121.

109. *ErW*, 250–51.

110. See chapter 1.

111. Robert Brandom, *Making It Explicit: Reasoning, Representing, and Discursive Commitment* (Cambridge, MA: Harvard University Press, 1994), 64–66.

112. *ErW*, 59–60.

113. Charles Taylor, "Modes of Secularism," in *Secularism and Its Critics*, ed. Rajeev Bhargava (New Delhi: Oxford University Press, 1998), 31–53.

114. *RoR*, 132–33 (translation slightly modified).

115. Schmitt, *Concept of the Political*, 19.

116. Schmitt, 26.

117. *ErW*, 231.
118. *ErW*, 531.
119. Cf. Erlewine, *Monotheism and Tolerance*, 156.
120. *ErW*, 559.
121. *ErW*, 558.
122. *ErW*, 586–87.
123. *ErW*, 587–88.

—⚏—

CONCLUSION

Some Minor Reflections
of Enchantment

LIBERALISM IS A PROBLEMATIC CONCEPT, almost by definition. In the story I have told, we have seen a few different aspects of the problem. On the one hand, I suggested that the history of liberalism is a story about the development of an explicitly public form of reasoning about the values and ideals that societies want to adopt for themselves. However, on the other hand, we have seen how this inherently public pursuit of those values opens up the additional problem of legitimacy: why should one set of values be worthy of pursuit as opposed to any others? If there is no ground that is more authoritative or compelling than any other ground, what is to stop the endless bickering and partisan dispute that will inevitably follow in such debate? As anyone who has ever been a member of an organization or community knows, debates can be endless, tiresome, and ultimately demoralizing. So, how to halt the descent into infinite—if not fruitless—exchanging of ideas? What is to keep this process from either entering into pure abstraction and irrelevance or else turning into an unavoidable impasse that leads to intractable consequences?

While I have suggested that enchantment provides one dimension of an answer to questions about legitimacy, I have also demonstrated how enchantment is an equally problematic concept. While public reasoning, as I have discussed in the example of Cohen's thought, takes up the issue of disenchantment, or the loss of that sense of the "most sublime values" described by Weber, I have also pointed to the vicissitudes of different paths of reenchantment. That is, nationalism, anti-Semitism, and racism also present themselves as paths of reenchantment, seeking to restore values believed to have been lost. And the inherently problematic aspect of enchantment, it seems, is that no matter how normative the experience of legitimacy and purpose provided by a set of values might be for some, the dialectic of enchantment can take place only within a liberal context where others remain unconvinced. In other words, one person or community's enchantment might be another's nightmare. Enchantment, it seems, offers only relative goods. So what, if any, is the answer? How might we avoid the pitfalls of the nineteenth and early twentieth centuries?

Unfortunately, an answer to this question is all the more pressing a century after Cohen's death and the end of imperial Germany. It is also an answer that seems ever more unattainable amid the resurgence of essentialisms in public discourse. Whether they are based in nation, ethnicity, class, or gender, identities are being claimed in increasingly irreconcilable forms. Each identity claims for itself the mantle of minority in relation to some other form of power; and each claim of minority is then invoked as exclusive.[1] Thus, the further liberalism's path of democratization drifts into a labyrinth of internecine conflicts, the more it seems enchantment takes shape as a new ground of essentialism.

However, the most basic claim of Cohen's thought is that knowledge—reasoning—is a public archive. Nobody has exclusive ownership over ideas. However, in the history of the later nineteenth and early twentieth centuries, liberalism was purported to be much more emphatically Christian, white, and European than it is today. Hence, to reconcile the claim that knowledge cannot be essentialized and that liberalism can be claimed as an identity by some, we must see how Cohen's account of public reasoning unsettled this coupling.

The connection between liberalism and its majority religious past, which Cohen made clear, was neither something kept secret nor something Cohen could accept wholesale. To the extent that the intellectual liberalism I have been exploring engaged in a kind of disenchanting neutralization of past values, this was not in pursuit of a more inclusive vision. Rather, this disenchantment was the result of a forgetfulness implicit in liberalism. By forgetting the minority protest of the Reformation, liberalism presented itself as universal and rational. This, as Schmitt claimed, ushered in the age of neutralizations. Nevertheless, liberalism was still more keenly aware of having an identity rooted in Christianity and Europe. Thus, in making the relationship between Protestantism and liberalism explicit, I have suggested that Cohen marks out a distinct path for the German-Jewish minority to inflect the majority culture anew, and that this minor protest was the result of reflecting on majoritarian norms. As a minor inflection, the German Jews negotiated a civic and social life within the context of a majoritarian culture that was neither interested in Jewish inclusion nor particularly invested in the kinds of questions that Cohen and the Jewish minority were asking themselves.

This is because minorities do not have the luxury of seeking enchantment in the world they already inhabit. Minority describes the disproportionate relationship between the goods, values, and reasons of a community that exists in two worlds in relation to a community that believes its own borders mark the edge of the known world. Minorities know they are different and have different needs and goals for their own communal flourishing. For most minority communities, just the opportunity to retain a social and communal identity can be enchanting. Whereas, for the majority, the claim to neutrality and disenchantment is itself a privilege unknown to groups struggling just to be themselves in transit between worlds. To believe that the most sublime values are threatened by others—by foreigners, by immigrants—is itself an expression of the blindness of myth.

But the pull of two worlds, of the need to reflect on oneself in the midst of a world that is other, is the root of sociality. It is the forgotten root of every majority and, as I have suggested, the root of liberalism as well. But liberalism's Protestant contours provide some respite from majoritarian essentialism. Protestantism, after all, demarcated religion as a category invoked in politics. And this is why religion expresses the meaning of *minority* so readily: the category of religion is by definition a protest of majoritarian politics. Majorities have the privilege of not being questioned by politics. Majorities also enjoy the illusion of a cohesive link between state and society. But this is the work of myth, as Cohen would say. And any politics that seeks to foist its own minor (in relation to the sum of all possible human) claims on the majority—any invocation of power for its own sake—follows a path of enchantment that leads to myth.

By contrast, the enchantment of minority is found in the *labor* of self-reflection, in the need to dwell on the threshold between the values of one world and the demands of another; this "tarrying with the negative,"[2] to borrow a phrase from Hegel, becomes the symbol of idealization, where difference must become part and parcel of what it means to claim an identity. In the story I have told, this kind of enchantment recognizes disenchantment as implicit within the two paths of Protestantism. And by emphasizing Cohen's account of Protestant epistemology, I have suggested we gain insight into how reasoning is pluralized to include this enchanted shade of liberalism as well: namely, reflection implies the protest and contestation of extremes within the space of reasons. Within the public sphere of liberalism we can therefore reclaim an ethical space of reasoning.

The ethical imperative to abide by justified reasoning is crucial to reconsidering the legacy of liberalism and modernity, because invoking the Protestant is an invitation to contestation. Protest contests the past; it contests tradition and signals a habituation and a habitation, the habitus of contestation. This conceptual space of Protestantism is a forum in which the meanings of spirit, nation, thought, and action are all frenetically exchanged and destabilized. Historically, it was a space where Christian tradition and dogma, both Catholic and Protestant, were no longer unquestioningly authoritative, where historical privilege and political entitlement were no longer sacrosanct, and where freedom and autonomy emerged as sources of legitimacy or new forms of rational explanation for human action. However, the question of who gets to reason and whose reasons get to count in the public sphere makes the Jewish Question and the rise of anti-Semitism emphatically epistemological as well as social and political problems, which are also part of this history of protest. Without clarity about the dialectic that underlies the history of liberalism, therefore, the risks are dire.

—∞—

For Cohen, the work of making the Protestant contours of liberalism explicit helped him negotiate Jewish difference within Germany. By articulating their struggle for civic rights in the language of Protestantism, idealization, and self-reflexive *Bildung*, the German Jews were thus articulating a kind of secular reasoning from their minority vantage point. But unlike Schmitt's indictment of Jewish liberalism, this appeal to secular reasoning was an attempt not to undermine religion but rather to undermine the politicization of religion. When Christianity becomes the basis for a political identity, the lesson of Protestantism—of separating institution and thought—is lost. Thus, Cohen saw a path toward civic equality for his Jewish minority community in articulating a minor reflection of the major tradition. And this ability of the minority to reflect the majority occurred within the space of reasoning, the social space between state and individual. This is the space of ideas, where enchantment still lingers.

While it may sound to some as if Cohen is saying that Jews are in fact the better liberal Protestants—the real Germans in Rosenzweig's earlier quoted sense—the responsibility to negotiate and articulate intersecting norms of religious and civic engagement was undoubtedly disproportionate. This one-way street of German-Jewish dialog is what Gershom Scholem infamously described as an "echo chamber" in which the Jews "heard only the sound of their own voices."[3] The demand for explicit self-reflexivity expressed by Cohen was not something Christian Germans were interested in because it was not something with which they—the majority—were burdened. Therefore, if we take seriously the degree to which Cohen's story demonstrates a disproportionate attention to self-reflexivity on the part of a minority that includes reflection on the majority—whether they are listening or not—then we can view Scholem's description as in fact an explicit goal of Cohen's public reasoning; that is, a practice of public reasoning requires that a minority community hear its own voices first. In doing so, however, the majority demands placed on the minority are also minoritized; in other words, the majority is reflected into the reasoning of the minority as part of a distinct moment, a node or stage, within the minority's act of self-accounting. German identity and Protestantism thus both become something minor, something reflected into German-Jewish communal identity.

It is for this reason that Cohen's account of the Noahide is both so significant and potentially limited. For, by speaking to Jews first, his account frames Judaism as the tradition within which minority is articulated. So, does that mean that the Noahide, as the figure *representing* minority—especially the legal configuration of the Noahide laws—is incontestable? Is the Noahide the exemplarity of all minority as such and, if so, by what right? Is the decision in favor of the Noahide an arbitrary one? What, if any, is the justification for these particular norms as opposed to any others, and can they too be contested?

As I noted in chapter 4, Cohen's account of ethical socialism places reasoning and the community of reasoners seeking their norms in the cultural and social sphere rather than in the political. This means that majority and minority are works in progress relative to one another; they are relative communities, as it were. In contrast to Schmitt, for example, who emphasizes the sovereign as the one who decides on the norm and its exception—a truly majoritarian prerogative—which constitutes the distinct sphere of the political, Cohen turns elsewhere. Cohen's account of the Noahide, by contrast, drew on the cultural and social sources of a minority community's reasoning. This does not mean that the specific norms reached by that community are determined as decisive, if by that term we mean final and absolute. Indeed, the Noahide remains a legal fiction par excellence within the body of Jewish law. Rather, as sources they remain resources that can catalyze continual occupation of the space of reasoning. The cultural and social space of reasoning is therefore prior to the political for Cohen, and the community of reasoners is therefore plural by definition. Because these norms are being worked out in the process of self-reflexively imagining what minority could look like for others, they are not decisive but rather hypothetical.

When Cohen suggests that reason is by definition a historical canon and that religion actively contributes to reason's expansion, as I noted in chapter 2, we should therefore understand this as the conceptual undercurrent of his account of the Noahide. The Noahide is the result of idealization. And as I argued in chapter 2, idealization places power in the hands of the reasoners who are reflecting on their sources and norms rather than in the sources and norms alone. This, as Cohen claims, is because the work of reasoning about such sources is an emphatically ethical affair, concerning human social relationships. It is neither the political sovereign nor the divine sovereign that decides. Such a shroud of mysterious transcendence over the sphere of sociality is precluded by ethics. While "the human being's relation to God may remain a mystery," Cohen claims, "his conduct to other people is not permitted to be considered such. With regard to the human, one has to judge and then decide. For the decision about good and bad is connected with this decision. The distinction between good and bad comes to nothing if it coincides with the distinction of well-being and ill."[4] For Cohen, one must judge and then decide, because the ethical judgment is prior to the political action.

Thus, the ethical relationship grounded in this judgment cannot remain a mystery but must be accounted for; it must be justified. And while some interpretations of the Noahide laws would place contemporary atheists and LGBTQ folks into the category of idolaters or those who commit acts of "sexual immorality,"[5] Cohen's account of reasoning would deem such interpretations as "political" by definition, pretending to majority when none can exist other than as a hypothesis. Cohen's ethics dictate that because both minority and majority are terms that are contested and re-worked in the space of reasoning, neither can be decisively final. In short, the figure of minority provides a conceptual mechanism for pluralizing the space of reasoning: if a minority can imagine itself as a majority in order to better understand itself, then so too can that idealized majority imagine itself minoritized by yet another minority—and so on. Because there are no ready-made or naturalized facts unless the community of reasoners reaches consensus about them, even if a majoritarian norm is achieved through its political deployment, the ethical labor of idealiza-tion demands the socialization of reasoning to continue to rejuvenate, refine, and contest the norms deemed decisive in the political sphere. This infinite process of self-reflexivity, reflecting the precarity of the minority onto the majority and thus destabilizing the latter's imagined immunity, provides a crucial corrective to public reasoning.

And while Cohen's own attention to minority self-reflexivity might speak to Jews first, it nevertheless demonstrates the Protestant sources of liberalism, indeed, especially German-Jewish liberalism. Protestantism is the majority minoritized in Cohen's German-Jewish liberalism. Cohen's vision for German Judaism therefore leaves us a parting message: we must make explicit the Protestant sources of liberalism if we are to negotiate the crisis of the liberal tradition today. For, as I write these words, we continue to witness the devolution of perhaps the sole remaining spark of enchantment in the liberal tradition: namely, the rule of law. Without a commitment to a standard beyond partisan politics, a source of legiti-macy above and beyond the relative goods of party and identity, we risk the descent into myth that characterized much of Cohen's lifetime. And we live in a world that needs correction. We live in a world that demands greater attention to how it can be made better.

Focusing on idealism as a model for justified reasoning and a faith in the power of ideas to shape the world, Cohen provided an example of how we might navigate the brute assertion of majoritarian identities. And his thought at least gestures toward an answer to the question of how we might vindicate a kind of enchantment. The process of minoritizing a tradition, which starts with the disproportionate demand placed on the minority, such as the Jews, to be self-reflexive, nevertheless begins a chain reaction. The minority is minoritized by majority demands; however, when the Jews reflect on their own history as well as the majority Christian one, they find a sense of self in history and its idealizations in which the majority tradition of Christianity is brought into historical focus. Minoritization breaks the spell of essentialism. Nobody owns an idea; hence, nobody can claim full possession of this space of reasoning.

My example of this process has traced Protestantism as the minoritized product of such reasoning. But the dialectic of enchantment that I have outlined has its various paths. The path into science leaves reason disenchanted and liable to reoccupations and reenchantments; the path into the political results in enchanted identitarianism. Neither can secure the space of reason that is articulated in a liberal tradition. But the enchantment of religion—of community and commitment to shared practices, histories, and ideas—can secure such a space; this is mainly because Protestantism describes how religion in the modern world consists primarily of ideas that persuade us to practice and practices that persuade us to think in a certain way. However, this enchantment is emphatically social—that is, neither private in the sense of individualist nor public in the sense of political. Rather, religion is social in the sense that individual and community occupy a space of reasoning that is coextensive with the space of reasoning about social goods, needs, and interests. Cohen's liberalism shows us how the belief in ideas enchants first and foremost because ideas transcend experience.

Cohen's ethical monotheism provides one example of an enchantment that limits, rather than authorizes, exclusive claims in the space of reasoning. This form of enchantment reminds us that each reason is minor when inflected through the space of reasoning. Thus, Cohen's monotheism points us toward the opening in sociality where religion—and really, this means any religion—must transcend the world of politics. This version of liberal enchantment does not seek to recruit religion but rather insists on religion serving as a buffer between individual and state. Religion is the most explicit form of idealism left in the modern world.

And the specifically diasporic history of Judaism provides Cohen with a model for how religion can avoid the idolatry of politics. Religion must insist on the separation of church and state.

Religion thus shows us the need for an idea of limitation; our reasoning is necessarily infinite in potential because it is only finite as the sum of human reasoners. Monotheism therefore helps idealize the implicit Protestantism of liberalism and claim this tradition as one in which infinite reasons might be offered but the singular goal is to preserve this space of reasoning by remembering that we are limited; hence, religion enchants this sociality by recalling that debate and reasoned exchange of ideas will always be limited by the idea of something greater: a concept that transcends partisan antagonism of identities and reminds us of something we share in common—namely, the idea of humanity.

With a focus on the purpose of reasoning rather than the pursuit of mythic origins and universals, liberalism therefore becomes a plural concept. It is scientific and enchanted. It is contested through reasons and myths. But most importantly, it is revised and reworked through the labor of minority inflections of its norms. If liberalism is to have any future, then it must be secured as an epistemological space in which the open possibility for meanings to be revised and reordered takes shape and where the past can be invoked anew. Liberalism can still be a public archive with sources that demand to be reinterpreted over and again; the question is whether we believe this work can be done.

NOTES

1. On the pitfalls of both a crude constructionism and the need for mapping greater attention to the role that group identities play can play in political advocacy, see Kimberlé Crenshaw, "Mapping the Margins: Intersectionality, Identity Politics, and Violence Against Women," *Stanford Law Review* 43, no. 6 (1991): 1241–99.

2. G. W. F. Hegel, *Phenomenology of Spirit*, trans. A. V. Miller (New York: Oxford University Press, 1977), para. 32.

3. Gershom Scholem, "On the Myth of German-Jewish Dialogue," in *On Jews and Judaism in Crisis: Selected Essays*, ed. Werner J. Dannhauser (New York: Schocken, 1976), 63.

4. Hermann Cohen, *Religion of Reason: Out of the Sources of Judaism*, trans. Simon Kaplan (Atlanta, GA: Scholars' Press, 1995), 132–33, translation slightly modified.

5. Compare, for example, the interpretations of Michael J. Broyde, "The Obligation of Jews to See Observance of Noahide Laws by Gentiles: A Theoretical Review," in *Tikkun Olam: Social Responsibility in Jewish Thought and Law*, ed. David Shatz, Chaim I. Waxman, and Nathan J. Diament (Northvale, NJ: Jason Aronson, 1997). On the distinction between "uncovering nakedness" as implying incest and "sexual immorality" implying homosexuality, see Steven Greenberg, *Wrestling with God and Men: Homosexuality in the Jewish Tradition* (Madison: University of Wisconsin Press, 2004), 70.

INDEX

Albrecht, Wilhelm, 210
Anderson, Benedict, 28
antiliberalism: development of, 109, 184; in German Empire, 13–14, 20, 29, 32, 43, 109, 184, 209, 211, 213–17, 221, 229, 232
anti-Semitism, 5–6, 7, 309–10, 312; Cohen's critique of, 9, 18, 29, 32, 110, 118, 159, 163, 165–66, 229, 231–33, 252, 254; 280; in German Empire, 12, 27–28, 122, 154, 159–52, 183–84, 187–88, 198–99, 202, 212–20, 229–33, 236, 275–76; and materialism, 122; and secularism, 211–14, 255–57; and social Darwinism, 130
Aristotle, 121, 279
atheism: and German idealism, 60–61, 65, 83; and pantheism, 52–57, 58, 63, 97n47
Augustine, 258

Bakhtin, Mikhail, 9, 116
Bamberger, Ludwig, 212
Bar Kochba, 220
Barth, Karl, 18
Bauch, Bruno, 217, 218–21, 222; and Cohen, 223, 225–26, 228, 229
Bauer, Bruno, 142; *The Jewish Question*, 162
Beiner, Ronald, 266

Beiser, Frederick, 18, 123
belief; Cohen's understanding of, 2, 58–59, 90, 110, 134, 196, 235, 269, 281, 287–93, 298–99, 316; and Heine, 63–64; and Judaism, 191, 212; and liberalism, 6, 8–9, 20, 188; and public reason, 29, 32; and Schmitt, 3, 256–59, 273; and science, 133–4, 159, 254; and secularism, 143, 263, 264; and *völkisch* movement, 216–17
Bell, Catherine, 260
Bernays, Jacob, 46
Biale, David, 84
Bildung, 11, 111, 113, 161; Cohen's account of, 28, 49, 86–87, 121, 159, 164, 202, 233–34, 291–93, 312
Bilgrami, Akeel, 262
Bismarck, Otto von, 13, 16, 46, 90, 117, 167–68, 198, 214, 237n7; and German unification, 48, 91
blood: Cohen's critique of, 160, 222, 228, 254; and German nationalism, 213–21, 236, 273; as racial essentialism, 25, 29, 31, 109, 184, 199
Blumenberg, Hans, 144–46, 147, 236
Boehm, Max, 220
Bonaparte, Napoleon, 46
Brenner, Michael, 3, 5

PAUL E. NAHME is Dorot Assistant Professor of Judaic Studies and Assistant Professor of Religious Studies at Brown University.